Jack Fay Robinson

The pictures below portray facial expressions representing twelve men
companying list below. In the parentheses before each mental state writ

( ) Astonishment ( ) Deli
( ) Bashful appeal ( ) Dete
( ) Contentment ( ) Grie
( ) Coquetry ( ) Phys

states.   The names of these twelve mental states are given in the ac-
he number of the picture which most nearly represents that mental state.

ht

·mination

cal suffering

(4) Rage

(3) Scorn

(12) Suspicion

(7) Terror

APPLICATIONS OF PSYCHOLOGY

BY

FRED A. MOSS, M.D., Ph.D.

Professor of Psychology, George Washington University
Visiting Psychiatrist, Gallinger Municipal Hospital

Formerly
Development Specialist in Tests and Measurements, First Division, U.S.A.
Staff Psychologist, Bureau of Public Personnel Administration

HOUGHTON MIFFLIN COMPANY

BOSTON · NEW YORK · CHICAGO · DALLAS · SAN FRANCISCO
The Riverside Press Cambridge

The Riverside Press

CAMBRIDGE · MASSACHUSETTS

PRINTED IN THE U.S.A.

TO
MY FORMER STUDENTS WHOSE
PATIENT ENDURANCE AND SYMPATHETIC COÖPERATION
HAVE MADE POSSIBLE
SEVERAL OF THE INVESTIGATIONS
DESCRIBED HEREIN

PREFACE

FOR a number of years, instructors of elementary classes in psychology have desired a book to be used during the second semester which would show how the principles taught in the general psychology during the first semester operate in the various professional and industrial fields. It is to supply such a need that this book was written. The book has been used for three years in mimeographed form with approximately six hundred elementary students each year. In that way it has been possible to prepare a book especially adapted to the particular needs of those whose training in psychology has not been extensive.

This book is written from the point of view which regards psychology as one of the natural sciences rather than as a branch of philosophy. An effort has been made to present the experimental findings of scientific investigators without indulging in a partisan discussion of controversial subjects.

The book is divided into three parts. Part I deals with those principles which apply equally to the behavior and efficiency of all men. Part II deals with the nature and causes of individual differences. Part III, which is the largest part, considers the specific applications of psychology in the professional and industrial fields.

In selecting the material for the various chapters, I have drawn heavily on the works of investigators in numerous fields. My experience in certain of these fields has been of distinct advantage in assisting me to choose material best suited to the aim of the book. My medical experience has been especially helpful in writing Chapters II, III, IV, XI, and XIII. Chapter XIV is an outgrowth of my work on the psychiatric staff of Gallinger Municipal Hospital. Chapter XII is largely the result of my experience in the field of tests, beginning with my work as Development Specialist in Tests and Measurements, First Division, United States Army. In writing Chapter XVII, I drew heavily on the experience gained as Staff Psychologist for the Bureau of Public Personnel Administration. Chapter XVIII is substantially a summary of my year's experience as Secretary of Hoover's Committee on the Causes of Accidents.

Acknowledgments are difficult to make. I have given credit in footnotes to the many authors and publishers who have permitted me to quote from their works. Particular acknowledgments are due to Professor Robert S. Woodworth, of Columbia University, and to Dr. William C. Borden, Dean of the George Washington University Medical School, for reading the manuscript and making many valuable criticisms. My greatest indebtedness, however, is due to my two colleagues, Dr. Katharine Omwake and Dr. Thelma Hunt, who have followed the book through from the beginning and have contributed so materially to its completion that there is scarcely a page in it which has not been improved by their efforts.

FRED A. MOSS

GEORGE WASHINGTON UNIVERSITY

CONTENTS

PART I

DETERMINING FORCES IN HUMAN BEHAVIOR

PART II

INDIVIDUAL DIFFERENCES

PART III

THE APPLICATIONS OF PSYCHOLOGY IN PROFESSIONAL AND INDUSTRIAL FIELDS

APPLICATIONS OF PSYCHOLOGY

. .

PART I
DETERMINING FORCES IN HUMAN BEHAVIOR

The same cause always produces the same effect, and the same effect never arises but from the same cause.

HUME

APPLICATIONS OF PSYCHOLOGY

.·.

CHAPTER I

BASIC PRINCIPLES OF BEHAVIOR

Things do not happen by mere chance in human life any more than in the fall of an apple or in an eclipse of the moon. The same situation acting on the same individual will produce, always and inevitably, the same response. If on different occasions it *seems* to produce different responses, it is because the individual has changed in the meantime and is not the same creature that he was.

THORNDIKE [1]

IF psychology is to have any practical applications in life, it must take as its fundamental hypothesis the principle that, if all the elements in the situation are known, human behavior can be predicted and controlled just as phenomena in the physical sciences can be predicted and controlled. The principle of cause and effect has for many years been generally accepted in the physical sciences, but it has only recently been applied to the understanding of human behavior. With the application of this principle, psychology loses its metaphysical element and becomes based on definite, understandable laws rather than on metaphysical guesses.

Modern psychologists declare that whatever a man does or becomes in life is the result of forces no more mysterious than are the forces involved in physical phenomena. When the apple falls from the mother tree, the physicist no longer looks on this as a chance phenomenon, but explains it in terms of the laws of *drives* and *resistances*; the *drive* of gravitation tending to pull the apple to the ground, and the *resistance* offered by the stem of the apple tending to keep it on the tree. Even so the modern business manager, in placing a certain young man in a position of trust, is anxious to know whether he will have sufficient resistance to withstand the drive of running away with the firm's money.

[1] Thorndike, Edward L.: *Education* (The Macmillan Company, New York, 1912), p. 60. Reprinted by permission of the publishers.

The fundamental principles underlying the science of human behavior are the same as the basic principles underlying the natural sciences. Just as the principle of cause and effect is basic to an understanding of every natural science, so the same principle is indispensable in the science of psychology. The physical sciences deal with the prediction, control, and cause of certain phenomena in nature. Psychology deals with the prediction, control, and cause of human behavior. As the natural sciences are much older than psychology, they have advanced much farther in understanding of the phenomena with which they deal.

Man is often able to predict phenomena before he is able to understand the forces that produce them. From the earliest times man has observed that water flows from higher to lower levels, but why it so behaved was not clear until the discovery of the law of gravitation. From time immemorial man has observed the restless and seeking behavior which occurs when the human being is deprived of food; but the cause of this restless and seeking behavior was not clear until the recognition of the hunger drive.

Although the natural sciences have gone far in the understanding of physical phenomena, certain phenomena are determined by forces so complex and intricate that scientists have only very limited success in predicting the phenomena and even less success in controlling them. Take the weather for an example. So many forces contribute to the determination of the weather that the predictions of meteorologists are often in error, and attempts to control the weather are so far futile. So it is with the more complicated phenomena underlying human behavior.

In the last analysis the behavior of any individual is the inevitable result of certain forces which act on him. His behavior is due to forces little more mysterious and uncontrollable than are the forces which govern the rest of the universe. This being true, the question naturally arises as to how it happens that when several individuals are confronted by the same situation and have apparently the same forces acting upon them, each may "choose" a different way of reacting to it. The answer lies partially in the fact that the structural make-up of the individuals was different to begin with. It would be as reasonable to expect the same reaction from an electric fan, an electric heater, and an electric desk light, when the cords connecting them are plugged into the current socket, as to expect all people to react the same when confronted by the same set of external stimuli. When the current is turned on, the electric fan "chooses" to revolve because it was made that way; the heater produces heat, and the desk light gives illumination for the same reason. The only reason that they "chose" to act differently is that they are structurally different. But if we have two structurally similar electric fans we shall invariably have similar behavior on their part; likewise given two human machines with structures sufficiently alike, we shall invariably have similar behavior when the same stimulus is applied. The main reason that the behavior of twins has so much in common is that their bodily structures are so much alike.

The human machine, like any other machine, responds in characteristic ways to the forces that act upon it. What its responses in any situation will be is determined in general by four factors: first, the kind of machine it was to begin with; second, the things with which it has come in contact so far; third, the chemical changes going on in it at the time; and fourth, the immediate elements making up the situation.

It is just as clear to the modern psychologist that he cannot put a feeble-minded individual in a responsible position and expect him to do the work of a genius, as it is clear to the mechanical engineer that he cannot expect a one-ton truck to do the work of a ten-ton truck. Every one recognizes that the behavior of the one-ton truck is conditioned by the fact that it was originally designed as a one-ton rather than a ten-ton machine, and no wise business man would place on it ten tons of goods and expect it to deliver them. Unfortunately, it is not so generally recognized that there are just as wide differences in the capacity of individuals to deliver intellectual results as there are in the capacity of these trucks to deliver goods, and that a "one-ton" mentality cannot carry a "ten-ton" load.

Not only is the behavior of any mechanism conditioned by the kind of machine it is to begin with, but it is also conditioned by the forces that have acted on it in the past. Whether the tires of the Ford truck will blow out or stand up when carrying a normal load is determined, not so much by the kind of tires they were at first, but by such factors as the number of miles they have been driven, and the number of cuts and bruises they have received in the past. So it is with human behavior; the nervous breakdowns of adult life are determined in no small part by certain unfortunate experiences of childhood. Just as the cuts and bruises of the automobile tire are often overlooked at the time they occur, so the wounds of childhood may not be apparent, but the results persist none the less and weaken certain elements in the fabric of resistance so that later on the same force or even a smaller force produces the crash.

The behavior of any organism is conditioned by the chemical changes going on in it. If there is an improper mixture of air and gas in the carburetor, the motor will spit, misbehave, and show other signs of inefficiency; and if there is an improper mixture of alcohol and other substances in the blood stream, the individual likewise will misbehave and show signs of inefficiency.

The human engineer holds that when all of the conditions are the same, if the same force is brought to bear upon the same individual his behavior will always be the same. And this is exactly the claim of the mechanical engineer. When an automobile rolls over a certain stone at one time without a blowout, and at another time a blowout is caused by rolling over the same stone, it may appear at first glance that the same force produced different results at different times; but the apparent exception to the rule is due to the fact that the forces acting on the tire were not the same in both cases. Perhaps the car was unloaded when it went over the stone without producing a blowout, and was heavily loaded when the blowout occurred; or it may have been that the tire was new and strong when it escaped the blowout and old and weak when the blowout occurred. In other words, in the second instance the *resistance* the tire could offer to the forces acting upon it was much reduced; i.e., it was no longer the same tire.

Thus the exceptions to the general rule that the same situation will always produce the same response are only apparent exceptions. In most cases the response is not the same because the situations are not the same. This is true of the human machine as well as of the inanimate machine. If at one time a man loves his wife and treats her kindly, and at another beats her, the cause of his behavior may be found in such explanations as those indicated above. When he beats his wife, the load may be an overabundance of alcohol; or his beating her may be due to the fact that the wear and tear of time have left their traces on his brain and he is no longer the man he once was. In the past the neglect of these contributing forces which make up so vital a part of the situation has led the human engineer into much error. When all contributing forces are kept constant, he finds that in the same situation the same individual will always behave in the same way.

Thus, back of any behavior there are underlying causes which act according to definite laws and which, with sufficient knowledge, may be demonstrated and analyzed. With this view of human behavior, psychology is raised from the realm of the mysterious and speculative medieval philosophy to its legitimate place among the sciences. By studying the laws of cause and effect in behavior the psychologists will in time to come be able to predict certain things in human behavior just as the astronomer can predict the reappearance of Halley's comet in 1986, and to control human behavior just as the physicist has done in the utilization of electricity. The succeeding chapters will show that psychology has already begun to predict psychological happenings, and to point the way to the control of these happenings. The prediction and control of any phenomena is based on an understanding of the forces that produce the phenomena. With this in view, we shall now consider some of the more important laws of behavior.

LAWS OF DRIVES AND RESISTANCES

As pointed out above, human behavior is produced by certain drives which act as motivating forces in the life of every individual. The strength of the *drives* depends upon the original nature of the individual, his physical condition, and his past experiences. As these three factors are not the same in all people, their *drives* likewise differ in strength.

Owing to the importance of the *drives* and *resistances* in the interpretation of behavior, the writer,[1] on the basis of a series of animal experiments, has attempted to formulate a few of the more general laws that apply to this field.   The chief reason for doing the experimental work on animals rather than on persons is the great difficulty of using human beings for such experiments.   The object of the experiments was to measure in terms of numerical units certain drives and resistances of the animals.   The method of conducting the experiments was that of balancing a drive against an opposing resistance, or against another drive, the conditions being always so arranged that one side of the balance would yield a numerical measure.

It is a fact of common observation that animals when confronted by certain situations tend to respond with rather definite, fixed behavior.   It is to these tendencies to action that the terms *drive* and *resistance* are applied.   By *drive* is meant the impelling forces in the situation that stimulate the animal toward certain positive behavior.   For example, if an animal is kept without food for a certain length of time, certain organic stimulations of the nerve endings in the stomach provoke in the animal restless and seeking behavior until food is found and the drive, for the time being, stopped.   It is to the motive force behind this seeking behavior that the term *drive* is applied.   By *resistance* is meant the repelling forces in the situation which stimulate the animal to negative re-

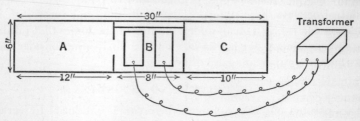

FIGURE 1. FLOOR PLAN OF EXPERIMENT BOX

actions, or tend to draw him away from certain behavior.   For example, the mere presence of cats produces in rats certain resist-

[1] Moss, Fred A.: "Study of Animal Drives," *Journal of Experimental Psychology*, VII, no. 3, June, 1924.

ances, and these resistances stimulate the rats to behavior tending to keep or remove them from a closer contact with cats.

In discussing these laws, we shall first state the law; second, describe the experiments on which it was based; and third, cite examples of its application in human affairs.

Law 1: *Any animal drive may be measured in terms of the resistance overcome, provided the strength of the resistance is known; or, where the strength of the drive is known and that of the resistance is not, the resistance may be measured in terms of the drive.* In other words, if one side of the balance is known, it is possible to measure the other in terms of the known. For example, if white rats are kept without food for some time and placed in section A of the experiment box shown in Figure 1, whether they will cross the electric plates in B to go to the food in section C depends upon two things — how hungry they are and how strong the current is on the electric plates; i.e., upon the strength of the *drive* as balanced against the strength of the *resistance*. If the animals have had sufficient contact with the plates before to know what to expect, and if there is sufficient current on the plates, they will not attempt to cross unless impelled by a very strong hunger drive. This was demonstrated in a series

of experiments, keeping the animals without food for from twelve to one hundred and forty-four hours and keeping the current on the plates at twenty-eight volts. Less than five per cent of the animals had sufficient hunger drive to overcome the resistance necessary to go to the food at the close of a twenty-four-hour hunger period. The drive increased within the

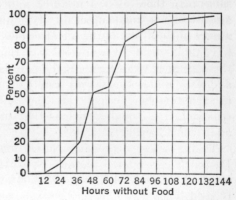

FIGURE 2. PER CENT HAVING CROSSED THE PLATES AT VARIOUS STARVATION PERIODS

next twelve hours so that approximately twenty per cent crossed at that time. By forty-eight hours the drive was sufficiently strong in half the cases to overcome the resistance, and the rats crossed to the food. And by seventy-two hours the hunger drive overcame the resistance in eighty per cent of the cases. By ninety-six hours ninety-five per cent of the rats had crossed, and by one hundred and forty-four hours every rat in the group had crossed. This is shown graphically in Figure 2.

From the above it will readily appear that the animals may be induced to cross for the food either by *increasing the drive* by keeping them without food for a longer time, or by *reducing the resistance* in the form of the electric current which they have to overcome to get to the food.

In human affairs, likewise, all acts are determined by the relative strength of the drives and the resistance. Take, for example, the most serious act ever committed by man, taking his own life. This can be explained as well by law 1 as can the behavior of the rats. Assume that a man is afflicted with an incurable disease which produces in his body one hundred units of pain per hour, which cause him to resort to any behavior possible to escape the pain. If death is the only way out of the pain, then these units become just so many units of force toward suicide. Assume further that in this same man there exist a hundred and forty-two resistance units against suicide, made up of fifty-two units of love for his wife, and ninety units of fear of the life after death. Now, in order for him to commit suicide, it is obvious that the pain must be increased or the resistance weakened. If the pain is increased to one hundred and sixty units, suicide will result; or if his wife should be killed in an automobile accident and these fifty-two units of resistance removed, it is equally obvious that unless some other factor is added suicide will result.

Taking a less depressing illustration, let us assume that the Detroit Tigers offered the owners of the New York Yankees one hundred thousand dollars for Babe Ruth. Whether Ruth would be sold is likewise governed by this same law. Assume, for example, that the Yankee owners considered Ruth worth more than that sum to them. It is obvious that in order to secure him the Tigers must *increase the drive* as expressed in the desire of the Yankee owners for money; or the trade might be brought about by a series of events which would *lessen the resistance* of the Yankee owners to parting with Ruth. For example, Ruth's batting average, instead of being above 300, might drop to a bare 150, in which case the *resistance* to parting with Ruth would be so weak that a very much smaller sum of money would suffice to bring about the change.

Law 2: Any drive that succeeds is stronger than the resistance overcome, and any drive that fails is not as strong as the resistance. For example, if a hunger drive caused by a forty-eight-hour starvation period will make the animal take an electric shock of twelve volts to get to food, but fails to induce him to take the shock of twenty volts, we may say that the strength of a forty-eight-hour hunger drive lies between a twelve-volt and a twenty-volt opposing stimulus, being stronger than the twelve-volt, but weaker than the twenty-volt shock. This law is illustrated in human affairs as follows: A bank messenger, who was entrusted with the transportation of varying sums of money amounting to as much as $900, always delivered the money safely until one day when he was entrusted with $1000, and on that occasion he ran away. Other things being equal, we should be justified in saying that the strength of his resistance to being a thief lay between $900 and $1000. To express the balance of drives and resistances in terms of the hunger drive, take the case of the crew of twenty men floating on a raft in mid-ocean without food, and with no immediate prospects of rescue. For the first four days no mention was made of eating each other, but on the fifth day the proposition was seriously considered, and on the sixth day they drew lots to see who should be the first victim. In this case it would be correct to say that their resistance to becoming cannibals lay in a hunger drive produced by being from four to six days without food.

Law 3: If two independent drives are opposed by the same resistance, and one drive overcomes the resistance while the other fails, the one that overcomes the resistance is the stronger drive. Using the experiment box the floor plan of which was shown in Figure 1, a current of twenty-eight volts was turned on the electric plates in B. Ten rats that had been kept without food for seventy-two hours were placed in section A and food in section C. Eight of the rats crossed the plates to reach the food. Keeping the resistance at twenty-eight volts, ten mature male rats were placed in section A and a female during the œstrous period (in heat) was placed in section C. Only five of the ten males overcame the resistance to crossing the plates to reach the female.

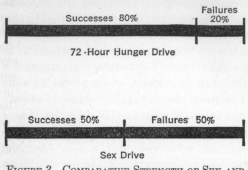

Successes 80%   Failures 20%

72-Hour Hunger Drive

Successes 50%   Failures 50%

Sex Drive

FIGURE 3. COMPARATIVE STRENGTH OF SEX AND HUNGER DRIVE

Unless some important factors have been overlooked, these results would tend to disprove the commonly accepted theory that the sex drive is the strongest of all drives, for the seventy-two-hour hunger drive overcame more resistance than the sex drive. This is shown graphically in Figure 3. These conclusions are borne out by the results obtained in other experiments.

The application of this law in human affairs is illustrated as follows: If the New York Yankees should refuse one hundred thousand dollars for Babe Ruth, but should be willing to exchange him for Rogers Hornsby, it would be logical to conclude that the desire for Hornsby is stronger than the desire for a hundred thousand dollars.

Law 4: Given two drives, both functioning at the same time, and so arranged that neither can succeed without neglecting the other, the one that succeeds is the stronger drive. This is illustrated in the balancing of the hunger drive against the sex drive, using the apparatus shown in Figure 4.

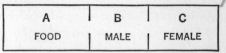

A	B	C
FOOD	MALE	FEMALE

FIGURE 4. FLOOR PLAN OF EXPERIMENT BOX USED IN MEASURING RELATIVE STRENGTH OF SEX AND HUNGER DRIVES

Five male rats, after being deprived of food for seventy-two hours, were placed in section B of the experiment box. A female during the œstrous period was placed in section C and food was placed in section A. In a series of preliminary experiments the males had learned that if they entered either section A or section C they could not escape from that section to go back into the other.   In other words, the animal was confronted with a "choice" between the drive for food and the drive for sex gratification.   Four out of the five chose the food instead of the sex.   It is obvious, therefore, that with the physical condition produced by going seventy-two hours without food, the food drive in rats is stronger than the sex drive.

In human affairs situations often arise in which one drive is balanced against another.   An historical illustration is seen in the case of Mark Antony, who had to choose between two forceful attractions — love and Cleopatra on one side balanced against Octavia and half of the world on the other.   The fact that Cleopatra was chosen in the face of such opposition indicates how strong was her hold on Antony.

Law 5: Given two antagonistic resistances, both functioning at the same time, and both so arranged that neither can cease to function without overcoming the other, the one that overcomes is the stronger resistance.   This choice of the less of two evils was demonstrated in animal experiments in the following manner: Section A of the apparatus represented in Figure 5 was constructed to hold water to the depth of one inch, and section B was covered with electric

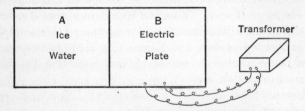

FIGURE 5. FLOOR PLAN OF EXPERIMENT BOX USED IN BALANCING RESISTANCES

plates joined to a step-up transformer ranging in voltage from ten to one hundred and ten volts.   When a rat was placed in section A and the temperature was reduced to 15° C. by pouring crushed ice into the water, the rat would climb on the electric plates if the current was twelve volts or less, but when the current was raised to sixteen volts, he would jump back into the icy water.   When more ice was fed in and the temperature of the water lowered to 10° C., he would once more climb on the electric plates, but when the voltage was raised to twenty volts, he again sought the water.

This choice between two evils, or the situation that the man in the street would call being "between the Devil and the deep blue sea," often occurs in human affairs. From the earliest times it has been known that certain situations are to all people, practically without exception, annoying, and tend to be avoided by them. For example, every one of the ten plagues of Egypt recorded in the Old Testament offered a resistance to some drive of the Egyptians: the lice and flies produced physical discomfort; the darkness and loss of the first born, mental discomfort; while the plagues of the hail, locusts, and murrain produced financial loss which might lead to both physical and mental suffering. Opposing these plagues was the resistance to letting the Hebrews go because the Egyptians desired to use them as slaves. In other words, He who designed those plagues was acting on the knowledge that an effective way to make people do a thing they object to doing is to make the results of not doing it more unpleasant than would be the results of doing it.

Law 6: When one drive by itself is not strong enough to overcome a resistance, it may be reënforced by other drives, until it is strong enough to overcome the resistance. This law was demonstrated by the following experiments with animals: Using the experiment box the floor plan of which is shown in Figure 1, a current of twenty-eight volts was turned on the electric plates in section B and the animals were placed in section A after having been kept without food for twelve hours. Food was placed in section C. As demonstrated in the experiment described in connection with the first law, a twenty-eight-volt resistance is stronger than a twelve-hour hunger drive, and none of the animals were willing to cross the plates so long as this single drive was pitted against so great a resistance. In order to reënforce the twelve-hour hunger drive, crushed ice was poured into section A, and, as the temperature gradually went down, one by one the rats crossed the plates and took the electric shock necessary to get over to the food in section C. In other words, neither the unpleasantness of standing in icy water nor the desirability of reaching the food would without reënforcement make the rats take the electric shock, but when both forces were acting together the resistance to crossing the plates was overcome. Such situations occur daily in human affairs. A man suddenly resigns his connections in a business office to take another position at a smaller salary. His salary is $6000 a year with the business concern, but in the new position he will get $2000 less each year. It is apparent that the drive of $4000 cannot overcome a drive of $6000 unless it is reënforced considerably. In this case the $4000 drive is reënforced by the fact that in order to receive the $6000 it is necessary for him to take orders from a very disagreeable section chief. The unpleasant chief corresponds to the ice in the experiment described above, and while the drive for $4000 alone was unable to overcome a drive of $6000, the drive of $4000 plus the desire to escape the unpleasant working conditions easily overcame the resistance.

Law 7: Other things being equal, every time a resistance is overcome the strength of that resistance is weakened. An experiment box with a floor plan similar to that shown in Figure 1 was used in demonstrating this law. For five successive days the rats, after having been without food for twelve hours, were placed in section A; a current of twenty-six volts was turned on the electric plates in B, and the food was placed in section C. As pointed out above, the hunger drive produced by going without food for twelve hours is not sufficiently strong to overcome a twenty-eight-volt resistance. Therefore the drive to cross into C was reënforced by feeding cracked ice into section A. On the first trial the temperature had to be lowered on the average to 10° C. before the animals crossed the plates. On the second trial the average temperature at which the animals crossed was two degrees higher, 12° C. On the third trial the average was 13.5° C., and by the fifth trial the animals crossed when the temperature was as high as 14° C. Thus we see that five trials reduce by approximately four degrees the amount of reënforcement necessary to make the twelve-hour hunger drive overbalance the twenty-eight-volt resistance.

From these experiments one may conclude that a resistance tends to lose its repelling force each time it is overcome; and this is borne out in human affairs. It is the idea expressed in the proverb, "We first endure, then pity, then embrace." In the case of the young woman who becomes a confirmed alcoholic, the first drink is probably taken with the reënforcement of a number of contributing elements, such as the example and encouragement of others at some social gathering where liquor is served. The young woman does not wish to appear to be a "goody-goody," and consequently yields to the urging of those about her to "try one little drink." On subsequent occasions less and less urging is required, until by and by her resistance to taking a drink has been converted into a positive liking for the beverage.

Law 8: *The strength of a drive is influenced by the physical condition of the individual.* Ten male rats were kept without food for twelve hours and placed in section A of the experiment box. A female when in œstrum was placed in section C of the box and a current of twenty volts turned on. (It should be noted that twenty instead of twenty-eight volts were used in this experiment.) Seven of the ten rats crossed the plates. Another group of ten males were kept for sixty hours without food and placed in the box under the same conditions. Five of the ten crossed. A third group of ten males were kept without food for ninety-six hours, and placed in the box, but only two of the ten crossed. From the above experiment it would appear that the strength of the sex drive in an animal is weakened if the animal is deprived of food. The application of this law to human affairs is well illustrated in the decreased strength of the hunger drive in individuals suffering from a gastric upset or any other condition accompanied by nausea. The dependence of drives on physical condition is clearly demonstrated in the total absence of the sex drive in animals after castration. It is further shown in the decreased strength of the sex drive in cases where the food has been deficient in vitamin E, as well as in cases of persons suffering from certain glandular deficiencies, such as an underfunctioning thyroid.

Law 9: *The strength of a drive is influenced by the environmental conditions.* By an ingenious method Kinder [1] studied the effect of temperature changes on the nest-building drives of rats. A

[1] Kinder, Elaine F.: "A Study of the Nest-Building Activity of the Albino Rat," *Journal of Experimental Zoölogy*, XLVII, no. 2, April 5, 1927.

litter of eight rats was divided into two groups of three each, and the two remaining rats were used as controls. Three rats of the first group were placed in cages out of doors with a temperature varying from 40° to 60° F.; the second group of three rats were placed in a heated room with a temperature of approximately 90° F.; and the control animals were placed in a room with a temperature of about 70° F. One hundred and forty strips of paper with which to build nests were placed in each cage. During the first forty hours the animals in the heated room built fewer nests than the outdoor animals or the controls, and after forty hours they built no nests at all. The total number of nests built by the three rats in the heated room was only fourteen, the average number of strips used by each rat per six-hour period being 11.5, 11.7, and 6.6. During the same period the outdoor animals built thirty-eight nests and used, respectively, 44, 52, and 38.6 strips of paper per six-hour period. It was found, however, that when exposed to extreme cold (below 50° F.) the nest-building activity dropped out almost completely and the animals remained inactive. Seventy hours after the beginning of the experiment, when the rats from the outdoor cages were placed in the heated room, their nest-building activity ceased almost immediately.

This law is illustrated in human affairs by the effect of weather conditions on the desire for alcohol as indicated by the greatly increased number of arrests for drunkenness during cold rainy days. The effect of spring weather in increasing the sex drive is seen not only in case of the lower animals, but in man as well. To keep the romantic feelings of youth within proper bounds, in the spring many jurisdictions find it advisable to detail additional police to take care of such violations as parking automobiles at night without lights along the highways. In some suburban communities arrests for this violation are from fifty to seventy-five per cent higher during May and June than during September and October.

Law 10: *The strength of many drives seems to have certain rhythmical variations.* In Kinder's experiment it was found that the nest-building drive in female rats after puberty shows a periodic variation in strength, being least during œstrum and strongest a

few days before the œstrum begins. Wang [1] found that restless
seeking behavior of the female rat, as measured by the revolving
drum, was highest during the œstrous cycle and much lower in the
inter-œstrous period. Several other animal experiments show that
with females the strength of certain drives has very marked periodic
variations accompanying the sexual cycle. How much this periodic
variation in strength of drives is due to the innate functioning of
the bodily organs, and how much to the conditioned or learned
functioning is difficult to say. We know, for example, that in cases
of prolonged fasting the hunger urge during the first few days shows
considerable increase in strength around the time of day that the
individual is accustomed to eat. This increase in strength is certainly due, in part at least, to habit.

  Law 11: The strength of a drive is influenced by age. Ten pubes-
cent and prepubescent rats (age 40 days) were placed in section A
of an experiment box similar to the one shown in Figure 1. A
female during œstrum was placed in section C, and a current of
twenty-eight volts turned on in section B. Only one crossed. Ten
adult male rats 120 days old were placed in the box under similar
conditions. Five of them crossed to the female. Then ten males
270 days old (senile) were placed in the experiment box. Only two
of them crossed.

  A parallel is seen in human behavior, beginning with the indifference of the prepubescent to sex stimuli, passing on through the
period of ardent pursuit of adult life, and ending with the apathy
of senescence.

  *Law 12: The behavior of any animal, be he rat, horse, or human,
is the resultant of his drives to action and the opposing resistances.*
This law is demonstrated in all of the preceding experiments. It
is as vital and generally useful to the psychologist as the law that
for every action there is an equal and opposite reaction is to the physicist.

----

[1] Wang, G. H.: *Comparative Psychology Monographs*, ii, no. 6.

CHAPTER II

EFFECT OF INTERNAL STIMULI ON BEHAVIOR

The variation of a few hundredths of one per cent in the glucose of the blood may make the difference between cowardice and courage; may determine whether a man shall be shot as a slacker or medaled as a hero.

EDWIN SLOSSON

ONE'S behavior at any time is in no small part determined by his physical condition. Given one physical state, the individual assumes an attitude of cheerful and kindly well-being toward others, while the same individual with another physical condition is so irritable and cross that no one can come near him with impunity. The practical significance of the effect of physical condition on behavior is almost universally recognized. The little child soon learns that "mama must not be disturbed when she has the headache," and that when father has "indigestion" it is worse than needless to try to interest him in a picnic. From time immemorial the soothing effect of a good dinner upon the disposition of a healthy person has been recognized, and few devices are more often employed by the diplomat in his profession of human engineering than is the invitation to dinner. More problems of "great pith and moment" have been solved over the dinner table than in all other conferences combined. The sick man and the same man when in perfect health are so unlike as scarcely to seem the same person. The behavior of the man who has lost two or three nights' sleep will be sufficiently different from his ordinary character that the difference will be readily apparent to the casual observer.

In this chapter we shall consider the effect on behavior of I, Fatigue; II, Loss of sleep; III, Hunger and malnutrition; IV, Disease processes.

I. FATIGUE

Fatigue is the temporary decrease in efficiency that rest can cure. There are usually recognized two main classes of fatigue; A, physical fatigue, and B, mental or nervous fatigue. The terms *physical fatigue* and *mental fatigue* are somewhat ambiguous, and it is to be regretted that we do not have more explicit terms. In the last analysis all fatigue is physical, for there can be no mental activity without bodily changes; but for the sake of discussion we shall consider mental fatigue as the fatigue of the connecting system and physical fatigue as the fatigue of the muscles and glands.

A. PHYSICAL FATIGUE. Probably the greatest problem of efficiency in industry is that of physical fatigue. Consequently a great deal of attention has been given to the causes and effects of fatigue, and to methods of avoiding it. Fatigue has been variously defined as (1) a temporary decrease in efficiency due to prolonged work, play, or any activity without adequate rest, and (2) a complex of feelings of lassitude or weariness. The concept of fatigue as a decrease in capacity for work is more useful than regarding fatigue as a feeling, for it is difficult to measure feelings accurately. But the definition of fatigue most useful to psychologists is one which explains the cause of the decreased capacity for work. Fatigue may best be defined as the consumption of energy-producing material and the accumulation of waste products which decrease the working efficiency.

1. **Causes of physical fatigue.** In activity the body uses up energy-producing material just as a steam engine burns up coal. This energy-producing material is glycogen, which is manufactured in the liver from materials taken from the blood stream. In strenuous activity the muscle uses up glycogen more rapidly than it can be supplied, and when the glycogen has been used up to a certain extent there is a loss of efficiency and finally fatigue. But in addition to the consumption of glycogen, continued work causes an accumulation in the organism of waste products which result from the breaking down and consumption of the glycogen. The accumulation of these waste products is usually the more important cause of fatigue, since it seldom happens that the supply of glycogen is anywhere near exhausted when fatigue sets in. The principal waste product given off by the active muscle is CO_2, which is absorbed in the blood stream, carried to other parts of the body, finally to the lungs, and given off in the expired air. But in very

strenuous muscular activity, CO_2 accumulates faster than it can be carried away, and the muscles are poisoned or fatigued. Exercise of one set of muscles causes decrease in efficiency throughout the body, for the accumulated fatigue products are carried in the blood stream to other parts of the body.

That fatigue is due to the accumulation of waste products in the tissues is demonstrated by various experiments on animals. The following will serve as an example of such experiments: From the body of a hunting dog that was completely exhausted by the chase, two pints of blood were transfused into the blood stream of a rested dog that had previously given up the same amount of blood to make room for the blood carrying the fatigue products. In a short time the rested dog showed all the signs of fatigue. The chief cause of fatigue in this instance was without doubt the waste products that were transferred in the two pints of blood. That fatigue is primarily due to an accumulation of waste products is also shown by the fact that *rigor mortis* sets in very much more quickly in an animal that is fatigued when it is killed than in one that is rested. Carrier pigeons killed immediately after a long flight grow stiff almost instantly after death, while those killed when in a rested state require from ten to twenty times as long for *rigor mortis* to set in.

2. **Factors in physical fatigue.** There are a number of factors in physical fatigue, among the more important of which are: *a*, adaptation to the job; *b*, age of the worker, and *c*, specific working conditions.

a. Adaptation to the job. Adaptation to the job is one of the most important factors in efficiency. The individual who is a "square peg in a round hole" cannot possibly work up to his highest efficiency. And many square pegs in round holes are such because they are not adapted to the job either physically or mentally. For example, a short stout girl cannot do as efficient work at a telephone switchboard as a slender girl, because it is harder for her to reach over the board. She also becomes fatigued more quickly than one who is physically better adapted to the job. The man who is slow in his movements soon becomes fatigued attempting to feed a machine which goes faster than his natural speed of movement. A great deal of extra energy is consumed in his efforts to keep up with the machine, and fatigue sets in early, greatly decreasing his efficiency.

The worker who dislikes his job cannot attain the highest efficiency of which he is capable. Constantly performing work which is repulsive leads to mental conflict, and decreased efficiency. The student learns two or three times more in an hour if he is studying his favorite subject than he would if he were studying a subject which he disliked. Thus, mental as well as physical adaptation to the job are factors in determining efficiency.

b. Age and fatigue. In recent years a good deal has been written in connection with child-labor legislation concerning the inability of young persons to compete in industry. The harmful physical and mental results of child labor have been brought out so forcibly that little need be added to that subject. The fatigue of industrial work affects the old as well as the very young, as is shown by the significant absence of old people in the more laborious types of industry. There is a widespread opinion that forty-five represents the average retiring age for most industrial workers. In trying to account for the very noticeable absence of workers beyond middle life in certain occupations, one student of the problem says: "The answer inevitably comes to mind that the rigor of the game incapacitates them at an age when human beings are expected still to be doing excellent work." If this is so, the accumulated fatigue of many years is the decisive factor. The remedy would appear to be a diminution in the hours of labor and the installation of other conditions not so severe for the human machine, and conducive to its longer usefulness.

c. Specific working conditions. The working conditions as such have a tremendous influence upon the quantity and quality of work done and upon the amount of energy consumed in the process.

(1) *Hours.* In the last few years there has been an almost world-wide movement to shorten the exhaustingly long working hours of industrial workers. And strangely enough, cutting down the working day by an hour or two does not as a rule involve a reduction of the day's production, but often brings an increase. This gain has been due largely, no doubt, to a partial elimination

of the element of fatigue.   Shortening the working hours and giving rest pauses during the day also decrease the number of industrial accidents.

The time of day at which the work is done also seems to be a factor in efficiency.   Night work is characterized by a greater fatigue than is day work; its total output is less than day work; and its accident rate and its proportion of lost time are in excess over those of the day.

(2) *Rest periods.*   An important factor in the elimination of fatigue is the rest period.   The frequency of pauses for rest and the length of the pauses are determined by the nature of the work and the length of the work period.   The heavier the work, other things being equal, the more essential is the rest period.   Taylor's study of the pig-iron handlers of the Bethlehem Steel Company is probably the best known case of the results achieved by regulating the pauses and the speed of work, and thus increasing production. Taylor[1] found that each man loaded on an average $12\frac{1}{2}$ tons of pig-iron per day.   After studying working periods and rest periods in relation to the size of the load, Taylor selected a number of men and directed their work.   He did not allow them to lift and to carry the loads as they pleased, but every movement was exactly prescribed by a foreman who timed accurately the periods of work and rest.   The work consisted in picking from a pile of pig-iron on the ground a single pig weighing 92 pounds, carrying this up an inclined plank, and dropping it upon a railway car.   Although simple, it required heavy muscular work.   By alternating work and rest periods the men managed to carry $47\frac{1}{2}$ tons per man each day instead of $12\frac{1}{2}$, and were under load only 42 per cent of the time. Their wages were increased 60 per cent, their output increased 266 per cent.

This case indicates that the individual cannot judge for himself the optimum work and rest periods, or the most efficient way of accomplishing the result.   Some people, keyed to a high pitch of excitement, continue work far beyond the limits of safety, not realizing or feeling fatigue.   Others become tired easily and give

[1] Taylor, Frederick W.: *Principles of Scientific Management.*   (Harper & Bros., New York, 1915.)

in to their feeling of fatigue long before actual capacity for work is decreased. Both of these types, however, other things being equal, profit in increased efficiency and feeling of well-being by alternate periods of work and rest.

(3) *Distraction.* Any distraction such as noise has a tiring effect on the nervous system due to the disturbance of attention. The worker can adjust himself more readily to continual noises such as the hum of machinery than unexpected noises such as dropping boxes, for the sudden noise calls up a sort of fear reaction. If the noise is continuous, the worker soon becomes negatively adjusted, but each time that the sudden noise occurs it calls for adjustment.

(4) *Complexity.* Complexity of the work by calling upon more muscles and exacting closer attention tends to make the work more fatiguing unless it is offset by greater interest on the part of the worker. In the latter case, although the element of fatigue is not eliminated, it may be more tolerable than monotony. Although uniformly repeated acts tend to become automatic and the nerve centers become less liable to fatigue, the sense of monotony may become fatiguing in itself. This is particularly true in the case of the worker who knows he is capable of doing more complex work. Workmen of a low grade of intelligence are not very likely to feel the monotony of doing a routine job, and in fact prefer doing the type of work that will require the least thinking.

(5) *Lighting.* Bad lighting not only makes an output of standard quality difficult, but it causes headaches and other effects due to eye strain. Adequate light for the work in hand is not enough; the light, to be the most efficient and least fatiguing should be so diffused that the shadows are at a minimum. This is more important in night work where the strain upon the eyes is especially great.

(6) *Posture.* Posture is a particularly important element in fatigue. A slouching posture cramps the lungs and other vital organs and weakens endurance. In industry the best measure to secure proper posture comes from providing the right tables and chairs for the work. Many States have legal requirements regarding seats in industry, but most of them specify only "provision of seats," and no distinction is made between a box and the best

constructed chair. In recent years considerable attention has been paid to the construction of working tables and chairs. A work table has been invented which may be used for sitting work, or adjusted for standing work. Several chairs for fatigue elimination have also been designed. These are provided with foot rests and backs and are so adjusted that the elbows of the worker are at the same distance from the work table when seated as when standing. The purpose is to lessen fatigue by alternate periods of standing and sitting while at work.

B. MENTAL OR NERVOUS FATIGUE. As pointed out above, mental fatigue is the fatigue of the connecting or nervous system. But it is extremely difficult to get pure nervous fatigue apart from muscular fatigue, for in all mental work the muscles are more or less involved; even such purely mental operations as mental multiplication, if continued long enough, necessitate keeping certain muscles under tension with the result of producing muscular fatigue as well as mental fatigue.

The nerve fibers are known to be indefatigable, and the cell bodies are apparently so. It would appear, therefore, that all the phenomena of nervous fatigue must be explained in terms of a heightened synaptic resistance.

There are two chief subjective symptoms of nervous fatigue: (1) sensations of weariness, and (2) the presence of a sense of effort in mental and physical activities. Sensations of weariness are supposed to orginate from impulses in specialized receptors. These impulses are apparently due to the accumulation of lactates and other waste products within them. The symptom, which is characterized by the feeling of increased effort, is probably due to the heightened synaptic resistance, necessitating the resort to previously unused paths, or to increase the effort necessary to force the impulses through the partially blocked paths. This latter would account for a change in the timing of the successive impulses, tending to slow them.

The chief objective signs of nervous fatigue are: (1) a decrease in the amount of work done, and (2) a decrease in the quality of the performance. The first is seen in the tendency of workers in any field to do less per unit of time as fatigue develops. The second is characterized by an increased tendency for the attention to wander; greater liability to accidents when exposed in hazardous work, and a greater liability to errors. Both of these signs are probably due to the heightened synaptic resistance in the more commonly and efficiently used nerve paths with a consequent détour of nervous activity to less well-organized paths.

Not only are the paths which deal with overt activity subject to fatigue, but the inhibitory paths also share in the fatigue. Fatigue of these inhibitory paths tends to release reactions ordinarily held in check. Thus a fatigued person is much more likely to fly into a rage than he would be if not fatigued.

Although what is usually termed "mental fatigue" may include certain factors other than those purely mental, separate mental functions, if exercised continuously without rest for long periods of time, do decrease in efficiency. One of the most extensive studies that has been made of the effect of long-continued exercise on mental functioning is the study of Arai [1] on the function of mental multiplication. The experimenter herself was the subject for the experiment. The problem was to measure the increase in time required to multiply mentally four-place numbers by four-place numbers continuously from 11 A.M. to 11 P.M. for four days in succession. Particular merits of the experiment are that it measured the fatigue due to exercise of a very difficult intellectual process; that sufficient practice was obtained during the week before the actual experiment to eliminate improvement due to practice; that it was as free as possible from sensory and muscular work; and that interest of the subject in obtaining the results eliminated much of the effect that might have been due to lack of interest or monotony. Her method is indicated in the following quotation from her report:

The subject relied on memory for the figures and multiplied them with closed eyes. The method made the task more difficult, but it helped to eliminate sensory fatigue. When the subject forgot the original figures, she looked at them again, but as the time was made longer on this account, the loss of the original figures was counted against her. But this seldom occurred, as the subject was careful to commit the numbers to memory.

[1] Arai, T.: *Mental Fatigue.* (Teachers College, Columbia University Contributions to Education, no. 54, 1912.)

The deleterious effect of mental fatigue on efficiency is indicated by comparing the time required to do the first eight problems on each day with that required to do the last eight. From these results it is seen that it required about twice as long to do the last eight as the first eight examples. This indicates that there is a considerable decrease in mental efficiency after a long period of continuous mental activity.

	Mar. 3	Mar. 4	Mar. 5	Mar. 6	Average
First eight....	46.9	45.2	35.8	46.1	43.9
Last eight	101.1	96.4	99.1	78.5	93.8

In interpreting mental fatigue, two things must be borne in mind. First, mental fatigue in a particular mental function may not and usually does not mean "general mental fatigue." Marked fatigue in one mental function may reduce the ability to perform other mental functions only very slightly. Second, mental fatigue may be caused by factors wholly extraneous to the work itself. In other words, one may be fatigued by what he does not do. This is illustrated in the more rapid onset of fatigue in the case of the college student who forces himself to stay in his room and study while his friends are having a grand and glorious time at a party. It requires much more effort for him to study due to the "pull" of his desire to go to the party.

Owing to the great importance of the effort and interest factors in mental achievement, work curves representing achievement over relatively long periods of time often correspond more closely to the agreeableness than to the difficulty of a task. Thorndike [1] has suggested the desirability of plotting a curve of satisfyingness of work as well as a curve of actual achievement in estimating the fatigue-producing qualities of any task. That mental fatigue is generally not a real decrease in capacity for work is indicated by the fact that, when fatigue is apparently present, the output of work can be greatly increased if an increased incentive is offered. The chief factors in mental fatigue are often only lack of interest and the mental conflict between the desire to be doing something else and the necessity for centering attention on the work in hand.

[1] Thorndike, E. L.: *Briefer Course in Educational Psychology.* (Teachers College, 1914.)

Neurasthenia is a condition of weakness or exhaustion of the nervous system, giving rise to various forms of mental and bodily inefficiency. It is thought to be produced by prolonged nervous strain. Worry and emotional stress acting on an unstable nervous system are very potent factors in the causation of neurasthenia.

Among the most commonly observed signs of neurasthenia are loss of weight, debility, despondency, and insomnia. The cerebral symptoms are connected with an inability to perform the ordinary mental work. The patient finds it impossible to add correctly a row of figures; the answering of a few letters is a source of the greatest worry; there is a loss of power of fixed attention, and the performance of his simplest duties requires considerable effort. As a rule such people are moody, irritable, and depressed. Complaint is made about everything. Advanced neurasthenia is practically never free from some form of anxiety and fear, and the classical "anxiety neurosis" is a frequent outcome of the condition.

Restorative processes. If the theory of nervous fatigue is correct which attributes it to accumulation of waste products in or about sensitive structures, the obvious basis for restoration is a discontinuance of activity so that time may be had to remove these products. The synapses are so minute and so well supplied with blood, that rapid restoration would be expected to follow the cessation of the flow of impulses across them. The rate of restoration is found, however, to depend on the amount of fatigue products carried by the blood; since the synapses tend to come into equilibrium with the blood which surrounds them, and, if there is a high concentration of fatigue products in the blood, the recovery must be slow, but if the concentration in the blood stream is low, there is a fairly rapid recovery.

The above explanation accounts for the recovery from daily fatigue, but does not satisfactorily account for the gradual lowering of nervous efficiency resulting from long periods of continuous work or mental stress. In such conditions as neurasthenia and nervous breakdowns due to prolonged mental stress, there is probably a more deep-seated impairment of the synapses than a simple accumulation of waste products. In such cases there is reason to believe that the primary cause of the prolonged "nerve fag" is due to a disturbance in the functioning of the ductless glands by which the environment of the nerve cell is affected for the worse, for it is definitely known that secretions from those glands have a marked influence on the functioning of the nerve cells. If this theory is correct, recovery would depend on such a mode of living as would restore these glands to their normal functioning.

The chief method of counteracting fatigue is by rest and recreation. Recreation is not inactivity, but another kind of activity. It is important in this connection to distinguish between work and play. In many cases the activity is the same. For example, to the person who for so many dollars plays the piano in a moving-picture theater, playing the piano is work; but to the other people who play the piano solely for the love of playing, the activity is play. It is thus obvious that work and play cannot be distinguished by the type of activity involved. The difference lies in the mental attitude toward the activity. Play is indulged in for its own sake, with no ulterior motive, the activity being satisfying in and of itself. Work, on the other hand, is not indulged in because of the enjoyment of the process, but because of some ulterior motive, as the desire to receive a salary with which to provide the necessities and luxuries of life, or to obtain the final result of the work, as the completed dress to wear to a party.

If the work performed is of such a nature that recreation comes from the work itself, little other recreation is needed, and the individual can work from twelve to fourteen hours a day with no fear of a breakdown. But if the work performed is monotonous or otherwise unsatisfying, more recreation is needed. Nervous breakdowns are very seldom caused by overwork alone, but are generally the result of prolonged worry or unhappiness. Because the worry or unhappiness is frequently associated with some phase of the work, what is primarily the result of worry is often attributed to overwork.

Recreation has two main purposes. The first purpose of recreation is to give expression to those fundamental drives which are thwarted by work. For example, the man who works alone most of the time does not give expression to the social side of his nature, and needs social recreation. The man who is of an artistic nature, and whose daily work makes no appeal to his æsthetic sense, needs recreation of the type that will enable him to develop his artistic side. Adequate recreation must satisfy all desires not satisfied by other activities. The second purpose of recreation is to take the mind away from worry and anxiety in connection with work. The best possible recreation is some activity or interest in which work is completely forgotten.

Recreation may be either physical or mental. The best recreation is given by the use of muscles or nerves which are not used in the daily work. A long walk affords little recreation to the letter carrier, while it will make the clerk, who has been bending over a desk all day, feel like a new person. Physical exercise has a beneficial effect upon those of sedentary occupation. It increases the circulation and heightens the tonicity of the muscles. More than that, it rests the higher brain centers, for it is a return to the primitive. The greater the similarity between the recreation indulged in and the activities of our forefathers, the greater appears to be the relaxation obtained. This explains the appeal of fishing, hunting, mountain-climbing, and camping, all of which are a "return to nature." Dancing, when not associated with late hours and dissipation, is an excellent recreation, involving, as it does, both physical and mental relaxation. Laughter, too, is a shock absorber of both physical and mental stresses and strains. It is a reaction against the repressing effects of society: an expression of glee at seeing the cogs of civilization slip momentarily. After tenseness and strained attention, laughter comes as a relaxation.

More strictly mental relaxation is offered by the moving pictures, card games, novels, radio, music, and art. These activities give physical rest and mental recreation or change. Religion, in giving a sense of peace and quiet, is a powerful mental recreation. The use of alcohol and drugs is a more harmful attempt to find relaxation from the stresses and strains of life. Still another popular recreation whose effect is chiefly mental is the trip, producing a change in scenery. The new environment has a beneficial effect in freeing the mind from unpleasant associations.

II. LOSS OF SLEEP

Every one knows from past experience that his mood and achievement during the day are dependent to no small extent upon the previous night's sleep. But many people insist that they must have nine or ten hours of sleep each night in order to feel well. Others, like Edison and Napoleon and Clemenceau, require only four or five hours of sleep per night even though engaged in strenuous work. Thomas Edison and eight of his men, in support of his theory that sleep is largely a useless habit, worked from one hundred and forty-five to one hundred and fifty hours a week for five weeks, or about twenty-one hours a day. During the period every man gained in weight and felt perfectly well. Edison believes that the average person sleeps entirely too much, and that one would feel much better if he slept only four hours a night instead of eight or nine. The length of time that people sleep is largely a matter of habit — an expensive habit, as it unnecessarily wastes valuable years out of the lifetime of the individual.

Although scientists have advanced various theories to explain the changes which occur in the body during sleep, very little is known of the actual character of sleep. By an ingenious series of recording instruments attached to the sleeper, Johnson,[1] Swan and Weigand secured records of the movements made during sleep. They found that the average length of the "rest period" — i.e., the average period during which no motions of sufficient magnitude to show on the record were made — was about twelve minutes. In other words, the average sleeper readjusts his position about five times an hour. They found marked individual differences in the length of the rest period, some averaging one change each eight minutes, and others changing about every seventeen minutes. They concluded that "the way an individual sleeps is a very definite personal characteristic." It was observed that extreme nervous fatigue was followed by increased restlessness rather than the reverse. This was probably due to the fact that increased fatigue of the higher brain centers tended to depress the inhibitory discharges from these centers which hold in check the reflexes con-

[1] Johnson, H. M., Swan, T. H., and Weigand, G. E.: "Sleep," *Psychological Bulletin*. (1926.)

trolled by the lower centers. In other words, the fatigue of the higher centers tended to take the brakes off the lower centers.

In 1925, the writer [1] and his co-workers conducted a series of experiments to determine the mental and physiological changes which accompany long periods of voluntary insomnia. Eight subjects in this experiment were kept awake for sixty hours, taking, at regular intervals, mental and physical tests, and tests in driving an automobile. Laboratory analyses of the blood and urine of those going without sleep gave indications of pathological changes similar to the changes which occur as a result of a mild infection. These pathological conditions were restored to normal by from seven to ten hours of sleep. The blood pressure decreased with increasing periods of insomnia. The lung capacity was little affected by loss of sleep, but the strength was slightly decreased. The visual and auditory apparatus were found to be less acute after sixty hours of insomnia than before. There was no corresponding mental change, the subjects doing just as well on mental tests after being awake for sixty hours or more as before. By the end of forty-five hours of insomnia, ability to drive an automobile was decreased markedly, for there was a strong tendency to fall asleep at the wheel. Ability to perform driving operations requiring only a short attention span, such as parking a machine in a limited space, was not decreased by insomnia.

The findings in this experiment lend support to the chemical theory of sleep, which holds that sleep is the result of the presence of certain poisons elaborated during wakefulness. These poisons tend to produce sleep by a purely chemical action. The toxins produced during wakefulness can be best eliminated during sleep, because in a state of complete rest, as in deep sleep, relatively few toxins are formed, since there is a minimum of nerve and muscle activity.

The important problem, then, is to determine how much sleep is necessary for the detoxication process. Some persons of the neurasthenic type go to sleep and after ten or twelve hours of disturbed slumber awake just as exhausted as when they went to sleep. Other persons of the type of Edison or Napoleon seem perfectly

[1] George Washington University, *Bulletin*, I. (1925.)

able to eliminate whatever toxins are present in four or five hours of sleep, and awaken thoroughly refreshed. The question, then, seems to resolve itself, not so much into how long one should sleep, as into how fast one should sleep. In other words, *sleep has not only length but depth.*

This idea is supported by the fact that the first two hours of sleep are proved to be very much deeper than the last two. In a series of experiments designed to determine the depth of sleep, Kohlschütter discovered that it requires an auditory stimulus approximately eight times as strong to awaken a person at the close of the first hour's sleep as it does at the close of the second hour; and a stimulus forty times as strong to awaken the person at the close of one hour of sleep as at the close of four hours; while it requires a stimulus more than one hundred times as strong to awaken a person at the close of one hour as it does after six hours. Although the restorative effects of the various hours of sleep may not con-

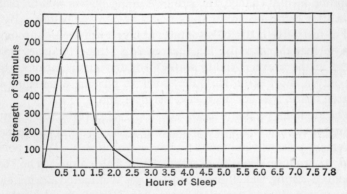

FIGURE 6. CURVE ILLUSTRATING THE STRENGTH OF AN AUDITORY STIMULUS (A BALL FALLING FROM A HEIGHT) NECESSARY TO WAKEN A SLEEPING PERSON

The hours are marked below. The tests were made at half-hour intervals. The curve indicates that the distance through which the ball required to be dropped increased during the first hour, and then diminished, at first very rapidly, then slowly. (After Kohlschütter.)

form very exactly to the ratios just quoted, yet these experiments certainly show that sleep has depth as well as length. This is shown in Figure 6.

The practical aspects of the problem of sleep are apparent. During the first twenty years of life a man can accomplish relatively little, for this is the period of preparation. The next forty years are the productive period, for as a rule the years subsequent to sixty are relatively unproductive. Of this forty years, two thirds are spent by man in sleep and unproductive recreation, leaving not quite fourteen years of life for productive activity. If, by building up new habits, or by some other means whereby the amount of sleep required by most persons can be cut down to six hours instead of eight hours a night, it would be possible to increase this period of possible productiveness one fourth. Whether an attempt to reduce the number of hours of sleep by gradually cutting off a few minutes from the total sleeping time each month would be followed by any injurious effects on the organism, no one is at present in a position to say. Only a series of carefully planned experiments can determine whether reducing the number of hours of sleep, if gradually done, would produce any bad effects whatever.

III. HUNGER AND MALNUTRITION

At every moment throughout life the tissues of the body are being exhausted and repaired. The tearing-down process and the building-up process are continuous. In strenuous work and in disease the tearing-down process is more powerful than the building-up process, whereas in rest, sleep, and recreation the reverse is true. Probably the most important single factor in the building-up process is food.

The importance of a proper diet for the upbuilding of the body has been greatly stressed in recent years. Surveys of school children in certain districts show an appallingly large proportion suffering from malnutrition, due to a deficiency of some fundamental quality in the diet.

The chief chemical compounds in foods which are necessary to a balanced diet are proteins, carbohydrates, fats, water, salts, and vitamins. The proper proportion of these constituents in the diet depends upon a number of factors. On the whole the best diet is a varied diet composed of meats, vegetables, and fruits in proper proportion and quantity. For fuel the body needs particularly fats and carbohydrates. For tissue-building the body needs iron, calcium, phosphorus, and iodine. For regulating the body processes vitamins are essential. Five vitamins have been discovered and there are doubtless others.

In experiments with rats it has been found that animals fed wholly on meat are much more vigorous than animals receiving a vegetable diet, but that neither the vegetable-fed nor the meat-fed rats are able to learn the maze as quickly as those animals with a balanced diet.

Malnutrition. The effect of food deficiency on behavior has long been recognized. During the World War the close relationship which exists between nutrition and reproduction was demonstrated. In all countries suffering from food shortage, the birth rate fell, a fact attributable in part to undernutrition. Slonaker's [1] experiments demonstrated that the activity of rats is closely related to the sexual cycle, and that this activity is highly responsive to changes in the nutritive plane of the animals. Stone [2] found that stunting by underfeeding delays the sex development and the behavior associated with the onset of puberty. Anderson [3] and Smith have shown that rats stunted by long periods of malnutrition do not learn as fast as control groups.

Vitamins. There are at least five vitamins: A, B, C, D, E. Vitamin A must be present if a mammal is to maintain good nutritive condition. Complete absence of this vitamin in the diet leads to decline and death. Rapid and complete recovery follows the administration of proper amounts of the vitamin. Deficiency in this vitamin results in zero-ophthalmia, an eye disease. Deficiency in vitamin B results in a type of nerve disease known as beri-beri, and in loss of appetite. Deficiency in vitamin C, which is found abundantly in such fruits as oranges, lemons, and tomatoes, results in scurvy. Vitamin D, which is present in large quantities in cod-liver oil, prevents rickets in children. Vitamin E is necessary for reproduction, and a deficiency in it lessens the sex urge.

Organic salts. The part played by mineral salts in controlling

---

[1] Slonaker, J. R.: *American Journal of Physiology.* (1924.)
[2] Stone, C. P.: *Journal of Comparative Psychology.* (1924.)
[3] Anderson, J. E., and Smith, A. H.: *Journal of Comparative Psychology.* (1926.)

behavior is only beginning to be appreciated.   It is an interesting fact that the salts found in the human body are the same as those found in the sea water, and, with the exception of magnesium, in the same proportion, but only in one fourth the concentration.   It probably means that in the distant past, when our animal ancestors began to forsake the sea life and to live on land, they had the proportion of salts now present in body fluids, and that they simply brought with them the salt mixture by which they had been surrounded, and to which their protoplasm was already adjusted.   Investigators have recently discovered that a disturbance in the calcium and phosphorus balance results in a marked instability of the nervous system which may be manifested in convulsions. Tetany in young children is an example.   Iodine, which has a marked influence on behavior, is an active constituent of the secretions from the thyroid gland and will be discussed in connection with the extracts from that gland.

A moderate diet is just as important as a balanced diet.   Most people probably eat much more than they actually require and select their food with little regard to food value.   Edison believes that people eat entirely too much.   He is quoted as saying: "On the average, men would get on better if they reduced their food consumption by two thirds."

A number of studies of the effect of prolonged fasting have been made.   In 1912, Langfield made a study of a forty-year-old man who fasted for thirty-one days.   During that time he drank daily seven hundred and fifty cubic centimeters of distilled water, but received no food of any kind.   Many tests were made of his mental, sensory, and motor ability.   In general there was a loss in muscular strength during the fast, and a gain in sensory acuity, while ability to learn was apparently little affected.

At the present time little is known about the effect of different kinds of food on the mental efficiency of an individual.   A well-planned series of experiments to determine the relation of food ingested to the intellectual and emotional traits is very much needed.

IV. DISEASE PROCESSES

Very little is known about the effect of the various disease processes on efficiency. It is generally believed that disease decreases efficiency, but whether this is true of all diseases, or whether it applies equally to mental and physical efficiency, is not known. Each year there is an average of one "cold" per person and many employees with colds continue to work at their regular tasks, but neither they nor their employers know what effects the cold has on their efficiency.

In 1928, the writer studied the effect of "colds" upon the scores made on intelligence tests. Complete records on only ten subjects were available for the study. Five of the subjects were first given the tests when they had colds, and the tests were repeated within a month when they had recovered. Tests were also given to a large number of other subjects, and when any of them got a cold the tests were repeated. The results were not very conclusive, but tended to show that subjects with colds attempted fewer items, and made more errors in those attempted.

Although there have been few scientific investigations in this field we have learned some things by observation. We know, for example, that a toothache lowers the threshold for emotional outbursts and paves the way to irritability. We know that it is very difficult to fix the attention when one has a headache, or to be the "life of the party" when one is suffering from an attack of indigestion. We have observed that patients suffering from certain diseases, such as typhoid fever, are dull and apathetic, showing a very depressed emotional tone; whereas patients suffering from such a disease as tuberculosis are more often bright and alert, having an optimistic outlook on life. This is true even though the tuberculous patient may be much nearer death than is the typhoid patient.

It is a fact of common observation that dyspepsia and a pessimistic philosophy of life go hand in hand, but we do not have positive evidence that the pessimism is the result rather than the cause of the dyspepsia. It is further observed that the man with an epicurean or hedonistic philosophy of life develops this philosophy during the time when his various bodily organs are working most efficiently. Had the internal chemistry of Cleopatra and Octavia been interchanged, how different the history of the world would have been!

That the various desires and cravings are very largely determined by the internal condition of the individual is seen in the peculiar food cravings which often accompany pregnancy. During this condition some women evince an almost uncontrollable desire for peculiar and sometimes revolting articles of food. A craving for such a substance as chalk is not infrequent. According to Williams,[1] we occasionally meet with women who diagnose their condition mainly from the occurrence of changes in their own temperament with which they have become familiar in previous pregnancies.

The effect of high or low body temperature on mental efficiency is well known. The range of temperature at which our mental mechanisms can function normally is very narrow. The continuance for more than a few minutes of body temperature two or more degrees either above or below normal is accompanied by symptoms indicating a disturbance in the tissues on which our mental life depends. If the temperature becomes sufficiently high the patient passes into delirium, and if the temperature becomes sufficiently low the patient passes into a dreamlike state of lethargy. The delirium of high temperature is often seen, but bodily temperature low enough to produce lethargy is seldom seen.

Endocrines. The effect of endocrine disfunction on one's mental and emotional life needs no better illustration than the dull and apathetic behavior of the person whose thyroid is underactive, or the restless and irritable behavior of the person with an overactive thyroid. This will be discussed more fully in connection with the administration of endocrine products in the next chapter.

Chronic infection. The influence of low-grade chronic infections on mental efficiency is not at present appreciated. The human body functions as a unit, and the various functions carried on by the body are all interrelated. Thinking and feeling are functions of the body just as digestion and the circulation of the blood are functions of the body. And just as low-grade infections may interfere with our digestive and circulatory apparatus, so they may

[1] Williams, J. W.: *Obstetrics.* (D. Appleton & Co., 1923.)

interfere with our thinking and feeling mechanisms. The importance of chronic infection in causing insanity is becoming apparent in the work of Cotton and will be discussed in connection with the chapter on Mental Disorders.

Dr. Anita Muhl [1] studied the personality trends of thirty tuberculous women, varying in age, social status, nationality, and occupation. In all of these she found certain fundamental personality trends which seem to be characteristic of tuberculous patients. A very characteristic thing about these tuberculous patients seems to be their twofold personality, the constant struggle in them between ambition and inertia. Nothing seems to blunt their ambition, and this often gives the patients an unusually optimistic appearance even in the face of great obstacles. Dr. Muhl says: "The tremendous ambition of these people, an ambition that is generally far in excess of their physical ability to carry out, is probably the factor that is responsible for the term which is so commonly and erroneously applied to tuberculous patients, namely, the 'pathological optimism' which is attributed to them and which has been interpreted as an abnormal hope of recovery." She further emphasizes the instability in the mood of the patients as follows: "They are people of easy ups and downs, easily elated and easily depressed, though they so often seek to cover the depression with a mask of gayety and facetiousness. Their mood is unstable, as I observed them bubbling over one day and blue the next." It is impossible at present to say whether the optimism and other personality traits of tuberculous patients are due to the specific toxins liberated by the bacteria which cause the disease.

While it is recognized that current diseases have a very marked influence on our emotional life, it is not so generally known that childhood diseases and other diseases from which we have apparently recovered have considerable influence on our emotional reactions. Dr. George M. Stratton recently made a preliminary study of this subject with about nine hundred students at the University of California. He confined his study to the effects of disease upon fear and anger. Each of the students was given a brief printed description of about twenty mildly anger-provoking situa-

[1] Muhl, A.: *Psychoanalytical Review.* (1923.)

tions, such as "a stranger jostles or crowds you without apology," and the students were asked to keep track of the occurrence of any of these twenty situations and to record after each incident what his reaction to the situation was.   There were six possible degrees of reaction to the situations, ranging from number one, which was, "You are not annoyed nor irritated in even the slightest degree," through number two, "You are slightly annoyed, but there are no physical symptoms of emotion, so far as you can notice"; and so on up to number six, "You are stirred to passionate, violent anger: your physical as well as your mental equilibrium is upset; and one or more of the following physical symptoms are present: trembling, nausea, loss of appetite, inability to talk coherently, weeping." A similar set of fear-provoking situations and a set of six degrees of fear were also given the students.

The student was expected to note, as soon as possible after a situation happened to occur, which of the six grades of fear or anger was called forth by the incident in himself.   After the records had been kept for some time, Dr. Stratton made a composite emotional score for each student.   The students were not told the purpose of the records.   The personal medical history of each subject was obtained from the university infirmary records, and twenty-three diseases were included, such as diphtheria, asthma, appendicitis, infantile paralysis, tonsillitis, nervousness, and headache.

In his report of the experiment Dr. Stratton [1] said:

There is a difference between the average scores of those whose history is free from disease and the average scores of those whose history is of disease. The difference is usually so exceedingly small that I should feel that it was probably quite accidental were it not excessively recurrent in the same direction and in different groups of persons and in different samples of the same group.   And this recurrent difference is such that individuals who have had disease show a somewhat more intense emotional reaction than do those who have not had disease.

Dr. Stratton goes on to say that the individuals who have had disease show more intense anger reactions than those who have not been ill to any extent.   But so far as fear is concerned, he found

[1] Stratton, George M.: "Emotion and the Incidence of Disease," *Journal of Abnormal and Social Psychology*, XXI, pp. 19–23.   (1926.)

that little or no connection appears between the history of disease and the intensity of the fear response.

Dr. Stratton says that the number of cases — nine hundred — was too small to show the relation between fear or anger and each separate disease, but that it seems far more probable than not that the twenty-three diseases are of unequal importance in their relationship to fear and anger. "A past which includes scarlet fever, for example, seems to give fuller promise of a heightened anger response than does a past which includes tonsillitis."

CHAPTER III

EFFECT OF DRUGS ON BEHAVIOR

There is no important part of us that cannot be influenced by powers vegetable and mineral of which every village doctor knows the properties. Little herbs that grow in the meadows can turn our brains, can fill us with a fever of loving, or with a little yellow juice stop forever the beat of our ambitious hearts. The spirits that live in little crystals and the virtues that belong to the soft-colored earths are quick to brighten or deaden the soul; and indeed all we are and do is actually the result of the coördination of innumerable and often indefinable forces — including the very humblest. An extra cup of tea, a glass of wine too little, or a forgotten pilule of energizing chemical, may decide one's fate. There is nothing too humble to be counted in that mysterious collaboration called a human deed.

RICHARD LE GALLIENNE [1]

IN the preceding chapter we have considered the effect on behavior of certain metabolic changes in the body. In the present chapter we shall consider the effect of introducing certain extraneous substances, such as drugs, into the body; and in the succeeding chapter we shall consider the effect on behavior of certain factors outside the body.

The use of drugs has a very noticeable effect upon both mental and motor efficiency. The administration of a drug can so change the behavior of an individual that his closest friends will not recognize him. The effect of a drug naturally varies with the drug used, and also with the individual using it. One man is made dead drunk by a single cocktail, while another is little affected by a dozen. One man becomes nauseated after smoking a single cigar; another smokes six without any appreciable effect. An eighth grain of morphine will have more effect on the novice than twenty times that amount will on the addict. In this chapter we shall consider only the more common drugs, including: I, opiates; II, alcohol; III, cocaine; IV, caffeine; V, tobacco; VI, glandular extracts; and VII, anesthetics.

I. OPIATES

For many centuries men have used the poppy to relieve their woes and reveal to them a more pleasant world. Medical men now

[1] Le Gallienne, Richard: *Love Letters of the King* (Little, Brown & Co., Boston, 1901), pp. 234-35.

use these drugs chiefly to produce sleep and rest in cases of nervous excitement, or to relieve pain. But the majority of drug-users do not get their drugs in therapeutic doses carefully measured by competent physicians, and prescribed only when actually needed. Instead, they depend upon illicit agencies as a source for their supplies, and upon their own whims to determine the amount that they take. In China, India, Persia, and many Western countries opium is smoked and chewed by almost as large a proportion of the population as use tobacco in the United States.

The use of stimulants and opiates is increasing, due doubtless to the increasing stress of modern life. The greater social and intellectual demands upon the individual lead him to seek stimulation or relaxation in drugs according to his particular need. In opium and morphine he finds relief from pain and temporary freedom from the sorrows of life. De Quincey, in his *Confessions of an English Opium-Eater*, described the pleasant effects of the drug as follows:

I took it; and in an hour, oh! Heavens! What a revulsion! What an upheaving, from its lowest depths, of the inner spirit! What an apocalypse of the world within me! That my pains had vanished was now a trifle in my eyes; — this negative effect was swallowed up in the immensity of those positive effects which had opened before me — in the abyss of divine enjoyment thus suddenly revealed. Here was a panacea for all human woes: here was the secret of happiness, about which philosophers had disputed for so many ages, at once discovered; happiness might now be bought for a penny, and carried in the waistcoat pocket; portable ecstasies might be corked up in a pint bottle; and peace of mind could be sent down by mail.

Four stages are usually recognized in drug addiction: 1, the honeymoon stage; 2, the stage of hesitation; 3, definite addiction; and 4, terminal cachexia.

1. **The honeymoon stage.** In the early stages the primary effect of opium, which lasts about eight hours, is to excite and stimulate the system. Vivid dreams and actual hallucinations appear. Concerning the joys of this stage De Quincey says: "Whatsoever things capable of being visually represented I did but think of in the darkness, immediately shaped themselves into phantoms of the eye: and by a process apparently no less inevitable, when thus

once traced in faint and visionary colors, like writings in sympathetic ink, they were drawn out by the fierce chemistry of my dreams into insufferable splendor that fretted my heart." After this dreamy stage the opium-user falls into a deep, dreamless sleep.

2. Stage of hesitation. Like most honeymoons, the stage of ecstatic pleasure is of short duration. By the end of the period, the groom begins to discover some of the defects of his bride. While she arouses in him many feelings of aversion, she still possesses an indescribable charm which makes it well-nigh impossible to abandon her. He wishes that he had never known her, but having known her she is now so much a part of him that he has not the courage to give her up. During this stage he goes through a very definite mental conflict and his mind is "like to a little kingdom divided against itself." Overestimating his will power, he swears off and promises himself never to touch the drug again. But absence makes the heart grow fonder, and the will weaker, and, forgetting her defects, he once more seeks his bride. But there is little joy in the reunion. He soon deserts her again, only to rejoin her in a few days. And so the see-saw game of reunion and desertion continues with less and less joy on each reunion and fewer and shorter periods of desertion.

3. Stage of addiction. In the end he is forced to recognize that he has waged a losing battle, and he accepts the bride just as the prisoner of Chillon accepts his chains:

> "My chains and I grew friends,
> So much a long communion tends
> To make us what we are, even I
> Regained my freedom with a sigh."

As the opiates are habit-forming drugs, the more they are used, the greater the craving for them, and the larger the dose necessary to satisfy this craving. Once the habit has become master, the victim is the slave and must obey. There are times when he would like to fight, but the odds are too great, and he yields apparently without effort to the whims of his tyrannical master. As the craving grows, the addict will satisfy it at any cost — and "dope" is now expensive. Poverty, wretchedness, and moral degeneracy usually follow. The amount of the drug necessary to secure the desired sensations must gradually be increased. When the effects of the drug wear off, sensations of lassitude and mental depression follow, accompanied by nausea and abdominal pains which may be mistaken for appendicitis. The patient is restless and irritable, and unable to remain quiet for any length of time. His sleep is disturbed, his appetite and digestion are deranged, and except when directly under the influence of the drug the mental condition is one of depression. Persons addicted to morphine and heroin usually become inveterate liars, and no reliance can be placed in what they say. Reasoning from the fact that dope-users will lie, steal, or in some instances even murder to get the drug, many students of the problem claim that the use of the drug in and of itself directly destroys the moral fiber and ideals of the addict. This is only partly true, for it is not so much that the moral resistance is so damaged that they have no compunction of conscience for committing the vices noted above, but that the desire for the drug is so strong that a normal resistance is powerless to prevent the commission of crimes when an obstacle is encountered in securing the drug.

4. **Terminal cachexia.** The practice may be continued for an indefinite time, and enormous quantities of the drug may be required to secure the desired relief. Finally the victim is reduced to a state of both physical and mental chaos. Physically he passes into a condition of asthenia, in which he takes little or no food and dies from extreme bodily debility. The accompanying mental havoc is no less marked than the physical wreck. His nights are spent in restless insomnia; a cloud of depression covers his days, and all his activity is accompanied by loss of will power and by moral delapidation.

The drug addicts are by no means all habitués of the underworld, criminals, or degraded wrecks of humanity, deserving of no sympathy. The testimony of expert physicians with wide experience in treating dope fiends contains many stories of thoroughly respectable people who have gained the drug habit while passing through a period of great mental or physical stress, during which they tried to get relief by taking the opiate to deaden their pain; and before they knew it, they found themselves slaves to the drug.

Most of them were highstrung, nervous, temperamental people, for that is the type most likely to fall a prey to the drug habit. Not all users of the opiates pass through the four stages enumerated above. Some are successful in breaking the habit at the second stage, and some few are apparently able to take moderate amounts of the drugs for long periods of time with very little apparent damage. Such cases are the exception rather than the rule. The path leading to physical and mental disaster is the one taken by most drug addicts.

II. ALCOHOL

Since the advent of prohibition, no subject has been the theme of more popular comment than alcohol. People under the influence of alcohol are so frequently seen that most of the qualities of this drug are known to laymen. Taken in moderate doses it produces a feeling of well-being and good-fellowship, and an increased confidence in one's mental and physical skill. Larger quantities are usually followed by a certain amount of excitement, characterized by boisterous exaltation, loquacity, and gesticulation. There is an early decrease in self-control and a weakening of the will power. Alcohol produces a descending paralysis of the nervous system, first attacking the inhibitory mechanisms of the cerebrum; next attacking the motor coördination and equilibrium centers in the cerebellum; and finally, if taken in sufficient quantity, affecting the vital centers in the medulla oblongata. In the early stages, due to the release of inhibitions, the individual's speech may sparkle with wit and brilliancy, but it usually betrays the source of the inspiration. While his movements are often clever and humorous, they are more often absurd and disgusting. Outbursts of furious anger or the indulgence in maudlin sentimentality are common occurrences. As the cerebrum becomes more and more affected, the sense of responsibility and the ability to discriminate between the trivial and the important are lost, and regard for the feelings of others as well as for the ordinary decencies of life is lost. As the cerebellum becomes involved, the movements become uncertain; the walk degenerates into a stagger, and the speech becomes slow and stammering. Later, the muscles of the legs refuse to work and the individual falls down and soon passes into a drunken stupor. Nausea and vomiting are usually present during this stage. On awakening from the stupor, the individual usually experiences great depression, together with nausea, vomiting, and a want of appetite. Due to the emotional depression, attempts at suicide are frequent during this time.

According to Cushny,[1] the effects of alcohol vary greatly in different individuals and in the same individual at different times.

One person is rendered sentimental, another bellicose, while in a third there may be no appearance of excitement, the first distinct symptom being profound slumber. When drinking is indulged in in company, the excitement stage is a very common phenomenon, but if alcohol is taken without the exhilarating accompaniments of bright lights and exciting companionship, it is much less frequently seen, and the question has therefore arisen how far the environment produces the excitement in alcoholic intoxication.

Most people are under the impression that alcohol is a stimulant. The carefully controlled experiments of Dodge [2] and Benedict indicate that, on the contrary, alcohol is in reality a depressant. Concerning the effect of alcohol, Clendening [3] says:

The sedative effect of alcohol in the form of whiskey or wine is too well known to need comment. It exerts its hypnotic effects by quieting apprehensions, by exercising a psychologic change, by inhibiting sorrow and all the restraining influences of judgment, so that the partaker forgets the burdens of the world, his own unimportance, and the illimitable stretch of time.

While there is not uniform agreement of all investigators, the majority agree that alcohol usually has a deleterious effect upon mental efficiency. McDougall and Smith found that varying doses of alcohol increased the number of errors in the dotting-machine experiment as follows:

Dose	Increase in errors (per cent)
10 cc.	21
15 cc.	42
20 cc.	39
25 cc.	113

[1] Cushny, A. R.: *Pharmacology*, 9th Edition (Lea & Febiger, Philadelphia, 1928), p. 186.

[2] Dodge and Benedict: *Psychological Effects of Alcohol*. (Carnegie Institute, Washington, D.C.)

[3] Clendening, L.: *Modern Methods of Treatment* (C. V. Mosby Co., St. Louis, 1928), p. 72.

A memory test also showed that alcohol lowers efficiency. Alcohol increases free association time and lowers the quality of the response. After reviewing all the work upon the mental and motor effect of alcohol, Rivers [1] concludes that in the case of mental work, the available evidence points to a decrease in the amount of work under the influence of alcohol when there is an effect at all; but there are very great individual differences, even the large dose of one hundred cubic centimeters failing to show any effect in some persons.

But alcohol has other more lasting effects. Prolonged use of it produces tolerance, which, although not so great as that acquired for morphine and nicotine, yet is sufficiently great to require double or triple amounts as the person becomes more and more accustomed to taking it. A large quantity of alcohol taken by an habitual drinker may not lead to the accumulation in the blood of a sufficient quantity to induce symptoms of intoxication. The brain of the habitual drinker also reacts less to alcohol and he is not intoxicated by a quantity that would probably carry an occasional drinker into a drunken stupor.

It is easy to understand how the person who has built up a tolerance for alcohol comes to the habitual indulgence in the drug to excess and finally becomes the victim of chronic alcoholism. The alcohol not only has a pleasing effect on the organs of taste, and on the mucous membranes of the mouth and stomach, but it also acts upon the brain, numbing the consciousness of unhappiness. The object sought by the drunkard is generally the action upon the brain. He finds that under alcohol his habitual depression disappears, and he loses the sense of degradation which possesses him when sober. The depression returns in exaggerated form after the effects of the drug have worn off, but it can be removed again by the same means, and in this way the habit is formed, each drink being made necessary by the depression produced by its predecessor.

The action of the alcohol on the brain greatly facilitates the descent into chronic drunkenness by the lessening of self-control.

[1] Rivers, W. H. R.: *The Influence of Alcohol and Other Drugs on Fatigue.* (Arnold, London, 1908.)

The victim may make the best of resolutions, but the habit which he has formed leaves him wholly unable to carry them out. The weaker and more susceptible often develop a psychosis. In this condition many hallucinations and delusions are manifested. The delusions are nearly always of a persecutory nature, the patient complaining that people are putting poison in his food or harming him in some other way. Delusions of marital infidelity and jealousy are also common.

A characteristic result of chronic alcoholism is delirium tremens, an acute attack of insanity, during which hallucinations of the various senses appear. These hallucinations generally take the form of snakes, rats, or dogs, but whispering voices and horrible words are also complained of. Needless to say, the victim manifests great fear and excitement. White [1] gives the following description of the condition:

At the height of his excitement the patient is in constant motion, picking insects from his nightdress, repelling the approach of terrible animals; in the extreme frenzy of his fright, he may make murderous assaults on those about him, believing them to be his enemies, or perhaps attempt his own life to escape from his horrible surroundings. During all this time the patient is constantly talking, shrieking in fear at times, at others carrying on an incoherent discourse with imaginary persons, fragments of which often relate to his former occupation and friends.

Statistics show that the percentage of feeble-minded persons in the families of alcoholics is much higher than in the families of non-alcoholics, even as much as thirty-five per cent higher. Hence the conclusion has frequently been drawn that alcoholism in the parents produces feeble-mindedness in the offspring. It seems more likely that the parents were also feeble-minded, and that the alcoholism in the parents was the result of the feeble-mindedness. The feeble-mindedness is thus transmitted directly to the offspring and alcoholism is only a coincidence in the process.

III. COCAINE

Unlike alcohol and the opiates, cocaine is a stimulant rather than a depressant. It acts first by stimulating the upper brain and con-

[1] White, W. A.: *Outlines of Psychiatry* (Nervous and Mental Disease Publishing Company, 1924), pp. 255–56.

tinues with a descending stimulation of the medulla and spinal cord. It gives a feeling of exhilaration, quickens the intellect for the time being, and makes the user appear very fluent in conversation. The garrulity is the result of the cerebral stimulation. The cerebral stimulation is further indicated by the perfect coördination of movements and the increased endurance when at muscular work. It has been used in South America for centuries to delay the onset of fatigue. The mountain-climbers of the Andes march for hours and days with very little rest or food when supplied with the coca leaves to chew. All laboratory investigations agree that much more work can be done after taking cocaine than before, and that it has considerable potency in hastening the recovery from fatigue. When taken, there is a general stimulation which is always followed by a depression. Unlike most drugs, it is doubtful if a tolerance is ever attained for cocaine.

Were it not for the danger of becoming addicted, cocaine would be much more frequently used, but the cocaine habit is one of the most dangerous and demoralizing habits. Since cocaine was introduced into medicine some twenty-five years ago, numerous cases of the formation of the cocaine habit have been reported. Many of these have become addicted to cocaine through the attempt to substitute cocaine for morphine in the treatment of morphinism, the treatment resulting in a craving for cocaine as well as for morphine. Chronic addiction results in digestive disturbances, tremors, and marked muscular weakness. The mental symptoms are characterized by hallucinations which are often associated with the skin. The patient imagines that insects cover him or are in the skin. In the intellectual sphere there is an impairment of reasoning and judgment, increased irritability, and a lessened moral sense. The moral degradation is often greater than from morphinism and the chance of ending the habit is less. According to one authority, "cocaine drives men crazy when they get it; morphine drives them crazy when they do not get it."

IV. CAFFEINE

Probably the most generally used and the most harmless stimulant is caffeine. It is the active principle in coffee and tea, and is used by many who refuse a more powerful stimulant. Caffeine is claimed to be an effective stimulant of both mental and physical powers, more especially of mental activity. It is also generally held that caffeine considerably delays the onset of fatigue. Coffee is therefore imbibed in large quantities by students cramming for examinations, by newspaper men on a big story, and by many others who feel the need of stimulation.

But those who drink coffee expecting great stimulating effects are frequently disappointed, for it appears that caffeine is often "like prosperous friends, most useless when most needed." The stimulating action of caffeine varies greatly in different persons and at different times in the same person, and sometimes fails to appear at all. In a recent experiment to determine the physical and mental changes caused by prolonged sleeplessness, caffeine in large quantities was used by four of the eight subjects. The other four had no stimulants of any kind. But the four who had relied on coffee to keep them wide awake and alert had their faith in caffeine severely shaken, for they found it just as difficult to stay awake as did those who had had no coffee.

Hollingworth [1] conducted one of the best controlled studies on the physical and mental effects of caffeine. The speed of movement and motor coördination of sixteen subjects were tested for a period of forty days to discover the physical effects of caffeine. An increase of about four per cent was found in the speed of movement, the amount of increase depending on the size of the dose. Doses of from two to six grains were used. The effect was noted in an hour after taking and lasted from one to four hours, according to the amount taken. There was no secondary depression following the stimulation for a period of seventy-two hours. In the mental tests, moderate doses of the drug tended to improve the performance. Concerning the effect of caffeine on typewriting, Hollingworth says:

The speed of performance in typewriting is quickened by small doses of caffeine and retarded by large doses. The quality of the performance, as measured by the number of errors, both corrected and uncorrected, is superior for the whole range of caffeine doses to the quality yielded by the

[1] Hollingworth, H. L.: *The Influence of Caffeine on Efficiency.* (Archives of Psychology, 1912.)

control days. Both types of errors seem to be influenced to about the same degree. The increase in speed is not gained at the expense of additional errors, but increased speed and decreased number of errors are simultaneously present.

Caffeine should probably be classed as a habit-forming drug. The person who develops a headache if he misses his morning cup of coffee is too well known to require further comment. The stimulating effects seem to be very greatly diminished in habitual caffeine-users; the continued use of small quantities of caffeine evidently gives rise to tolerance. The habitual coffee-drinker appears unaffected by a quantity of coffee that would make another person, unaccustomed to coffee, actually ill, with headache, confusion, nervousness, and decreased motor efficiency.

V. TOBACCO

Tobacco in one form or another is used by a very large proportion of the population in varying degrees from the novice who tries to smoke to be sociable to the inveterate smoker who has a cigarette between his lips from morning to night. Both men and women use tobacco in one form or another. Some authorities state that as many as forty per cent of the women of the country smoke, from the high-school girl to the grandmother.

The "kick" in tobacco is nicotine, which is an alkaloid. Nicotine is a deadly poison. In fact, it is claimed that its poisonous effects are as powerful as those of hydrocyanic acid. In small quantities it has an effect similar to that of other alkaloids (morphine, strychnine, and cocaine). The commonly alleged soothing effects which are produced by the smoking of tobacco are due primarily to the nicotine, and it is safe to say that tobacco without nicotine would be about as satisfying as wine without alcohol.

Since tobacco is so widely used, it is natural that a great variety of investigations should have been made to show how the smoking of tobacco affects efficiency. Two methods of attack have been used. One is to measure the efficiency or achievement of smokers and non-smokers over a long period of time, as shown, for example, in academic grades. The second is to measure physical or mental efficiency after smoking a cigar or cigarette and comparing it with efficiency before smoking the tobacco.

The following cases are cited as being typical of investigations of the effect on efficiency of the habitual use of tobacco: Dr. J. W. Seaver found that, of 100 students taking highest honors at Yale, 95 were non-smokers, and only 5 smokers. An examination of the class records of Harvard University showed that for fifty years not one tobacco-user has stood at the head of his class, and this notwithstanding the fact that five out of six students are smokers. Decaisne concluded that smokers stand lower in their classes in the French colleges. Bartillon, G. Doré, and Elia Joubert came to the same conclusion regarding students of the Polytechnic School. A Clark University professor found that of 201 students 93 were smokers and 108 not; of the latter 68 per cent won honors; of the former, only 18 per cent.

Athletes when in training are not allowed to smoke. Dr. Black, of the University of Utah, made a careful study of the relation of smoking to football. Data were gathered from fourteen state universities and colleges, and led to the following conclusions: First, in the try-outs for football squads, only half as many smokers as non-smokers are successful. Second, in the case of able-bodied men, smoking is associated with loss of lung capacity amounting to practically ten per cent.

The following investigations are typical of those in which the immediate effects of smoking a cigar or cigarette upon efficiency are noted. Dr. Fisher conducted a series of experiments at the Y.M.C.A. College in Springfield, Massachusetts, upon young men between the ages of twenty-one and twenty-five. The plan of the experiments was to use both smokers and non-smokers so as to note the immediate effects of smoking on each; to have them go through a given test first without smoking, and then try the same test after smoking. As a rule they smoked a single cigar or cigarette. Dr. Fisher concluded that smoking is not beneficial. It quickens the heart rate, affects in slight degree the blood pressure, and disturbs the circulatory apparatus so that it takes some considerable time for the heart to return to normal. He reported that smoking affects muscular precision in fine movements such as writing, and in larger movements such as lunging at a target with a fencing foil, or in baseball pitching. The case seemed to be against tobacco.

These investigations indicate that smoking decreases both physical and mental efficiency. It is therefore of no value in increasing the ability to work, for which purpose it is frequently used. From the point of view of efficiency, its use is a handicap rather than an asset.

The results obtained in the investigations should perhaps not be accepted at their face value as an indictment of tobacco smoking. The differences in performance of the smokers and non-smokers may be due to differences in original temperament and ability rather than to smoking. The same original traits which made one group smokers may be the traits which produce differences in performance. It is the general impression that smokers are more social than non-smokers. A few years ago Bulwer-Lytton said, "The man who smokes, thinks like a sage and acts like a Samaritan." In a study of nearly two hundred students the author found that there is very little difference in the abstract intelligence test scores of smokers and non-smokers. The smokers appear somewhat higher in social intelligence as measured by a test of social intelligence. Of course this should not be interpreted to mean that smoking causes an increase in social intelligence. The explanation probably is that those who by original endowment had more social intelligence tended to begin smoking as the result of the desire not to be "odd" when in a group of smokers. Study of one hundred cases of inveterate smokers shows that in a very large percentage of cases they began to smoke as a result of social pressure, or rather as a result of being in a group where most of the others smoked.

The emotional factor is very important in determining the number of times a man will smoke each day. In the study mentioned above, the author found that periods either of great depression or of extreme joyousness are characterized by more smoking than periods when the emotions are at the normal level. It seems that periods of depression are characterized by more smoking, however, than periods of happiness. The soothing effect of tobacco is brought out in the old song:

"Contented I sit with my pint and my pipe,
Puffing sorrow and care far away;
And surely the brow of grief nothing can wipe
Like smoking and moistening our clay."

Not much of a thoroughly scientific nature is known of the effect on behavior of tobacco, coffee, or alcohol. It is difficult to secure reliable data in this field because of individual differences in tastes, habits, and in susceptibility to the drugs. Prejudice and propaganda have also tended to befog the field. Exaggerated accounts of the evils of the use of alcohol, of opium, of tobacco, and even of tea and coffee, are spread abroad by those organizations which oppose the use of these drugs. The liquor-dealers, tobacco-growers, and other interested parties have countered by publishing the most glowing descriptions of the joys and beneficial effects derived from the use of alcohol, tobacco, or coffee. So-called scientific experiments on the effects of these drugs, when managed by a prejudiced organization, are only so much more propaganda, and not a reflection of the true state of affairs. Moreover, there are wide differences between the individuals who use the same drug. Balzac, the great writer, did practically all his writing at night. As he worked, he kept near him a steaming pot of coffee, and drank five or six cups of coffee each evening. Another person becomes nervous and unable to work after one cup of coffee. Goethe is said to have consumed fifty thousand bottles of wine during his lifetime. Mark Twain did not drink alcohol in any form, but smoked about three hundred cigars a month. An extensive series of experiments designed to secure more reliable data on the effect of these drugs is urgently needed.

VI. GLANDULAR EXTRACTS

The behavior of any individual is closely tied up with the condition of his ductless glands. These glands synthesize some very powerful substances known as *autocoids*, which are poured out into the blood stream and influence metabolism in a variety of ways. These substances are extracted from the glands of such animals as the sheep and the ox and are sold in various preparations for medical use.

1. **Thyroxin.** Thyroxin is an iodine compound which is synthe-sized in the thyroid gland.   If a sufficient quantity of thyroxin is given to an individual whose thyroid gland is already functioning properly, it increases both his speed of reaction and his sensitivity, and lowers his threshold for nervous irritability.   He becomes very nervous, is unable to stay still, finds great difficulty in fixing his attention on one subject, and if the administration is continued, not infrequently suffers from insomnia.   On the other hand, if an individual's thyroid gland is producing an undersecretion, none of the objectionable effects outlined above will appear with the ad-ministration of thyroid extract, but, instead, the patient will be very much benefited.   There are two conditions due to under-functioning of the thyroid gland in which thyroxin is especially helpful in correcting the individual's behavior, namely, cretinism and myxedema.

a. Cretinism.   Cretinism is a condition resulting from the pro-longed underfunctioning of the thyroid gland in childhood, produc-ing a dwarf both physically and mentally.   According to Clenden-ing, it is a condition in which "the burning taper we call life flickers and smoulders and smokes."   If the condition continues to adult-hood, the individual retains the mind of a child coupled with an abnormal physical development.   He is apathetic, awkward, and obviously idiotic.   This condition can be greatly improved if recog-nized early and treated with administration of thyroid extract.

b. Myxedema.   Myxedema is the condition resulting from the underfunctioning of the thyroid gland in adulthood.   In this condi-tion the skin is dry, the hair falls out, and the face is pale and puffy.   This type of person has a downtrodden view of life, and often de-velops a mental state closely bordering on insanity.   He becomes indifferent, and listless; his reaction time is markedly slowed up and his sexual urge much diminished.   Most of these symptoms can be removed and the patient restored practically to normal by administering thyroxin.

2. **Pituitary extract.**   While the extract from the pituitary gland has not proved so valuable in correcting conditions due to the underfunctioning of the pituitary gland, as is the case of thyroid extract in remedying thyroid deficiencies, still there is one condition

in which it can be of considerable service. If the pituitary gland fails to secrete properly before adolescence, we have a condition known as *Fröhlich's syndrome*. Clendening [1] describes this condition in boys as follows:

The boys are fat, feminine, weak, and misunderstood. Their manifest deformities are regarded by their parents, teachers, and playmates as natural and inevitable variations of human structure, rather different but within the normal limits. They are sissy because they are sissy: some boys are sissy. They are fat because some people are fat. They are weak and do not play *boys'* games because they are sissy. That is the usual view. It is not commonly recognized that they are definitely in a mutual deficiency group, that the deficiency is an affair of internal secretion, and that treatment to be effective at all must be begun early in life.

We have all seen such fat, sissy boys, the tragedies of whose lives might have been largely prevented by the early administration of pituitary extract.

3. Adrenin. The secretions from the suprarenal glands are very closely associated with the emotions of fear and anger. According to Crile, the body goes on a war footing when these glands get into action. The skeletal muscles are toned up, the heart beats faster, blood pressure is increased, the clotting time of the blood diminished, and digestion inhibited. Cannon claims that 68/100,000 of a milligram of adrenin (the active principle of adrenal extract) thrown into the blood stream will increase the heart rate as much as thirty-four beats per minute. At the same time the liver gives up immense quantities of its glycogen supply into the blood stream, thus raising the sugar content. The effect of sugar upon the body is, generally speaking, like fuel in a furnace. By means of it the muscles needed for offense or defense are provided with greater energy. Fatigue is also warded off because the adrenin neutralizes fatigue products. Thus adrenin acts as a sort of Paul Revere to emotional excitement, putting the body in a condition for defense or attack. When adrenin is injected into a heart which has stopped beating, it sometimes succeeds in starting the heart to beating again. It thus has the effect of bringing the dead back to life.

[1] Clendening, L.: *Modern Methods of Treatment* (C. V. Mosby Co., St. Louis, 1928), p. 232.

4. **Parathyrin.** Parathyrin, which is the active substance of the parathyroid glands, influences very closely the calcium metabolism of the body. Removal of the parathyroids of animals is followed by a kind of convulsion known as "parathyroid tetany." Animals from which all parathyroid tissue has been removed are protected completely from tetany by a small injection of parathyrin every twenty hours. Acting on the suggestion that epilepsy may be due to a deficiency of parathyrin, several investigators are trying it in treating epilepsy, but it is too early to judge the value of it for this purpose.

VII. ANESTHETICS

Anesthetics are substances, which, when taken in sufficient quantities, abolish consciousness and eliminate sensation. Anesthetics are used chiefly to prevent pain, produce relaxation, and to suppress the reflexes in a patient undergoing operation. While it is now generally recognized that any agent that will accomplish these purposes is a very definite friend of suffering humanity, such has not always been the common view. The difficulty with which anesthetics were introduced into the medical world is illustrated by the case of Sir James Simpson, who about the middle of the last century proposed to use anesthetics as a means of abolishing the pains of childbirth. No sooner had he made the proposal than the Scotch theological authorities became very indignant on the ground that it was an "impious interference with the will of the Lord." In those days the theologians ardently believed in the original sin of woman and in the justice of her suffering. After many well-written arguments had failed in Scotland to justify the use of anesthetics for such a purpose, Simpson won his point by showing that, according to the twenty-first verse of the second chapter of Genesis, the Lord himself, in the first recorded operation, before taking a rib from Adam's side, "caused a deep sleep to fall upon Adam." In that way was the use of anesthetics introduced into Scotland.

1. **Ether and chloroform.** The action of ether and chloroform is usually divided into three stages: first, that of imperfect consciousness; second, that of excitement; and third, that of surgical anesthesia.

First stage: One of the first effects following the inhalation of ether or chloroform is a feeling of suffocation, this feeling being especially marked in the case of ether. At the same time the face feels very warm, and the whole body becomes bathed in perspiration. The patient has a dull, far-away feeling, and all his senses are less acute; the voices in the operating room seem to come from a distance, and his vision is considerably dimmed. His kinesthetic sense is so dulled that his limbs feel stiff, and he has considerable difficulty in moving them. As a rule, however, the sensations, with the exception of the initial choking sensation, are pleasant.

Second stage: During the excitement stage, the patient, while practically unconscious, is as a rule very active. He attempts to remove the inhalation mask from his face, and sometimes kicks and struggles so that it takes three or four people to hold him on the operating table. His movements are not coördinated, and seem to be the result of some dreamlike condition of consciousness. This behavior varies extremely with different individuals, and seems to depend in no small part upon his past associations. According to Cushny,[1] "One person prays aloud and sings hymns; another abuses the surgeon, the hospital, and all his immediate surroundings; while yet another is overcome with the fear of impending death and laments his unfortunate position." If the anesthetic is continued, however, the patient soon becomes less active, the muscles relax, and he enters the stage of surgical anesthesia.

Third stage: During deep anesthesia the face has a calm, death-like expression, due to relaxation of the muscles. All the reflexes are abolished; even the eyelids fail to close when the cornea is touched. Consciousness is entirely blotted out. The respiration is slow and shallow. This stage of anesthesia may be kept up for hours by continuing to give the patient small quantities of the anesthetic. When the administration ceases, the patient once more passes through the excitement stage, which, however, is not as a rule so violent as the excitement accompanying the induction of anesthesia. After passing through this last excitement stage, the patient usually sinks into a deep sleep which continues for

[1] Cushny, A. R.: *Pharmacology*, 9th Edition (Lea & Febiger, Philadelphia, 1928), p. 211.

several hours. It sometimes happens, however, that, instead of sleep, nausea, vomiting, and dizziness appear simultaneously with the recovery of consciousness.

2. **Nitrous oxide.** Unlike ether and chloroform, nitrous oxide is pleasant to take. At the commencement of inhalation there is a very slight feeling of suffocation, which is quickly replaced by a pleasurable sensation and a feeling of exhilaration. Numerous cases are recorded of people taking "laughing gas" (nitrous oxide) in order to experience the "grand and glorious feeling" which accompanies the initial stages of this type of anesthesia. If the anesthetic is continued, the patient quickly passes into the stage of analgesia (inability to feel pain). During this stage the patient retains control of his intellect, but is entirely without pain or emotional reaction. Crile says that if one were to say to a patient in this stage of anesthesia, "You will die in a few moments," this would be to him merely a statement of a fact in which he was not particularly interested, since the anesthetic had rendered him incapable not only of expressing but even of feeling an emotion. According to Crile, analgesia completely separates the patient from his emotions, affords him great relief from the sensation of pain, and at the same time allows his brain to function sufficiently to aid him in "carrying on." If the anesthetic is continued in sufficient quantity, consciousness is lost in a whirl of confused and incoherent ideas and impressions, and the stage of analgesia deepens into the third or true anesthetic stage. This stage of anesthesia, when introduced by nitrous oxide and oxygen, is not unlike natural sleep. The patient may have dreamlike experiences which can be recalled several hours later. The average time required to anesthetize a patient with this gas is seventy-five seconds, and when the anesthetic is discontinued, the patient usually regains consciousness in about a minute.

In the case of anesthesia as in that of various other drugs, we see very definite proof of the chemical basis of behavior. If an individual is allowed to breathe nothing but nitrous oxide for a period of one minute, he becomes unconscious, and knows nothing of the things that are going on around him. But if the same individual, even when in the surgical stage of anesthesia, is given a few breaths of oxygen, he immediately regains consciousness, and is wholly aware of the events occurring near him. This shows that thought, feeling, and even consciousness itself are nothing more than the reactions of our bodies to certain internal chemical conditions. When a certain chemical union exists in our organism, such as that produced by the inhalation of nitrous oxide, we become unconscious, but when a different chemical union exists, such as that produced by inhaling oxygen, we become mentally alert.

CHAPTER IV

EFFECT OF EXTERNAL STIMULI ON BEHAVIOR

We poor human beings pride ourselves amusingly upon what we call our free will, and yet there is perhaps nothing in creation more at the mercy of external influences than man.

LE GALLIENNE [1]

THE strength of the different drives to action depends not only upon the innate constitution and the physical condition of the individual, but also upon the immediate stimuli, both external and internal, which he receives. It is generally recognized that surrounding conditions have a decided influence upon the feelings and the accomplishment of the individual. We are, in no small part, creatures of our environment, reflecting in our mental condition changes in weather and other environmental factors. The leaden sky depresses us and suggests all kinds of unpleasant thoughts. The bitter sayings of friends are brought to mind. Gloomy forebodings arise with regard to the future. When the sky is overcast, our emotional tone is low, but when the morning sun arises bright and cheerful, our depression is replaced with hope and joy.

The importance of one's immediate surroundings in determining his behavior is nowhere recognized more than in literature. From the remotest antiquity, attention has been paid to the circumstances or setting under which the action occurs. It is realized by all that the individual's mood and emotional background of behavior are very much influenced by the surrounding conditions. Poe introduces the depressing story of *The Fall of the House of Usher* with the following words: "During the whole of a *dull, dark,* and *soundless* day in the *autumn* of the year, when the *clouds* hung *oppressively low* in the heavens, I had been passing *alone*, on horseback, through a *singularly dreary* tract of country; and at length found myself, as the *shades of the evening* drew on, within view of

---

[1] Le Gallienne, Richard: *Love Letters of the King* (Little, Brown & Co., Boston, 1901), p. 234.

the *melancholy* house of Usher."[1] Here the darkness, the clouds, the season, the time of day, and the loneliness combine to set the stage for some dreary or terrible event.

Some of the immediate stimuli which particularly affect behavior are: I, Climate; II, Season; III, Weather; IV, Time of day; V, Altitude; VI, Ventilation; VII, Light.

I. CLIMATE

Climate has an important influence in determining the character and behavior of a people as well as their physical qualities. Huntington,[2] who has made an exhaustive study of the effect of climate on civilization, says that character, in the broad sense of all that pertains to industry, honesty, purity, intelligence, and strength of will, is closely dependent upon the condition of the body. How much of the European energy and initiative are due to stimulating conditions of climate is shown by a comparison of the character of Europeans in tropical countries with their character in the temperate zone. "Whatever differences we may find are presumably due largely to physiological causes, but they manifest themselves chiefly through the will. In tropical countries weakness of will is unfortunately a quality displayed not only by the natives, but by a large proportion of the northerner sojourners. It manifests itself in many ways. Four of these, namely, lack of industry, an irascible temper, drunkenness, and sexual indulgence are particularly prominent, and may be taken as typical." The climate of many countries seems to be one of the chief reasons why idleness, immorality, dishonesty, stupidity, and weakness of will prevail.

Huntington shows the influence of climate on the rise and fall of nations. He advances the hypothesis of pulsatory climatic changes, the idea being that there are not only small cycles, such as in five-year periods, and large cycles causing glacial periods, but also intermediate ones of a length of several hundred years. The climate in any one locality tends to one extreme or another. These changes influence the progress of nations, causing the decline of

---

[1] Italics inserted by the writer.

[2] Huntington, Ellsworth: *Civilization and Climate* (Yale University Press, New Haven, 1922), p. 41.

one and the rise of another. He considers the rise and fall of such empires as Eurasia and those of Northern Africa examples supporting his hypothesis.

The changes in climate may mean filling a country with a lot of stagnant pools which serve as incubation centers for the spread of malaria. The climate in Greece was almost ideal about 400 B.C., but was followed by a rapid climatic degeneration from 300 to 200 B.C. Malaria followed, and to this day has been the curse of Greece. Malaria is one of those chronic devitalizing diseases that sap initiative. Sufferers from it are for weeks in chills and fever, and for years subsequent to the disease, their energy is depleted. Although recovered from the active attack of the disease, those who have had it go languidly to their necessary tasks, and as soon as possible sit down and rest. One cannot expect much initiative or energy from a nation in which for centuries almost half of every generation has been devitalized by this baneful disease. It is not mere accident that the introduction of malaria coincides with the beginning of the decline of Greece and Rome, and by the time it became thoroughly endemic, the greatness of those nations was only history.

The nearer the equator the race, the smaller the individual tends to be; the hotter the climate, the darker the skin. We find in hot climates races which have developed black skins to protect themselves from the burning rays of the sun; a little farther north, but still under warm skies, we find the swarthy Italian and Spaniard; still farther north, where the weather is cold, we find the blond German and Scandinavian.

Mental differences between races of different climates are no less striking than physical differences. The inhabitants of hot climates are as a rule listless, easy-going, ambitionless, uninventive, and emotional. They are generally interested in philosophical speculation and in religion. Indeed, practically all the great religions of the world have originated in hot climates. Inhabitants of warm countries are as a rule passionate and hot-headed. Murder is the act of the quick-tempered individual; and it is interesting to note that murders are proportionately much more numerous in warm than in cold climates. In the warmer climates of Spain and Italy, we find the highest murder rate in Europe, while in the cooler climates of England, Scotland, and Holland are the fewest murders in proportion to the population. Suicide, on the other hand, is more often an act of cold deliberation. In this connection it is interesting to note that suicide is more common in the temperate or colder climates than in the tropics. Statistics show also that the more enlightened and scientific a race becomes, the higher is the rate of suicide for that race.

In very cold climates as in very hot climates the people tend to be unprogressive. The nearer a race is to the poles, the more vital energy is expended in furnishing body heat and the less energy there is left for the activities which make for progress and civilization. In the cold climates conditions of life are extremely hard, and the time and attention of the inhabitants are completely occupied by the attempt to obtain food and shelter. Aristotle said wisely, "When pressing needs are satisfied, man turns to the general and more elevated." But the pressing needs are never satisfied in the cold zones where Nature is so inhospitable to life.

Neither excessive heat nor excessive cold is conducive to the greatest achievement of the individual, and consequently the dominant peoples the world over are found in temperate climates. Aggressiveness and vitality are greatest in nations living where the average temperature is between 50° and 70° F., and these nations have led the world in the march of civilization. It has been suggested that the hustle and bustle of which most Americans boast is neither a virtue nor a thing to be proud of, but only a form of nervous irritability produced by certain elements in our climate.

It is interesting to see the effect of contrasting climates upon the same types of people. Such an opportunity is offered to-day by comparing the inhabitants of the Province of Ontario in Canada with the white inhabitants of the Bahamas.[1] The original white settlers of both sections were drawn very largely from the English Tories who left the United States at the time of the Revolutionary War. To-day the descendants of those settlers who went to Canada constitute the strongest element in making Ontario the best governed and most progressive of the Canadian provinces. The

[1] Huntington, Ellsworth: *Civilization and Climate* (Yale University Press, New Haven, 1922), p. 27.

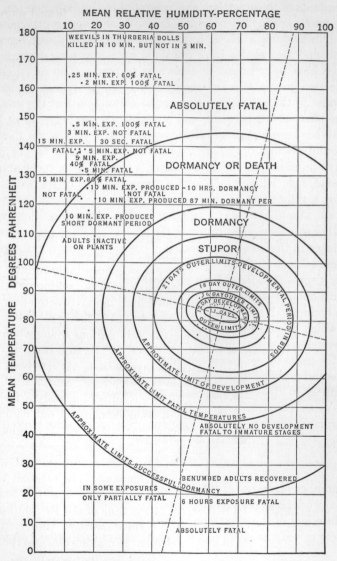

FIGURE 7. THE RELATIONS OF TEMPERATURE AND HUMIDITY TO
COTTON BOLL-WEEVIL ACTIVITY

(After Pierce.)

descendants of those settlers who migrated to the Bahamas, on the other hand, are inefficient, unprogressive, and apparently incompetent individuals. Large numbers of them have never been to school, and many who have obtained an education, through indolence have later forgotten even how to read. The racial stock of the two groups was the same; therefore, the climate must be the cause of the wide differences in the attainments of the groups.

The effect of temperature and humidity on the behavior of boll weevils has been experimentally investigated by W. Dwight Pierce.[1] He found a small optimum zone around 82° F. and 65 per cent relative humidity in which the animals studied were most active; a second zone where their activity was practically reduced to a stupor; a third zone where they were dormant; and another zone that was absolutely fatal. In other words, as the conditions vary on either side from the optimum, the animal tends to pass through the stages in the order enumerated. His idea is shown graphically in Figure 7.

The depressive effect, both physical and mental, of a frigid or a tropical climate is generally admitted by travelers and explorers in these regions. Nansen, in *Night and Ice*, tells of the dreamy state into which he and his crew of the Fram fell while "lying still" in the winter and spring of 1895. He adds: "There is slight inclination for æsthetic or moral estimates. The most beautiful landscapes and grandest music leave one tolerably cold." Probably no climate is so de-energizing as is that along the equator. The white settler, filled with enthusiasm and fired with ambition, enters the tropics, but before very long the tropical sun has melted his enthusiasm and evaporated his ambition.

II. SEASON

A number of studies of the effect of the season upon physical and mental work have been made. Huntington collected data concerning the effect of the season on the quality of work done by factory workers in various parts of the United States and Cuba. Among

[1] Pierce, W. D.: "A New Interpretation of the Relationships of Temperature and Humidity to Insect Development," *Journal of Agricultural Research*, March 20, 1916. Courtesy U.S. Department of Agriculture.

factory workers in New Haven the lowest point of efficiency is reached in the latter half of January. The curve of efficiency rises slowly to June, drops slightly through July and August, rises quickly in September, and reaches the highest point about the first of December. Southern workers hold the high level of efficiency till about the middle of January, while farther north they show a decrease in working capacity somewhat earlier. Very cold and very warm weather apparently lessen efficiency in manual work, while moderately cold weather has an invigorating effect.

Huntington also studied the effect of seasons upon mental efficiency by compiling the grades on recitations of students at West Point and Annapolis, grades in both institutions being recorded daily throughout the school year. His results resemble those of physical activity, and show a decided increase in efficiency in the spring and fall, and a falling-off in the summer and winter.

Dexter [1] made a study of the effect of the season upon the accuracy of the calculations of bank clerks. The record of efficiency was kept in terms of errors. Most errors were made in October, November, and December, and fewest in April, May, and September. During the hot summer months a large number of errors were made. These results may be explained by the lack of energy from excessive heat in the summer, the stimulating character of change in temperature during spring and fall, and the increased business and holiday rushes, which probably were as important as weather conditions in causing errors during the winter months. In any kind of work moderate seasons seem to produce the best results; neither the very coldest season nor the very hottest being conducive to highest efficiency.

There appears to be a close relation between the season and the type and number of crimes committed. The curve of crimes of assault and battery shows a marked peak about August, with the lowest point in December. The maximum of crimes against persons is reached during the summer months. Dr. G. F. Lydston said that the tonic effect of cold weather in maintaining the nervous and mental equilibrium of neuropaths, and thus inhibiting crimes

[1] Dexter, E. G.: *Weather Influences.* (The Macmillan Company, New York, 1914.)

of violence, is obvious. The physiological turmoil in the sexual system ushered in by spring is well known. It bears relation not only to sexual crimes, but to other crimes of violence. Heat has a marked influence on the passions, and crimes of violence increase almost in proportion to the increase in temperature and humidity. The maximum of crimes against property is reached during the winter months. This is doubtless explained by the fact that conditions of life are harder during cold weather.

The seasons are closely connected in the popular imagination with certain emotional states. Spring is associated with joyousness, with the awakening of new impulses; summer is associated with voluptuousness; autumn with melancholy; and winter with discontent and gloom. Spring represents youth; summer, maturity and fruitfulness; autumn, old age and decay; and winter, death and gloom. Spring is without doubt the accepted mating period for both plants and animals. Flowers bloom at that time and the nuptial flights or swarming of many insects take place only during this season. At that season the human being, too, is stirred to feelings of love and romance. As the poet puts it:

"In the spring a young man's fancy lightly turns to thoughts of love."

III. WEATHER

Few things in human affairs are more talked about than the weather and few things are more universally recognized as exerting a marked influence upon human behavior.

1. **The effect of weather on school children.** Studies based on the observations of teachers indicate that the deportment of pupils is at its best in the cold months of the year. It is also better on rainy or cloudy days than on fair days. On rainy days the pupils lack some of the energy necessary for being mischievous; they feel less the beckoning to more enjoyable activities outside the schoolroom. The mental efficiency of the pupils shows also a variation with weather conditions, cold days apparently producing greater efficiency than hot ones. Rainy days, if not continued, bring good results, but cold, cloudy weather with a high humidity continued through several days is unfavorable to mental abilities.

2. The effect of weather on employees in industry. Clerical errors are frequent during warm seasons, with a marked increase during excessively hot spells, and are fewest on cool days. They show slight increases also with high barometer readings, high winds, and cloudy, wet weather. The results obtained by Huntington, in his study of the effect of weather conditions on factory workers in various parts of the United States, correspond to those obtained for clerical workers. For all types of work there seems to be something in very cold or very hot, or abnormally cloudy or windy weather that affects the activities of man in an unfavorable way. Dexter accounts for this by a lowering of the vital energies, while the more favorable days produce an excess of reserve energy, or as we say "pep" which must be worked off.

3. The effect of weather on drunkenness. Although it can hardly be possible that the weather alone can "drive a person to drink," it has its influences. If it is admitted that weather has a marked effect upon the mood and behavior of the individual, it is only natural to expect it to exert an influence on his desires for drugs and stimulants. The close relation between certain weather conditions and drunkenness is shown by a study of 63,117 cases of arrest for drunkenness. The investigator obtained from the police department of a large city the number of arrests each day over a period of three years. From the weather bureau station of the same city, the mean temperature and weather condition of each of the days were secured, and the average number of arrests for each type of day was compared with the number of arrests per day throughout the year. It was found that there were fewer arrests in the hot summer months and more for the cold months, the arrests in July being forty-seven per cent less than in December. An increase in drunkenness was shown for days of abnormally high and abnormally low barometric reading, and for days of high winds, although the effect was somewhat less than the effect produced by temperature.

4. The effect of weather on insanity. The few studies that have been made of the relation of weather and insanity indicate that there are certain conditions which tend to throw a person, already predisposed to insanity, over the border line. At the extremes of heat and cold there is an increase of mental disturbances. This is probably closely tied up with the physical condition of the individual; physical suffering or discomfort produced by the extremes of weather often being the important factor. There are fewer arrests for insanity during the colder months and more than normal during the warmer seasons.

It is generally believed that our moods and emotions are very much influenced by the weather. A rainy day brings with it many things conducive to an unpleasant mood — extra uncomfortable preparations in dress, perhaps wet feet, extra hazards in driving automobiles, poor light, miscarried plans, and broken-up picnic parties. On cloudy days most people feel gloomy and depressed. They work with a lower efficiency than on clear days. On the other hand, clear days bring with them fewer conditions conducive to unpleasant moods. On clear days the individual is cheerful and energetic. Winds likewise affect the mood and attitude of the individual — an occasional windy day has a stimulating and energizing effect, but a long-continued period of prevailing winds is found to be depressing and irritating.

The greatest poets have all recognized the effects of weather on human emotions. In Shakespeare's plays the weather is used to intensify and correspond to the emotions of the characters. In *Macbeth* there is a storm just before the murder of Duncan; King Lear wanders about the heath during a frightful storm; and the night on which the conspirators persuaded Brutus to join the plot against the life of Cæsar is described as a "tempest dropping fire," with "scolding winds" and "threatening clouds."

IV. TIME OF DAY

The effect of time of day upon behavior is as pronounced as is the effect of season or weather. One feels different physically, mentally and emotionally in the morning before breakfast and after the evening meal. It is generally recognized that an individual's performance varies during the day. Curves of working efficiency for various types of workers show distinct periods of increased or lowered efficiency.

Hollingworth [1] has conducted experiments which indicate the

[1] Hollingworth, H. L.: "Variations in Efficiency during the Working Day," *Psychological Review*, xxi, pp. 473–91. (1914.)

basis for the variations in efficiency throughout the working day. In a series of experiments upon ten individuals for ten days, two of which consisted of almost continuous work for twelve hours, he found that efficiency at any time of the day depends, not upon any organic rhythm, but on the amount of work that has preceded that period. The curve of efficiency of work begun at 7.30 is similar to the curve of work begun at 10.30, except that the second curve is shifted ahead three hours, the period of highest efficiency occurring three hours later. Thus the degree of efficiency at a particular time is due primarily not to organic rhythm, but to the amount of work previously done and to the accompanying fatigue.

Certain activities are so habitually pursued at the same time of day that that particular hour seems to provide the emotional background best fitted to them. Dawn is the hour of hope, of beginning, when the mind is filled with energetic ambitions of a practical nature. Midday is the time of business negotiations and of greatest activity. Twilight is the hour of mysticism and sentiment, the hour of vague longing and of undefined desires. Night is traditionally associated with wild parties, crimes, and conspiracies. It is then that thieves, witches, fairies, and bootleggers are said to be most active. During the darkest hours ghosts are reputed to appear, "doomed for a certain time to walk the night."

V. ALTITUDE

Very great differences are noticeable between people of different localities, even within the same general limits. These differences in character have been produced, not so much by the factor of location or altitude itself as by the different modes of living that the localities have necessarily brought with them. The differences are perhaps most striking between the mountaineer and the man living in the lowlands. The life of the mountaineer is very hard, and his attention is turned toward wresting a living from the barren soil of the mountain-sides. Due to the ruggedness of the mountains and the consequent difficulty of constructing roads, his means of communication with the outside world are extremely limited. Even to-day thousands of mountaineers live to a ripe old age without having once seen a train. Coming in contact with others but seldom, the mountaineer becomes taciturn and introspective. He is suspicious of strangers because he is not accustomed to dealing with them. He has few friends, but is extremely loyal to them. His strong hatred of an enemy and desire for revenge are demonstrated in the feuds of the Kentucky mountaineers, which last for generations. The typical mountaineer is fixed in his ideas and wary of any sort of change. Being much alone, he has the opportunity to do considerable thinking; this and the hard conditions of life surrounding him usually produce in him a stoical philosophy of life.

The man living in a comfortable lowland town, subjected to an opposite set of conditions, shows a quite different character. Whereas the mountaineer talks little and thinks much, the lowlander talks easily and ponders less. Coming in constant contact with people, the lowlander has a great many acquaintances, but fewer loyal friends. Seeing many "foreigners," he is less a slave of custom and more ready to adopt new ideas than is the mountaineer. He has more interests and more pleasures than the mountaineer, and lives a more comfortable life. His more hospitable surroundings foster in him an epicurean attitude toward life. The differences in the character of the lowlander and the mountaineer are due in no small measure to the different surroundings in which they live.

Differences in altitudes affect behavior in part at least through the amount of available oxygen in the various altitudes. As the distance above sea level increases, the oxygen supply decreases, and *vice versa*. Mental and physical efficiency are closely tied up with the amount of oxygen taken into the lungs. If an individual takes from ten to thirty breaths of pure nitrogen without any oxygen, he becomes unconscious, and consciousness is quickly restored by the inhalation of oxygen. Except in controlled laboratory experiments, oxygen is always available in the surrounding air to a greater or less degree; much more is available in the valleys and much less on the tops of high mountains. Owing to the reserve ventilating power of the lungs, an altitude as high as nine thousand feet is borne without discomfort by nearly all healthy persons. At the altitude of Pike's Peak (fourteen thousand feet), a considerable proportion of unacclimatized persons develop marked symptoms of oxygen-want.

As the altitude is further increased, there is a dulling of the senses, the intellect is less keen, and the judgment is characterized by a "fixation of ideas." In extreme cases epileptiform seizures, partial paralysis and coma may occur. These symptoms are fairly sudden in their onset and occur as a rule before an altitude of twenty-five thousand feet is reached. This is a matter of practical importance, since aeroplanes frequently ascend to altitudes well above twenty-five thousand feet. In such altitudes it is necessary to provide oxygen tanks from which to breathe. But since the early effects of oxygen-want include depression of judgment and intellectual acuity, with no warning from painful or subjectively disturbing symptoms, it is imperative that the aviator be warned to begin inhaling oxygen from his tank as dangerous altitudes are reached regardless of his own feelings.

VI. VENTILATION

Ventilation is a comparatively recent innovation. A few centuries ago houses were built without chimneys, and in that day there was as much attention given to avoiding "fresh air" as there is to-day to securing it. In recent years the desirability of adequate ventilation has been generally emphasized, and "bad air" is said to be injurious to health. It is the popular impression that the drowsiness and lassitude induced by a crowded, poorly ventilated room is due to an increase in the carbon dioxide and to a decrease of oxygen in the air. The air is made up of the following gases in the proportion given, with other constituents in smaller proportions; nitrogen, 78.20 per cent; oxygen, 20.76 per cent; carbon dioxide, 0.04 per cent.

In the most poorly ventilated buildings the carbon dioxide is increased to only about 0.3 of one per cent and the oxygen is decreased to 19 per cent. But before any very bad effects can come from the air, the proportion of carbon dioxide must be increased to at least 3 per cent or the oxygen must be decreased to 14 per cent. It is obvious, therefore, that the ill effects observed in poorly ventilated rooms must be due to some other cause than increase in carbon dioxide. The increased temperature, high humidity, and lack of movement of the air are the most important factors in producing these unpleasant effects through their operation on the heat-regulating functions of the body.

An excellent series of experiments was conducted by the New York Ventilation Commission under the direction of Thorndike,[1] Chapman, and McCall. In these experiments on human beings confined in a small, airtight chamber, it was found that when the air had become sufficiently vitiated to induce marked discomfort in the occupants, the discomfort disappeared very quickly when a fan was set in motion and the air brought into active circulation. That the discomfort is due to interference with evaporation from the skin is shown by the fact that a person confined in such a room, but breathing fresh air brought in through a tube from outside, experiences an equal degree of discomfort with those breathing the air in the room. On the other hand, a person outside the room, with his body exposed to fresh air, who breathes the air of the room through a tube, experiences no discomfort. The cause of the discomfort, therefore, cannot be an increase in carbon dioxide and a decrease in oxygen. These experiments show that one may breathe vitiated air for a considerable time without experiencing discomfort or apparent injury so long as the air is kept in motion sufficiently to allow evaporation from the surface of the body.

Thus far comfort and discomfort under different atmospheric conditions have been considered. It is equally important or more important to determine the effect of different atmospheric conditions on efficiency as measured by quantity and quality of work done. There is a falling-off in efficiency in physical work when temperature and humidity are raised. In mental work the results obtained by the Ventilation Commission were as follows:[2]

When an individual is urged to do his best, he does as much, and does it as well, and improves as rapidly in a hot, humid, stale, and stagnant air condition (86° F., 80 per cent relative humidity, with no air or only recirculated air, and with no movement of the air save what is caused by events

---

[1] Thorndike, E. L., McCall, W. A., Chapman, J. C.: *Ventilation in Relation to Mental Work.* (Teachers College, Columbia University, New York, 1916).

[2] *Ibid.*, p. 75.

in the room, and in the case of recirculation, by the recirculating force) as in an optimum condition (68° F., 50 per cent relative humidity, 45 cubic feet per person per minute of outside air introduced).

When the subjects were allowed to follow their own inclinations — do mental work or read stories, talk, or sleep — they did as much work per hour when the temperature was 75° as when it was 68° F. But when the temperature was 86° F. and the relative humidity 80 per cent, there was a slightly diminished inclination to do mental work. This probably means that mental work required more effort when the temperature and humidity were high. Thus it is seen that the ability to do mental work under test conditions is not materially decreased by high temperature and high relative humidity. The inclination to work is, however, lessened, and the result is generally a decreased amount of work performed during warm weather or in a poorly ventilated room.

In 1928 the writer coöperated in a series of experiments designed to measure the effect on mental and physiological efficiency of extreme changes in the oxygen and carbon dioxide content of the air. On each of two days, at about 7.30 A.M., seven adult men, including the author, entered a small metal tank which was then sealed and made airtight. The group remained in the tank for from nine to ten hours. Preliminary tests of mental and physical efficiency were given, and the tests were repeated at regular intervals, as the carbon dioxide in the air increased.

Chemical analyses were made of the surrounding air at stated periods. During the first day the CO_2 was permitted to increase and the oxygen to decrease simultaneously, but on the second day the oxygen was kept above twenty per cent by releasing additional oxygen as necessary.

There was no noticeable effect either mentally or physically until the CO_2 was almost four per cent. At that time it became increasingly difficult to breathe. The lung ventilation increased enormously. No constant mental effect was noticed until the CO_2 had increased to above five per cent. With the CO_2 between five and six per cent, there was considerable difficulty in concentrating, and by the time that the CO_2 had reached six per cent, most individuals found it practically impossible to do either mental or physical work.

The decrease in mental efficiency was not gradual, but decidedly abrupt. These results, together with those dealing with the effect of prolonged periods of loss of sleep and lack of food, indicate that there is probably a critical point beyond which one is not able to maintain coördination of his thinking apparatus. It seems that such a point is reached at about six per cent CO_2 with most people.

The average person has a tremendous reserve of the factors which maintain mental efficiency. Just as in pneumonia an individual may retain his mental integrity during a crisis when only one lobe of his lung is functioning, so, for a short period of time, his mental efficiency may show very little impairment when the external conditions are quite objectionable. No one is able to say, however, how long a high level of mental efficiency would remain under such conditions.

Humidity must always be considered in relation to temperature. As the temperature of the air increases, its ability to take up moisture increases; hence the optimum humidity increases as the temperature increases. A relative humidity of less than 25 is unusually dry; from 25 to 40 is dry; from 40 to 60 is most agreeable and gives rise to no discomfort; a relative humidity of 60 to 80 gives a sensation of moist air. With a temperature of 68 degrees, the humidity should be about 50 per cent. A very high relative humidity produces discomfort by preventing the evaporation of perspiration from the body.

VII. LIGHT AND ULTRA-VIOLET RAYS

The importance of light in mental and physical efficiency is not yet realized. The value of the ultra-violet rays of the sun in preventing or curing such diseases as rickets and tuberculosis is beginning to be appreciated, and we are hearing more and more about heliotherapy or the use of the sun's rays in the treatment of such diseases. Exposure to the sun's rays causes an increased blood supply to the skin and makes for a better elimination of waste products through the skin. It increases the fat tissue beneath it and improves muscular development. Not only do the sun's rays tend to improve the physical well-being of an animal, but, if the temperature is not too hot, they have an invigorating effect on the mental condition. The contrasting effect of bright, smiling, and dark, gloomy days on one's emotional condition has already been discussed under the section on weather.

It is interesting to speculate how our prehistoric ancestors first discovered artificial light. The savage may have seen a tree struck by lightning; or he may have thought of producing fire when he saw the spark produced by accidentally striking two stones together; or, less probably, he may have thought that, as he produced warmth by rubbing his hands together, he might get greater warmth by rubbing two sticks together. Regardless of how the discovery was made, by the dawn of history man had learned the efficacy of fire to provide heat and light.

During the last few years considerable experimental work has been done on illumination. A careful study of the mechanism of the eye and of the efficacy of various methods of illumination was made by Ferrée and Rand. They pointed out three characteristics of the visual apparatus which condition the efficiency of illumination. First, every individual by original nature has a tendency to turn his eyes toward any bright object in the field of vision so that the light may cast an image upon the center of vision. From earliest infancy the individual has a tendency to turn his eyes toward a bright light. Voluntarily keeping the eyes on something else when there is a bright light in the field of vision is accomplished by the contraction of antagonistic muscles, which consumes energy and hastens fatigue. A second characteristic of the eye is the varying sensitivity to light of the different portions of the retina. The center of the retina is adjusted to bright lights, the periphery to dim lights. This is shown by the fact that dim lights, as the stars, are first seen from the corner of the eye. As the peripheral region of the retina is permanently adjusted to dim lights, a bright light falling on this portion of the eye produces an uncomfortable or painful glare. The result is eye-strain. A third characteristic is the contrast produced when neighboring parts of the retina are stimulated by lights of different intensity. By contrast with the dark field the light appears even brighter, and the result is a painful glare.

An examination of these characteristics of the eye makes it evident why natural light is the best form of illumination. Sunlight conforms to the most important rule of illumination — that the light should be evenly distributed, with no bright spot where the eyes tend to focus. Moreover, natural lighting is generally not too intense, and, as the source of the light is distant, sharp contrasts are less common than in artificial lighting. While sunlight is the best method of illumination, it must be supplemented by artificial lighting in many instances. All systems of artificial lighting, however, are not of equal merit. The best system of artificial illumination is an indirect light such as is given by entirely enclosing an electric light in a translucent globe. The second best method of artificial lighting is the semi-indirect light; and third and worst is the direct light, which is frequently too intense. To secure the best results, it is much more important to have evenness of illumination than high intensity. Until recently the latter has been the ideal in lighting, because the test of lighting efficiency has been how small an object can be seen. A better way to measure the efficiency of the lighting system is by the output of work under different lighting conditions. Probably the best method of measuring the effect of a lighting system, however, is to determine the rapidity of onset of fatigue under different conditions of illumination.

One of the most important problems of illumination is street lighting. Many of the traffic mishaps in large cities could be eliminated by better street lighting. The ideal street light is not glaring; it does not attract the attention of the automobile driver from the roadway; it does not send most of its light up into the air where it is wasted instead of lighting the street; and lastly, it conserves electricity. The difficulties attendant upon driving at night due to darkness and glaring headlights are shown by the disproportionately large number of accidents occurring after dark.

The most important factor in lighting which causes differences in emotional feeling is color. Color therapy, or the use of colored lights for the treatment of various nervous and mental diseases, has attracted considerable attention recently. Ferrée studied the effect of colored light upon muscular activity as measured by a special apparatus for testing the strength of grip in the hand. In ordinary light the strength of grip was found to be 23 units; it increased to 24 for blue light; to 28 for green; to 30 for yellow; to 35 for orange; and to 42 for red. This shows the stimulating effect of the "warmer" colors.

PART II
INDIVIDUAL DIFFERENCES

The most universal quality is diversity
MONTAIGNE

CHAPTER V

THE IMPORTANCE AND NATURE OF INDIVIDUAL DIFFERENCES

My general impression is that certain aptitudes, as for mathematics and music, are mainly innate, and that kinds of character and degrees of ability are mainly innate, but that the direction of performance is mainly due to circumstances, and that the environment imposes a veto on any performance not congenial to it.

CATTELL [1]

INDIVIDUALS are neither born equal, live equal, nor die equal. Some persons from the beginning to the end of life are practically free from disease; the majority are handicapped with only an occasional failure of health; while others are apparently born with a bodily mechanism so susceptible to disease that at no time in life are they free from it. Some are born into homes of culture and luxury, and are given all the advantages that wealth and influence can provide; in the homes of the majority the necessities of life, but few of the luxuries are provided; while others are born into homes where their earliest heritage is poverty, disease, and ignorant parentage. A limited number are born geniuses; most have average intelligence; while an unfortunate few have such a defective mentality that they must live and die as idiots. Some are endowed with such high social ability that they could be elected to Congress on the Republican ticket from Georgia; the majority have no special ability either for making or for losing friends; while others are born with such thorny dispositions that no one can come in close contact with them without injury. Some persons have such uncanny insight into mechanics that no appliance is so complicated but that they can repair it or reproduce it; most individuals have only enough mechanical ability to do such things as making minor repairs on their automobiles; while others are so devoid of mechanical insight that they cannot screw a nut on a common bolt without stripping the threads or wringing off the head.

[1] Cattell, J. McK.: *A Statistical Study of American Men of Science*, III. (The Distribution of American Men of Science. *Science*, New Series, XXIV, pp. 734–35.)

In constructing a building the mechanical engineer must know the strength of the materials he is using, the amount of stress and strain each will withstand, and the best material to use for each different purpose. He must know that cast-iron beams and steel beams do not give the same results, and that concrete will hold or crack depending upon the quality and proportion of the materials used in it. The applied psychologist may be considered the human engineer who deals with human beings as the mechanical engineer does with his materials. It is the business of the human engineer to recognize that individuals differ; that one man is capable of making an invention that will benefit the world, while another is capable of no higher type of work than that requiring a strong back and a weak mind; that one person will lose his head in an emergency, while another will do whatever the situation demands in a similar emergency; and that a person may be a miserable failure as a salesman and a shining success as a mechanic. In other words, the applied psychologist must know in what respects individuals differ, and the nature of these individual differences. He must recognize the fundamental fact of applied psychology, namely, that the individual is the unit. All applications of psychology must depend upon knowledge of the laws that govern individual behavior, and the conditions that modify it.

I. INDIVIDUAL DIFFERENCES IN VARIOUS FIELDS

Let us consider briefly the importance of individual differences in various vocational fields.

1. **Employment.** The significance of individual differences in employment is clearly apparent. The employer's methods of selecting employees will be determined to no small extent by his opinions concerning individual differences, their causes, and the possibility of modifying them. And having selected his employees, he is again brought face to face with the problem of individual differences in deciding upon methods of training, working conditions, shop incentives, transfers, promotions, and lay-offs. The problem of individual differences is the most difficult one facing the industrial engineer to-day, for although he can easily standardize his machines and other purely mechanical elements, when it comes to

standardizing the human element, he faces a much more difficult problem.

2. Selling. No one realizes more clearly than the salesman that people differ. An appeal that is quite successful with one person has no effect when used with another. The "good schools" argument, for example, is often used effectively by a real estate salesman in selling a house to a man with a number of small children. But the same argument often has the opposite effect when used on a prospective buyer without children, for he immediately foresees high taxes to pay for those "good schools," and, not wanting to pay for educating the other man's children, he prefers to buy a home in a community where less money is spent on the schools.

3. Advertising. Why does a certain advertising concern spend more than one hundred million dollars a year on advertising, and put out advertisements with one hundred and eight different types of appeals? Once more the answer is the existence of individual differences. People differ, and an advertisement that will persuade one person to buy will fail utterly with others, and so a large corps of experts must be kept on the staff to develop advertisements that will appeal to all types of prospective buyers.

4. Medicine. One of the first facts that is brought to the attention of the young medical student is the existence of what are called idiosyncrasies; i.e., individual peculiarities so that a drug which will work very satisfactorily with one person may have the opposite effect on another. From the beginning to the end of the medical course it is drilled into the future practitioner that people differ, and that he must treat the individual rather than the disease. Some persons must be given bread pills and treated with soothing suggestions and harmless potions, while others must be made to realize the seriousness of their condition, and the need for greater care.

5. Medico-legal field. In the medico-legal field many phases of the problem of individual differences are encountered, for here such questions as the following must be answered: When is a person not responsible for the crimes he commits? How may feeble-mindedness be detected? What should be the treatment of the criminal insane? What provision should society make to take care of epileptics? These and many similar questions depend for an answer to no small extent upon the psychology of individual differences.

6. Law.   In the detection of crime the problem of individual differences is always of importance.   Why does a certain criminal with a long record of burglaries always enter through the basement the house which he intends to rob, while another, equally proficient in his art, always effects his entrance through second-story windows? In placing a man on the witness stand it is no small concern to the lawyer to know whether the witness will become frightened and break down, or whether he will tell his story with the same assurance with which he told it in the lawyer's office.   In the matter of punishment and reform individual differences are of major importance.   The chief difficulty with such enlightened methods of treating criminals as those instituted by Osborne at Sing Sing is the fact that while some prisoners will react admirably to kind treatment, there are always others who take advantage of any humane consideration that is given them.   In passing sentence upon an individual who has committed a crime, one should recognize that the punishment should be meted out, not according to the crime, but according to the criminal.

7. Politics.   In few professions is the problem of individual differences of more practical importance than in that of politics. While running for office the politician, in order to attract the votes of the church people, often makes a very substantial contribution to the building fund of a new church.   But late in the evening of the same day he may be found making merry with a radically different crowd, singing "one jug of liquor for the four of us" and pledging his whole-hearted support to any bill designed to destroy the Eighteenth Amendment.   His behavior in both cases is based upon a recognition of the differences between his two groups of supporters. This same principle is illustrated in the fact that for the last twelve years, in order to catch the vote of the Anti-Saloon League and other dry organizations, the platforms of both major parties have carried planks promising to make America dry. But the private lives of many elected on these platforms have been exceedingly wet, and, in spite of all platform promises, America continues to be damp.

8. Education.   The importance of individual differences in the field of education is generally recognized. One of the outstanding results of the use of intelligence and standardized educational tests in our schools has been to show how widely pupils differ. We often find in a class one child who can learn twice as fast as the others. At the present time few would deny that it is absurd to expect all the children in a class to progress at the same rate. In the last few years, as a result of the recognition of these differences in the mental ability of children, there has been a complete revolution of our educational philosophy. The whole emphasis has shifted toward making the individual child rather than the group the unit of instruction. Special schools for the defective and for the superior child are now quite common.

9. Traffic. The problem of individual differences is of daily increasing importance in the control of automobile traffic. With twenty-six thousand people killed in 1927 in automobile accidents, it is a matter of no small concern to determine the persons capable of safe driving and those not to be entrusted with the operation of such a death-dealing machine as the automobile. Statistics show that a very large proportion of the accidents are caused by persons who have previously been involved in accidents, although this class makes up less than four per cent of the total number of drivers. If some method can be found of eliminating this very small number of drivers, accidents can be reduced almost one half. It is easy to understand why so much attention is being given to the problem of discovering how this small group of dangerous drivers differs from the safe driver.

II. THE NATURE OF INDIVIDUAL DIFFERENCES

From earliest childhood we are made to recognize the fact that people differ. We know that there are tall people and short people, fat people and lean people, clever people and dull people, with some representing every degree of tallness and cleverness in between. Investigators in the past have not been content merely to recognize the fact that individuals differ, but they have attempted to determine the extent of these differences and have spent considerable time in studying them with the hope of discovering, in so far as possible, the principles underlying such differences.

1. **Difficulties of separating individuals into clear-cut classes.** In the past there has been a marked tendency to attempt to separate individuals into definite groups or classes. The philosophers of old recognized four types of personalities — the sanguine, the phlegmatic, the choleric, and the melancholic. And down through the ages similar classifications of individuals have been made in accordance with some specific human trait. But with the development of more reliable methods of measurement, it has been found that the grouping of individuals into classes is often misleading and inaccurate. The chief reason for this is the difficulty of establishing definite limits which separate one class from another. Should all men, for example, who are less than 62 inches in height be considered as dwarfs, all who are more than 74 inches as giants, and those whose height falls between 62 inches and 74 inches as persons of normal height? An objection to such a classification is readily seen when it is noted that the difference in height between the 62-inch normal and the 74-inch normal is 12 inches, while the difference between the 62-inch normal and the 61-inch dwarf is only 1 inch. The same objection applies to any attempt to place individuals in clear-cut classes in accordance with any one trait, for there is always a tendency for one class to fuse with another. The student should bear this in mind when studying any classification of human beings.

2. **Normal distribution curve.** Various investigators using the modern methods of science have shown that people differ in any one trait somewhat as follows: The vast majority possess an average amount of the trait, while there are a few who possess a very small amount of the trait and likewise a few who possess it in great abundance. It is further found that those who possess it in great abundance are about equal in number to those who possess a small amount of the trait. In other words, the vast majority of humanity possess a mediocre amount of any one trait, and the farther away the amount is from the average amount possessed by humanity as a whole, the smaller will be the number of people possessing that amount. To illustrate: A thousand men in a certain regiment were carefully measured as to height. The range and distribution of the height of the thousand men are shown in Figure 8. The left end of the line AB represents the height of the shortest man, the right end

that of the tallest. The number of men of the various sizes is represented by the height of the curve above the base line AB. This bell-shaped curve is called the *normal distribution curve*. The peak of the curve, representing the largest number of cases, corresponds to the point in the base line representing approximately 68 inches; i.e., more men are about 68 inches tall than of any other height. Half of

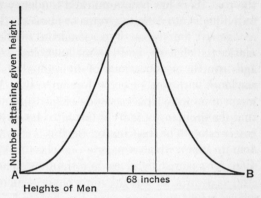

FIGURE 8. CORRECT VIEW OF INDIVIDUAL DIFFERENCES. NORMAL DISTRIBUTION CURVE FOR HEIGHTS OF MEN

the thousand men are between 66 and 70 inches in height. This middle fifty per cent is indicated by the space between the vertical lines in Figure 8. This type of figure represents not only individual differences in physical traits, but holds equally well for the differences in mental traits. Individuals tend to differ as shown in Figure

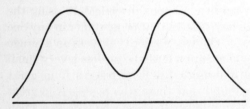

FIGURE 9. WRONG VIEW OF INDIVIDUAL DIFFERENCES

8 and not as in Figure 9, for types as such do not exist. They are only extreme deviations from the normal. All the distributions obtained from measurement of traits of unselected individuals tend to fall into the typical groupings pictured above in the normal distribution curve. The facts illustrated can be summarized as follows: 1. Graphs showing the distribution of abilities in any trait have the same general shape. 2. There is a marked piling-up of "mediocrity" near the center of the distribution. 3. There is a tendency for symmetrical shading-off on either side with less and

less frequency the farther away one goes from the center of the group.   4.   These and many other measurements demonstrate the fact that individuals are very unequal in ability.

The student with an inquiring mind may seek an explanation for the fact that individuals, when measured in any one trait, tend to fall into the normal distribution curve as described above.   The explanation seems to lie in the fact that the normal distribution curve represents the shape of any distribution of chance happenings, and that human traits are determined by a variety of factors operating in a more or less chance fashion.   For example, if you should toss up four coins sixteen times, and count the heads and tails each time, you would get close to the following results:

```
4 heads and 0 tails 1 in 16 times
3   "    "  1   "  4 "   "    "
2   "    "  2   "  6 "   "    "
1   "    "  3   "  4 "   "    "
0   "    "  4   "  1 "   "    "
```

If you should toss ten coins 1024 times, there would be only 1 chance in the 1024 of throwing 10 heads and also just 1 chance of zero heads.   There would be 10 chances of throwing 9 heads, and also 10 chances of throwing 1 head.   There would be 45 chances for either 8 heads or 2 heads; 120 chances for either 7 heads or 3 heads; 210 chances for either 6 or 4 heads; and 252 chances for 5 heads.

The results of various measurements would indicate that human traits are determined by a similar law of chance combinations, which produce a large number of mediocre individuals and smaller numbers both of superior and inferior individuals.

III.   BASIS OF INDIVIDUAL DIFFERENCES

Individual differences in behavior are determined by differences in bodily structure and by differences in past experiences.   Differences in structure depend very largely, but not wholly on heredity and maturity.   Large parents tend to beget large children, and tall parents beget children who likewise grow up to be tall.   Children of negroes have the thick lips, flat noses, kinky hair, and other anatomical characteristics of their race.

The structural changes that develop as the result of age or

maturity produce their corresponding differences in behavior. On this point Myerson [1] says:

> The evolution from helpless infancy through lusty maturity to decrepit old age runs the same course in regard to body and mind. There is the same extreme plasticity in childhood, there is a similar gain in power, though loss of plasticity, in maturity by the establishment of organized habits and reflexes, and bodily old age resembles mental old age in the increased rigidity which physically shows itself in the stiffened face, stiffened bones, stiffened arteries, and mentally shows itself by the disappearance of the power to adjust in a fine and plastic way to new situations and experiences. Death is the final immobility, but life itself is manifested by an increasing immobility in all qualities.

Sex differences in behavior are also greatly influenced by differences in bodily structure. The larger and more powerful bodies of men predispose them to certain kinds of behavior just as the greater weight and strength of the truck tend to limit its use to certain kinds of activity, while the lighter bodies and greater speed of the passenger car predispose it to a different sort of activity.

While structural differences better equip an individual for some lines of endeavor than for others, they do not confine his activity within very narrow limits. Just as the passenger car may be used for hauling freight, so the truck may be pressed into service for a joy ride. And just as the man may in an emergency render to the injured the service usually performed by the Red Cross nurse, so the woman in cases of necessity may perform some of the more strenuous duties of the soldier.

Structural differences tend to determine the gross nature of one's performances, but differences due to experience and training determine the technique and skill of the performances. Woman's less frequent achievement of eminence is due not so much to her innate inferiority as to her restricted opportunity. And the poorer showing of negroes on intelligence tests is in part to be explained by their inferior environment. Lack of success in life may be due to an inborn lack of brains, but it may also be due to the lack of proper training in a propitious environment.

As pointed out above, structural differences depend only in part

[1] Myerson, Abraham: *The Psychology of Mental Disorders* (The Macmillan Company, New York, 1927), pp. 7–8. Reprinted by permission of the publishers.

on heredity.   The dwarfed form may be due to the fact that the parents were dwarfs, but even children of tall parents are dwarfs when the thyroid and pituitary glands of the children fail to develop properly.   Hunchbacks may in rare instances be due to heredity, but are in most instances due to tuberculosis of the spinal vertebræ. The part played by inheritance in causing knock-knees and bow-legs is small, but the part played by rickets is large.   Imperfect brain development may be due to heredity, but it is more often due to such diseases as congenital syphilis and meningitis.

For convenience of discussion the problem of individual differences will be considered in more detail under the following heads: 1. Differences due to Race.   2. Differences due to Family Inheritance.   3. Differences due to Past Experiences.   4. Differences due to Age.   5. Differences due to Sex.   6. Differences in Emotional Outlets.   7. Personality and its Measurement.

CHAPTER VI

DIFFERENCES DUE TO RACE

Oh, East is East and West is West, and never the twain shall meet
Till Earth and Sky stand presently at God's great Judgment Seat.
RUDYARD KIPLING

A DISTINCT race is a group of people having the same remote ancestry, and consequently having certain physical and mental traits different from those of other races with a totally different ancestry. Thorndike [1] made the following statement in this connection:

Men are more like one another and unlike dogs or horses because men spring from a presumably common remote ancestry which was not the ancestry of dogs and horses. Men, dogs, and horses are more alike mentally than men, dogs, horses, earthworms, and clams are, because presumably men, dogs, and horses spring from a common ancestry which was not the ancestry of earthworms or clams. Certain men, for example the American Indians, springing from a common ancestry which was not the ancestry of Europeans, may be expected to be mentally more like one another than like Europeans, if their common ancestry differed mentally from that of Europeans.

On the basis of physical characteristics most authorities divide mankind into three races, the black race, the yellow race, and the white or Caucasian race. Each of these three races has both physical and mental peculiarities. The black skin, flat nose, and kinky hair of the negro are no more characteristic of his race than are certain mental peculiarities. And the Mongolian possesses mental twists no less distinctive of his race than is his yellow skin. There is a widespread belief that there are great differences in the strength and variety of emotions in the different subdivisions of the races. The excitable Frenchman, the phlegmatic German, the hyper-emotional Latin, the passionate Russian, the witty and good-natured Irish, the bland and stolid Chinese, and the joyous, irresponsible negro are popular conceptions common in literature and in conversation. The extent to which these traits are due to

[1] Thorndike, Edward L.: *Educational Psychology*, III, 206. (Teachers College, Columbia University, New York, 1914.)

heredity and the extent to which they have been influenced by environment is impossible to determine. But whatever the causes of these differences may be, common observation shows that they do exist.

In the following discussion attention will be given primarily to the race differences existing among the peoples in the United States, and we shall consequently consider the racial peculiarities of the two American-born races, the American Indian and the negro, and of the foreign-born or immigrant races. The fact that these races are existing side by side makes the development of race prejudice inevitable, and the problem of race crossing of considerable importance.

I. THE AMERICAN-BORN

1. **The Indian.** Although the American Indian was the original inhabitant of this country, and has been here since the white man first took possession of it, little of a scientific nature is known concerning the traits peculiar to the Indian race. The most reliable data that we have concerning the Indian relate to his intelligence. The results of various investigations indicate that the Indian is inferior in intelligence to the whites, although the evidence for this conclusion is not very abundant. In a study of the intelligence of 1050 full-blooded Indian children, Garth found their median Intelligence Quotient [1] to be 67 as compared with an Intelligence Quotient of 100 for white children. Rowe also found that 94 per cent of the Indians tested below age on the Binet Scale as compared with only 21 per cent of the whites who tested below age on this same scale. Hunter gave the Otis Group Intelligence Test to comparable groups of Indians and whites and found a median score of 83 for the Indians as compared with a median score of 123 for the whites. When the full- and mixed-blood Indians are compared, the mental superiority of the mixed bloods is clearly demonstrated. Garth found that the mixed-blood group was 11 per cent better than the full-blood group in tests of higher mental processes. Hunter found that the scores on the Otis test decreased with a decrease in

[1] The Intelligence Quotient is secured by dividing the mental age by the chronological age.

the amount of white blood. This gradual decrease in ability from the quarter to the full-blood Indian is shown by the median scores on the intelligence test as follows: quarter Indian, score 109; half Indian, score 91; three quarters Indian, score 78; full Indian, score 67. In general intelligence, then, the Indians are apparently inferior to the white race. A possible explanation of this poor showing will be given later in this chapter.

Certain emotional and character traits are attributed to the Indian by tradition. Their stoical endurance of suffering, the cruelty with which they take revenge upon their enemies, and their loyalty to friends are very generally recognized mental characteristics. Unlike the negroes, the Indians have never made good slaves. The early settlers tried at various times to use them as slaves, but the proposition did not work. Their independence and bravery ill adapt them to play the part of a subservient race. As a race they are not very demonstrative, but give little outward indication of either joys or sorrows.

2. **The negro.** The number of Indians is too small and their contacts with the whites not sufficiently close for them to be of the greatest interest to us. Such is not the case, however, with the negroes, and consequently the negro offers a more acute problem than the Indian. By extensive studies and by observation we know more of the racial characteristics of the negro than we do of any other race except our own. A comparison of the negro and white races offers the best illustration of the fact that races differ in physical, mental, and emotional traits.

a. *Physical differences.* There are certain striking physical characteristics which mark a member of the black race. We recognize a negro at a glance by his black, shining skin, his kinky hair, flat nose, thick lips, and gleaming teeth. His brain weighs less than that of the white man, even though his body is slightly larger than the body of the white man. The negro has a peculiar quality of voice, and possesses an innate sense of rhythm which appears in his songs and dances.

Likewise certain racial differences in immunity to disease are evident. The negro is almost immune to certain diseases. He is not seriously affected by yellow fever, which is generally fatal to

Caucasians, but he is extremely susceptible to other diseases, such as tuberculosis. This difference in immunity to disease is no doubt due to the fact that the negro, having lived in yellow-fever countries for centuries, has developed an immunity to yellow fever, but has not yet developed immunity to tuberculosis, which was a disease unknown to his forefathers in Africa.

b. *Differences in mental disorders.* Not only do races differ in their susceptibility to the somatic diseases, but they differ as well in their mental disorders. Kirby [1] tabulated according to race all mental disorders of patients admitted to hospitals serving the city of New York for the year 1908. His data are shown in the following table. It will be observed that the Irish are most liable to

PSYCHOSES	IRISH (per cent)	JEWISH (per cent)	GERMAN (per cent)	UNITED STATES (per cent)	ITALIAN (per cent)	NEGRO (per cent)
Senile psychoses.........	9.80	2.87	6.70	7.14	3.70	9.80
General paralysis (paresis)	7.59	14.05	20.10	17.46	9.87	29.41
Alcoholic psychoses....:	27.69	0.32	11.85	11.90	8.64	7.82
Dementia præcox.......	13.48	27.47	14.95	16.66	23.44	13.72
Manic depressive psychoses...............	16.66	28.43	12.89	18.25	13.58	9.80
Epileptic psychoses.....	2.20	1.59	4.64	3.17	4.93	3.92
Other psychoses........	22.58	25.27	28.87	25.42	35.84	25.53
Total number of each race.............	418	313	194	126	81	51

Rosanoff, Aaron J.: *Manual of Psychiatry* (John Wiley and Sons, New York, 1927), p. 14.

alcoholic psychoses, while the Jews are practically free from this; but the Jews are especially high in dementia præcox and the manic-depressive psychoses. The negroes are most susceptible to paresis (general paralysis). How much such differences can be explained in terms of different social conditions of the races is hard to say. If the negroes and Irish are compared in the diseases of paresis and alcoholic psychoses, it appears that the Irish have about one fourth as many paretics as the negroes, and that the negroes have about one fourth as many alcoholics as the Irish. It is known that paresis is caused by syphilitic infection and that the alcoholic psychoses are caused by an overindulgence in alcohol. It may be that race tradi-

[1] Kirby, George H.: *A Study in Race Psychopathology* (New York State Hospital Bulletin, N.S., I, 1909), p. 663.

tions cause the Irish as a race to drink very much more than the negroes, and due to a greater sex promiscuity the negroes may develop more cases of syphilis and consequently more cases of paresis.

c. *Intellectual differences.* (1) *Intelligence of Adults.* Just as races differ physically, so they differ mentally. Galton said that, making allowances for differences in environment, he believed that negroes are inferior in intelligence to Europeans by about one eighth the difference between the intelligence of Aristotle and that of the lowest idiot. A comparison of the intelligence test scores of negroes and whites in the army showed the negro to be decidedly inferior. On the Army Alpha Intelligence Test the median score obtained by the negro recruits was 23, and that obtained by the white recruits was 63 on a 212 point scale.

These differences may be due in no small part to factors other than innate race differences. That environment played some part in determining these differences is indicated by the fact that the negroes in different sections of the country made radically different scores on the test. Comparing the intellectual ability of Northern and Southern negro recruits, it was found that the Southern negro is as much inferior to the Northern negro as negroes in general are inferior to whites. This difference in intelligence may be accounted for by the selective force at work in causing migration of the negroes to the North. The more intelligent and ambitious negroes move North where opportunities are greater; while those who are less intelligent and ambitious tend to stay in the South where they can manage to exist with less effort. But it is also true that those who go North have better educational advantages. A comparison between the letter ratings ("A" being the superior rating) on the army tests of Northern and Southern negroes gives the following:

GROUP	No. OF CASES	PERCENTAGE RATED						
		D–	D	C–	C	C	B	A
Northern negroes *..	4,705	14.4	31.2	25.8	18.0	7.2	2.7	0.7
Southern negroes ...	6,846	57.0	29.2	9.6	3.4	0.7	0.2	0.1

* *Memoirs of the National Academy of Sciences*, xv, part iii, chap. viii, p. 707.

Those who are counted as negroes range in color from the pure black negro to the light mulatto. The differences between these various types are not limited to color alone. A considerable intellectual difference exists between the mulatto and the pure negro. In the army a large number of negro recruits were separated on the basis of skin color, and the intelligence ratings of the darker and the lighter groups were compared. The darker class contained pure negroes and those whose skin color indicated that they had a smaller proportion of white blood than mulattoes. The lighter class contained those whose skin color indicated that they were true mulattoes or persons who had a larger proportion of white blood than mulattoes. On the Army Alpha Intelligence Test the darker group made a median score of 30; the lighter group made a median score of 50. Negroes with considerable white blood are distinctly superior in intelligence to the pure negro, but still inferior to the white man. This color difference is recognized by the negroes themselves, as is shown in the following verses:

"De yaller gal rides in de limousine,
De high brown rides in de train, ·
De po' black gal rides de ol' gray mule,
But she gits thar just de same.'

Pintner[1] summarizes the reports of various investigations into the comparative intelligence of white and colored by saying:

All results show the negro decidedly inferior to the white on standard intelligence tests. These results are sufficiently numerous and consistent to point to a racial difference in intelligence. The overlapping of the two races is great, and the most liberal estimate seems to be that at most 25 per cent of the colored reach or exceed the median intelligence of the whites. No qualitative difference in intelligence between the two races can explain this marked quantitative difference. Indeed, it is doubtful whether real qualitative differences exist with reference to the traits measured by our intelligence tests.

(2) *Intelligence of Children.* A number of studies of the intelligence of the negro school children have been made, of which the

---

[1] Pintner, Rudolf: *Intelligence Testing* (Henry Holt & Company, New York, 1923), p. 345.

following is typical: Strong [1] used the Goddard Revision of the Binet Scale in comparing 125 colored children with 225 white children from 5 to 15 years of age. The percentage of each group retarded mentally is shown below:

	COLORED	WHITE
More than one year backward	29.4	10.2
Satisfactory — or normal	69.8	84.4
More than one year advanced	0.1	5.3

A child is said to be retarded mentally if his mental age, as indicated by a standard test of intelligence, is less than his chronological age. A ten-year-old child with a mental age of eight is two years retarded mentally. About three times as many colored children as white children studied were more than one year backward, while a very small percentage as compared with white children were advanced more than one year.

(3) *Scholastic standing.* Due in part to the fact that negroes are lower in general intelligence, and in part to their attitude toward school and methods of study, we find that the scholastic standing of negro children is generally lower than that of white children. McCall's study of the achievement on standardized educational tests of white and colored students in the Baltimore schools is typical of investigations along these lines. His conclusions are presented in terms of the grades that the Baltimore school is ahead of the average school system, as measured by standardized tests. The relative standing of the white and colored schools as compared with the average school is presented in terms of the grades that the Baltimore schools are ahead of the average school system.

The eighth grade of the colored school is 2.7 grades behind the average eighth grade in achievement, and the eighth grade of the white schools is 0.1 grade ahead of the average eighth grade. The eighth grade of the colored schools in this city, then, is almost three years behind that of the white schools, the achievement of colored eighth-grade students on standardized tests being equal only to that of the average fifth grade. The colored students fall farther behind the white students each year. The fourth grade of the colored schools

[1] Strong, A. C.: "Three Hundred and Fifty White and Colored Children Measured by the Binet-Simon Measuring Scale of Intelligence," *Pedagogical Seminary*, xx, 485–515.

is only 0.7 of a grade below normal, but the eighth grade is almost three years below. This fact brings out the difference in the rate of progress of the white and colored students. The average for all grades from fourth through eighth, shows the white schools 0.1 grade ahead of the average school and the colored schools 1.76 grades behind.

d. Race inferiority. Every race thinks itself superior, and, as a matter of fact, is superior in some respect. On all quantitative measurements of abstract intelligence or school achievement both negroes and Indians are inferior to whites. Their contribution to our civilization in scientific discoveries is almost nil. But the above facts are not just cause to consider these races inferior in other respects to the white race. Races have different philosophies of life and consequently radically different sets of values which lead them to develop very diverse civilizations. We have only our own word for it that our civilization is superior to that of the American Indians or of the African negroes in the fifteenth century. If the chief aim of life is the acquisition of pleasure and the escape of annoyances, their civilization might have been superior to ours. But certain it is that the white man is on the whole better adapted for this particular civilization than are the negroes or Indians. And it is possible that if tests were designed in terms of the civilization of the negroes and Indians, the boasted superiority might be changed to inferiority.

In defending the poor showing made by the negroes on intelligence and other objective tests, Watson [1] says that the negroes have never been given a chance.

If you sent each and every negro to Harvard and then through law and medicine and gave him a year for travel and a million-dollar-a-year income, he would still not have an equal chance. Even in Boston or in Washington the negro would still be a negro; he would still be made to feel his inferiority. There is a sporadic attempt in New York on the part of a sophisticated group to lionize the negro. They go to the Harlem night clubs, eat and drink with him on a plane of social equality, ask him to their homes, and in general wine and dine him. But let one negro try to marry a son or daughter of any member of this clique, and the devil's to pay. In Jamaica and on the Continent there is less of the social barrier and the

[1] Watson, John B.: *The Ways of Behaviorism* (Harper & Bros., 1928), p. 38.

negro consequently has more nearly an equal chance with the white. Why, then, didn't he develop in Africa where he was king? Because where food, sex, and shelter offer no problems, there is nothing in the environment to force the trial-and-error movements that lead to discovery. Even white races dwelling in the tropics slow down.

While there is considerable truth in what Watson says, the evidence now available would indicate that race differences depend on more factors than social opportunity. No amount of social opportunity will make the average negro equal to the average white in abstract intelligence. And it is also probably true that no amount of training would make the average white equal to the average negro in certain other traits. In short, where there are structural differences there must be behavior differences. The white man's structure gives him an advantage in certain traits, the negro's structure gives him an advantage in other traits.

e. Qualitative differences. Differences in emotional make-up between the negro and the white man are so apparent that they have become proverbial. The joyousness and optimism of the negro race are well known. Like a child the negro is ordinarily cheerful and good-natured; childlike, too, is his speedy recovery from grief or depression. Living in the present as he does, savings banks and life insurance policies hold little appeal for him, for he believes that the sunny days should be enjoyed as they come, not spent in saving up for a rainy one. The negro's firm belief in enjoying life is shown in the following verses:

> "I ain't agwine t' work t' my dyin' day.
>   If I ever lays up enough,
> I'se gwine off a while an' stay.
> I'll be takin' a few days off.
> 'Case de jimpson weeds don't bloom but once,
>   An' when dey's shed, dey's shed.
> An' when you'se daid, 'tain't just for a month,
>   'Case you'se gwine t' be a long time daid."

The negro views life optimistically. Privations appear to disturb him little, and in situations which would cause a white man to give up in despair, the negro sings merrily and goes on. Due in part to the joyous temperament of the negroes, suicides among them are comparatively rare. The average suicide rate per 100,000 population of white and colored in the Southern States from 1919 to 1923 was as follows:

	1919	1920	1921	1922	1923
South:					
Average white............	6.9	6.3	8.7	7.7	6.9
Average colored.........	1.6	1.8	2.4	2.1	2.0
Whole United States:					
Average for both races....	11.4	11.2	12.6	11.9	11.6

In every instance the suicide rate of the white population is about four times as high as that of the colored population, even after ample provision has been made for the differences in the numbers of the two races. Since the suicide rate in the South is considerably lower than in the country as a whole, the difference in the suicide rate among whites and colored is even greater if the rates for the whole nation are taken.

As a rule negroes do not desire responsibility. They prefer to enjoy themselves in idleness, working only when work is unavoidable, and to depend upon some one else to supply the necessities of life. As a race they are inclined to be lazy and shiftless, to which cause is due the abject poverty in which many live. The typical negro irresponsibility and tendency to look to the whites for support is illustrated in the following verses:

"I don't has to work so hard
   'Case I'se got a gal in the white folks' yard,
An' eb'ry ev'nin' at half-past eight
   I comes along by the garden gate.
She gives me butter, an' sugar, an' lard.
   Now I don't has to work so hard."

The superstition of the negro is probably largely due to his ignorance and to his great emotional excitability. The negro has a firm belief in charms to entice "Lady Luck" or to keep away evil spirits. The following quotation from an advertisement circulated in the Harlem district of New York bears witness to the superstition of the negro. The circular was sent out by a negro who called himself "Professor," and who did a thriving business until his place was raided by Federal agents.

> Sahara Lucky Cords: For men only. Well seasoned with psychic. Instruction for use will be forwarded according to order. Price $25.
>
> Bring Back Powder: Whatsoever you desire to bring or send away, just burn this powder in the fire and call the name of the person seven times at midnight. Price $55; for quick service $75.

Negroes are especially gregarious, loving big crowds and much display. Secret organizations flourish among them. Their church services are an occasion of much enjoyment to all the family. A dance, a circus, or a funeral, anything serves as an excuse for a large gathering. Even at funerals the negro's customary joyous nature is not entirely sobered, for a funeral is an occasion for a great gathering.

The negro love of display is shown by the bright colors, extreme styles, and flashy jewelry worn by them on gala occasions. Their fondness for display also appears in their liking for big words, appropriate or inappropriate. Negro children called by such names as *Hyacinth, Nebuchadnezzar, Insense,* and *Adiposa* are not uncommon. At a Southern negro camp-meeting the preacher closed with the following impressive jargon: "Brethren and sistern, thanking you all most severely for your infectious distraction, I will now rambulate to my seat with odoriferous feelins of concentration toward each and every one of you."

As the negro is by nature extremely emotional, his religion is of the most primitive sort, relying for its appeal upon many threats of "hell and damnation." In the typical negro revival the nights are made hideous by the wails and heartrending groans of the mourners. At these revivals they delight in singing such songs as:

> "Nigger man settin' on the gates of hell,
> Gates flew open and in he fell,
> No hiding place down there.
> Went to the rock to hide my face,
> Rock cried out, 'No hiding place,
> No hiding place down here.'"

In all their songs, and in the sermons they preach as well as in the prayers they pray there is a weird melody characterized by a rhythmic beauty which is lacking in the worship of the whites. This is seen in such songs as:

> "I couldn't hear nobody pray.
> Well — I couldn't hear nobody pray.
> O, 'way down yonder by myself,
> I couldn't hear nobody pray."

The shouting, which is very evident in all negro worship, also has this rhythmic quality. Many times as the shouter grows more enthusiastic he keeps perfect time to the song by jumping up and down in a sort of dance. The negro attitude toward shouting is shown in their song:

> "I really do believe without a doubt
> That all good Christians ought to shout."

The colored race is especially fond of music and dancing. The white child has to learn to dance, but the little pickaninny apparently dances instinctively. With the negro, rhythm seems to be an innate quality, and he can extract music from any sort of instrument. Most negroes have good voices and love to sing. They sing at their work in the fields, whereas the white men work in silence. If there are twenty negroes, they will sing twenty different parts, but the total effect will be a very pleasing harmony.

The negro has made his chief contribution to civilization in music, literature, and dramatics. What the negro is to music and jazz is everywhere evident. He has a keen sense of the dramatic, and is a natural mimic, acting with more abandon than his white fellows. In poetry the section of religious songs is larger than any other, and constitutes his most precious gift to the American artistic field. Indeed, the negro's finest æsthetic and artistic qualities seem to spring from his religious intensity. Famous scientists of the negro race are conspicuous for their absence, for the negro genius apparently lies in other lines.

f. Differences in working efficiency. For several years Superintendent Daniel DeNoyelles,[1] who is superintendent of a large in-

---

[1] DeNoyelles, Daniel: "The Negro as Laborer," *Journal of Industrial Psychology*, February, 1926, pp. 91–93.

dustrial plant in New York State, has been employing native whites and negroes to do the same type of unskilled work in his plant. In that way he has had the opportunity to study at first hand several hundred workers of each race. Concerning the comparative working efficiency of the two races he says:

Taking all the men who had been one year or more in the plant so as to eradicate learning conditions, their realized earning power was charted. This could be accomplished because the work is largely piecework and a laborer may complete only three fourths of a day or even one half of a day. Thus a man's desire to claim his full earning power may be seen in the way he completes or leaves incomplete his working time.

The data on which his conclusions are based are shown in Figure 10. From the foregoing it is seen that the working efficiency of the

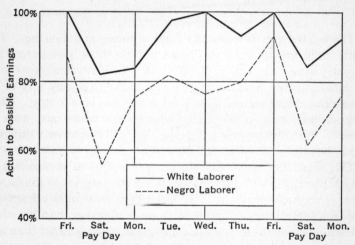

FIGURE 10. REALIZED EARNING POWER OF WHITE AND COLORED
LABORERS
(After DeNoyelles.)

white laborers is superior to that of the negroes, for at no time does the realized earning power of the negro equal or surpass that of the whites. The native whites also maintain more steadiness; the negroes have many very high and very low levels of efficiency, from which one may infer that their work is concentrated on certain days.

It should be noted that on Saturday (pay day) the efficiency of both whites and colored is at its lowest, but that of the whites is much higher than that of the negroes.

What they do with their pay is also indicative of race differences.

When he [the native white] receives his pay envelope, he does not breathe a sigh of relief and murmur "at last." He does, however, feel as if one more rung in the ladder of achievement was ascended. The achievement may be a betterment of the condition of their families or themselves. Seldom is pay a greater disadvantage to them than it is an advantage. Most of the negroes, though, are broke the day after being paid. Many of them on Monday wish to have advanced some money from the pay-to-come. The native white lives a life, the negro a day.[1]

A difference in the relative effectiveness of incentives is also noted.

Another difference is the way in which the groups respond to praise. The native whites can be generally excited to better work by words tactfully used. It can be done either by showing enthusiastic pride in his work or else by bringing rivalry to the fore by comparing him with another worker in the plant. In the case of the negro, however, I have found that some object catches his attention more. Words are wasted on him while a pack of cigarettes is not. But even then with any kind of object, praise is many times without effect on him.[2]

In the same plant it was found that those negroes who were born and brought up in the country were on the whole more reliable and dependable workers than those who were born and brought up in the city. Most of the trouble-makers came from the city.

The closing paragraph of Superintendent DeNoyelles's report is also significant in this connection.

White gangs with white bosses do the best and most satisfactory work. Next in line would come negro gangs with white foremen. Last would come, taking as a criterion the amount and kind of work done, negro gangs with negro bosses. The native whites seem to be the best leaders, and under their guidance both whites and negroes do best work.

II. THE FOREIGN-BORN

1. **The European races.** Race differences and the measurement of these differences present an important problem in connection

---

[1] DeNoyelles, Daniel: *op. cit.*, 92.   [2] *Ibid.*

with immigration. Much has been written concerning the relative desirability of the different people as immigrants, and many conflicting opinions exist concerning the comparative intelligence of various foreign peoples. Few of these opinions, however, are based on the results of actual measurements, and the majority are in the last analysis only opinions. Since the World War several investigations have been undertaken with the object of devising some better means for selecting our immigrants. Yet there is considerable uncertainty as to the proper interpretation of much of the objective data. In many investigations the number of cases was too small to give very reliable data, and in others the factor of selection evidently played an important part, and the results of the investigations do not give a true picture of the ability of the races. These facts should be borne in mind when interpreting these data.

During the World War thousands of men born in various foreign countries were tested by means of the army tests of intelligence. Those who could read and write English were given the Army Alpha test; those who could not read and write were given the Army Beta,

RANK ORDER OF COUNTRIES ACCORDING TO PERCENTAGE OF FINAL
LETTER GRADES BETTER THAN D AND ALSO ACCORDING TO THE
PERCENTAGE OF A AND B LETTER GRADES COMBINED *

RANK ORDER	PER CENT D, D-, E	RANK ORDER	PER CENT A, B
England................	8.7	England..............	19.7
Holland................	9.2	Scotland	13.0
Denmark...............	13.4	White draft...........	12.1
Scotland...............	13.6	Holland..............	10.7
Germany...............	15.0	Canada..............	10.5
Sweden................	19.4	Germany.............	8.3
Canada	19.5	Denmark.............	5.4
Belgium...............	24.0	Sweden..............	4.3
White draft...........	24.1	Norway..............	4.1
Norway...............	25.6	Ireland..............	4.1
Austria................	37.5	All foreign countries....	4.0
Ireland...............	39.4	Turkey..............	3.4
Turkey................	42.0	Austria...............	3.4
Greece................	43.6	Russia...............	2.7
All foreign countries.....	45.6	Greece...............	2.1
Russia................	60.4	Italy................	.8
Italy................	63.4	Belgium..............	.8
Poland................	69.9	Poland..............	.5

* (*Memoirs of National Academy of Sciences*, xv.)

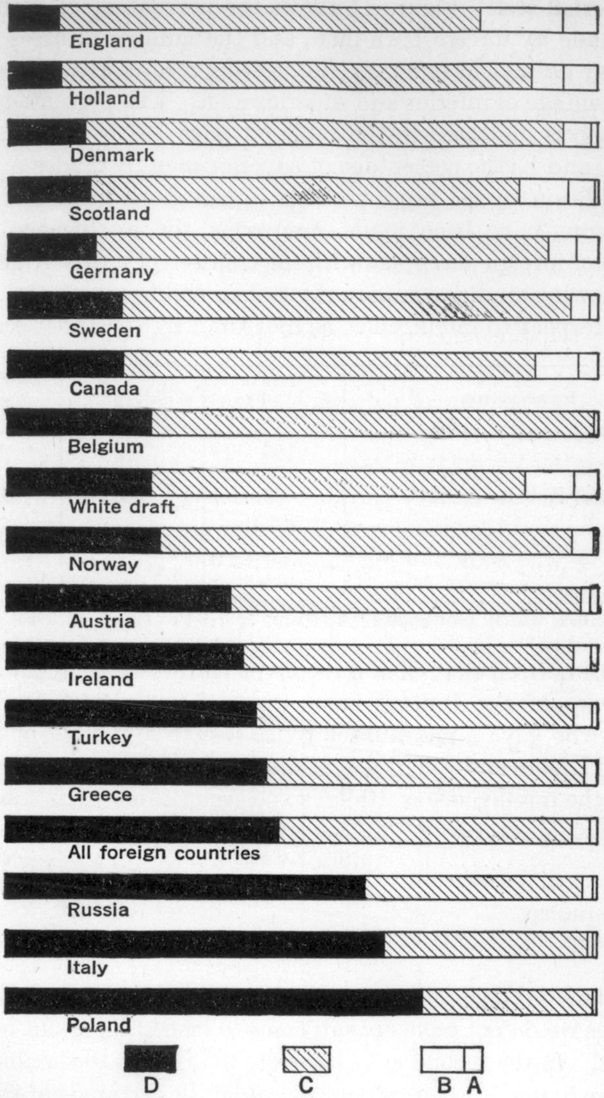

FIGURE 11. PERCENTAGE DISTRIBUTION OF LETTER GRADES IN INTELLIGENCE BY NATIVITY OF FOREIGN-BORN MEN IN THE DRAFT

a non-verbal test. Figure 11 shows the percentage of each letter grade made by foreign-born men, and the number of cases tested. The army data yield some very interesting results with reference to the percentage of inferior and superior men. The percentage of inferior men is indicated in the table on page 107 by the grades of D, D −, and E; the percentage of superior men by grades A and B.

In addition to the army tests of foreign-born men, several investigations have been made comparing the intelligence of the children of foreign parentage with the children of native Americans. The following studies compare the Italian children with the Americans in respect to intelligence, as measured by the Binet scale:

INVESTIGATOR	MEDIAN I.Q. OF AMERICANS	MEDIAN I.Q. OF ITALIANS	NUMBER OF CASES OF ITALIANS
Arlitt..........................	106	85	87
Pintner and Keller..............	95	84	313
Brown.........................		77.5	51
Young		84	25

(After Pintner, Rudolf: *Intelligence Testing* [Henry Holt & Co., New York, 1923], 352.)

It is to be noticed that all of these investigators agree in placing the intelligence of the Italians below that of the native Americans. Young, who gave a group intelligence test to a number of twelve-year-old Italian and American children, found much the same difference in the intelligence of Italians and Americans. His results are as follows:

	I.Q.	No OF CASES
Americans....................................	107	402
Italians	88	248

The data on the foreign-born are open to two criticisms. In most instances we do not have enough cases to be certain about our conclusions. In the second case, the tests were given to the foreigners who were living in America, and we cannot be certain that these are typical of their race. For all we know, there may be some selective influence which is causing us to get a more highly selected group of northern Europeans, and a less highly selected group of southern Europeans.

The author is at present coöperating in a study to determine the relative intelligence of nationalities. In this study a test is being used which has no local items, and is so constructed that the children of no nationality would have an advantage. The test is being given to approximately two thousand children in each country. The study will not be completed for two more years. At present returns are available on only five countries, but arrangements are completed to extend the study into a large number of countries.

2. The Oriental races. At present very little objective data are available concerning the intellectual qualities of the Oriental people. The investigations carried on by Miss Murdoch in Honolulu give us the opportunity to compare a number of the Oriental races. Between five and six hundred twelve-year-old children in the schools of Honolulu were the subjects of this research. Care was taken to avoid, in so far as possible, the element of selection by including all the children of this age who were in the public schools where the tests were given, and by selecting those schools whose pupils appeared to be the most typical representatives of the various races. The results of this research are given in the accompanying table. The school grade which a twelve-year-old pupil has attained gives some indication of his native ability. According to this criterion the North-European Americans are much the most intelligent, followed in order by the Chinese, American-Hawaiians, Japanese, etc.

In order to overcome the language handicap under which many of the groups labor because English, the language of the schools, is not spoken in the home, non-verbal tests of intelligence were used. The Army Beta is a non-verbal test, and the National Intelligence Test is made up of both verbal and non-verbal elements. That the language factor is of tremendous importance seems evident from an inspection of the table, particularly of the last two columns. The Oriental races, especially the Japanese and Chinese, do comparatively much better in non-verbal intelligence tests than in verbal intelligence tests or in school standing.

Miss Murdoch [1] makes the following comment on the investiga-

[1] Murdoch, Katharine: "Racial Differences Found in Two American Cities," *Industrial Psychology*, February, 1926.

tion: "In every race in every trait measured there was great variability within the race itself, and in every case I found overlapping of the races. There was always at least some member of each race who did better than the average of any other. Even though only one tenth of one per cent of Filipinos did better than the average of Americans, some Filipinos made this good record."

PERCENTAGE OF EACH RACE GROUP WHICH OVERLAPS THE
AMERICAN MEDIAN

	No. of Cases	School Grade Attained	National Intelligence Test	Army Beta Test	National Intelligence Test, Verbal Elements	National Intelligence Test, Non-Verbal Elements
Americans (North European descent)	57	50	50	50	50	50
American-Hawaiians	59	20	11	14	8	29
Chinese............	58	24	14	23	4	42
Japanese...........	61	15	4	42	2	50.6
Portuguese........	57	9	1.6	5	1.5	16
Korean............	33	11	8	32	4	26
Chinese-Hawaiian..	33	11	2	9	1	19
Hawaiian..........	58	9	2	3	3	12
Country Japanese..	56	1	.6	1	.1	9
Porto Rican.......	23	2	.3	.5	.2	1
Filipino..........	23	1	.1	.2	1	.7

(After Murdoch, Katharine, "Racial Differences Found in Two American Cities," *Industrial Psychology*, February, 1926, p. 100.)

III. RACE PREJUDICE

Every race has certain customs and manners which have grown up through the centuries, as well as certain physical characteristics which are typical of the race. Other races with different physical and mental characteristics resent these, and the result is race hatred or race prejudice. Such epithets as "frog-eating Frenchman," "pig-tailed Chink," "flat-footed nigger," "Russian Whiskerino," and "unspeakable Turk" are but a few of the uncomplimentary expressions of race prejudice to-day.

Wherever two distinct races live in close contact with one another, we find race prejudice, and the greater the differences between the two races, the greater the prejudice. As regards physical beauty, for example, the most attractive traits of a race are regarded as the ideal. If fairness is characteristic of the race, the ideal beauty is fair; darkness is ugly, and *vice versa*. This explains why the acclaimed beauties of other races frequently appear quite revolting according to our standards of beauty. The farther away a race is from our own racial ideal, the more hideous it seems, and the stronger our prejudice.

Yet another cause of racial prejudice is the fact that a conquering nation generally forces its customs and civilization upon the peoples it conquers. Fear is an important cause of race prejudice — the fear of the people of one race that those of another race will usurp their place in the economic or social world.

Wherever two races come in contact with one another, race prejudice is found, and the closer the contact the greater the prejudice. In the United States we find the prejudice against the Oriental much greater in the West than in the East. We find the Northerner arguing for social equality for the negro, while the Southerner considers the negro race too inferior to possess this equality. The negroes realize the prejudice against them in this country, and some react with bitterness, others with resignation. The negro expresses his feeling of the injustice done him in the following:

"Well, it makes no dif'unce how you make out your time,
  White man sho' to bring nigger out behin'.
If you work all the week, and work all the time,
  White man sho' to bring nigger out behin'."

IV. RACE DIFFERENCES IN ACHIEVEMENT

Is the achievement of a race a fair measure of its ability? If the question is answered in the affirmative, we have a fairly easy means of comparing the ability of races. Yet there are several objections to considering the achievement of a race a fair measure of its ability, chief among which are the following: (1) The civilization and culture of one race may have been borrowed from other races, and so indicate little as to the ability of the race which possesses it. For example, in Japan to-day we have a civilization that compares favorably with that of the leading Western nations, but if we had examined the civilization and culture of Japan some fifty years ago, we should have found an entirely different state of affairs; the change being due to the fact that since that time Japan has adopted the civilization of the Western nations. (2) The achievements and civilization of a race may have been due to the efforts of men long since dead, and so be a very poor measure of the present generation. For example, the civilization and culture of China are due very largely to the work of such men as Confucius and others who have been dead for more than two thousand years. (3) The progress and achievements of any race are made by a few superior men. That being true, the larger the race, the more variable it is, the more likely it will be to produce these superior men. For example, the achievements of which our nation boasts were produced by such individuals as Edison, Burbank, and Henry Ford, and, other things being equal, the more people we have, the more likely we shall be to have more Edisons, Burbanks, and Fords.

CHAPTER VII

DIFFERENCES DUE TO FAMILY INHERITANCE

I never heard tell of any clever man that came of entirely stupid people.

CARLYLE

FOR years a very bitter controversy has been waged among biologists, psychologists, and scientists in the social fields concerning the relative part played by heredity and environment in determining one's behavior and potential achievement. In general this controversy has been much more energetic than scientific, the advocates of environment attempting to explain everything as the result of training and other environmental factors; and the partisans of heredity being equally dogmatic in their emphasis on the inheritance factor. Numerous studies have been published in support of their claims by the opposing sides, and the conclusions of these studies have in turn been warmly contested by those of the opposite point of view.

The nature of the problem renders it extremely difficult of solution, for the two variables, heredity and environment, are both of necessity present in every study, and it is impossible to isolate or completely control either. Heredity has made its contribution at the time the ovum from which the child develops is fertilized. At the moment the ovum is fertilized, environment begins to exert its influence and continues to do so at every step through life, until the individual, due to the weight of the environment and his own inherent weakness, breathes his last, and goes "to mix forever with the elements." Every act of intellect, character, or skill has its environmental setting and depends on past experiences as well as inherited tendencies. It is this impossibility of separating the two factors which renders the problem so difficult.

The issues involved are of such consequence to social control and betterment that they are involved in the basic principles of all the social sciences. If ignorance and illiteracy are due very largely to poor educational opportunities, they can be wiped out by the proper type of school facilities; but if they are due to poor heredity, all the school can do is to provide the type of differentiated training best adapted to inferior ability. If crime and delinquency are due to environment, we can prevent them by altering the environment; but if they are due to heredity, we can avoid them only by eugenic measures designed to prevent the birth of inferior stock. If the various types of insanity are caused by such environmental factors as microscopic organisms, in a short time by the proper measures we should be able to wipe out insanity just as we are now wiping out typhoid fever. But if a predisposition to insanity is passed on through the germ plasm from generation to generation, we can reduce the number of insane only by taking the proper measures for birth control.

This chapter and the one following will give a brief survey of the extent of our present knowledge concerning the problem. In this chapter we shall consider: I, The inheritance of physical traits; II, The inheritance of mental traits; III, The mechanism of inheritance, and IV, Improvement of the racial stock.

I. INHERITANCE OF PHYSICAL TRAITS

Just as individuals possess certain distinctive characteristics as the result of their remote ancestry or race, so they possess traits, both physical and mental, as the result of immediate ancestry or family inheritance. Traits such as baldness, obesity, or polydactylism (six fingers instead of five) are said to "run in families." Members of some families all live to a ripe old age; members of other families all die young; some families are fat; others thin; and these traits are apparently influenced little by environment or by efforts to change them.

Study of inherited traits reveals certain laws of inheritance which appear to be borne out in general in considering a large number of cases, although inheritance in any particular case cannot be determined thereby. It is found that children tend to be more or less like their parents in any particular trait. Taking height for an example, some of the children may be taller than their parents, some the same height, and others shorter than their parents, but the children of tall parents are generally above the average in height, while the children of short parents are usually below the average. Children deviate from the average of the population in the direction of their parents; but extreme characteristics of parents are usually less extreme in children. Children of similar family inheritance vary less among themselves than an equal number of unrelated persons. We seldom find in the same family children who are very tall, very short, and of average height. As a rule members of the same family are either all tall, all short, or all about average in height.

Physical traits offer the best material in the study of inheritance, for they are more readily measured than are mental and emotional traits. Obviously such characteristics as the color of the eyes, the height, the cephalic index (ratio of the width to the length of the head), and color of the hair are very little influenced by environmental factors. Similarities in these traits in closely related individuals must, then, be largely due to family inheritance. Using his mathematical formula to determine the amount of relationship, Pearson gives the following correlations [1] for physical traits in families:

[1] *Correlation* is a term used to express relationship between two variables. The significance of correlation may be best understood by reference to the "gas laws" in physics. 1. As the *temperature* increases, the *volume* also increases. Here we have two variables, *temperature* and *volume*, bearing a direct or positive relationship to each other. 2. As the *pressure* increases, the *volume* decreases. In this case we have two variables, *pressure* and *volume* bearing an inverse or negative relationship to each other. 3. The *volume* is not affected by the *height* of the person measuring it. Here we have two variables, *volume of gas* and *height of examiner*, not related in any way.

The same thing is seen in school grades. 1. As the *intelligence* of the pupils increases, their *school grades* also tend to increase. Here the variables *intelligence* and *school grades* have a direct or positive relationship. 2. As the number of *days of absence* from school increases, the *school grades* decrease. In this case, the *days absent* bear a negative relationship to the *school grades*. 3. *School grades* are not affected by the *height* of the pupils. Here we have a zero relationship. Thus it is seen that two variables may have a positive relationship, a negative relationship, or a zero relationship.

Take, for example, the two variables mentioned above, *intelligence* and *school grades*. If, when these variables are plotted, it is found that the most intelligent individual makes the highest scholastic record, the second highest in intelligence makes the second highest record, and so on down to the least intelligent, who makes the lowest scholastic record, the correlation is perfect, or + 1.00. If, on the other hand, the lowest in intelligence makes the highest record, the next lowest in intelligence makes the next highest record, and so on, the correlation is again perfect, but negative, or − 1.00. The first case represented a perfect direct relationship, the second, a perfect inverse relationship. But the relationship is practically never a perfect

		Correlation
Color of eyes	Brothers	.52
Height	Brothers	.50
Height	Father and son	.30
Cephalic index	Brothers	.49
Color of hair	Brothers	.55

It should be noted that the correlation between the height of brothers is .50 and that between the height of father and son only .30. The factors making for similarity of brothers are transmitted through the germ plasm of both the father and the mother, while the factors that make for similarity of father and son are transmitted only through the germ plasm of the father. In the case of half brothers, one would expect about the same correlation as that between father and son, for here only one person is contributing the factors making for resemblance.

If a large number of individuals are selected at random from a given neighborhood and paired off, also at random, the correlations for these physical characteristics (height, color of eyes or hair) between the pairs will be approximately zero; i.e., there is no factor at work causing resemblances in chance-selected individuals. But in the case of pairs of brothers a correlation of approximately .50 indicates that there is some factor causing a resemblance. As the two groups, brothers and unrelated individuals, have fairly similar environment, the close resemblance of the siblings (children other than twins of the same parents) must be very largely due to heredity.

Certain individuals seem to have an inborn tendency toward multiple pregnancy, since it is not unusual for the same woman to give birth to twins or triplets upon several occasions. Twins normally occur about once in every ninety births. In a study of 1252 cases of multiple pregnancy, Puech found that 48 of the mothers had given birth to twins twice, 3 thrice, and 1 upon four oc-

positive or a perfect negative one, but somewhere in between. The nearer the correlation is to zero, the less its significance, and the greater becomes the evidence that there is little relation between the two variables. On the other hand, the greater the magnitude of the correlation, the closer is the relation between the variables in either a direct ratio or an inverse ratio according to whether the sign be positive or negative. A correlation of + .48 shows a reasonably close relation between intelligence and scholastic standing, but a correlation of + .59 shows a much closer relationship.

casions. According to Williams, multiple pregnancy has been known to occur in all the females of a family throughout several generations. Mirabeau found an hereditary tendency toward triplet pregnancies in 13 out of the 75 cases collected by him. In one family the birth of triplets had occurred in five successive generations.

Twin pregnancy may result either from the fertilization of two separate ova or of a single ovum, the first giving rise to fraternal and the second to identical twins. Fraternal twins are not necessarily of the same sex and may not resemble each other more than other children of the same parents. Identical twins are always of the same sex and show very close physical and mental resemblances. About one out of every five pairs of twins are of the identical variety.

Twins of the two ova variety may be the offspring of different fathers. This is a well-recognized occurrence in dogs and other lower animals, and undoubtedly occurs in human beings. Williams related the case of a white woman who had had connection with a white and a colored man respectively within a short period and was delivered of twins, one of which was white and the other a mulatto.

At first glance it would seem that heredity is solely responsible for the phenomenon of twins, especially of twins of the identical type, but environment plays its part. Biological investigations have shown that identical twins can be produced experimentally and at will in several varieties of fish. According to Stockard, retardation of the growth of the ovum at critical periods of development is the essential factor concerned. This may be done by exposing the fertilized egg to cold or by diminishing its supply of oxygen. He has also shown that the degree of duplicity can be altered by changing the time at which the retarding influences are brought into play. In other words, if the retarding influences are applied for one period of time, identical twins will result; if at another, Siamese twins, and if at another period the double-headed, double-bodied, or double-legged monster. Thus, much that has passed for heredity may be due to pre-natal environment.

Heredity seems to have an influence in producing certain physical defects.   Studies of congenital blindness and deafness indicate that a rather large proportion of these defects occurs in a relatively small proportion of families.   Loeb made a study of 304 families in which a form of cataract was found.   This disease is characterized by the appearance of an opaque area in the usually transparent part of the eye, which finally renders the person blind.   In the particular form of the disease studied, the cataract does not develop until middle age.   In the 304 families there were 1012 children, 58 per cent of whom developed the disease.   This form of cataract must clearly have been inherited, for in the general population the percentage of people afflicted with the defect is very small.

Statistical studies of deafness have shown that, out of every four persons who have a brother or sister who was born deaf, one is deaf. Of those persons who have no deaf brothers or sisters only about one in a thousand is deaf.   A person, then, who is of the same ancestry as a congenitally deaf person is 250 times as likely to be deaf as is a person who has no congenitally deaf relatives.   There seems to be little doubt that congenital deafness is an inherited characteristic, as no other factor could account for the disproportionately large number of cases of deafness in certain families.

II. INHERITANCE OF MENTAL TRAITS

The many studies of the inheritance of mental characteristics indicate that there is a close relationship between members of the same family in mental abilities.   Thorndike's investigation of 168 families, each having two children, is typical of those studied.   In 138 of the 168 families he found that either both children were bright or both were dull.   In only 30 did he find one dull child and one bright one.

Studies of the similarity of mental characteristics of twins as compared with those of siblings offer fairly definite evidence that certain mental abilities and traits have an hereditary cause, for identical twins have most nearly the same heredity.   In these studies the training of the two groups (twins and siblings) was about equal.   The question, then, is in what respects and how much do twins resemble each other, and to what extent can we discredit similar environment as a cause of their likeness.   Thorndike, who studied certain mental abilities in fifty pairs of twins and in siblings by their achievement on certain tests, found the resemblance between twins to be about twice as great as the resemblances between brothers and sisters who are not twins.

1. **Resemblance of siblings.** In a study of a large number of high-school students, Thorndike [1] found a correlation of .60 between siblings in mental ability. He sums up this investigation as follows: "If we may accept Pearson's results for the resemblance of siblings in eye color, hair color, and cephalic index (.52, .55, and .49), and regard .52 ± .016 as the resemblance in traits entirely free from environmental influence we may infer that *the influence upon intelligence of such similarity in environment as is caused by being siblings two to four years apart in age in an American family to-day is to raise the correlation from .52 to .60.*"

Unfortunately we do not know that mental and physical traits are transmitted in exactly the same manner. Physical traits may depend much more than mental traits on heredity. Until this point is settled, we are not justified in assuming that siblings, if unaltered by environment, would correlate .52 on mental traits.

2. **Resemblance of parents and children.** Willoughby [2] administered a battery of verbal and non-verbal group tests to parents and children in 141 families. He found an average resemblance between mothers and children of .37, between fathers and sons of .36, and between fathers and daughters of .31, and an average between parents and offspring of .35. He also found a correlation of .44 between the scores of husbands and wives.

Jones [3] obtained intelligence test records on 2500 persons ranging in years from three to sixty-five in rural New England. Among his conclusions are: (1) The correlation between the scores of the mother and the children is on the average five points higher than

[1] Thorndike, Edward L.: "The Resemblance of Siblings in Intelligence," *Twenty-Seventh Yearbook*, National Society for the Study of Education (Public School Publishing Company, Bloomington, 1928), part I, p. 52.

[2] Willoughby, Raymond R.: "Family Similarities in Mental-Test Abilities," *Twenty-Seventh Yearbook*, National Society for the Study of Education (Public School Publishing Company, Bloomington, 1928), pp. 55-59.

[3] Jones, Harold E.: "A First Study of Parent-Child Resemblance in Intelligence," *Twenty-Seventh Yearbook*, National Society for the Study of Education (Public School Publishing Company, Bloomington, 1928), pp. 61-72.

between that of father and children. This may be due to the influence of the mother on the child through the pre-natal and post-natal environmental factor, or it may be due to the fact that paternity may extend outside the family, while the maternity is never in doubt. (2) Where one parent possessed superior intelligence and the other inferior intelligence, their union resulted in intermediate offspring rather than in strong offspring. Superior intelligence is not a dominant or a unit trait.

3. **Resemblance of twins.** In a study of the scores on intelligence tests of identical and non-identical twins, Miss Tallman found the order of resemblance to be as follows: identical twins, like-sexed twins, non-identical twins, siblings.

The comparative school standing of siblings has been studied by various investigators, and in all cases a positive correlation is found between the school grades of members of the same family. Starch found that the correlation of the scores of brothers and sisters, when measured on such capacities as reading, spelling, writing, etc., was .42. Thorndike's statement that one can prophesy as much concerning a pupil's rank in college from the rank his elder brother had in college as from his own rank in entrance examinations, is an excellent summary of the findings. Thorndike [1] makes the following statement concerning the school standing of twins: "If one knew nothing whatever about two pupils in a city's schools save that A was a twin of a boy who was in the top fifteenth of children of his age in intellect, while B was the twin of a boy who was in the bottom fifteenth, he could still be practically certain that A would be brighter than B, that A would in nineteen cases out of twenty be in the upper half of the class, and that B would have the same probability of being in the lower half."

4. **Inheritance of inferior ability.** (a) *Feeble-mindedness.* It is fairly well established that feeble-mindedness or inferior mental ability is inherited, and that feeble-minded parents generally have children who are also of inferior ability. One of the most widely known investigations of the inheritance of feeble-mindedness was made by Goddard, who studied mental defects in two lines coming

---

[1] Thorndike, Edward L.: *Education* (The Macmillan Company, New York, 1912), 69. Reprinted by permission.

from related ancestral stocks. A man of good ability had a son by a feeble-minded girl, and later married a normal woman. From this illegitimate son, called Martin Kallikak, have come 480 descendants. One hundred and forty-three of these were classed as feeble-minded, while only forty-six have been found normal. The mentality of the others was unknown or doubtful. In this branch of the family there was a long line of drunkards, drug-users, prostitutes, and incompetents. Among the descendants of the normal woman there were a large number of professional people, and almost all were people of good standing.

A significant investigation of the inheritance of inferior mental ability was reported by Moorrees in 1924. He studied the mental make-up of the parents of forty-five feeble-minded children in a public institution. Several standardized tests of intelligence were given to each parent, and the occupation of the parents was also investigated. He found that approximately three fourths of these feeble-minded children have either one or both parents who are feeble-minded. About twice as many of the mothers as fathers were feeble-minded.

(b) *Mental disorders.* Not only is heredity important in feeble-mindedness, but certain tendencies to mental disorders seem to be inherited. Dementia præcox and the manic-depressive psychoses seem to run in families. Hysteria, neurasthenia, and psychasthenia can often be accounted for on an hereditary basis. For data supporting these statements, the reader is referred to the section on the causes of mental disorders, Chapter XIV.

5. **Inheritance of superior ability.** In his statistical study, "Hereditary Genius," Galton has brought out four facts concerning the inheritance of mental ability: (1) An individual who attains eminence is more than two thousand times as likely to have eminent relatives as is a person who does not attain eminence. (2) The more distantly related a relative is to an eminent man, the less likely is the relative to become eminent. (3) There is a tendency for the inherited ability to be specialized. (4) Individuals who attain eminence tend to be very precocious and to show marked manifestations of their superior ability early in life. These conclusions are based on his study of the relatives of 262 judges, 130

statesmen, 89 of the world's greatest military commanders, 119 literary men, 148 men of science, 57 poets, 97 artists (musicians and painters), and 75 divines, making a total of 977 persons. A few individual cases from his study will serve to illustrate his work.

Statesmen. Among the statesmen we shall consider the case of William Pitt, second son of the first Earl of Chatham, who was described by Galton [1] as follows: "Illustrious statesman; Premier, 1783–1801; and 1804–06. Precocious and of eminent talent; ... æt. 14 an excellent scholar. . . . He was Chancellor of the Exchequer æt. 24, and Prime Minister æt. 25; which latter office he held for seventeen years consecutively." *Relatives:* His father was the first Earl of Chatham and also Premier of England. He was "one of the ablest of statesmen, most brilliant of orators, and the prime mover of the policy of England." His mother was Hester Grenville, sister of George Grenville and aunt of Lord Grenville, each of whom served as Premier of England. Among his other relatives who attained eminence is his niece, Lady Hester Stanhope.

Military commanders. In the military field let us take as chief representative Alexander the Great, who, Galton [2] says, is "commonly reputed to be the commander of the greatest genius that the world has produced. When only æt. 16, he showed extraordinary judgment in public affairs, having governed Macedonia during the absence of his father. He succeeded to the throne, and began his great career of conquest æt. 20, and died æt. 32. . . . He inherited much of the natural disposition of both of his parents; the cool forethought and practical wisdom of his father, and the ardent enthusiasm and ungovernable passions of his mother." *Relatives:* His father, Philip II of Macedonia, was "an illustrious general and statesman, who created and organized an army that was held together by a system of discipline previously unknown, and kept the whole of Greece in check. Æt. 24 he had shown his cool forethought and practical skill in delivering himself from embarrassing political difficulties. . . . Cicero praises him for having been 'always great.'" His mother, Olympia, was "ardent in her enthusi-

[1] Galton, Francis: *Hereditary Genius* (The Macmillan Company, New York, 1892), 112. Reprinted by permission.

[2] *Ibid.*, 143.

asms, ungovernable in her passions, ever scheming and intriguing."
His half brother, Ptolemy Soter I, was the founder of the famous
line of Ptolemys who became rulers of Egypt.

Poets. As an illustration not only of certain special abilities, but
of unsettled temperament as well, let us take the case of Lord
Byron.[1] "His 'Hours of Idleness' was published æt. 19, and the
'English Bards and Scotch Reviewers,' which made him famous,
aet. 21." *Relatives:* Honorable Admiral Byron, circumnavigator,
author of the "Narrative," was his grandfather. His father, Captain Byron, is characterized by Galton as "imprudent and vicious."
His mother was "strange, proud, passionate, and half mad. 'If
ever there was a case in which hereditary influences, arising out of
impulses, passions, and habits of life, could excuse eccentricities of
character and extremes of conduct, this excuse must be pleaded for
Byron, as having descended from a line of ancestry distinguished on
both sides by everything calculated to destroy all harmony of
character, all social concord, all individual happiness.'"

Artists.[2] "The Bachs were a musical family, comprising a vast
number of individuals and extending through eight generations. . . .
There are far more than twenty *eminent* musicians among the
Bachs; the biographical collections of musicians give the lives of
no less than fifty-seven of them." Sebastian Bach was "a tran-
scendent musical genius. He was very precocious and arrived at
the full maturity of his powers at the age of 22." *Relatives:* His
father, J. Ambrose, was a distinguished organist. His great-great-
grandfather, "the founder of the family, was a baker at Presburg,
who sang to the guitar." A second cousin, J. Christopher Bach,
was one of the greatest musicians of Germany. A son, Guillaume
Frederick, called "Bach of Halle," was a man of great power and
very learned. Another son, C. P. Emanuel, called "Bach of Ber-
lin," was "the founder of our pianoforte music; whom Haydn and
likewise Mozart regard as their direct predecessor and teacher."
A third son, J. Christopher, called "Bach of England," was a
charming composer.

---

[1] Galton, Francis: *Hereditary Genius* (The Macmillan Company, New York, 1892),
222. Reprinted by permission of the publishers.

[2] *Ibid.*, 233.

In making his study, Galton based his conclusions on 977 men, each of whom was selected as being the most eminent in 4000 of his age. These 977 eminent men had relatives of that degree of eminence as follows: fathers, 89; brothers, 114; sons, 129; all three together, 332 for the first degree relatives. Grandfathers, 52; grandsons, 37; uncles, 53; nephews, 61; all four together, 203 for the second degree relatives. The probable numbers of that degree of eminence for 977 average men are as follows: fathers, sons, and brothers together, 1; grandfathers, grandsons, uncles, and nephews, together, 3.

He found that the more distantly related a relative is to an eminent man, the less likely is the relative to become eminent. The eminent sons are almost without exception more numerous than the eminent brothers, and the latter are slightly more numerous than the eminent fathers. In passing from the first to the second degree kinships, there is a sudden dropping off of the numbers; and in the third degree of kinship, another abrupt dropping off in the numbers is found.

To meet the argument that training and opportunity rather than inherited ability largely account for the eminence attained by relatives of eminent men, Galton made a comparative study of adopted sons of popes and real sons of eminent men. From this study he concluded that the adopted sons of the popes did not attain eminence nearly so frequently as the sons of eminent men, although training and opportunity were apparently equally conducive to eminence in the two cases.

The following statement of Galton,[1] coming as it does from a scientist of such high rank, is very significant: "I feel convinced that no man can achieve a very high reputation without being gifted with very high abilities."

Galton believed that the frequency with which all those members of a family who attained eminence did so in one special field, as music, poetry, or painting, indicated that not only was superior ability inherited, but that superior ability was highly organized in special lines and passed on from generation to generation. Galton [2]

---

[1] Galton, Francis: *Hereditary Genius* (The Macmillan Company, New York, 1892), 43. Reprinted by permission of the publishers.
[2] *Ibid.*, 61–62.

makes the following statement concerning the judges of England between 1660 and 1865:

> Do the judges often have sons who succeed in the same career, where success would have been impossible if they had not been gifted with the special qualities of their fathers? ... Out of the 286 judges, more than *one* in every *nine* of them have been either father, son, or brother to another judge, and the other high legal relationships have been even more numerous. There cannot, then, remain a doubt but that the peculiar type of ability that is necessary to a judge is often transmitted by descent.

Specialization of inheritance also appears in many other fields. Of twenty-six eminent sons of eminent scientists, twenty-two achieved their eminence in science. All except four of the eminent relatives of eminent painters were gifted in that line, and the four were specially talented in closely related lines, as sculpture, embroidery, and music. Musical ability seems especially to fall in certain family groups. Of the musicians studied by Galton there were only two, Mendelssohn and Meyerbeer, whose eminent kinsmen achieved their success in careers other than music.

6. Family resemblances in mental and emotional traits in white rats. It would seem that the resemblances between members of the same family of the lower animals might afford the best opportunity to study the part played by heredity in determining mental and emotional traits. So far as we can observe, such factors as home training, schooling, and various other socializing influences are not present with the lower animals. If such is the case, similar behavior on their part must be due to similarity of structure and hereditary organization.

(*a*) *Resemblance in ability to learn.* Burlingame [1] and Stone studied the learning ability of 224 white rats comprising 40 different litters. A maze was used to measure their rate of learning, and the number of errors made by each pair of rats in runs 6 to 15 of the maze was tabulated. The correlation between the performance of the pairs of rats was $.31 \pm .04$. The correlation of human siblings is about .50, which is distinctly higher than that of rats. The authors

---

[1] Burlingame, Mildred, and Stone, Calvin P.: "Family Resemblance in Maze-Learning Ability in White Rats," *Twenty-Seventh Yearbook*, National Society for the Study of Education (Public Schools Publishing Company, Bloomington, 1928), 89–99.

explain the lower correlation of the rats by suggesting that they probably had a selected group of animals, and that, if they had been able to draw from an unselected population of rats, the correlation would have been higher.

(b) *Resemblance in emotional drives.*   In a study of emotional drives, in which methods described in Chapter I were used, some fairly constant family resemblances in the strength of these drives were observed.   The hunger and sex drives of fifteen pairs of white rat siblings were measured, by putting the rats one at a time in the experiment box described on page 8, with an electric shock of 28 volts between them and the food or sex reward, and noting how long the animal remained in section A before crossing the plates. A correlation of .29 was found between rats of the same litter for the hunger drive, and a correlation of .38 for the sex drive.   The number of cases is too small to be very conclusive, but the study is at least suggestive of a method of attacking the problem of family resemblances in emotional traits.

III. MECHANISM OF INHERITANCE

In all the inherited characteristics considered thus far, there is a tendency for children to be like their parents, but there are wide variations in individual cases.   Thorndike [1] describes the reason for these variations of children of the same parents as follows:

In all thought of inheritance, physical or mental, one should always remember that children spring, not from their parents' bodies and minds, but from *the germs of those parents*.   The qualities of the germs of a man are what we should know in order to prophesy directly the traits of his children. One quality these germs surely possess.   They are variable.   Discarding syntax and elegance for emphasis, we may say that the germs of a man include some six-feet germs, some six-feet-one germs, some six-feet-two, some five-feet-eleven, some five-feet-ten, etc.   Each human being gives to the future, not himself, but a variable group of germs.   This hypothesis of the variability of the germs explains the fact that short parents may have tall sons; gifted parents, stupid sons; the same parents, unlike sons.

The work of Mendel in 1865 was the starting-point of our knowledge of the biological facts underlying heredity.   While experi-

[1] Thorndike, Edward L.: *Educational Psychology, Briefer Course* (Teachers College, Columbia University, New York, 1924), 356–57.

menting with peas, he found that if you cross tall peas with dwarf peas the offspring will be as tall as the tall parent; in the first generation of offspring there are no dwarfs. But if you sow the seeds from these tall offspring, one fourth of their seeds will produce dwarfs, and three fourths will produce tall peas. If you select at random four plants from this generation — that is, grandchildren of the original pair — taking one dwarf and three talls, the seeds from the dwarf will produce only dwarf plants; and one of the tall plants will produce only tall plants, while the other two "tall" peas will produce three tall plants to one dwarf.

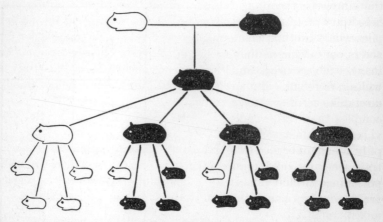

FIGURE 12. ILLUSTRATION OF MENDELIAN LAW IN GUINEA PIGS

Mendel explained these phenomena on the assumption that there are two types of inherited traits, dominants and recessives. Tallness is a dominant trait, while shortness is a recessive trait. The recessive traits apparently vanish in the first generation of offspring, but they are still carried in the germ plasm of three fourths of the offspring. The dominant traits are also carried in three fourths of the grandchildren of the original pair. Of the grandchildren, one fourth carry only the dominant traits; one half carry both dominant and recessive traits; and one fourth carry only recessive traits.

Mendel's principles of heredity are seen in animals. When purebred black guinea-pigs are crossed with albinos, the offspring are all black — blackness is thus the dominant trait. If these blacks are mated with each other, the offspring turn out one white to three blacks. (See Figure 12.) The white guinea-pig of this generation is a pure recessive, and if mated with another of like kind produces only whites. Only one of the blacks is a pure dominant, and the other two still retain the recessive traits, and if mated with their kind will produce one white to three blacks. This statement covers only the more elemental Mendelian principles.

1. **Factor hypothesis.** The situation described above represents the simplest type of the hereditary process and applies where two unit characters, one of which is dominant, such as black and white, are found. But in most cases heredity is more complex than this. Individuals containing only the pure dominant or recessive trait are rare; the largest percentage of individuals are hybrids containing mixed traits.

	R	r
R	RR	Rr
r	rR	rr

FIGURE 13. RESULTS OF CROSSING RED AND WHITE MIRABILIS
(After Correns.)

1 RR = Red
2 Rr = Pink
1 rr = White

The factor hypothesis is the best explanation of these more complex forms of heredity. It may be illustrated by reference to Correns's work.[1] He crossed red and white mirabilis ("four-o'clocks"), and secured for the second generation a pink blend which apparently followed no law of dominance. He then mated this hybrid group among themselves. The result of mating two hybrids is best shown by

[1] Correns, C.: *Der Übergang aus dem homozygotischen in einen heterozygotischen Zustand in selben Individuum bei buntblättrigen und gestreift blühenden Mirabilis-Sippen.* Ber. Deutsch. bot. Gesell. 28. 1910.

reference to Figure 13, in which R stands for the color factor and r for absence of color factor. Each hybrid entering into the production of offspring may produce germ cells containing either the R factor or the r factor, this possibility being represented for one parent by R and r along the top horizontal row of the figure, and for the other parent by R and r along the left vertical row. No gamete (sexual cell) can contain both of two alternate characters. If two germ cells, both containing the factor for color, unite, a pure red form results, shown in the Figure by the square marked RR.

	RR	Rr	rR	rr
RR	RRRR	RRRr	RRrR	RRrr
Rr	RrRR	RrRr	RrrR	Rrrr
rR	rRRR	rRRr	rRrR	rRrr
rr	rrRR	rrRr	rrrR	rrrr

FIGURE 14. RESULTS OF CROSSING VARIOUS TYPES OF WHEAT
(After Nilsson Ehle.)

1	$RRRR$	= Pure Red
4	$RRRr$	= Light Red
6	$RRrr$	= Pink
4	$Rrrr$	= Light Pink
1	$rrrr$	= Pure White

If two germ cells, both containing the factor for absence of color, unite, a pure white form results, shown in the Figure by rr. And if two germ cells, one containing the factor for color and one the factor for absence of color, unite, a mixed form (pink) is obtained, represented in the squares marked Rr and rR.

What Correns obtained, therefore, on mating hybrid forms was offspring in a ratio of one pure red, two pink, and one white, which is the ratio of a normal distribution curve. This experiment indicates that pure dominance need not be present to produce an occasional individual of the dominant type; two "doses" of one factor (R), one from each of the hybrid parents, are cumulative in their effect, and produce a red offspring (RR).

The inheritance which we find in human beings and higher organisms is much more complex than this, however. We may carry our illustration a step farther to indicate how the more complex blends may be obtained. The work of Nilsson-Ehle [1] indicates how various blends were produced in wheat. He crossed red and white wheat, getting the pink form, and, upon crossing this hybrid stock with its kind, he got varying shades of color ranging from pure red to pure white.

The dihybrid ratio with both factors similar will show how this occurs. In this case, a pure red gamete (sexual cell) is RR instead of R, and the pure white is rr instead of r. With two alternate factors present in each gamete instead of one, there may be gametes of the Rr variety. Chance would give a proportion of one RR gamete, to two Rr, to one rr in the sperm and the same proportion in the ova. These proportions are represented in Figure 14 along the top horizontal row and along the left vertical row.

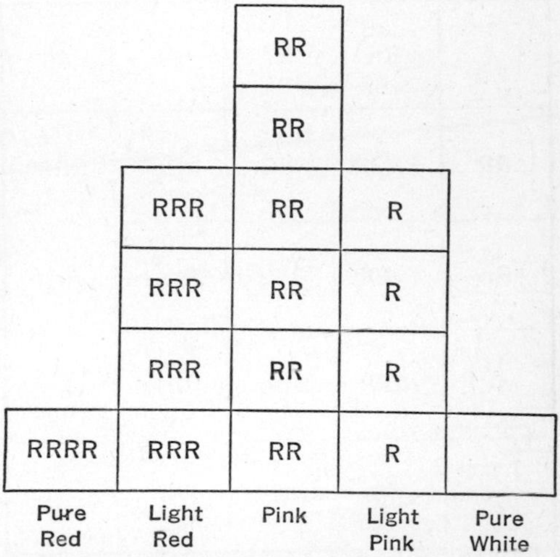

FIGURE 15. NORMAL DISTRIBUTION OF TYPES OF WHEAT ON SUCCESSIVE CROSSINGS OF RED AND WHITE VARIETIES

Now, by reference to Figure 14, it is seen that the chance possibilities of union of the gametes give offspring which may be represented by $RRRR$, $RRRr$, $RRrr$, $Rrrr$, or $rrrr$. These respectively are pure red forms, light red forms, pink forms, light pink forms, and white forms. The ratios of the various colors produced, as may be seen from the figure, are one pure red, four light red, six pink, four light pink, and one pure white. This may be represented in a normal distribution curve, using one R to represent one color factor present in the somatic cell. (See Figure 15.)

[1] Nilsson-Ehle, H.: *Kreuzungsuntersuchungen an Hafer und Weizen.* Lund's Univ. Arsskrift. 1909.

If we had trihybrid gametes — a pure red plant having three colors instead of two — and crossed them, we should get the following results: one pure red; six light red; fifteen dark pink; twenty pink; fifteen light pink; six tinted white; one pure white.   When we realize that most human traits contain not one, two, or three, but probably many factors, we can appreciate how complex is the whole mechanism underlying heredity.

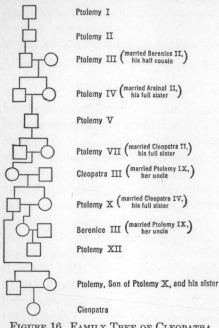

Ptolemy I

Ptolemy II

Ptolemy III (married Berenice II, his half cousin)

Ptolemy IV (married Arsinol II, his full sister)

Ptolemy V

Ptolemy VII (married Cleopatra II, his full sister)

Cleopatra III (married Ptolemy IX, her uncle)

Ptolemy X (married Cleopatra IV, his full sister)

Berenice III (married Ptolemy IX, her uncle)

Ptolemy XII

Ptolemy, Son of Ptolemy X, and his sister

Cleopatra

FIGURE 16. FAMILY TREE OF CLEOPATRA
(After *Journal of Heredity*.)

2. Inbreeding. In most Christian countries today the marriage of people who are closely related is looked upon with horror.   Marriage of brother and sister is now almost everywhere taboo; and many States have laws preventing the marriage of first cousins.   But this wide-spread aversion to inbreeding has not always existed.   In ancient Egypt, for example, inbreeding of the closest kind produced the family tree of the famous Cleopatra, who was generally recognized as a woman of surpassing beauty and of intellectual powers seldom equaled.   Her family tree is shown in Figure 16.

There was also very close inbreeding in the family of Charles Darwin, who married his first cousin Emma Wedgwood.   Four of their sons attained such eminence that they were elected Fellows of the Royal Society, which is one of the highest scientific honors bestowed.   If offspring like these are the result of inbreeding, why does society have such a horror of it? The effect of close inbreeding is apparently to accentuate whatever dominant traits are present, and bring out the recessive traits. If the stock is poor, inbreeding tends to accentuate and bring to light any defects. Animal breeders get their finest and purest stock by inbreeding if the stock is good to begin with; but if the stock is poor, there is a rapid deterioration. The way society is organized to-day, the individuals who inbreed tend to come from inferior stock, and the offspring are consequently inferior.

IV. IMPROVEMENT OF THE RACIAL STOCK

As heredity is of vital importance in determining the physical and mental character of the offspring, any attempts to raise the general level of the population must take heredity into account. There are two methods of improving the racial stock; by preventing the reproduction of the unfit, and by encouraging the reproduction of those who are best fitted to benefit society. As mentally defective parents produce mentally defective children, and as on the average they have more children per family than do those farther up the social scale, they constitute a real problem. Under the present social order, it is neither considered humane nor practicable to kill undesirable children after they come into the world. Four methods are proposed of preventing the reproduction of various kinds of deficiency, as feeble-mindedness, epilepsy, or venereal diseases, and of encouraging the reproduction of the best stock. They are: (1) sterilization; (2) segregation; (3) doctor's certificate for marriage; (4) eugenics.

Those physical or mental defectives whose offspring would be a menace to society should be prevented from reproducing. This may be accomplished by the drastic measure of sterilization or asexualization to prevent the possibility of offspring. Over a dozen States now have laws providing for the performance of operations to prevent the reproduction of various kinds of physical and mental defects. A second method by which the procreation of undesirable individuals is prevented is by segregation of the sexes. In almshouses, hospitals for the feeble-minded or insane, prisons, and similar institutions, the sexes are segregated. This method of segregation, however, is expensive, as it necessitates the confinement in institutions almost for life. The requirement of a doctor's certificate for marriage would prevent defectives from marrying and thus reproducing their kind. Most of the States have enacted laws prohibiting the marriage of feeble-minded persons, epileptics, and those afflicted with venereal diseases.

In improving the general level of society, it is necessary, not only to prevent the reproduction of the unfit, but also to encourage the reproduction of the best. This is the problem of eugenics. Eugenics is the study and cultivation of conditions that may improve the physical and moral qualities of future generations. Statistics show that the families of professional men are on the average far smaller than those of laborers. The long period of preparation for professional life, the consequent late marriage, and the wish to give the children every advantage limit the size of families in the most desirable portion of society. If the period of preparation for life were shortened, and the maximum income attained early in life instead of late, so that the men could afford families, the eugenic ideal would be more nearly approximated.

CHAPTER VIII

DIFFERENCES DUE TO PAST EXPERIENCES

I am a part of all that I have met

TENNYSON

I. HOW PAST EXPERIENCES CAUSE INDIVIDUAL DIFFERENCES

THE part played by past experiences in shaping our behavior is not generally appreciated. From the time life begins until it ends, one's personality is being changed by his experiences. Past experiences determine whether one will swim or drown when alone in water over his head; whether his conduct will be moral or dissolute depends on his training; whether he will belong to the Methodist church and vote the Democratic ticket rests largely on his early experiences; whether an object will provoke a feeling of love or aversion is determined by one's previous experiences with the same or similar objects. According to James, nothing that ever happens to an individual is entirely forgotten, but its effect is stored up and influences his future behavior.

Every act is a step in forming a new habit, in strengthening an old reaction tendency, or in breaking down an existing response tendency. From the very beginning of life the child may be taught to nurse at regular periods, and only at these times, and to sleep at regular hours. Through experience the child may learn that crying is the sure method of securing what he wants. Through experience he learns that fire burns, dogs bite, and green apples cause stomach-ache. Experience is constantly changing the *meaning* of the outside world.

1. **Pre-natal influences on individual differences.** Much that passes for pre-natal influence is mere superstition, and much that passes for heredity is due to pre-natal environment. Birth-marks are supposed by the layman to be due to such things as emotional disturbances in the mother. The parents of an imbecile child who

drooled a constant stream of saliva once brought him to the author, explaining that the child's deficiency was due to the fact that his mother had been badly frightened by a mad dog a month before the child's birth.   After investigating the case, there was no difficulty in finding that the real cause of the drooling was feeble-mindedness, and that the feeble-mindedness was due to a brain injury which the child received at the time of birth.

As pointed out in Chapter II, due to the physiological disturbances which accompany pregnancy, the pregnant woman sometimes craves some particular kind of food or drink that she cannot get.   According to popular superstition, the child in such cases may be born with a birth-mark or an abnormal craving as a result of this emotional thwarting in the mother.   A mother sometimes explains a red splotch on the child by saying that she longed for wine or cherries while carrying him.   A case was reported this year of a mother pleading with the judge to mitigate the prison sentence of her alcoholic son by saying that she longed for whiskey during the last months before his birth, and that his chronic intoxication was her fault.

There is no more evidence for such beliefs than for any other superstition.   It would be just as reasonable to expect every child born on Friday the thirteenth always to have misfortune as to believe that the thoughts or feelings of the mother directly affect the child.   But there is evidence that certain pre-natal experiences of the child himself do affect the later behavior of the child.

(a) *Disease*.   Syphilis is not inherited, but it is often acquired before birth from a syphilitic mother.   Congenital syphilis may be just as disastrous to the future mental efficiency of the individual as a case acquired after birth.   Nor is syphilis the only disease which the child may contract pre-natally.   If the mother has scarlet fever, the child has it; if the mother has measles a few days before the child is born, the child will be born with an active case of measles.   The fact that an individual had such a disease before birth may account for his later immunity to the disease.

(b) *Handedness*.   It is generally supposed that right-handedness or left-handedness is determined by heredity, but there is now considerable reason to believe that such is not the case.   The slight preference for one hand which a child shows from birth may be explained by the position which he occupied in the mother's uterus during the last few weeks before birth. More than seventy per cent of all babies for weeks before birth occupy such a position that the left arm is against the mother's hip bone and the right arm is free to move against her soft parts. For this reason, the right arm gets more exercise for several weeks before birth, and the child will show a slight preferential use of it at birth. In another position, the reverse is true. The right arm is firmly wedged against the bony parts and the left arm is free, and the child is born with a preference for the left hand. In a third position neither hand has the advantage, and the child is probably born with no tendency to use one more than the other. The author is at present coöperating in an investigation which should establish the truth or falsity of this hypothesis.

2. **Physical differences due to nurture.** While many physical characteristics, such as eye color and height, are due almost wholly to heredity, there are others that are due to experience or nurture. The size of the blacksmith's arm, and the shape of the Chinese woman's foot, are not seriously affected by heredity. Whether one possesses the endurance of the athlete or the short wind of the office worker is determined primarily by his previous training. The stooped shoulders of the ancient bookkeeper and the erect posture of the army sergeant are not the result of heredity. Whether the flapper's hair will hang in straight strands or will fly out in a permanent wave might possibly be due to heredity, but is more often due to the work of some hairdresser. Previous experiences largely determine susceptibility to disease. A case of measles in childhood means immunity in later life; but a case of pneumonia in childhood probably means an added susceptibility to the disease in later life.

3. **The mechanism of the conditioned reflex.** Past experiences affect our behavior chiefly by means of the conditioned reflex. The conditioned reflex is based on the fact that for every fundamental reaction that we are capable of making, there is an unlearned stimulus which by original nature is joined to this reaction and is able to produce it. For example, the flashing of a bright light in one's eye causes the muscle fibers located in the colored part of the eye, the iris, to contract and the pupil to become smaller. Like-

wise the presence of acid in the mouth causes the salivary glands to become active.   The light and the acid are the unlearned or natural stimuli which provoke the reaction of pupillary contraction and an increased flow of saliva respectively.   If along with the natural stimulus, or light, an indifferent stimulus, such as the sound of an electric bell, is simultaneously presented, the individual will finally react to the bell alone by a contraction of the pupil.   Or if the bell is rung every time a drop of dilute acid is placed on the tongue, in a short time the mere sound of the bell will cause an increased flow of saliva.   Thus, through past experience, one man may respond to the sound of the bell by a contraction of the pupil and another by an increased flow of saliva.

In an excellent piece of work Cason [1] has shown how, by training, the same stimulus may produce in different persons diametrically opposite reactions.   He demonstrated that, by training, the sound of a bell can be made to cause pupillary contraction in one group of hearers, and pupillary dilatation in another group.   The formula by which he accomplished this is:

Unlearned Stimulus	Unlearned Response
A bright light $\longrightarrow$	Contraction of pupil
A very dim light $\longrightarrow$	Dilatation of pupil

With one group of subjects, simultaneously with increasing the light intensity he sounded the bell, and with another group, simultaneously with decreasing the light intensity he sounded the bell. In the end he could sound the bell and the pupils of members of the first group would contract, while the pupils of those of the other group would dilate.   The following scheme will show what happened.

During training period

First group:

Bright light + Sound of bell $\longrightarrow$ Contraction of pupil
(unlearned stimulus)   (indifferent stimulus)

Second group:

Dim light + Sound of bell $\longrightarrow$ Dilatation of pupil
(unlearned stimulus)   (indifferent stimulus)

[1] Cason, Hulsey: "The Conditioned Pupillary Reaction," *Journal of Experimental Psychology* (1922), v, 108–46.

After conditioning had been accomplished

First group:

> Sound of bell $\longrightarrow$ Contraction of pupil
> (learned or substituted stimulus)

Second group:

> Sound of bell $\longrightarrow$ Dilatation of pupil
> (learned or substituted stimulus)

It will be noticed that we end by two divergent reactions to a stimulus which in the beginning was powerless to cause any pupillary change, the same stimulus causing the pupils in one group to grow smaller and the pupils in the other group to grow larger.   By the methods described above, the individuals became conditioned, that is, the indifferent stimulus became the substituted stimulus and caused a reaction which at first it was unable to produce.   It should be noted further that this process was wholly independent of the "will."   One can will from now until Doomsday without causing a change in his pupils.   The reaction was also independent of consciousness.   The individuals were no more conscious of their pupillary behavior than we are conscious of any other purely physiological process.

The conditioning process is going on throughout life.   Things which have no *kick* (that is, are powerless to produce certain responses) are constantly acquiring a *kick* by becoming substituted stimuli for things which originally have a *kick*.   Our response to any object is largely determined by our previous experience with it.   Given the proper history, the same object may provoke fear in one person, love in another, and rage in a third.   Why one group cheers and another hisses when Al Smith's picture is shown is to be explained in the different training of the two groups.

4. The effect of experience on emotional differences.   Watson has shown that the unlearned emotional reactions of the child are few.   He found only the three primary emotional reactions of fear, rage, and love present in the infant, and the stimuli capable of calling out these reactions very limited.   A loud noise and the removal of support provoke the fear reaction; hampering movement provokes the response of rage; and stroking certain erogenous zones induces the love reaction.   But through experience or conditioning, the emotional life of the adult becomes much more complicated.

Through conditioning, many stimuli which at first had no *kick* can provoke the fear reaction. Watson has shown that the child is not instinctively afraid of such furry animals as the rabbit, cat, or rat. But by conditioning, any one of these animals may produce the fear reaction. A child may stroke the fur of a cat, and not be afraid of it in any way, but if, every time the child touches the cat, some one strikes a bar, making a loud noise immediately behind the child's head, the child will soon manifest the fear response by beginning to cry and turning away as soon as the cat is presented. The cat has borrowed its fear-producing *kick* from the loud noise.

It is by such transfers of feeling from one thing to another that the complex emotional life of the adult is built up. The child is afraid of few things; the adult of many. The child has few attachments; the adult loves the old home, the old scenes, the old faces, the old songs, and even the automobile may set off a reaction of tenderness. The objects borrow their *kick* in the same way the cat got its fear-producing power.

In his essay on *Witches and Other Night Fears*, Charles Lamb gives a concrete example of how fears are conditioned. "I was dreadfully alive to nervous terrors. The nighttime and solitude and dark were my hell. . . . I never laid my head on my pillow, I suppose from the fourth to the seventh year of my life, so far as my memory serves in things so long ago, without an assurance, which realized its own prophecy, of seeing some frightful specter." He attributes these fears and hideous visitations to a picture in Stackhouse's *History of the Bible*, of the raising of Samuel by the Witch of Endor.

That our likes and dislikes for certain kinds of foods are very largely built up through experience is indicated in an experiment reported by the author.[1]

The experimental conditions were as follows: Three cups were prepared, one filled with orange juice which had been made very sweet with sugar, another filled with vinegar which was very, very sour, and the third filled with pure water. A medicine dropper was provided for each liquid. The child was blindfolded and told to open his mouth. A portion of orange

[1] Moss, F. A.: "Notes on Building Likes and Dislikes in Children," *Journal of Experimental Psychology* (December, 1924), 475–78.

juice was squirted into his mouth. He was told to open it again and again, and each time for the first six times he was rewarded with orange juice. By this time the strangeness of being blindfolded and receiving orange juice in this unusual way had in a measure worn off, and he was no longer excited. So when he opened his mouth for the seventh time, I administered a large portion of vinegar. The effect was instantaneous. He began spitting, shook his head, gritted his teeth, and seemed to shiver all over. He also began to cry, but by a speedy administration of orange juice his tears were soon dried and the investigation again proceeded. Orange juice was again given continuously for five times, but on the sixth time the vinegar was substituted. Simultaneously with the giving of the vinegar, I clicked a little telegraph snapper with which he himself had previously been playing and clicking. Practically the same reaction appeared this time as the first time the vinegar was given. The orange juice was again given four times, followed by the vinegar and snapper. After repeating this ratio of orange juice and vinegar twice, Billie's patience was exhausted and the experiment had to be discontinued until the next day.

On the second day of the experiment the first conditioned reaction appeared. This was accomplished by clicking the snapper at the same time I administered a medicine dropper filled, not with vinegar, but with pure water. The conditioned reaction appeared twice on this day. On the third day it appeared twice, on the fourth day five times, and after that it gradually became more and more firmly established until in the end when the snapper sounded the same reaction almost invariably occurred regardless of whether the dose be vinegar, orange juice, or water.

The blindfold was removed and after he had gone back to playing I clicked the snapper and got no response. It seemed, therefore, that the reaction was more or less conditioned by the whole situation of being blindfolded and receiving liquid into his mouth under such unusual conditions, and could not at that stage be set off by the sound of the snapper alone. However, after the experiment had been continued for twelve days, I clicked the snapper while he was quietly playing by himself and the shivering reaction occurred. After that I tried him at various times, and was often able to get the response by clicking the snapper when he was not noticing me. This would seem to indicate that conditioned reactions in their initial states occur in response to a whole group of stimuli, and that it is only in their later stages that a single element is abstracted, and can serve as an adequate stimulus.

Billie manifested an excellent example of conditioned likes and dislikes. Before the experiment, he liked the snapper and often played with it. But after the experiment had been continued for two weeks, he didn't like it and threw it down when it was placed in his hands. Before the experiment, he was very fond of oranges, but subsequently he lost all his desire for oranges and very much preferred apples.

Past experiences also account for the appearance of love and hate at first sight. Every day we meet people who at first sight arouse in us a feeling of repulsion or dislike colored with dread. Although we have never seen them before, there is something about them which makes us feel:

> "I do not like you, Dr. Fell,
> The reason why I cannot tell,
> But this I know, and know full well,
> I do not like you, Dr. Fell."

All of us have our Dr. Fells, and usually find it impossible to account for our attitude toward them.

Psychologists explain these dislikes as the left-overs of some former unhappy experience. Somewhere in the remote past we came in contact with a person who for one reason or another aroused our intense enmity. This particular individual had certain characteristics peculiar to himself. Among these characteristics was probably included a hooked nose, squinting eyes, or an Andy Gump chin. We saw the man on numerous occasions, and each time he had these same peculiar features. Every time we saw him our feeling of aversion was aroused. At first our dislike was not for any particular facial feature, but for the individual possessing the particular feature. We should have disliked him just as heartily if he had had a Roman nose, or a massive chin. During all the time we came in contact with him our attention was probably never actively directed to his hooked nose or short chin. Years pass, and we forget about the man who originally provoked our enmity, and especially about his particular facial architecture. But our dislike for hooked noses, squinting eyes, and Andy Gump chins is stored up in our nervous systems, ready to provoke the same feeling of aversion whenever that characteristic appears. We meet Dr. Fell, who happens to possess a hooked nose, and no sooner do we see him than we dislike him. The hooked nose may be the only characteristic he has in common with our former enemy, and our failure to recognize that the nose is the cause of our hate leaves us totally unable to account for our dislike.

Not only do we dislike people at first sight, but even love at first sight is more than a myth. Every one has had the experience of passing on the street some one whom he had never seen before, and feeling toward him an immediate reaction of sympathetic interest and a desire to meet him and know him better. And here once more our action depends upon the left-overs of some former experience. Some one who held our affection in the past had the same type of curly hair, or some other characteristic, that is possessed by our prospective friend, and it is this common feature that arouses our feeling of love and desire to know him better.

It is this tendency to react to a whole group of elements in terms of one element that accounts for our blind but intense hatred for whole races, or for our equally strong affection for the same race. If, for example, two Italians swindle you out of your home, and then give you a beating for telling them about it, you may easily manifest a bitter feeling toward all Italians. But if you happen to fall in love with an Italian girl, and her relatives welcome you into their family, your attitude toward the whole Italian nation is likely to be one of tenderness and kindly good will.

Every person, friend or enemy, is essentially a compound stimulus, and any part of the stimulus may be prepotent in producing the response.

Not only can liking, disliking, or fearing a certain thing be caused by training, but these fears, likes, or aversions can be done away with, also by training or re-education. One method of breaking down learned fears is by tying them up with pleasant reactions and by gradually accustoming the individual to the thing feared. Watson [1] reports the removal of the fear of animals in the case of Peter, a three-year-old child. Peter was afraid of all animals and all furry things. This fear was removed by the following procedure: When he was given his lunch a rabbit was displayed in a cage just far enough away not to disturb his eating. The second day it was brought nearer, the third, nearer still, and so on, until finally the rabbit could be placed upon the table, then in Peter's lap, then he would eat with one hand and play with the rabbit with the other. In other words, Peter was completely retrained. His fear of the

---

[1] Watson, John B.: *Behaviorism* (W. W. Norton & Company, Inc., New York, 1924), 137–38.

rabbit was entirely gone. His fear of other furry objects had likewise disappeared.

5. The effect of training on attitudes. Not only are our emotional patterns largely built up through experience, but the more permanent mental and moral attitudes depend for their origin on training and experience. This accounts for the wide differences which we find in the current ideas of right and wrong in different countries and at different times in the same country. Polygamy was practiced by the "best people" in Solomon's time, but now the youth are taught a very different attitude. Stealing was generally condoned in Sparta, and infanticide was widely practiced in numerous countries. A few years ago slavery was socially approved, and the institution of war is even now approved in practically all lands. Gladiatorial combats were approved in Rome just as bull fights are approved in Mexico and prize fights in the United States. We have definite attitudes of aversion to slavery and gladiatorial combats, but no such aversion exists to war and prize fights.

Why is one man a Republican and another a Democrat, or one man a Catholic and another a Baptist? Heredity certainly cannot be held the principal cause of these differences. There is no original tendency to be either a Republican or a Democrat. Such differences are almost entirely the result of training. Most of the people who belong to a particular religious denomination do so, not because after impartially studying all denominations they became convinced that that particular one was the best, but simply because their parents were members of that church and they were brought up in the church. Environment or training thus determines in a very large measure the particular church with which the individual will affiliate. Most Republicans vote the Republican ticket because their fathers and grandfathers did, and because, almost from infancy, they heard politics discussed from the Republican point of view. In short, training very largely determines the individual's stand in religion, in politics, and in standards of conduct.

Occasionally an environment may have an effect exactly opposite from that expected. A man may not always continue to act throughout life as he did in his youth, and his environment may be the cause of changes in his beliefs and opinions. Men may be at-

tracted to one creed or point of view through having been exposed
to the opposite influences. It is just as possible to drive a person
from a particular creed by sickening him with an overdose of the
beliefs of the creed, as it is by overfeeding a person with a particular kind of food to build up in him a dislike for the mere sight of
that food.   So a given environmental force, when overacting, may
stimulate opinions and behavior opposite to those it was intended
to foster.

**6. The part played by past experience in causing mental dis-
orders.**   Certain mental disorders, such as feeble-mindedness and
dementia præcox, may be largely due to heredity, but there are
several types of disorders in which the hereditary factor plays only
a minor part.   "Yesterday this day's madness did prepare" is true
in many of the more common disorders.   Such important diseases
as paresis and the alcoholic psychoses are environmental in origin,
definitely caused by specific physical agents.   Syphilis following
the debaucheries of youth often means paretic delusions twenty
years later.   The alcoholic sprees of to-day often mean the delirium
tremens of next week.

According to two very popular schools of psychology, the Behaviorists and Psychoanalysts, all the minor mental diseases are
caused by certain unfortunate experiences of the individual.   This
theory is discussed in more detail in Chapter XIV.

7. The effect on ability of previous experiences.   It is generally
recognized that training makes considerable difference in one's scholastic attainment and cultural status.   The most apparent difference between the professional and the non-professional man is that
the former has a certain background of training and experience
which the other lacks.   Differences in intelligence often determine
who can become professional men, but if two men have the same
native intelligence, and one is given the advantage of professional
training in an environment of culture, while the other, surrounded
by a vicious neighborhood, is trained in ways of crime, the activities of these two will be so different that one could hardly believe
them of equal native ability.

Many psychologists and educators believe that the I.Q., as determined by standard tests of intelligence, is not affected by train-

ing. That such is not the case was shown by Freeman [1] and his co-workers. After a careful investigation of the influence of environment on the intelligence of 401 foster children, the investigators conclude:

1. A group of children were tested before placement and then retested after several years of residence in a foster home. A comparison of their ratings on the two tests gave evidence of a significant improvement in intelligence (as measured by intelligence test scores). A study of certain sub-groups showed that the children in the better foster homes gained considerably more than did those in the poorer homes. Furthermore, the children who were tested and adopted at an early age gained more than those adopted at a later age. These facts appear to indicate that an improvement in environment produces a gain in intelligence.

2. A comparison was made between the intelligence of siblings (brothers and sisters) who had been reared in different foster homes. The correlation between their intelligence was found to be lower than that usually found for siblings raised together. The usual coefficient of fraternal resemblance is about .50, but it was found that for siblings separated before either of the pair was six years of age the correlation was only .25. When the comparison was made for those whose foster homes were of different grade, the correlation was found to be only .19. These facts make it appear that a part of the resemblance between siblings reared together is due to the influence of a similar environment.

3. A group of siblings was divided into two groups by putting into one group the member of each pair who was in the better foster home and into the other group the one in the poorer home. The mean I.Q. of the group in the poorer homes was found to be 86 while that of those in the better homes was 95. An analysis of the conditions of adoption made it seem unlikely that there was any marked tendency for the brighter member of a pair of siblings to be taken into the better foster home. A random formation of two groups from pairs of siblings would give groups of equal intelligence. The superior intelligence of the siblings in the better homes appears, therefore, to give evidence that the character of the home affects the child's intelligence to a marked degree.

4. Two unrelated children reared in the same home were found to resemble one another in intelligence. The correlations between the intelligence of such unrelated pairs ranged from .25 to .37. This resemblance is probably due for the most part to the similarity of their environment.

5. The available information on the own parents of the foster children

[1] Freeman, F. N., Holzinger, K. J., Mitchell, B. C.: "The Influence of Environment on the Intelligence, School Achievement, and Conduct of Foster Children," *Twenty-Seventh Yearbook*, National Society for the Study of Education (Public School Publishing Company, Bloomington, 1928), 209–11.

indicated that a large percentage were of defective mentality.   If heredity were the only factor in the determination of intelligence, it would be expected that their children would be decidedly below the average.   It was found, however, that their mean I.Q. was practically equal to the standard for children in general.   Only 3.7 per cent rated below 70, and these were those placed at relatively late ages.   These facts seem to point quite clearly to the influence of environment upon intelligence.

6. In the case of 26 children studied, both parents were rated as feeble-minded.   It was found, however, that only four had an I.Q. below 70 and these only slightly below.   The average I.Q. of 81 for these 26 children is higher than would be expected according to the Mendelian law, but is considerably below that of the entire group of children studied.   These facts appear to indicate that heredity and environment are both influential factors in the development of intelligence.

7. The school progress of the children studied compares very favorably with that of the children in several large school systems.

8. In various groups comparisons were made between the intelligence of the children and the grade of foster home in which they had been reared. For the entire group of 401, the correlation between home rating and intelligence was found to be .48.   The correlation between the intelligence of the children and the intelligence of their foster parents as measured by the Otis test was found to be .37.   In the case of the children who had been tested before adoption, an initial correlation of .34 with home rating was raised to .52 after a period of residence in the foster home.   These correlations would indicate that the character of the home is an important factor in the development of the child's intelligence.

9. The influence of the home is further shown by the fact that there is a correlation between early placement and intelligence and a slight relationship between the child's intelligence and the length of time he has spent in the foster home.

10. A large percentage of the children studied had parents who were morally defective.   In spite of this poor heredity, however, few cases of serious misbehavior were found among the foster children.   It seems probable, therefore, that environment has been an important factor in determining their conduct.

11. In interpreting certain data of the study it was necessary to know whether the apparent effect of good home environment could be accounted for by a selection of initially bright children by superior foster parents. The analysis of the data led to the conclusion that selection was not a large factor in the relationships.   In the extreme cases in which the children were given a mental test before adoption, the correlation between this initial I.Q. and home rating was .24.   In over eighty per cent of the cases no test was made before adoption.   Furthermore, a survey of the circumstances of adoption indicates that the intelligence of the child is not usually

taken into account as a major consideration. Finally, for certain groups in which it would have been least possible to estimate the intelligence of the child the correlation with home rating is as high as for other groups.

II. THE CONTROVERSY OF NATURE *vs.* NURTURE

As pointed out in the previous chapter, the two variables, heredity and environment, are constantly influencing our behavior. The influences of the two are present in every act, and it is extremely difficult to say how much is due to original nature and how much to past experience. Moreover, the environmental influences are so complex, and their action is so overlapping that it is hard to single out for study any one particular factor. The complexity of the whole problem is apparent when one considers that the variety of environments is endless and that the same environment exerts different influences upon individuals with different original natures.

1. Attributing to one what belongs to the other. The mistake of attributing to training effects which are in reality due to original nature or selection is frequently made. The greater achievement of college graduates as compared with the achievement of those who do not go to college is often attributed entirely to the training given by a college education. But the possession or the lack of college training is not the only difference between the two groups, for they were different even before college age. This difference probably caused one group to go to college, while the other entered the industrial world. The college group is, in general, a highly selected group, distinguished from the non-college group by greater ability, greater ambition, and more educated parentage. While no doubt the training received in college proved of value to these men, yet this training could not have brought success had they by original nature been of inferior ability. Again, training is too often given as the primary cause of the greater proportion of eminent men among those born in the cities, especially those containing universities, as compared with those born in rural districts. It is difficult to determine whether the achievement of these men is due primarily to the advantages of city life and university training, or to the fact that the more intellectual people, the parents who are able to transmit to their children a better heredity, are those who gravitate toward the cities and centers of learning.

In studying the effects of a bad environment, such as that existing in the slums where immorality and vice abound, the question of heredity *vs.* training comes up again.   Children brought up in such an environment are almost certain to be of morally inferior parentage.   In general, they belong to a group possessing inferior mentality, immorality, and poverty.   Their environment is inferior, in part at least, because their ancestors were also mentally and morally inferior.

The advocates of heredity are equally prone to claim the whole field for heredity.   If in the same family one son is a shining success while the other has only a mediocre or even sub-normal ability, the partisans of heredity, basing their conclusions on the fact that both sons were reared in the same home and by the same parents, attribute the differences in their achievement to differences in the germ plasm from which they sprang.   A more common-sense view would be to attribute part of the difference, at least, to certain subtle factors in the environment which are different for the two boys.   Watson [1] shows the fallacy of attributing to heredity differences which in reality belong to training, by giving an illustration of the effects of different environments on members of the same family living in the same home:

"Look at the musicians who are sons of musicians; look at Wesley Smith, the son of the great economist, John Smith — surely a chip off the old block if ever there was one."   You already know the behaviorist's way of answering these questions.   You know he recognizes no such thing as mental traits, dispositions, or tendencies.   Hence, to him, there is no sense to the question of the inheritance of talent as the question is ordinarily raised.

Wesley Smith was thrown into an environment early in life that fairly reeked with economic, political, and social questions.   His attachment for his father was strong.   The path he took was a very natural one.   He went into that life for the same reason that your son becomes a lawyer, a doctor, or a politician.   If the father is a shoemaker, a saloonkeeper, or a street cleaner, or engaged in any other non-socially recognized occupation, the son does not follow so easily in the father's footsteps, but that is another story.   Why did Wesley Smith succeed in reaching eminence when so many sons who had famous fathers fail to attain equal eminence?   Was it

[1] Watson, John B.: *Behaviorism* (W. W. Norton & Company, Inc., New York, 1924), 77–79.

because this particular son inherited his father's talent? There may be a thousand reasons, not one of which lends any color to the view that Wesley Smith inherited the "talent" of his father. Suppose John Smith had had three sons who by hypothesis all had equal abilities and all began to work upon economics at the age of six months. One was beloved by his father. He followed in his father's footsteps and due to his father's tutorship this son overtook and finally surpassed his father. Two years after the birth of Wesley, the second son was born, but the father was taken up with the elder son. The second son was beloved by the mother, who now got less and less of her husband's time, so she devoted her time to the second son. The second son could not follow so closely in the footsteps of his father; he was influenced naturally by what his mother was doing. He early gave up his economic studies, entered society, and ultimately became a "lounge lizard." The third son, born two years later, was unwanted. The father was taken up with the eldest son, the mother with the second son. The third son was also put to work upon economics, but receiving little parental care, he drifted daily towards the servants' quarters. An unscrupulous maid taught him to masturbate at three. At twelve the chauffeur made a homosexual out of him. Later, falling in with neighborhood thieves he became a pick-pocket, then a stool-pigeon, and finally a drug fiend. He died in an insane asylum of paresis. There was nothing wrong with the heredity of any one of these sons. All by hypothesis had equal chances at birth. All could have been the fathers of fine, healthy sons if their respective wives had been of good stock (except possibly for the third son *after* he contracted syphilis).

Watson [1] further emphasizes the effect of early conditions and training in the following:

Let us take a hypothetical case. Here are two boys, one aged seven, the other six. The father is a pianist of great talent, the mother an artist working in oil, a portrait painter of note. The father has strong large hands, but with long, flexible fingers (it is a myth that all artists have long, tapering, finely formed fingers). The younger son has the same type of hand. The father loves his first born, the mother the younger. Then the process of "creating he them in his own image" begins. The world is brought up on the basis largely of shaping the young you are attached to as you yourself have been shaped. Well, in this case the older becomes a wonderful pianist, the younger an indifferent artist. So much for different training or different slanting in youth. But what about different structure? Please note this. The younger son, under ordinary conditions, could not have been trained into a pianist. His fingers were not long

[1] Watson, John B.: *Behaviorism* (W. W. Norton & Company, Inc., New York, 1924), 81.

enough and the muscular arrangement of the hand was not flexible enough. But even here we should be cautious — the piano is a standard instrument — a certain finger span and a certain hand, wrist, and finger strength is needed. But suppose the father had been fond of the younger child and said, "I want him to be a pianist and I am going to try an experiment — his fingers are short — he'll never have a flexible hand, so I'll build him a piano. I'll make the keys narrow so that even with his short fingers his span will be sufficient, and I'll make a different leverage for the keys so that no particular strength or even flexibility will be needed." Who knows — the younger son under these conditions might have become the world's greatest pianist.

From a superficial examination it would appear that Watson [1] is giving the whole field to nurture, and is wholly ignoring the effect of heredity. He does, however, provide indirectly for the influence of heredity in his provision for differences in the structures that make up the body:

Some human beings are born with long fingers, some with short; some with long arm and leg bones; some with short; some with hard bones, and some with soft; some with overdeveloped glands; some with poorly functioning glands. Again you know that we can identify human beings by differences in their finger prints. No two human beings have ever had the same finger prints, yet you can mark off man's hand and foot prints from the tracks of all other animals. No two human beings have bones exactly alike, yet any good comparative anatomist can pick out a human bone (and there are over 200 of them) from the bones of every other mammal. If so simple a thing as the markings on the fingers differ in every individual, you have absolute proof that general behavior will and must be different. Infants crawl differently, cry differently, differ in the frequency with which defecation and urination occur, differ in early vocal efforts, in requirements for food, in the speed and rapidity with which they use their hands — even identical twins show these differences — because they differ structurally and differ slightly in their chemical make-up. They differ likewise in the finer details of sense organ equipment, in the details of brain and cord structure, in the heart and circulatory mechanisms and in the length, breadth, thickness, and flexibility of the striped muscular systems.

Whence came these differences in structure? Very largely from the ancestors through the complicated mechanism of heredity. In-

[1] Watson, John B.: *Behaviorism* (W. W. Norton & Company, Inc., New York, 1924), 79–80.

asmuch as behavior depends so largely on structure, it follows that if different structures are inherited, different drives to behavior are likewise inherited. The behavior of a Ford automobile differs from that of a Rolls-Royce primarily because the two machines are structurally different.

On the whole, however, Watson [1] believes that the part played by heredity in determining human behavior is, like the report of Mark Twain's death, "slightly exaggerated." The pride we take in our ancestry makes us overemphasize the part played by heredity.

The truth is society does not like to face facts. Pride of race has been strong, hence our Mayflower ancestry — our Daughters of the Revolution. We like to boast of our ancestry. It sets us apart. We like to think that it takes three generations to make a gentleman (sometimes a lot longer!) and that we have more than three behind us. Again, on the other hand, the belief in the inheritance of tendencies and traits saves us from blame in the training of our young. The mother says when her son goes wrong — "Look at his father or his grandfather (whichever one she hates) and what could you expect with that ancestry on his father's side!" And the father, when the girl shows wayward tendencies— "What can you expect, her mother has always let every man she came in contact with make love to her." If these tendencies are inherited, we can't be much blamed for it. Traits in the older psychologies are God-given and if my boy or girl goes wrong, I as a parent can't be blamed.

2. Effect of the same environment upon individuals of different original natures.

As pointed out above, two individuals with different original natures will be influenced differently when exposed to the same environment. When duck eggs and hen eggs are placed in the same incubator and the same amount of heat applied, ducklings are hatched from the duck eggs and chicks from the hen eggs. Moreover, when a hen is given a few duck eggs to hatch and rears the little ducks along with her own chicks, when she takes her mixed brood into the vicinity of a lake, the little ducks react to their environment by jumping into the water, while the chicks steer clear of it.

If two children are adopted into the same family, they may have very similar environments, but if one of the children is of a mechani-

[1] Watson, John B.: *Behaviorism* (W. W. Norton & Company, Inc., New York 1924), 83.

cal turn of mind while the other is musical, different phases of the
environment will have a predominant influence on each.   The
mechanical child pays attention to those portions of his environment which give him the opportunity to express his mechanical
ability.   The musical child may ignore the mechanical elements of
his environment and seize with avidity upon anything connected
with music.   Each pursues those phases of his environment most in
accord with his aptitude.

That a good environment cannot compensate for poor heredity is
indicated by the failure of many an adopted child to measure up to
the level of the family in which the child is brought up.   The author
made a study of an adopted child which demonstrates the limitations placed by heredity.   A wealthy family in Washington with a
baby daughter adopted another baby of the same age to be brought
up with their daughter.   Nothing was known about the heredity of
the adopted child.   As time went on, great differences between the
two children were apparent, although both were given the same advantages.   The adopted child could not succeed in school, and never
went beyond the third grade, while the daughter graduated from
Vassar.   The adopted daughter finally was brought to a home for
unmarried mothers.   When given a mental test she showed a mental
age of seven years, eight months.   Evidently environment was
unable to overcome the influence of the poor heredity of this girl.

The effect of equal amounts of practice of a mental function upon
individual differences in respect to efficiency in it has been studied
by various investigators.   If differences in achievement in any
given line are largely due to differences in amount of practice, then
provision for equal amounts of practice should tend to reduce these
differences.   But if the addition of equal amounts of practice does
not reduce the differences, it would appear that those differences
are largely due to heredity rather than to inequality of training.

While the findings of those who have studied this problem are not
all in agreement, their results indicate that equal periods of practice
tend to decrease the relative differences, but to increase the absolute differences.   If, for example, fifteen students (five of superior
ability, five of average, and five of low ability) worked arithmetic
problems for one hour, and if, at the close of the hour, the average

of the highest five students was 50 problems solved, of the middle five, 25 problems, and of the lowest five students only 10 problems; and if all the students were given 100 hours of intensive drill in problem-solving, at the close of this practice period we should probably find scores somewhat as follows: for the highest group, 150 problems; for the next, 100; and for the lowest, 50. During the first hour the highest group did twice as many as the middle group, but after the hundred hours of practice they did only one half more than the middle group. At first the highest group did five times as many as the lowest, but after practice they did only three times as many as the slowest group. Thus the relative differences between the groups were decreased by practice. But during the first hour the highest group surpassed the middle group by only 25 problems, and surpassed the lowest group by 40 problems, while at the close of the practice period the highest group surpassed the middle group by 50 problems, and surpassed the lowest group by 100 problems. Thus the absolute difference between the groups was increased by practice. This is shown graphically in Figure 17.

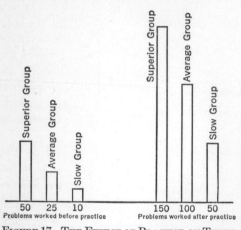

FIGURE 17. THE EFFECT OF PRACTICE ON THREE HYPOTHETICAL GROUPS OF DIFFERENT ABILITIES

This hypothetical case considerably oversimplifies the question of the effect of practice on individual differences. For a more complete discussion of the problem the reader is referred to the excellent article by M. Kincaid [1] which summarizes the experimental work.

[1] Kincaid, M.: "A Study of Individual Differences in Learning," *Psychological Review* (1925), 32, 34–52.

In summarizing this section it may be said that heredity or original nature determines *how far* the individual can go; the environment determines *in what direction* his progress will be.   An intelligent, ambitious young man may have the potentiality of success in law, business, or medicine; i.e., he can go far along any one of several lines.   Which of these careers he chooses is determined largely by his environmental influences.   Intelligence depends very largely on his inheritance, but moral qualities depend almost wholly on environmental factors.   It is here that training is most effective.   The individual's character depends in no small degree upon liking certain things and disliking others; and his likes and dislikes are largely built up by training.   While a good environment cannot entirely compensate for a poor heredity, it may modify for the better certain characteristics and abilities.   Likewise, a poor environment and lack of opportunities for advancement may prevent an individual of ability from accomplishing much in life.   There is no doubt that human beings are materially influenced by the customs, ideals, laws, friends, and occupations to which they are exposed.   But what the final character of the individual will be depends in part upon his hereditary equipment.

As stated above, one's success or failure is determined by the joint action of his heredity and of his training.   Inasmuch as his heredity remains constant throughout life, the only hope of bettering him is by improving his environment, the effectiveness of the environmental influences being dependent to a large extent upon its adaptation to the limitations offered by heredity.   This is brought out with particular force in the case of training the person of moron or slightly sub-normal ability.   If we attempt to train such a person to perform tasks requiring superior ability, our efforts are doomed to end in failure, but it may be quite possible so to adapt his training to his innate ability that he will be able to earn a good living and to contribute his part to society.   The fact that he is only of moron ability and not of superior ability must be recognized and he must be trained accordingly.

An individual's accomplishment or adaptation is the product of his heredity multiplied by his environment.   Let us represent the highest type of heredity by 10, and the lowest type by 1, with the various intervening grades. Let training also be represented on a ten-point scale, with 10 representing the highest type of training and 1 the lowest. Then the moron, for example, may start life with an heredity factor of 3, and may receive a training which on a scale of 10 would be rated 8. His achievements in life may be represented by the product of these two numbers, or 24. But the person of very superior ability may start out with an heredity factor of 9, and may receive a training of 2 on a scale of 10, yielding a product of 18. If the training were of the highest type, rated 10 in both cases, the product in the case of the moron would be 30, while that in the case of the superior individual would be 90, giving a net result of three times as much for effort in the case of the superior individual as compared with the results attained by the same effort in the case of the moron. The one place, therefore, where we can least afford to have poor training is in the case of the person with superior ability. The individual of moron ability, no matter how good his training, will never be able to make any very important contributions to this or future civilizations. The person of superior ability may also accomplish little if he is handicapped by lack of training, and his potential value to society is thus allowed to go to waste. But if the superior individual is given a training that will allow him to make the most of his superior inheritance, he may become a scientist, an inventor, or such a leader in his chosen field that he can render society a very distinct service.

CHAPTER IX

DIFFERENCES DUE TO AGE

> All the world's a stage,
> And all the men and women merely players.
> They have their exits and their entrances;
> And one man in his time plays many parts,
> His acts being seven ages. At first the infant,
> Mewling and puking in the nurse's arms.
> Then the whining school-boy, with his satchel
> And shining morning face, creeping like snail
> Unwillingly to school. And then the lover,
> Sighing like furnace, with a woeful ballad
> Made to his mistress' eyebrow. Then a soldier,
> Full of strange oaths, and bearded like the pard,
> Jealous in honor, sudden, and quick in quarrel,
> Seeking the bubble reputation
> Even in the cannon's mouth. And then the justice,
> In fair round belly with good capon lin'd,
> With eyes severe and beard of formal cut,
> Full of wise saws and modern instances;
> And so he plays his part. The sixth age shifts
> Into the lean and slipper'd pantaloon,
> With spectacles on nose and pouch on side,
> His youthful hose, well saved, a world too wide
> For his shrunk shank; and his big manly voice,
> Turning again toward childish treble, pipes
> And whistles in his sound. Last scene of all,
> That ends this strange eventful history,
> Is second childishness and mere oblivion,
> Sans teeth, sans eyes, sans taste, sans everything.
>
> SHAKESPEARE

THE individual's life from beginning to end is more or less regulated according to his age. A certain age is the first step toward his education, his occupational status, his recognition by law, and many of his liberties and pleasures. In fact, age limits have been set up for most activities in life, but in practically no case is there a scientific basis for their establishment. The different age qualifications demanded by the different States for the same thing point out the lack of a reliable foundation. Age specifications seem to be based upon the assumption that the number of years, months, weeks, days, hours, and minutes an individual has lived gives an accurate measure of what the individual is physically or mentally. But chronological age is far from being identical either with physiological maturity or mental maturity. People are not born equal, nor do they progress through life at the same rate. Therefore chronological age, or the number of years lived, cannot give a reliable indication of fitness. The intelligent child of six years has often progressed much farther mentally than the feeble-minded youth of sixteen years.

Just as all persons do not develop at the same rate, so all parts of the same person rarely show the same development. This at once suggests the possibility of measuring the individual's capacity in terms of the development of any one of the parts; i.e., age in terms of development as well as in terms of time. Modern science recognizes five ages in terms of which the capacity of the individual may be defined: (1) chronological age; (2) physical age; (3) mental age; (4) educational age; and (5) emotional age.

1. **Chronological age.** The most widely recognized and one of the most ancient measures of the powers of an individual is the number of years, months, weeks, and days he has been in the world. As chronological age is the most obvious and easily determined age of the individual, it has been used as the basis of classification for centuries. The Spartan boy was taken from home and placed in barracks at the age of seven; the Roman youth assumed the toga of citizenship at sixteen. Even at the present day chronological age is the most common basis of classification. The child starts to school at six (in some States five or seven years of age); at sixteen he may leave school and go to work. He may not be employed in industrial concerns under the age of fourteen (in some places sixteen). He cannot vote until he is twenty-one, nor can he make a valid contract before that age, with one exception; this exception, strangely enough, is the marriage contract. At sixty-five or seventy the man is retired. His whole life is controlled by definite age specifications for certain things.

One way to check the effect of age upon occupational efficiency is to correlate the efficiency ratings of employees with their chronological ages. O'Rourke did this for Civil Service employees, and found a correlation of only .06. With a group of clerical workers, Thurstone secured a correlation of .35 between grade of work done and age. With insurance salesmen the amount of sales correlated with age at the initial contract to the extent of .15. Burtt found that with a group of telegraphers there was a negative correlation (−.09) between age and receiving ability.

The influence of age may also be investigated by noting the relative efficiency of workers at different ages, and seeing whether there is an optimum age for a given occupation. Using this method, Kenagy and Yoakum found that, with a group of superior salesmen, the average age was about 39. Eleven per cent of them were under thirty and only ten per cent over fifty. The men below thirty probably had not had sufficient experience to reach their highest efficiency, while those above fifty were beginning to slow up. For other types of work the optimum age might be either more or less than thirty-nine; statesmen as a rule are older, and baseball stars younger.

The relation between labor turnover and age has also been studied. Kitson [1] reports a study that was made in two large industrial concerns between the age at time of entering the firm's employ and number of weeks worked before quitting of their own accord. His results are shown in the following table.[1] There is in both instances much more turnover with the younger workers. There is a marked stability for men over fifty.

| | AVERAGE NUMBER OF WEEKS | |
AGE	COMPANY A	COMPANY B
Under 21	18	10
21 to 25	19	9
26 to 30	23	11
31 to 35	31	24
36 to 40	28	19
41 to 45	29	12
46 to 50	30	8
51 to 55	58	15
Over 55	56	25

The influence of age on mental disorders is shown in Figure 18. The chart is based on data from the Twenty-Third Annual Report of the New York State Hospital Commission. The length of the

[1] Kitson, H. D.: "A Critical Age as a Factor in Labor Turnover," *Journal of Industrial Hygiene* (1922), IV, 199–200.

line indicates the relative number of each age who are admitted to hospitals for the insane.   In general, susceptibility to mental disorders increases very rapidly with advancing years.   The age of greatest susceptibility is not the same for all psychoses.   Dementia præcox and the manic-depressive psychoses usually begin before thirty-five.   More than half of all the cases of paresis occur between the ages of thirty-five and fifty.   Involution melancholia is rarely seen before the age of forty, and senile dementia practically never occurs before sixty.

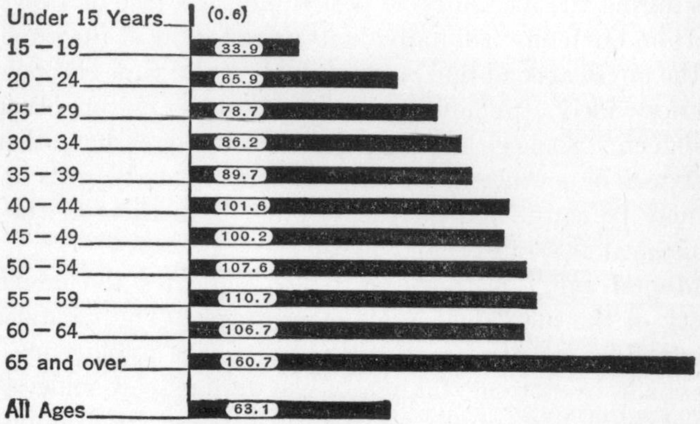

FIGURE 18. THE RELATION OF AGE AND MENTAL DISORDERS

2. Physical age.   Chronological age, however, is not always a reliable index of physical age.   Physical age depends primarily upon growth, and its relation to chronological age depends upon the rate of growth.   But all men do not mature physically at the same rate, neither do all men decline at the same rate.   Some men of seventy, for example, are physically younger than other men of forty-five.   The physical failing and death of an individual usually result from the failure of some one of the complex mechanisms making up his body, as the heart, kidneys, lungs, or blood vessels, and not from the wearing out of the organism as a whole.   And the changes in heart, lungs, and blood vessels are not so closely related to the number of years the individual has lived that chronological age can be taken as a sign of physical age.   This fact was brought

to the attention in an arresting manner during the World War, when 500,000 young men between the ages of eighteen and twenty-five were rejected as being physically "too old" and worn out for military service. Many men of forty, on the other hand, were in excellent physical condition, and showed remarkable endurance under trench life.

It is generally thought that the rate of growth shows no decline until maturity, and then declines as old age sets in. On the contrary, senescence appears at birth, for the maximum rate of growth occurs during the intra-uterine period, and the rate of growth declines from birth on. All individuals do not grow at the same rate. Thus the physical condition of individuals of the same chronological age varies widely. Some boys reach puberty at eleven, others not until sixteen. Some girls reach puberty at ten or earlier, others not until sixteen or seventeen. Those who mature early in these functions may be considered physically older than those of the same chronological age, but of later maturity.

3. Mental age. A third age which indicates the intellectual capacity of the individual is his mental age. The mental age is determined by use of some standardized test of intelligence. The scores made by normal children of the various chronological ages are used as the basis of measurement. Suppose, for example, that the child to be tested is ten years old. On the intelligence test he makes the score which is generally made by normal ten-year-olds, so he is said to have a "mental age" of ten. A ten-year-old child who makes the score generally made by nine-year-old children is said to have a mental age of nine. In like manner a mentally defective child of ten may have a mental age of four years, while a young genius ten years old may have a mental age of thirteen or fourteen. It is not uncommon to find a twenty-year-old youth with the body of a man and the mind of a six-year-old child. Nor is it uncommon to find a twisted, crippled body and a mind of unusual keenness.

The mental age of an individual tells little about him unless his chronological age is known. A four-year-old child with a mental age of six offers quite different possibilities from a nine-year-old child with a mental age of six. The former is a young genius, the

latter feeble-minded.   The Intelligence Quotient, or I.Q., is used
to show the ratio between the mental and the chronological age.
The I.Q. is secured by dividing the mental age by the chronological
age.   A ten-year-old child with a mental age of ten has an I.Q. of
100, or normal.   A four-year-old child with a mental age of six has
an I.Q. of 150, which is attained by only one in several thousand.
The nine-year-old child with a mental age of six has an I.Q. of 66,
and is definitely feeble-minded.   So it is obvious that as chronological age alone does not tell the whole story, so mental age alone
is not a reliable measure of the capacity of the individual.

The mental age, as indicated by scores on standard tests of intelligence, does not continue to increase throughout the whole of

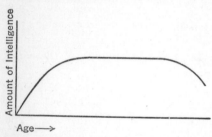

life.   Mental ability, like
physical ability, has a rapid
growth during early life,
slows up during the late
teens, and probably ceases
to increase during the early
twenties.   It remains fairly
stationary till the pre-senile
changes begin, then slowly
regresses.   This is shown
graphically in Figure 19.

FIGURE 19.   CURVE SHOWING HYPOTHETI-
CAL RISE AND DECLINE OF MENTAL AGE

Many die from accident or concurrent disease before there is much
decline in mental alertness.   Individuals also seem to differ very
widely in the time when they begin to decline.

4. Educational age.   A fourth age of the individual is his educational age.   By educational age is meant the development of an
individual in the knowledge and skills taught in schools.   If John
Doe can read, spell, and solve arithmetic problems in standardized
educational tests as well as the average child of ten, we say that
John Doe has an educational age of ten.   A number of excellent
educational achievement tests that have been standardized on
thousands of children are now available for the various school
subjects.

Usually in children who have gone to school there is a fairly close
relation between mental age and educational age.   But this does

not hold true for those who lack educational advantages. During the World War some Kentucky mountaineers were recruited who showed a mental age of eighteen years on intelligence tests, but who had no more formal education than a six-year-old child. Their educational age, therefore, was six years. These men, possessing good intelligence but lacking educational advantages, when put in school were able to raise their educational age four years within a single year; that is, a year from the first testing their educational age was ten years. All illiterates have a low educational age, but they may have a high mental age. There is a wide difference in educational age between an illiterate and a college professor, but there is not necessarily an equally wide difference in mental age.

5. Emotional age. People are not born equal, nor do they progress through life at the same rate. Some women of sixteen are older emotionally than others of thirty-six. Some men of thirty-five are from an emotional standpoint already in their senescence, while others of sixty are still dabbling in the problems of youth, love, and romance. It sometimes happens that a child with a high mental age has a relatively low emotional age; i.e., his intellect grasps the facts of the situation, but his emotional reaction indicates that his emotional development has not kept pace with his intellectual development.

The emotional development of the individual depends to a large extent upon the development of such physiological functions as the onset of puberty, or menopause, or the beginning of old age. Children who reach puberty at an early age are more mature emotionally than those of the same chronological age who have not yet reached puberty. As old age sets in, there is a marked change in the emotions.

The emotions are closely connected with the development and functioning of the ductless glands. An overactivity of the thyroid gland, for example, results in hyperexcitability and hyperemotionality. An oversecretion of the suprarenal gland makes the individual more susceptible to the stronger emotions. Undersecretion of these glands results in lack of emotion in situations that normally would call out the emotions. Disease of the ductless glands often results in some emotional abnormality.

In most people there is generally not a great deal of difference between mental, physical, emotional, and chronological ages. This being true, tradition has handed down certain divisions of the life of man into definite periods or "ages," each of which was supposed to be characterized by certain mental and emotional traits. Most of these schemes for dividing the life of the individual use the chronological age of the individual as the basis for division.

Plato's fourfold division of the life of man is one of the schemes making provision for the age differences. His plan divided human life into four periods of twenty years each. The first twenty years he designated as childhood, the second twenty as the period of preparation, the third twenty as the period of accomplishment, and the fourth twenty as the period of old age.

It has thus been recognized, since the days of ancient Greece, that the motives producing human behavior are considerably modified with age. The things we care for in adolescence interest us little in senescence; and the projects of age are equally uninteresting to youth. The marked difference between age and youth is seen in the constant battle of youth against age. From the camp of the aged we hear much talk of the corruption of youth, and youth in turn derides the shams of age, and condemns the "old hypocrites who talk about what they don't understand." It is just as natural for youth to be wild and radical as for age to be tame and conservative. Wildness and tameness are largely outward manifestations of the glandular work within.

In order to bring out in more detail the outstanding traits which tradition assigns to the different ages, let us take the well-known method, used by Shakespeare, of dividing the life of man into seven ages, and try to find the predominant interests of each age.

First age — the helpless stranger. What are the things that count most to the infant? Certainly no factor in the life of the child is more important than his mother. The chief needs of the child are for food and care, and these needs are supplied by his mother, who therefore receives a large share of his affection. But the mother is not the only influence in the life of the child at this age. The child is getting acquainted with the world into which he has come. He therefore has the propensity for manipulation, and for studying the properties of things. He takes them to pieces, and puts them together; he builds up his block tower, and knocks it down again, apparently for no other motive than to see it go up and then see it come down. This is the age that Pope had in mind when he said:

> "Behold the child, by nature's kindly law
> Pleased with a rattle, tickled with a straw."

This is also the time when the child is getting control of his muscles. It is at this age that he learns to crawl, to walk, and to talk. The outstanding characteristics of the first age may be summarized as the age of the three "M's" — *mother, manipulation*, and *movement*.

Second age — the heir of the ages. The second age of life is the age of glorious air castles. At no time in life does the world look quite so promising as at this age. Hope reigns supreme, and careers of singular daring and achievement are planned. The child is active, both physically and mentally. His games hark back to the activities of his prehistoric ancestors; he digs caves, climbs trees, chases animals, and does many other things attributed to our forefathers. He has no sense of cleanliness or propriety, and is perfectly willing to carry frogs' legs or dead snakes in his pockets. The little girl, while not so heathenish as the lad, nevertheless shows certain archaic tendencies as evidenced in her behavior with dolls.

In later life it is generally agreed that "the days of our youth are the days of our glory," and when the burdens of later life bear heavily upon us we often look back to the oasis of youth and sigh.

> "Ah happy years! Once more who would not be a boy!"

But all is not happiness and light-heartedness in this age, for the youngster in looking at life is confronted with certain questions that the greatest philosophers of all times have been unable to answer. He gains some idea of the vastness of the universe and of the illimitable stretch of time. He sees the irresistible forces of Nature turn day into night and life into death, and he is puzzled when he attempts to explain how Nature does it. After his various futile attempts to understand the "how" of Nature, he readily agrees that

> "'Tis a strange world we came to, you and I,
> Whence we know not, and surely none know why.
> Why we remain, a stranger question still,
> And yet another, whither when we die?"

But the boy refuses to become discouraged by his inability to answer these questions, and, avoiding the unsolved problems of the universe, he turns to the idolatry of some popular hero. Every boy has his hero, and the hero is usually chosen for his physical skill or daring. One boy will know the batting average of Ty Cobb, and sundry facts about this hero of sportdom. Another boy will be equally well informed of the doings of Charles Lindbergh. This is distinctly the age when the child is interested in the most active sort of human undertakings, when his highest ambition is to be a cowboy, a policeman, a railroad engineer, or a giant-killer. His favorite reading is also along such lines. During the latter part of this age the doings of Jesse James and Buffalo Bill strike a sympathetic chord in the boy's imagination. The outstanding characteristics of this age may be summarized by the three "H's" — *hope, heathenism, hero-worship.*

Third age — youth, love, and romance. The transition from the second to the third age is often quite abrupt. It is usually ushered in with the "first fitful fever of infatuation." From then on the youth is never the same again. He no longer prefers the crude companionship of his own sex to the more gentle manners of the opposite sex. He takes advantage of all opportunities to participate in social life, and in doing so there is a complete change in his attitude toward his appearance. For the first time he voluntarily combs his hair, and takes an interest in seeing that his clothes are pressed and his shoes shined. At this age for the first time he washes behind his ears without having to be forced to do so; he willingly scrubs his hands, and uses a toothbrush. This age is characterized more than any other by "wild parties" and convivial companionship.

> "Unthinking, idle, wild and young,
> They laughed and danced, and talked and sung."

It is characterized by good health, good humor, good affections, and good times. The philosophy of this age is usually hedonistic, characterized by a marked tendency to seize the fleeting pleasure before it is too late. The youth's philosophy is seen in the following quatrain:

> "Set not your heart on any good or gain,
> Life means but pleasure or it means but pain.
> And when time lets slip a little perfect hour —
> Take it, for it may not come again."

The outstanding characteristic of this age is the awakening of the three "S's" — *self*, *society*, *sex*.

Fourth age — the struggle. The third age usually ends in marriage, and with this event the interests of the man undergo a radical change. Ambition becomes his motivating force. His period of preparation being finished, he is now ready to apply the results of his training in furthering his ambitions. Moreover, he has a real incentive to exert himself to the utmost in order to better his position either in a business or a social way. Marriage brings with it the necessity for an adequate income and for a home, and ushers in a number of responsibilities unknown to the previous age. No longer is the individual free to take life as a song and to live it as he pleases, for there are others to whom he must account. Marriage exerts a "settling" influence and curbs the tendency to move from job to job, for moving becomes an arduous undertaking, and loses all the thrill which accompanied it when he had only himself and a suitcase to move. This is the time when he first understands the full meaning of the lines:

> "Down to Gehenna or up to the throne
> He travels the fastest who travels alone."

The fourth age is preëminently the age of struggle. It is the time when the success or failure of one's life is largely determined. Here the individual applies all his energies to further his ambitions, and in the end either accomplishes his objectives or is forced to abandon his projects and admit failure. This application of his abilities in his endeavor to further his ambition ends in either accomplishment or abandonment of his projects, thus indicating the dividing point in the life cycle for the next two ages. The outstanding characteristics of this age are *ambition* and *application*, followed on the one hand by *accomplishment* and on the other by *abandonment*.

Fifth age — victory or defeat. For the favored few whose struggles of the fourth age ended in accomplishment, this is the age of realization. The man has "arrived" and his future is assured. He has amassed a large fortune, and the fortune is in turn utilized in the pursuit of fame. If he has sufficient money, he may get himself placed in various positions of power and prestige. When he has achieved both fortune and fame, many strangers will feel impelled to become his "friends," and being surrounded by these flatterers, he in turn often forgets those earlier real friends through whose efforts he has been able to "arrive."

But if, as is more often the case, the efforts of the fourth age were not attended with success, his state, instead of being characterized by *fortune, fame,* and *friends,* as indicated above, would be better described by fortune adverse, leading to failure; and having failed many of his former friends lose interest in him and he tends to become friendless. His failures, coupled with the desertion of his friends, depress him, and produce in him a feeling of futility. He feels that the fates dealt him an impossible hand, and he continues the game with the attitude of one who knows that higher cards are out against him. In this condition he looks to the future, not with joy, but with apprehension. And so, the liquid dew of youth having evaporated, life drags through the sultry hours of the noonday sun, and heads for eventide.

This age will have to be summarized by two sets of "F's," depending upon whether success or failure has gone before. Those that accompany success are *fame, fortune,* and *friends,* while those attending lack of success are *failure, friendlessness,* and *futility.*

Sixth age — regression. The divergent courses of success and failure, seen in the preceding age, are continued into the sixth age. He who is successful in the struggles of the fourth and fifth ages now begins to fail in his physical strength. His voice is less loud; his hand is less steady, and his judgment less certain. His face shows all the marks of age, for the faces of the rich, as well as those of the poor, take on the color of the faded leaf, and "wrinkles, the damned democrats, won't flatter." His sight is no longer keen, and the expression, "he is getting a little deaf," means much. His power of walking shows a marked decrease, and he manifests an intense dislike for going upstairs. As age increases, he becomes more intolerant of opposition. His memory is also beginning to fail, and it is not uncommon for him to say, "I know this, but I can't name it." Many other weaknesses develop both in mind and body, and, like the proverbial old woman, he is made to learn his limitations.

The writer of Ecclesiastes [1] gives the following excellent symbolic description of this age:

Remember now thy Creator in the days of thy youth, *while the evil days come not,* nor the years draw nigh, when thou shalt say, *I have no pleasure in them;* while the sun, or the light, or the moon, or the stars, be not darkened, nor the clouds return after the rain: in the day when *the keepers* of the house shall tremble, and the strong men shall bow themselves, and *the grinders cease because they are few,* and *those that look out of the windows be darkened,* and the *doors shall be shut in the streets* . . . and all the *daughters of music* shall be brought low; also when *they shall be afraid of that which is high,* and fears shall be in the way . . . and *desire shall fail.*

How better could palsied age be described than "when the keepers of the house shall tremble," or toothless age than "the grinders cease because they are few," or sightless age than "the windows be darkened"? The general failure of all our sense organs is indicated by "the doors shall be shut in the streets," and the failure of physical strength by "they shall be afraid of that which is high" — do not like to climb hills or stairs. Glandular failure accounts for the time when "desire shall fail."

Consequently, having waned both physically and mentally, it is necessary to withdraw from active participation in the more weighty affairs of life, and, having withdrawn, man finds sufficient time to think and wonder. This is the age to which King Lear has arrived when the play opens, and he calls his daughters to him, saying, "It is our fast intent to shake all cares and burdens from our age, while we, unburdened, crawl toward death." Having plenty of leisure, the more intelligent man at this age begins to think about the life to come, and to wonder about those gone before. The following verse indicates the trend of his thoughts:

"Strange, is it not, that of the myriads who
　　Before us passed the door of darkness through,
Not one returns to tell us of the way
　　Which to discover, we must travel too."

[1] Ecclesiastes XII, 1–5. Italics mine.

If the struggles of the fourth and fifth ages led to failure, the final result is for practical purposes the same, but the terms applied to it are different. The unsuccessful man does not wane, he just weakens; nor does he withdraw, for he has nothing to withdraw from; he merely waits, and waiting he spends his time in lonely memories. Thoughts of earlier friends lead to feelings of intense loneliness. As a result of such feelings he wishes for the days of his prime, or, failing that, for a new deal in the "Land of Beginning Again." The key words of this age are the three "W's," which are different depending upon whether they follow success or failure. Those that follow success are *wane, withdraw,* and *wonder* — those that follow failure are *weaken, wait,* and *wish.*

Seventh age — the helpless senescent. Regardless of which path they have traveled in the fifth and sixth ages, those who travel through the seventh age travel practically the same path. By this time the physical and mental resources have waned and weakened to such an extent that rest is the imposed result. The previous ages have left man with mental fatigue, physical fatigue, and emotional fatigue. He no longer wishes for change and variety, but insists upon things being left just so. He wants the same chair, the same bed, the same position at the table, the same fashions, the same customs, and the same old homestead. The recognition of the physical weakness which accompanies this age is expressed by the old man of eighty as follows:

"I'se wufless as de rotten pole of las' year's fodder-stack.
 De rheumatiz done bit my bones; you hear 'em crack and crack?
 I can't sit down 'dout gruntin' like 'twas breakin' o' my back.

"What use dé wheel, when hub and spokes is warped and split and rotten?
 What use dis dried-up cotton-stalk, when Life done picked my cotton?
 I'se like a word dat somebody said, and den done been forgotten."

A second characteristic of this age is reverie. This is second childhood, and it should be remembered that childhood is the time when air castles were built. But in the first childhood the beautiful dreams are of the future, while in the second childhood the most happy dreams are those of the past.

"Old hopes which long in dust have lain,
Old dreams come thronging back again."

The old man turns back to the days of his youth and endows them with a grandeur which is increased by the distance he is from them. The rest and reverie continue until finally death brings release. The characteristics of the seventh age can be summed up in the three "R's" — *rest, reverie,* and *release.*

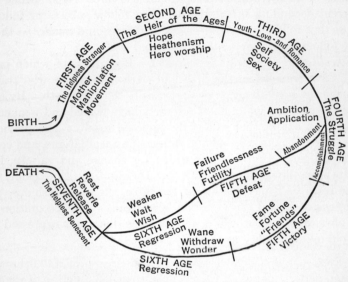

FIGURE 20. THE CYCLE OF THE AGES

The emotional characteristics of the seven ages are summarized in Figure 20.

CHAPTER X
DIFFERENCES DUE TO SEX

In the world of everyday things . . . we find that men and women are different; their bodies are different and their minds are different; most men are physically stronger than most women; women have produced fewer writers, poets, musical composers; they are emotionally likely to react in another direction from the average man; they can almost be said to have another set of virtues and vices; *now of all these differences, which are ordained in the biological nature of things, and which, using the word in its widest sense, are the result of education?*

LANGDON-DAVIES [1]

DOWN through the ages the woman has cried "O that I were a man!" and her little daughter has complained, "If I were only a boy I could do" thus and so, but no one has yet heard man or boy express a desire to be of the opposite sex. In this chapter we shall try to account for the seemingly greater desirability of being a male. The following problems will be considered: I, What is Sex; II, How Sex is Determined; III, Physical Differences between the Sexes; IV, Differences in Intelligence; V, Differences in Scholastic Standing; VI, Emotional Differences; VII, Differences in Training; VIII, Differences in Variability; IX, Differences in Achievement.

I. WHAT IS SEX

In the animal world we observe that most species are divided into two sexes, each of which has fairly constant structural and behavior characteristics. We find, for example, that one function of the female, be she woman, cow, hen, or flea, is to have offspring. But when it is contended that it is an innate function of the female to stay at home and to prepare food and to mend the clothes of the male, one must reply that such traits are the exception rather than the rule in most animals. If it is contended that the quality of being a female deprives the individual of her work and insures for her a parasitic existence, including alimony when the male tires of the parasite or she of him, one must ask whether in a state of nature the female butterfly, deer, horse, ape, or primitive man shows such traits.

[1] Langdon-Davies, John: *A Short History of Women* (The Viking Press, 1927), 27–28.

Sex as such is by no means universal; there are many of the lower animals that dispense with it altogether. Originally all animals were sexless. When they wished to reproduce, they simply split into two, and each half had its independent existence. In certain animals we find the two sexes in the same individual. They are called hermaphrodites, containing both the male and the female germs. In other animals like the hydra we have both the a-sexual (simply splitting off a part of the body and starting a new individual from it) and the sexual methods of reproduction, but when the hydra uses the sexual method, there is only one individual concerned, the parent hydra being both father and mother. In such higher forms as man we have only the sexual method of reproduction, with the male and female cells in separate individuals.

In order to get some light on the question *What is sex?* let us consider the life history of some tiny animals called Copromonas that live in frog ponds. When food is plentiful, the Copromona reproduces by simply splitting, and becoming two individuals. These two new ones continue the process until we may have hundreds where we had only one. But in the end the Copromonas apparently become fatigued and exhausted and no longer split up. Instead of splitting, two individuals come together and so mix themselves into one another that they lose their identity as separate individuals. Thus we see the beginning of sex. Apparently the protoplasm becomes exhausted and can no longer reproduce by simple splitting. By the mingling of the protoplasm of the two individuals, the protoplasm is apparently rejuvenated, and is enabled to begin splitting again with its original vigor.

Further light is thrown on the question by studying a minute animal that lives in the gastro-intestinal tract of the centipede. Like the Copromonas, these animals consist of one cell and increase for a long time by simple cell division, and later they also apparently become exhausted and mix their protoplasm with another to revive its potency. But they adopt a more complicated method to produce this result. Some individuals split into smaller sperm cells, while others grow into larger egg cells. The egg cells have a lot of nourishment stored in them, and remain at rest until sought out and penetrated by the sperm cells. The sperm cells, having very little nourishing food stored in them, are adapted for movement; they accordingly seek out the egg cell and bore into it. From this union an individual results that can start the whole process of division over again. Here we see the beginning of division of labor of the two sexes; the eggs storing food and waiting to be sought by the sperm cell; the sperm cells being characterized by considerable movement and slight storage of food. The division of labor and specialization of function are carried much further in the higher animals.

Variation is another thing accomplished by sex. When the male and the female cells mix, the resulting individual is not an exact duplication of either. Certain variations occur which may better adapt the organism to its environment. Sex may be looked on as a mechanism producing variety or diversity.

In the one-celled animals the single cell serves for motion, digestion, and reproduction. In the higher animals we find a certain group of cells set apart for movement, others for sensation, others for digestion, others for the transportation of food to and waste products from the other cells, and still others for the specific purpose of reproduction. In such animals the question naturally arises as to the relation of the reproductive cells to the various other cells. Is the animal male or female only in the reproductive cells, and are the other parts of the body neuter?

In order to throw some light on this question, let us look at some of the secondary sex characteristics. In all the higher animals, including man, the characters of sex, anatomical, physiological, and psychological, are divisible into two classes, called primary and secondary. Primary characters pertain to the sexual organs themselves and to their functions. The secondary sex characters are not directly connected with the sex organs, but nevertheless constitute marked differences between the sexes.

Men and women differ in size and shape, as well as in physical strength. The voice of man is deep and hoarse; that of the woman higher and softer. The hair distribution of the sexes differs markedly. The breasts of men do not develop and are apparently vestigial structures. Those of women show considerable development. Thus it would appear that sex concerns more than the reproductive system, for it apparently influences all the cells of the body.

The influence of sex on the various somatic cells — that is, cells other than reproductive cells — is indirect, depending for its effect on the internal secretions of the sex glands. If the sex glands of a cock are removed at an early age, his comb and spurs fail to develop, his body takes on a different shape from that of an uncastrated cock, and his behavior is that of a very poor, unvirile being. Steinach found that the removal of the ovaries or testes of guinea pigs causes the animals to grow up much less masculine or feminine in their appearance. By grafting an ovary into a male guinea pig whose testes had been removed, the animal grew up to resemble a female. It is reported to have developed perfect milk glands, suckled young ones, and behaved in other ways like a female guinea pig. He also found that a female whose ovaries had previously been removed, and testes grafted in their place, grew large and powerful, and would fight with males and court females. These experiments show that the sex traits of an animal depend, in part at least, on its internal secretions from the ductless glands, and that the structure of its body, as well as its habits, emotions, and general nature, can be altered by changing these secretions. Every cell in the human body has the possibility of being changed into either the male or the female pattern by the secretions from the ductless glands.

II. HOW SEX IS DETERMINED

Like most other human traits, sex is determined jointly by heredity and certain environmental factors. Until a short time ago, and even at the present time many scientists believed that sex is solely a product of inheritance, and is in no way influenced by environment. They base their conclusions upon such investigations as those of Painter.[1] He has shown that the sperm cells contain forty-eight chromosomes, one of which is of the "x-y" variety. In the ripe sperm cells and the ripe egg cells the number of chromosomes will be only twenty-four, for each cell splits into two before they meet in the act of fertilization, and half of the

---

[1] Painter, T. S.: "The Spermatogenesis of Man," *Journal of Experimental Zoölogy* (1923), XXXVII.

chromosomes go into each half. When the sperm and ovum mix, they regain the characteristic number of forty-eight. After division there are two types of spermatozoa, each containing twenty-four chromosomes, but one type contains an x chromosome, while the other has a y chromosome. Inasmuch as all the chromosomes of the mature ovum are of the same type, it is apparent that there would be two types of ova after fertilization, one containing forty-six typical chromosomes and two x chromosomes, and one containing forty-six typical chromosomes and an x and a y chromosome. The first type develop into females, and the second type into males. It would thus appear that sex is primarily determined by the male cell which fertilizes the ovum. Ripe spermatozoa containing the x chromosome produce females, while those containing the y chromosome produce males.

But the determination of sex is much more complicated than the advocates of the chromosome theory might lead us to believe. A number of recent investigations have shown that several environmental factors influence the determination of sex. Feeding rotifera entirely on chlorophyll protozoa causes all the offspring to be female, while a diet without any protozoa containing chlorophyll causes all to be male. A pond snail growing in close quarters with little room to move around develops into a male, but if given more room will develop into a female. Thus we see that in some animals sex is influenced by diet and crowded conditions.

If the worm benellia grows to the adult stage alone, it becomes a female; but if during growth it comes in contact with a female, it attaches itself to her as a parasite and develops as a male. Here to be a male is the reward for successful parasitism.

In some species sex determination is influenced by certain factors that may affect the basal metabolism. Witchi reported that in water at a normal temperature the ratio of frogs was about as many females as males, but if the temperature of the water was raised to 90° F., all were males. It has also been found that pigeon eggs laid in winter hatch out 153 males to every 100 females, and that eggs laid in hot weather hatch only 70 males to 100 females.

There are some facts which might indicate that in the human species sex is determined sometimes after conception. It is almost impossible to tell the sex of a fetus that has not had more than three months' development.   The organs of the two sexes develop indiscriminately, and all that is necessary to make one male or female is to enlarge some organs, diminish others, and change the position of others.   All observers agree that during the early months of human pregnancy there are many more males than female fetuses. In human fetuses of four months, there are supposed to be about 180 males to 100 females, but at birth there are only about 105 males to 100 females.   This might indicate that the sex had been altered in a number of cases — several males changed to females; or it might be explained by supposing a greater pre-natal mortality of the males.

III. PHYSICAL DIFFERENCES BETWEEN THE SEXES

Differences in structure mean differences in behavior.   According to Loeb, men and women are physiologically different species. In all races, men on the average are larger and stronger than women. Women are traditionally known as "the weaker sex," and from a physical standpoint this is true.   It is important to know whether this physical inferiority is due to innate qualities in the woman, or to ways of living which are conducive to physical weakness.

In answer to this question we are safe in stating that the average woman is very much less powerful than she might be owing to her protected life in her conventional, labor-saving environment.   But when equal provision is made for women to develop their potential physical strength, a balance in favor of men still remains.   Dr. Ales Hrdlicka has studied the sex differences in physical strength of American Indians.   The Indian women do all the hard work and have every opportunity to develop their muscular strength, and social custom does not mitigate against a fine female physique. As a result of his investigation he concluded that the average Indian woman is only two thirds as powerful as an average Indian man.   This is not as much as the difference between white women and white men, and while it indicates that part of the difference in the white race is due to the debilitating lives led by the white women, still it shows that, in spite of hard work and healthy living, women remain weaker than men.   Regardless of their different modes of living, Indian men are as much taller than Indian women as white men are taller than white women. Although the heart-beat among Indians is slower than among whites, the Indian woman's heart beats as much faster than the man's as the white woman's heart beats faster than the white man's heart.

In this connection it should be noted that entirely apart from environment and training, differences between the sexes exist. At birth boy babies possess relatively more muscle tissue, the girl babies relatively more fat tissue. The strength of man is considerably greater in proportion to the body weight than that of woman. In men the ratio of weight to strength is approximately 1 to .87; in women the ratio is 1 to .54. Women, however, equal the men in such physical characteristics as visual and auditory acuity and reaction time. In reaction time the women even appear to be slightly quicker than the men. There seems to be little difference in the acuteness of the special senses, although there may be a sex difference in certain defects of these senses, such as color blindness, a defect which afflicts three times as many men as women. Men have from 6 to 7 per cent higher basal metabolism rate than women.

In almost every organization where the question has been studied, it has been found that women employees have records of more rest-room treatments and more absences on account of illness. A study of the relative number of days of sick leave taken by men and women during a six months' period in a government department, in which the number of men is approximately equal to the number of women, showed that women take about three times as much sick leave as men. Such records, however, cannot be taken to indicate that women are sick three times as much as men. Other factors must be considered, such as the attitude of the employees toward their work, the leniency of rules regarding leave, or the relative grade of the positions held by men and women. The men are usually in the more important positions and find it more difficult to take sick leave.

IV. DIFFERENCES IN INTELLIGENCE

In order to make reliable investigations of the differences in intelligence due to sex, it is desirable in so far as possible to eliminate all factors except that of sex. The individuals of both sexes to be compared should be near the same age; should have received approximately the same education; and should have been subjected to similar training and social surroundings. If under these conditions studies show an appreciable difference between the two sexes, it must be due to real sex differences, and not to a different environment or to hereditary factors other than sex. It is impossible to fulfill these conditions completely. The best that can be done is to select boys and girls of about the same age attending the same grammar school, or young men and women of approximately equal age and educational advantages attending a co-educational university.

The intelligent person is the one who has the ability to adjust himself satisfactorily to new situations. The situation may present a problem dealing with ideas, with people, or with things. What the person will do when confronted by a problem involving ideas depends upon the amount of abstract intelligence he has; how he will get along with people depends upon his social intelligence; and to what extent he can see the mechanical relations between things depends upon his mechanical intelligence. Let us see how the sexes compare in respect to these three kinds of intelligence.

1. **Abstract intelligence.** (a) *Intelligence of university students.* The best method of ascertaining how men and women compare in abstract intelligence is to compare their scores on tests which measure this ability. At George Washington University a study was made of the abstract intelligence of 561 women students and 477 men students. The test used was the Army Alpha Intelligence Test. The median [1] score of the women was 144 and that of the

[1] The median is the center score of the group. There are as many persons making scores above the median as there are making scores below the median. For example, a class of 25 pupils attempts to spell a list of fifteen words with the following results:

SCORE	NO. OF PUPILS	SCORE	NO. OF PUPILS
15	1	8	3
14	0	7	0
13	2	6	2
12	2	5	0
11	1	4	2
10	4	3	1
9	5	2	1
		1	0

The score of 9 is the score of the middle case, for ten pupils made more than 9 and ten pupils made less than 9. In other words, 9 is the median score.

men 142.   The highest score possible on the test was 212.   In several other universities differences in favor of the men have been found, but everywhere the difference between the median scores of the men and the women was very small, so small that it is probably due to chance selection, and indicates that there is no real difference in the mental alertness of the two sexes.

b. *Intelligence of elementary-school children*.   Terman studied the abstract intelligence of a thousand unselected school children between the ages of five and fourteen.   The measure of intelligence which he used was the Intelligence Quotient determined by means of the Stanford Revision of the Binet-Simon Intelligence Test. The median of the girls of every age up to thirteen was a trifle higher than that of the boys of the same age, but the boys over thirteen were slightly superior to the girls of the same age.   On the whole, the boys and girls were approximately equal in abstract intelligence.

2. **Social intelligence.**   By social intelligence is meant the ability to deal successfully with people, to understand the feelings and motives of others and to be able to get along with them.   Which sex is superior in social intelligence?   In order to measure the social intelligence of the two sexes, a standardized test of social intelligence was given to a thousand freshmen at George Washington University.   The men and women comprising this group were about equal in abstract intelligence as indicated by the average scores on an abstract intelligence test.   An analysis of the results of this examination shows that the median score of the five hundred men is about five points lower than the median score of the five hundred women. The highest score possible was 160 points.   On this test the women excelled in the ability to recognize a person's mental state from his facial expression as indicated in a series of twelve photographs representing as many mental states.   The women also excelled in ability to recognize the mental state of the speaker or the motives back of the spoken word.   They excelled in judgment as to the best course of action in social situations requiring tact, and in accuracy of observation of human behavior.   The men excelled in breadth and variety of interest; while the sexes were approximately equal in memory for names and faces.   As in all mental traits, however, the

differences between individuals of the same sex are far greater than the differences between the median scores of the sexes. Woman's superior social intelligence is not a new idea. Several years ago Havelock Ellis was discussing the "greater affectability of the female mind"; and the origin of the expression "woman's intuition" is lost in antiquity. Immediate responsiveness to the emotions of others, ability to size up a social situation quickly, understanding of motives governing others, and interest in people are distinctly feminine traits.

3. **Mechanical intelligence.** In mechanical intelligence, or in seeing things in their proper mechanical relationship, the men excel. From earliest childhood the little boy wants to build things, to take his toys apart to see how they work, and to try to put them together again. This innate curiosity as to the mechanism of things is probably not so strong in the little girl. Moreover, the boy is encouraged in his interest in mechanics, while the girl is discouraged from evincing any interest in this field which tradition has decreed should belong preëminently to man. The majority of the occupations dealing with mechanical things are followed exclusively by men. Few women have been given the opportunity to demonstrate their ability as engineers, draftsmen, or electricians.

In automobile driving, however, the two sexes have approximately an equal chance to show their mechanical ability. A test consisting of questions concerning the mechanism of the car and problems in driving was given to about five hundred university students (men and women), all of whom had had more than one thousand hours' driving experience. The scores on this test indicate that forty per cent of the women know as much about the mechanics of a car and how to operate it as fifty per cent of the men. Thus, if the average score of the men was 75, forty women out of every hundred made a score of 75 or higher. These results apparently indicate that, in a field where knowledge of mechanics is useful to both sexes, women do not prove very inferior to men.

Thus we see that on abstract intelligence the two sexes are about equal, women are slightly better in social intelligence and men in mechanical intelligence. These latter differences may be due to differences in training. The following quotation from Thorndike [1] sums up the question of sex differences in intelligence:

The most important characteristic of these differences is their small amount. The individual differences within one sex so enormously outweigh the differences between the sexes in these intellectual and semi-intellectual traits that for practical purposes the sex differences may be disregarded. So far as ability goes there could hardly be a stupider way to get two groups alike within each group but differing between the groups than to take the two sexes. As is well known, the experiments of the last generation in educating women have shown their equal competence in school work of elementary, secondary, and collegiate grade. The present generation's experience is showing the same fact for professional education and business service. The psychologist's measurements lead to the conclusion that this equality of achievement comes from an equality of natural gifts, not from an overstraining of the lesser talents of women.

V. DIFFERENCES IN SCHOLASTIC STANDING

Scholastic standing or school record depends in part upon abstract intelligence, and in part upon other factors such as social intelligence, mechanical intelligence, and certain character traits. To make good marks in school, a pupil must have sufficient abstract intelligence to learn the required subject matter; sufficient social intelligence to get along with teacher and pupils; and sufficient perseverance or industry to do the work required. In such courses as physics and other laboratory courses he must also have a fair degree of mechanical intelligence in order to succeed. Lack of any one of these qualities may lead to poor scholastic standing. Thus, a comparison of the scholastic standing of the two sexes involves factors other than the factor of abstract intelligence.

Using a battery of standardized achievement tests, Burt measured over 5000 school children in 19 different schools, taking approximately 2500 of each age. His results are shown in Figure 21. It will be noted that on the whole there is very little difference in the school standing of the sexes in the grammar school. More difference, however, is found in college students.

Thorndike [2] reports a comparison of the two sexes, attending the

[1] Thorndike, Edward L.: *Educational Psychology, Briefer Course* (Teachers College, Columbia University, New York City, 1924), 345–46.

[2] Thorndike, Edward L.: *Educational Psychology*, III (Teachers College, Columbia University, New York, 1914), 183.

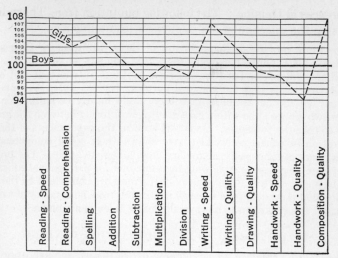

FIGURE 21. SEX DIFFERENCES IN CHILDREN IN VARIOUS
SCHOOL SUBJECTS

The boys are represented along a constant line. (Adapted from Gates.)

same high-school classes, in various abilities, shown in objective
tests and in school marks.   The percentage of boys reaching or exceeding the median of the girls is as follows:

In English (Regents' examination and school mark)........ 41
In mathematics (Regents' examination and school mark).... 57
In Latin (Regents' examination and school mark).......... 57
In history (Regents' examination and school mark)........ 60

In college the percentage of men students reaching or exceeding
the median of the women students is as follows:

In English............................. 35 (approximately)
In mathematics........................ 45 (approximately)
In history and economics................ 56 (approximately)
In mental science...................... 50 (approximately)
In modern languages................... 40 (approximately)

A study of the scholastic standing of the men and women at one
of the large co-educational universities showed the scholastic average of the women to be considerably higher than that of the men;
although the scores on the abstract intelligence tests showed the
sexes to be about equal in mental ability.   Grading on a 9 point

scale, in which 9 is high, the average scholastic record of the women was 6.5 and that of the men only 5. The correlation between the scholastic average of the women and their intelligence scores was only .48, while that of the men was .59. That is, there was a closer relation between the intelligence of the men and the grades they made than there was between the intelligence of the women and their grades.

VI. EMOTIONAL DIFFERENCES

One's emotional life depends on the chemical balance in his organism. Anything that affects this chemical state affects his emotional life. The sum total of the chemical changes in an individual are called metabolism. Every cell in the body is at all times undergoing metabolic changes. As pointed out above, the metabolic changes in men are between six and seven per cent higher than in women. The calcium metabolism is of considerable interest in this connection, for it seems that neurological irritability is very intricately connected with the calcium balance. Women need more calcium than men, especially when they are pregnant, for a great deal of calcium is used to build the skeleton of the child. After the child is born, an extra amount of calcium is required to produce milk. Moreover, the metabolism of a woman is more or less disturbed at her menstrual periods.

It is well known that metabolism affects an individual's attitude toward life and its problems. With the increasing calcium salts which remain fixed in the body of the old person, he gradually changes from the rollicking vivacity of youth to the jaundiced conservatism of old age. As the chemical changes are decreased both in amount and in variability, the individual's behavior and emotional attitudes become more fixed. This being true, we can see some physiological basis for the common belief that woman's emotional life has more ups and downs than does man's. Not only is her behavior more changeable, but she is probably more responsive to stimuli than man. To claim, as some writers do, that this greater emotional instability is a detriment is to argue that the conservatism of age is a virtue. It is this changeableness in her emotional life that makes the young woman so interesting.

Differences in drives. Very little experimental work has been done to show the sex differences in emotional drives. The few experiments which have been performed in this field used the lower animals as experimental subjects, and we cannot be certain how indicative the findings in these experiments are of the drives in case of the human.

In 1924 the author [1] reported a series of experiments designed to measure the strength of the sex drive in white rats in terms of the amount of punishment the animal would take to satisfy that drive. The experiment was conducted along the lines described in Chapter I. Five males were placed in section A of the experiment box (see Figure 1) and a female during her œstrual period was placed in section C. A current of twenty-eight volts was turned on the electric plates in B. Only two males crossed in the hour that they were left in the box. The complement of the experiment was performed by confining the males in section C and leaving the female when in œstrum in section A, free to cross the plates if she had sufficient drive to overcome the resistance. Of the five females thus tested, three crossed.

It is significant that when driven by the sex urge, three of the females crossed and only two of the males. These results might also throw the shadow of suspicion on the correctness of the statement that "the male is essentially the pursuer and the female the pursued." Whether the above statement is correct or not, these results certainly show that some females will overcome more resistance to place themselves in a position to be "pursued" than will the average male in order to pursue. The behavior of the female when admitted to section C would, at first glance, tend to support the statement that she is the pursued rather than the pursuer. On the approach of the male, she responds with the proverbial fleeing behavior, only she doesn't flee very far nor into inaccessible places such as back across the plates into section A. A quotation from Thorndike [2] would very accurately describe this situation: "The female responds by coy advances and retreats: the male by caressing pursuit and capture. The former is satisfied by, and so instinctively maintains, whatever augments the aggressiveness of the male; he responds similarly to the hopeful difficulties which her behavior offers. Capture and submission are responded to by the mutual absence of fear ... and by satisfaction in bodily contact,

[1] Moss, F. A.: "A Study of Animal Drives," *Journal of Experimental Psychology*, VII, no. 3 (June, 1924), 172.

[2] Thorndike, Edward L.: *Educational Psychology*, I (Teachers College, Columbia University, New York, 1913), 98.

including as the final element the contact necessary for the fertilization of the ovum."

There are certain general differences, noted by both psychologist and layman, between the emotional activities of men and women. Although these differences are not subject to exact measurement, they are apparent to the careful observer. Thorndike traces some of the differences back to the relative strength of the parental and fighting instincts in the two sexes, the assumption being that the parental instinct is stronger in the female and the fighting instinct in the male.

Opposite views as to the origin of the love of the mother for her child are held by Thorndike and Watson. Thorndike holds that the love of a mother for her child is instinctive, and cites as evidence mother love in the lower animals. Watson holds that it is acquired by caring for the child. He quotes such facts as that there is relatively little grief at the loss of a child which is born dead, but that when the child dies after living a few months the mother is frantic with grief and cannot be consoled. Both points of view have something to recommend them, and the truth will probably be found in a compromise. There is possibly an innate tendency in all women to love their offspring, but this tendency is no doubt greatly accentuated by caring for the child. If, then, the love for the child is in part acquired by contact, it is natural that it should be stronger in the mother than in the father, because the mother more often comes in contact with the child.

Being physically stronger, man tends to dominate woman, and woman finds little annoyance in submitting to his dominance. In large organizations, women employees prefer men to women bosses. One woman hates to take orders from another, but submits without hesitation to the supervision of a man. On the whole, women submit to authority much more gracefully than men do. From the habit of submission, women have developed a degree of patience far beyond that possessed by most men. Doctors and nurses agree that women make better patients than men because they complain about pain less. Women may have developed their patience through the annoyances which they have had to endure in connection with menstruation and childbirth.

The desire for social approval is very strong in both sexes. Practically any person is uncomfortable when his circle of friends disapproves of his action, and is happy and contented when society smiles upon him and praises him. Though man and woman both desire the approval of others, they desire to be approved along different lines. For example, a girl usually takes pride in being pretty, or in having small hands, trim ankles, and wavy hair. A man is more likely to take pride in possessing powerful muscles and physical skill. A girl does not choose a husband for his handsome face; she considers other factors to be of more importance. But beauty plays an important part in the selection of a bride. Consequently we have nation-wide beauty contests for women, but none for men; but we seldom have prize fights, baseball, football, or other competitions of strength, skill, or daring for women. In adorning the person so as to gain social approval, the sexes again differ. Women are thought of as slavishly following the styles. But what of men? At a formal ball the women wear clothes of every cut and color, but all men wear the same, drab, stereotyped suits. Women, seeking individuality, show much more originality in their clothes, while men show little innovation in their dress.

An important sex difference is seen in suicide statistics. Three times as many men as women commit suicide; moreover, there is a striking difference in the age at which most men take their own lives as compared with the age of women suicides. Women commit suicide most frequently between the ages of twenty and forty, the period when love affairs are ending unhappily. Men commit suicide more frequently from forty to sixty, the period when business affairs and financial failures are most depressing. This tends to support the claim that women are more interested in persons, men are more interested in things.

Still another emotional difference between the sexes is found in the interest in religion evinced by men and women. If women are more responsive emotionally than men, it is not strange that the emotional appeals of religion should prove more effective with them. The fact that going to church affords the woman a chance to dress in her best, to drop home cares, and to mingle with other people also influences the greater church attendance of women. The men are away from home all the week, meeting people in the business world, and their desire for society having been satisfied, they prefer to remain at home and read while their wives go to church.

VII. DIFFERENCES IN TRAINING

From early childhood the two sexes are subjected to radically different training. The little girl is forbidden to do many things which her brother is encouraged to do. She is told that it is not ladylike to climb trees, play football, or dig caves, and if she does such things she is called a "tomboy." The little boy is told that he must not sew, play with dolls, or make mud pies, and if he persists in doing such things he is called a "sissy." Santa Claus brings the boys footballs and erector sets, but he brings the girls dolls and doll carriages. The boy is encouraged to play rough-and-tumble games such as wrestling and boxing. The girl is scolded if she runs and gets overheated, but is urged to play with dolls and practice her music. The boy is taught that it is unmanly to cry when frightened or hurt, and that he must protect his sister from dangers such as a dog or a mouse. The little girl learns that tears are her best weapons, and that jumping on a chair and screaming is the socially approved way to greet a mouse.

In considering sex differences, the differences due to training should be distinguished as far as possible from the differences due to sex alone. The male is naturally larger and stronger than the female, and everything in his training tends to develop muscular strength and independence. The female is physically smaller and has less strength than the male, and her training tends to prevent muscular development and to foster a spirit of dependence. Just how much of the differences which are evident in the conduct and attitudes of adult men and women is innate and how much is built up by training is a moot question, but it is certain that training and custom exert a great influence in building up the different codes of behavior peculiar to men and women. Take the double standard for an example. There is logically no more reason why a man should be permitted to have promiscuous sex affairs than there is for a woman having such affairs. But down through the ages we have had two codes of sex morality, a very stringent one for women and a much more liberal one for men.   At the present time many people are proclaiming the dangers of women smoking.   As a matter of fact, there is no known physiological reason why smoking should be more injurious to women than to men.   Without doubt consuming immoderate amounts of alcohol is injurious to a woman, but the practice is equally injurious to a man.

VIII. DIFFERENCES IN VARIABILITY

Many scientists hold that men are more variable than women, that women cluster more about the normal and that men more often depart from the normal, falling in the classes of genius or feeble-minded.   In support of the theory of the greater variability of men are cited such facts as that twice as many men as women are found in institutions for the feeble-minded, and that a disproportionately large number of men attain eminence as compared with the number of women of like achievement.

Recent investigations show that there is very little difference in the variability of the two sexes.   It is probable that facts other than that of variability enter in to produce the greater proportion of men in institutions and also in positions of eminence.   For example, the fact that more men than women achieve eminence may be due to the fact that until recent years women have been very largely excluded from the professions in which it is possible to achieve eminence, and that, in addition, a large number of those who do embark upon a career where eminence is possible, soon marry and devote a major portion of their energy to home-making.   The greater number of men in institutions for the defective may be due to the fact that feeble-minded men, when forced into economic competition with their normal fellow workers, go down in the struggle, and are placed in institutions where they can receive the care their condition demands.   Many feeble-minded women, however, not having to meet such severe competition, succeed in caring for their families after a fashion, or, if wholly helpless, are cared for by relatives, so that society never learns their true condition.

The author made a study of the Army Alpha Intelligence Test scores of five hundred men and five hundred women university students.   The average scores of the men and women were about equal. The men were slightly more variable, the women clustered more closely about the median. A score of 180 or above was made by 55 men and by only 32 women, while at the other end of the scale a score of below 120 was made by 88 men and only 60 women. In a similar study of elementary-school children, Terman failed to find any difference in the variability of the sexes.

It is sometimes claimed that the physical variability of males is greater than that of females, but investigations fail to bear out this contention. Hollingworth and Montague [1] studied accurate measurements of two thousand newborn babies, one thousand of each sex, and failed to find any significant differences in the variability. In a study of physical characteristics of adults of both sexes, Pearson failed to find any differences in variability. From the data now available, it seems reasonable to doubt that there is any constant tendency for the male to be more variable than the female.

IX. DIFFERENCES IN ACHIEVEMENT

The argument of those who believe that women are mentally inferior to men is supported by the fact that there have been a greater number of geniuses and eminent persons among men than among women. Concerning the thousand persons he selected as being the most eminent as represented in history, Cattell [2] says:

I have spoken throughout of eminent men as we lack in English words including both men and women, but as a matter of fact women do not have an important place on the list. They have in all thirty-two representatives in the thousand. Of those, eleven are hereditary sovereigns, and eight are eminent through misfortune, beauty, or other circumstances. Belles-lettres and fiction — the only department in which woman has accomplished much — give ten names as compared with seventy-two men. Sappho and Jeanne d'Arc are the only other women on the list. It is noticeable that with the exception of Sappho — a name associated with certain fine fragments — women have not excelled in poetry or art. Yet these are the departments least dependent on environment, and at the same time those in which the environment has been found as favorable to

[1] Hollingworth and Montague: "Comparative Variability of the Sexes at Birth," *American Journal of Sociology* (1914), xix.

[2] Cattell, J. McK.: "A Statistical Study of Eminent Men," *Popular Science Monthly*, 62 (1903), 375.

women as to men. Women depart less from the normal than men — a fact that usually holds for the female throughout the animal series; in many closely related species only the male can be readily distinguished.

The fact that modern civilization is offering women greater opportunity for achieving eminence is brought out by Castle.[1] The following table shows that the number of eminent women is steadily increasing; 24.5 per cent of the total number of women of eminence in all history have lived in the eighteenth century and 38.5 per cent in the nineteenth. When given an opportunity, women show that they are capable of achievements little, if any, less noteworthy than those of men.

DISTRIBUTION OF EMINENT WOMEN BY CENTURIES

CENTURY	NUMBER OF CASES	CENTURY	NUMBER OF CASES
7 B.C.	3	7	7
6	3	8	5
5	8	9	6
4	8	10	6
3	4	11	9
2	1	12	12
1	10	13	10
A.D. 1	11	14	17
2	4	15	32
3	14	16	45
4	6	17	84
5	7	18	213
6	8	19	333
		Total ...	868

Hampered by the weight of custom, as they undeniably are, yet women are steadily penetrating into occupational fields from which they have long been excluded. More and more women are achieving economic independence, many of them in pioneer fields. Statistics show that a little more than one fifth of all the women who are ten years of age and over are employed at tasks for which they receive monetary rewards. The occupations in which they are engaged and the percentages engaged in each are as follows: [2]

[1] Castle, Cora S.: A Statistical Study of Eminent Women (1913), Table II, 26.

[2] Reed, Ruth: "Where Women Work Today," Industrial Psychology (April, 1926), 257.

OCCUPATIONS | PER CENT
Domestic and personal service......................... 25.6
Manufacturing and mechanical industries.............. 22.6
Clerical occupations................................. 16.7
Agriculture.. 12.7
Trade.. 7.8
Transportation....................................... 2.5

Evidence of the important place held by women in industry is offered by the fact that in 1920 there were thirty occupations employing more than fifty thousand women. Many of these positions were those in which women were traditionally employed, as in domestic service, but within the last ten years many others, such as those of the bookkeeper, saleswoman, and cashier, have come to be regarded as offering as good opportunities for women as men. In fact, the numerical increase for women in clerical work between 1910 and 1920 was greater than for all other general divisions of occupations combined.

There are, indeed, few occupational fields afforded by industry and the professions, for which women are physically fitted, into which they have not penetrated in greater or less number. And as opportunities for professional work became more numerous, many women entered upon professional careers, in which many have achieved noteworthy success. During the last decade the number of women in the professions increased thirty-eight per cent. Statistics show that to-day about one ninth of all women who work away from home are engaged in professional pursuits. In the last few years there has been a tremendous increase in the number of women employed as lawyers, clergymen, theater owners and managers, doctors, chemists, and draftsmen. The number of women college presidents and welfare workers has trebled in the last decade.

During this time the success which has followed the advent of women in fields heretofore regarded as man's special prerogative indicates that the relatively unimportant achievement of women in the past must be due to lack of opportunity rather than to lack of capacity for achievement.

CHAPTER XI

DIFFERENCES IN EMOTIONAL OUTLETS

To be, or not to be: that is the question:
Whether 'tis nobler in the mind to suffer
The slings and arrows of outrageous fortune,
Or to take arms against a sea of troubles,
And by opposing end them.

SHAKESPEARE

As pointed out in Chapter I, the behavior of any individual is the resultant of his drives and resistances. When the drive and the opposing resistance are approximately equal in strength, neither being strong enough to overcome the other without considerable effort, the individual is in a state of mental unrest, or internal strife, a condition known as an *emotional conflict*. An emotional conflict is the mental state resulting from the thwarting of a powerful drive, or from the necessity for overcoming some strong resistance. It includes the arrayment of the opposing forces and the resulting battle between them. The conflict may be of short duration or it may last for years.

What is the cause of an emotional conflict? Why does the individual not yield immediately to the urge every time he feels strongly impelled to a certain course of action? The answer lies in the fact that his impulses are often thwarted by the conditions of life which surround him. For his desires to secure expression certain opposing forces must be overcome. These opposing forces preventing the immediate satisfaction of his impulses have their origin in three sources: (1) antagonistic drives or resistances; (2) the teachings of society; and (3) external reality.

1. Conflict with antagonistic drives or resistances. One fundamental drive may come into conflict with another or with a strong resistance. Thus, the tramp's desire for good food and family life may come into conflict with his desire for new scenes or his resistance to labor. The desire of the small boy for immediate revenge for the insult from the larger boy may come into conflict with his fear of physical suffering at the hands of the stronger boy.

2. **Conflict with the teaching of society.** It not infrequently happens that our natural drives or resistances are opposed by the customs and teachings of society. There were many examples of this during the war when the impulse of the soldier to preserve his life came into conflict with his ideas of patriotism and society's teaching of loyalty to his country. Man's tendency to love more women than her to whom he is married is opposed by his religious teachings as well as by accepted social customs. The boy's impulse to take any fascinating object or mechanical contrivance that he can carry away is soon inhibited by his ideals of honesty and his habit of respecting the other man's property.

3. **Conflict with external reality.** A third cause of mental conflict arises when something in the external environment opposes the satisfaction of a drive. The death of one's fiancée may thwart the normal consummation of his love life; a hunched back or a scarred or deformed face may block one's desire for social approval; business disaster, inhibiting the attainment of numerous desires, comes into conflict with a great number and a great variety of drives.

Emotional conflicts are everywhere at all times. They are like growing pains; we all have them. No age of the individual is free from emotional conflicts and no position in life avoids them. No environment is so favorable but that many of our strongest emotional drives must be constantly thwarted. Most of these conflicts, like the minor ills of childhood, do not leave any permanent damage although they are distinctly annoying at the time. It occasionally happens, however, that an emotional conflict is much more like a malignant disease in the severity of its attack and in the permanency of its damages.

The emotional unrest which accompanies the thwarting of some of our most powerful emotions is not unlike the physical turmoil which accompanies some of our most dreaded maladies. In speaking of the conflict accompanying the thwarting of love Shakespeare says:

> "O, beware, my lord, of jealousy:
> It is the green-eyed monster which doth mock
> The meat it feeds on: that cockold lives in bliss
> Who, certain of his fate, loves not his wronger;

> But, O, *what damned minutes tells he o'er*
> *Who dotes, yet doubts, suspects, yet soundly loves.*"

The mental torture of emotional conflict is further seen in the case of Macbeth in his conflict between fear and the desire for social approval.

> "Better be with the dead,
> Whom we to gain our peace have sent to peace,
> Than on the torture of the mind to lie
> In restless ecstasy."

Having traced the origin of emotional conflict and having noted the universal prevalence of conflicts between drives and resistances which produce in the individual annoying emotional stresses and strains, the question arises: What does the individual do when a strong impulse is blocked? A general answer is indicated by observing animal behavior. If a dog which has been accustomed to sleeping inside the house at night is accidentally left out on a cold night, the thwarting of his impulse to get within leads to such behavior as scratching on the door, pushing against it with his forefeet, seeking other points of entrance, barking, or finally seeking some other place to stay to avoid the cold. In other words, when confronted by an annoying situation, the animal makes various attempts to get out of that situation. While it will not be feasible to discuss all the diverse ways by which the human being seeks to avoid annoying conflicts, it will be possible to enumerate some of the more common ways by which he attempts to get out of the conflict.

Various means of escaping emotional conflicts are resorted to, some of them good, some bad. Certain ones permit the individual to carry on his duties in life with a minimum of interference from emotional stresses; others incapacitate him for normal work and human adjustments. We shall accordingly consider these ways out of emotional conflicts under two main heads: I, Normal Ways Out; and II, Abnormal Ways Out. The normal ways out are employed by all of us at one time or another, and no one considers us particularly queer for that reason. The following normal ways out of emotional conflicts will be considered: (1) Memory; (2)

Imagination; (3) Dreams; (4) Inactivity; (5) Migration; (6) Sour grapes; (7) Negative sour grapes; (8) Logic-tight compartment; (9) Compensation; (10) A bid for sympathy; (11) Projection; (12) Rationalization; and (13) Substituted activities. Any one who employs one of the abnormal ways out markedly incapacitates himself, and is immediately recognized by society as being queer. The following abnormal ways out of emotional conflicts will be considered: (1) Insanity; (2) Imaginary illnesses; and (3) Suicide.

I. NORMAL EMOTIONAL OUTLETS

1. Memory. One of the most frequent ways out of an annoying mental conflict is through the memory of happier days. The individual admits to himself that to-day is bad, but not being able to change the conditions of to-day, he consoles himself with the memories of yesterday when things were more in accord with his heart's desire. During the times of his most bitter thwartings, he turns to the past as the desert traveler to the oasis, and reënacts scene by scene his most happy experiences. Those whose early life has been most rich in experiences have the largest store house to draw from at such times. For this reason it has been suggested that during the spring and summer of life the individual should obtain a number of worth while experiences and store them up in order to provide "canned memories," to be utilized during the lonely days of the bleak winter time of life. On such days he can take down from memory's store house a can of rich experiences and in that way re-live the more pleasant days of youth.

2. Imagination. But not all people have had experiences that bring consolation in the dark hours of conflict. These individuals who find the present bad and the past empty may seek a way out of the stresses and strains of an emotional conflict by looking to the future. This is the method of reverie and day dreams. The individual, oblivious of the past and of the present, builds himself a

"Land of Heart's Desire,
Where beauty has no ebb, decay no flood,
But joy is wisdom, Time an endless song."

During such times the imagination enables the individual to strip the present of its sorrows and vicissitudes and to recast it in a more pleasant form.

3. Dreams. In the case of the individual whose days are too occupied for imagination and reverie, this same method of alleviating present conflicts may act at night in the form of dreams. His loved ones who have recently died are once more in his dreams living and well; his ship which was lost at sea arrives safely in port; and it develops that it was all a mistake about the lover who had proved untrue; and the child who was refused a ride across the lake in a boat, dreams of riding all around the lake and seeing many wonderful things. Thus is the thwarted desire satisfied in the dream.

4. Inactivity. When the conflict is very annoying and has persisted for some time without the individual being able to find an adequate solution for it, he frequently settles it by deciding not to settle it. This is seen in the case of Macbeth's conflict between his feeling of duty to the king and his desire for the throne, when he says:

> "If chance will have me king, why, chance may crown me
> Without my stir."

This way out of the conflict is, as a rule, only a postponement, and brings only temporary relief. Eventually the problem must be settled, the individual must resort to another more decisive attempt.

5. Migration. Another way out of the conflict which is often employed is that of migration, or the leaving of one's immediate surroundings. The individual who is jilted by his sweetheart suddenly becomes athirst for far-away things, and "his soul goes out in longing to touch the skirt of the dim distance." The politician who is defeated in an election suddenly has a desire to hunt big game in South Africa or to travel in some other far-away place. The business man who fails likewise seeks a new place to start over again. This desire to find a place where one can get away from the failures of the past and the unhappiness of the present is expressed in the various attempts to find a "Land of Beginning Again." Ponce de Leon, having failed to accomplish his desires, sought the fountain of youth so that he might start over again.   Byron, being disgusted with affairs in England, spent his last days fighting for Greece and thus hoping to rebuild a land more to his heart's desire.

6. Sour grapes.   Another common way out which is often employed when our emotional longings are thwarted is the sour-grapes mechanism.   Just as the fox in the fable, who, being unable to secure the grapes which he desired, went away and consoled himself by asserting that the grapes were sour and no good anyway, so the human being also finds consolation in belittling the things for which he has sought in vain.   If a man is in love with a beautiful girl who declines his attentions, he consoles himself by saying that "beauty is only skin deep."   He creates in himself the belief that in all probability she would not know how to take care of a house, and would be an extremely expensive luxury, and that she might be very domineering and want to interfere with his most comfortable habits.   He thinks of the pleasure he gets in smoking, and picturing her telling him to give up his cigar, he consoles himself by saying:

"And a woman is only a woman, but a good cigar is a Smoke."

This same way out is used in many of the other affairs of life. If an individual loses his job he convinces himself that the loss was a blessing in disguise, that the job was ruining his health, and that a change of work will be good for his future progress.   If he attempts to make money and fails, he declares that money is the root of all evil.   This tendency to underevaluate the desirable things that one does not or cannot have, is well shown in some of the well-known traditions around the college campus.   The student who is less fortunately endowed intellectually is very prone to believe that the man who learns quickly forgets quickly, and that the very intelligent people are nervous and physically inferior; or the student who finds his memorizing ability below that of others looks upon his superior classmates as students with "parrot memories," but no brains; and the girl who is not so highly endowed with beauty often asserts that the pretty girl is a "dumb Dora."   Numerous other instances of the sour-grapes way out of an emotional conflict can be observed in everyday life.

7. Negative sour grapes. The Pollyanna type of individual finds, that no matter how bad the situation may be, one ought to be pleased because it might have been so much worse. This is the individual who is perpetually happy. He minimizes his disappointments by magnifying his enjoyment of what he has attained. Being forced to live in a two-room cottage, the individual declares that this is very desirable because the work of keeping it up is not so great. Being turned down by the girl he loves, the Pollyanna type of man stresses the advantages of bachelorhood. To again use the fox parallel, in this case the fox goes hunting for good grapes, but, finding only sour grapes, decides that the sour grapes are exactly what he wanted, and consequently he ceases to hunt for sweet ones, and tells the other foxes that sour grapes are best.

8. Logic-tight compartment. Another way out of emotional conflicts, which is represented by the Jekyll and Hyde situation, is that in which the individual builds up two opposing lines of activity, both of which are to him pleasing. His behavior is at one time guided by one drive or one set of drives, and at another by the opposing drives. He refuses to face the facts and to permit the impulses which are diametrically opposed to come into conflict. He desires to have the good opinion of his fellow men, and consequently wants to preserve the Jekyll activities, but he also desires to satisfy certain unconventional longings, and thus he finds that part of the time it is most convenient to live the life of Mr. Hyde. The question arises as to how Dr. Jekyll and Mr. Hyde get along together in the same individual. The solution lies in the fact that a mental wall is built between them, so that the impulses which govern the Jekyll activities are never permitted to come into conflict with those of Mr. Hyde. This is the usual mechanism of the proverbial hypocrite who is a swindling sinner during the week and a shouting saint on Sunday.

9. Compensation. Another way out is seen in the case of the man who, blocked in his activities in one direction, tries to make up for his thwarting by activity in another direction. The student who was poorly prepared in an examination makes up for his lack of facts by writing an unusually large volume of meaningless generalities. The clerk who is bulldozed by his boss, but who is unable to take revenge on him for fear of losing his position, finds satisfaction in domineering his own wife and children.   The major reprimands the captain, and the lieutenant receives a similar "bawling out" from the captain; but the lieutenant, not content to let it stop with him, scolds the sergeant, who then passes it on to the corporal, and the corporal to the private, who probably kicks the mule.   And thus through life we compensate by "taking it out on the under dog."

10. **A bid for sympathy.**   The individual who is thwarted in his desires frequently seeks a way out by putting forth a plea for sympathy.   The child who is refused something that he very much desires straightway refuses to eat.   Under certain conditions the individual may even go to the extent of starving himself, as seen in the case of McSwiney and other "martyrs" who sought to arouse sympathy for Ireland.   The lover, being unfortunate in his suit, proceeds to get beastly drunk, hoping in that way to make his sweetheart sorry.   Many of those who make unsuccessful attempts at suicide hope to arouse sympathy by so doing.   It is the most common escape mechanism employed by the "individual with the world ag'in' him."

11. **Projection of faults on others.**   Closely akin to the bid for sympathy is another mechanism by which the individual projects his own faults on others.   It is not surprising that this mechanism should often be employed as a method out of an emotional conflict, since it is based upon a tendency which is almost universal in human behavior.   If we interview one thousand persons involved in automobile accidents, we shall be fortunate if we find as many as ten out of the thousand who will admit that they were at fault in causing the accident.   The man who is a confirmed alcoholic says that his wife is so mean that he has to drink to keep from going crazy, or he may project the fault of his own drunkenness on his father, saying that he inherited the taste for liquor from him.   No matter how low in the gutter a man may get, he can always find some one else to blame it on.

12. **Rationalization.**   There is another type of defense mechanism employed in emotional conflicts whereby the individual calls upon his reason to justify his act to himself.   The motive assigned

for his act is always personal and subjective. When a person is driven by blind impulses into primrose fields, he tells himself that he is seeking experience and knowledge of life in order to make himself more useful to his fellow men, and to enlarge his capacity for service. He is not honest enough with himself to call it plain illegitimate curiosity. Perhaps no person is entirely guiltless of the subterfuge of rationalization. We justify not only our actions, but our opinions and points of view; our likes and dislikes; our approvals and disapprovals. If it were not for rationalization, some persons would be eternally at war with themselves. The man with a thirst for whiskey, desiring a drink, justifies taking it by saying that it is good to keep off the influenza. Our neighbor insults us. If he is larger than we are, we justify our not hitting him by saying that we are too proud to fight, or cannot stoop to his level; but if he is smaller than we, we give him a good thrashing and say that our honor demanded it. If the student is tempted to go to a dance when he knows that he should spend the evening studying, he camouflages his real motives by telling himself that he has been hard at work and deserves a rest; that, moreover, he must be careful of his health, and that a little pleasure to-day will increase his efficiency to-morrow. These excuses and explanations probably fool no one except himself, but to him they appear quite satisfactory.

13. Substituted activities. One of the most common, and, on the whole, one of the most satisfactory ways out of an emotional thwarting is by substituting some other activity for the desired or forbidden activity. The politician who is defeated after a number of years of faithful service drains off the sting of defeat by writing his autobiography. The girl whose lover proves untrue finds comfort in music; the youth whose longing for romance and adventure has been thwarted finds comfort in reading stories of adventure and in identifying himself with the knights of old.

For the normal adult one of the best ways out of an emotional conflict is work. When the individual is harassed by desires for the forbidden, one of the best ways out of the annoying situation is so to engross himself in work that he will not have time to think of the thwarting. At first this may be hard, but habit cures all things, and makes endurable what at first appears unendurable. Many of our desires are soon forgotten, and by engaging in some activity that requires all our attention, we give our memories time to forget.

II. ABNORMAL WAYS OUT OF AN EMOTIONAL CONFLICT

The ways out of emotional conflicts that have been discussed in the preceding section are usually considered normal; they may be employed by the average man on the street without his being considered abnormal or queer; in fact, all of us have resorted to some of these ways at one time or another. There is another group of ways out, however, that instantly stamp the individual who employs them as abnormal, for no one can employ them without incapacitating himself for the normal execution of his life work. These are the methods of (1) Insanity; (2) Imaginary illnesses; and (3) Suicide. Such methods are utilized when the thwarted drive is very strong and the individual is unable to make an adjustment through one of the normal emotional outlets.

1. Insanity. With an unstable individual, especially one whose nervous system has been damaged by some organic disease, the constant thwarting of any strong emotional drive may lead to insanity. The grandiose delusions of the paretic may, in part, be explained on this basis. The thing that makes a delusion possible is the organic disturbance, but the type of delusion may be due to the emotional thwarting. The thwarting of the desire for companionship is illustrated by the story of a farmer whose wife became insane. The farmer is frankly puzzled. He tells that he had to send her off to a place the state provides, and that the doctors say the case is hopeless. He then adds:

"But to this day I'm blessed if I can tell what turned her queer:
She hadn't stepped foot out o' doors for nigh on thirty year."

Avoiding emotional conflicts by insanity may take several forms, of which the following are the most important: (a) the conquering hero; (b) the suffering hero; (c) regression; (d) amnesia; and (e) negativism.

a. The conquering hero. In tracing the previous history of an insane patient of the conquering-hero type it is frequently found that throughout his life his ambitions were constantly thwarted. The discrepancy between his desires and his attainments produced in him an unpleasant state of conflict, from which he eventually attempted to escape by a "flight from reality." He consequently develops and systematizes the delusion that he is eminently successful, and imagines that he is Napoleon or some other great hero. In order to account for his being a man long since dead, he may use the theory of the transmigration of souls. One patient suffering from delusions of grandeur insisted that he was originally Adam, but had since been born seven times, being in turn Moses, Ezekiel, Alexander the Great, Jesus Christ, George Washington, Napoleon, and Robert E. Lee. Another patient in the same hospital thought that he was the President of the United States of the World. These delusions not only take the form of self-aggrandizement in the social realm, but are equally extravagant in attributing to the patient great physical strength or skill. One patient thinks that he is able to hold up the world; he says that Atlas did it, and that Atlas was one of his forefathers. Another believes that he is immensely wealthy, his wealth amounting to quadrillions; in fact, he has so much money that one thousand certified public accountants cannot begin to give an accurate estimate of how much he has. On hearing that France was in great financial straits, and unable to pay her debt to the United States, he asked how much she owed. He then calculated the interest and wrote a check to the Treasury of the United States for the whole French debt with interest. He explained by saying that France has always been a "wild child," but that she "means well" and should be helped along until she gets on her feet. Others imagine that they are great poets or musicians. During the last few years the author has examined in hospitals for the insane two Shakespeares, one Homer, and three Christs. And so throughout the whole category of the goals for which the average man strives, they gain by a simple act of the imagination that which in reality they are unable to obtain.

b. *Suffering hero.* A second type of insanity which is utilized to escape emotional conflicts is that of the suffering hero. Like the conquering hero, the individual who follows this path has failed in his ambitions, and in his flight from reality pictures himself as a great person. But he does not complete his picture of grandeur in the way that the conquering hero does. Others do not recognize him as a hero; on the contrary, the world is persecuting him; he is therefore deserving of sympathy and pity. In this method out of the unpleasant, annoying situations, the individual finds gratification, for after all he is a hero, and sympathy and pity, by making his persecution endurable, contribute not a little to his satisfaction. He cannot satisfy his desires in reality, and therefore in unreality imagines himself the hero, and the degree to which his heroism is unrecognized is due to a misunderstanding world.

The insane person of the suffering-hero type is the victim of a conspiracy: he believes that he has been robbed of a fortune; that in childhood he was kidnaped by gypsies; and that he is in reality the son of the King of England, but kept from the throne by his enemies. These delusions of persecution sometimes make such patients extremely dangerous, as they frequently try to take revenge upon those whom they believe to be persecuting them.

c. Regression. The individual, finding the present bad, refuses to live in the present, but regresses to some earlier period in his life when conditions were much more pleasant. We consequently find in many institutions for the insane adults of middle age who think that they are children of only ten or twelve years. They want the type of playthings that they had at that stage of life, and insist upon acting the part of a child. The author once had as a patient a young woman whose parents were killed in an automobile accident when she was sixteen years of age. It was necessary for her to go to work, and she had considerable difficulty in eking out a living. When she was twenty-four she fell madly in love, but in about a year her lover married another woman. A few months after his marriage, the patient began to act queer, to play with dolls, read fairy stories, and do other things characteristic of the girl of eight or nine years. On investigation it was found that she believed she was only a child of nine, and that she was once more happy in her old home surroundings. By ignoring the unpleasant realities of the present, and reverting to a happier state, she had escaped the annoying conflicts which tormented her.

d. Amnesia. Among the other types of insanity that appear as an attempt to get out of an emotional conflict may be mentioned amnesia, or the loss of memory.   Here the patient attempts to escape a state of mental turmoil by building up total forgetfulness of his entire past, sometimes even forgetting his name.   Not long ago the son of a middle-aged lady attempted suicide.   Two days after the incident the mother could not even remember the name of the hospital to which he was carried, or the name of her family physician who was treating him, although she had lived in that city all her life and had known the physician for more than ten years.

   e. *Negativism*.   Another way out is that of negativism, in which the patient refuses to recognize the existence of the unpleasant facts.   His loved one dies, and although he attends the funeral, he persists in believing that she still lives.   He loses his reputation and social position, or perhaps is sold out of house and home, but refuses to recognize the situation.

   In practically all of the ways out of an emotional conflict through insanity the individual is wholly unconscious of the falsity of the mechanisms which he is employing.   The patient does not deliberately shut his eyes to reality, nor does he deliberately with malice aforethought forget his past, or assume the pose of the suffering hero or the conquering hero.   But these methods of escape are probably hit upon in a blind trial-and-error way.

   2. **Imaginary illnesses.**   It not infrequently happens that when confronted by an annoying conflict the individual attempts to escape it by either consciously or unconsciously feigning illness. The housewife, suffering from a strong emotional thwarting and desirous of getting away from her unhappy surroundings, becomes ill, and must be sent to the mountains or the seashore for her health. The "get-rich-quick" swindler who is summoned to testify concerning certain of his transactions which are likely to land him in the chain gang, becomes seriously ill, and may even convince the doctors that it would be disastrous for him to go out of his room. In the World War thousands of cases of shell shock were reported. The soldier, torn between fear of mutilation and death if he faced the enemy, and of a bayonet in the back and the reputation of being "yellow" if he ran, developed a nervous breakdown as the way out of the situation.   The shell-shocked individual accom-

plished two results: he forgot the horrible position in which he was placed, and he was sent back behind the lines to a hospital. Many soldiers developed blindness, deafness, or paralysis as a result of shell shock, although the loudest explosives they heard may have been the armistice fireworks.

None of these individuals are deliberate malingerers. They are not deliberately feigning illness, but believe themselves really ill. Their illness, however, exists only in their minds, and can be cured only by treating the diseased habit system. But while it lasts the individual is incapacitated just as truly as if he were suffering from a cancer of the stomach instead of a "mind diseased."

3. Suicide. It frequently happens that when the conditions of life are extremely repulsive to the individual, and when none of the ways out of a conflict hitherto cited are acceptable to him, he resorts to the one sure end of all emotional worries, namely, suicide. As pointed out in Chapter I, suicide, like all other human actions, is the result of certain drives and resistances. In the case of the person resorting to suicide as a method out of emotional conflict, the unrest or torture resulting from the conflict constitutes the drive toward suicide, and all the forces tying the individual to life constitute the resistance to this way out. If the individual's dread of life under the conditions presented is greater than his fear of death, and the forces producing in him a desire to live, he commits suicide. Suicide is probably always chosen as the less of two evils, an unpleasant means of escape from a still more unpleasant situation. If an individual commits suicide it is because the resistances to life are stronger than the resistances to death.

When confronted by defeat and humiliation Brutus said:

> "Our enemies have beat us to the pit:
> It is more worthy to leap in ourselves,
> Than tarry till they push us in.
>
> .   .   .   .
>
> So fare you well at once; for Brutus' tongue
> Hath almost ended his life's history.
>
> .   .   .   .
>
> Cæsar, now be still.
> I killed thee not with half so good a will."

We seldom pick up a paper but we read that some one has chosen this way out of a painful situation. The business man, with certain failure staring him in the face, welcomes death as the one sure means to escape his creditors. The lover who has loved "not wisely but too well" looks forward to death as the one certain way of bringing balm to his hurt mind. The student, despondent over having failed, sighs for the eternal sleep where there is neither giving nor taking of examinations. And thus through the whole category of thwarted desires do we find individuals seeking suicide as the one panacea for all the "heartaches and the thousand natural shocks that flesh is heir to."

Individual differences in ability to tolerate thwarting. Individuals differ as widely in their ability to stand up under emotional conflicts as they do in their ability to withstand physical ills. Some persons can withstand the harassing annoyance of almost any emotional worry, and seem little affected thereby, while others are thrown out of balance by the slightest emotional conflict. Between these two extremes are the bulk of our population, representing every intermediate degree, but tending to cluster around the middle of the group. Those at the unstable end of the curve make up a large part of the hospital population of psychotics and neurotics. Those in the center and the upper end of the curve, possessing a more stable emotional make-up, manage to adjust to the situation, or to make their escape from an emotional conflict by some of the normal ways out.

CHAPTER XII

PERSONALITY AND ITS MEASUREMENT

Whatever exists at all exists in some amount, and anything that exists in amount can be measured.

THORNDIKE [1]

WE may not be able to measure a trait to-day, but if it exists, it will some day be measured. There was a time in the history of the race when our forefathers were pleased to be able to measure things in pounds, for it was so much more accurate than guessing. They were even more pleased at the results when they were able to measure in ounces. Measurement in the physical world has now been reduced to a definite science. It is no longer a matter of opinion as to the strength of a steel beam; construction engineers can very accurately measure the amount of stress and strain that it can withstand. It is reasonable to expect that the human engineer will eventually make similar progress in methods of measuring the materials with which he deals, and that although he is not yet even to the pound stage in the measurement of many human traits he will, in the future, be able to measure them with a high degree of accuracy.

One of the most important groups of traits which the human engineer has to measure is the group constituting personality. The value of measuring these traits is apparent when we consider their significance. Personality traits determine an individual's interests in life; his ability to live socially with his fellow beings; his success in school and his attainment in his chosen profession. The accurate measurement of these traits is invaluable to the teacher, the business manager, or the employer in industry.

Personality consists of the individual's native traits, modified or accentuated by his training and environment. His personality is the result of what he is born with and what he has lived through. The components of personality which are relatively fixed at birth

---

[1] Thorndike, E. L.: *Seventeenth Yearbook*, National Society for the Study of Education, Part II, 16 (Public School Publishing Company, Bloomington.)

include such traits as comprehension, judgment, ability to see relationships, ability to learn, and other traits which are generally classified as intelligence. In this same group should be included certain emotional and physical traits which depend primarily on the original make-up with which the individual started life. Other traits, especially those constituting temperamental qualities, are more largely the result of the influence of training on original nature. While other more general traits of personality, including attitudes of conventionality and ethical ideals are almost entirely built up by training and environment. Inasmuch as one's personality depends so largely on his physical condition and past experiences, and since these are constantly changing, we should think of personality as a dynamic rather than a static thing. We shall now consider some of the traits that make up personality and the methods that have been used to measure some of these traits.

I. INTELLIGENCE

According to Thorndike, there are three types of intelligence: (1) Abstract intelligence, or ability to deal with ideas; (2) Social intelligence, or ability to deal with people; and (3) Mechanical intelligence, or ability to deal with mechanical contrivances. These types are not distinct, nor mutually exclusive. A person may be high in all three or low in all three, or high in one and low in the others, just as he may be tall and fat, short and fat, tall and thin, or short and thin.

1. Abstract intelligence. Methods of measuring abstract intelligence were the first to be developed in the field of objective measurement of mental traits. The pioneer work in this field was done by Alfred Binet, a French psychologist who developed the first intelligence test. He had noticed that by a certain age normal children have sufficient knowledge and ability to handle successfully intellectual problems of a specific difficulty. By the age of three, for example, the average child can point to his nose, eyes, mouth and hair, and can give his last name. By the age of six he can distinguish right from left, and count thirteen pennies. By the age of nine he can give the date (including day of week, month, day of month, and year), and can tell how much change he would receive if he gave the merchant twenty-five cents after having purchased four cents' worth of goods. By twelve he can define such abstract words as *pity*, *revenge*, and *envy*, and can point out the lessons taught by fables. The superior adult can repeat, after hearing them once, such a series of numbers as 8-3-7-9-5-4-8-2, and has a vocabulary of 13,500 words. Binet devised other problems of equal difficulty for each of these years and also a group of problems of the proper difficulty for each of the other years. In that way he was able to measure the child's intelligence in terms of the difficulty of the mental tasks which he was able to accomplish. Inasmuch as these tasks were evaluated in terms of age level, the child's intelligence rating was expressed in terms of mental age. If the child could answer the questions and perform the tasks that the average nine-year-old child was able to do, but could not do those of the ten-year level, he was considered to have a mental age of nine years. A six-year-old child who can do mental tasks of the nine-year difficulty is considerably accelerated mentally, but a child who is twelve years old, and can only do the nine-year tasks, is three years retarded mentally.

In order to indicate the degree of acceleration or retardation, Terman devised the *intelligence quotient* as a method of indicating the individual's intelligence quality. This quotient expresses the relation between the mental age and the chronological age, and is secured by dividing the mental age by the chronological age. The original Binet tests have been considerably revised and improved by Terman and his colleagues, and in fact, the Terman revision is the form of the Binet tests most widely used in this country.

The type of test developed by Binet must be administered individually to every person tested. It has the double disadvantage of consuming a large amount of the examiner's time and of being rather difficult to administer. These disadvantages were instrumental in leading to the development of group methods of measuring intelligence, although in special cases the individual tests yield more satisfactory results, and are still widely used in spite of these disadvantages.

The army intelligence tests, developed under the direction of the Psychological Staff of the Surgeon-General's Office and the National Research Council, and used in testing army recruits, will serve as an example of objective group intelligence tests. At a time when it was essential to find some method of classifying in a short time large numbers of men for assignments in the army and in the training schools, it was necessary that a test suitable for examining large groups at one time should be developed to replace individual testing methods. The Army Alpha Test requires only about fifty minutes to administer, and can be given to two or three hundred people at the same time. It consists of eight parts which test: (1) ability to follow directions; (2) arithmetical reasoning; (3) practical judgment; (4) knowledge of the meaning of words; (5) ability to see the meanings of disarranged sentences; (6) ability to complete numerical progressions; (7) ability to see relationships; and (8) general information.

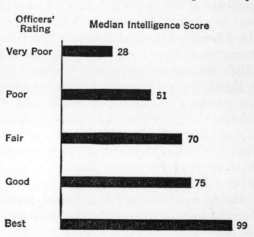

FIGURE 22. RELATION BETWEEN INTELLIGENCE SCORES AND OFFICERS' RATINGS

By the end of the World War this test had been given to over a million and a half men. On the basis of the examinations over seven thousand had been recommended for discharge, more than ten thousand for labor battalions, or other service organization, and over nine thousand for further observation. A comparison of Army Alpha scores and officers' ratings of the intelligence of over nine hundred men in the army showed a close relationship, as indicated in Figure 22.

Figure 23 shows the distribution of intelligence ratings in typical army groups showing the value of the tests in the identification of officer material. Intelligence scores found in various occupations indicated the value of this test for use in selecting men for occupational assignment. Intelligence levels of occupations were established from the lowest ones of laborer, miner, teamster, or barber, to the higher levels of civil engineer, medical officer, or engineer officer.

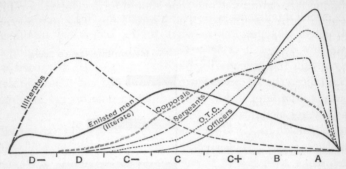

FIGURE 23. DISTRIBUTION OF INTELLIGENCE RATINGS IN TYPICAL ARMY GROUPS

A number of tests similar to Army Alpha have been developed since the war. Many of these are being used by industrial organizations and educational institutions to aid in a better understanding of their personnel. In connection with the testing of college personnel, the tests devised by Thorndike and other psychologists are widely used and seem to be giving very satisfactory results. In the chapter on education these tests will receive further consideration.

2. Social intelligence. Having seen the value of measuring abstract intelligence, administrators both in school and industry are now becoming interested in measuring social intelligence. In the college it often happens that a student may have a high abstract intelligence and make a wonderful college record so far as grades are concerned, but be utterly lacking in social intelligence, or ability to get along with people. Yet when it comes to succeeding or failing in the world, ability to understand people is much more important than ability to understand books. In industry, the administrator is realizing that for certain of his employees social intelligence is a more important quality than is abstract intelligence.

A careful study of the qualities of the so-called successful man will reveal, in nine cases out of ten, that his success depends, not on his deep and profound knowledge which puzzles the brains of the average man, but on the simple and more commonplace qualities which please the understanding of the common folk, and arouse in their hearts a feeling of sympathy. For all practical purposes of life, social intelligence wins over abstract intelligence, ten to one. Abstract intelligence knows what to do, but social intelligence knows how to get it done. Those with high social intelligence rarely attain the best grades, but they are usually rewarded with all the offices that it is within the power of their fellow students to bestow, and later in life their former instructors are astounded that they get along so fast.

In no trait do people differ more than in their ability to get along with others. And, as just pointed out, social intelligence or ability to get along with others is one of the most important elements making for success. Recognizing the importance of social intelligence, the administrators of a number of colleges and universities are giving a social intelligence test to all their entering students in order to assist them more intelligently in selecting courses and in planning a career in keeping with their natural aptitudes. The first series of tests designed to measure social intelligence were devised by members of the department of Psychology at George Washington University and given to all students who entered that university in 1925. Since then this test has been used in various other universities and industrial concerns. The test consists of six parts, measuring six different factors of social intelligence.

Part I is a test of judgment in social situations, consisting of a number of situations in which judgment and an appreciation of human motives are required. Four solutions are suggested for each situation and the person taking the test is instructed to check the one which in his opinion most satisfactorily meets the situation. The following is a sample:

You have an employee who is very efficient, but he is continually complaining about the work he has to do. You have noticed that his complaints have a bad effect on the other employees. It would be best to:

_____ Request the other employees to try to overlook his faults.
_____ Find out why he has that attitude and try to make an adjustment.
_____ Change him to some other department where he will have a different boss.
_____ Let him do most of the planning for his work.[1]

Part II measures the ability to recognize faces and to associate the correct names with them. This ability is tested by giving the person taking the test a sheet showing twelve faces and the names that go with them, which he is to study for four minutes, at the end of which time he must recognize these twelve faces when he sees them again in a group of twenty-five and must also recall the accompanying names.

Part III tests the ability to appreciate correctly the mental state back of certain facial expressions. This is a valuable factor in getting along with people, for to know the true thoughts of others one must depend more on the eye than on the ear. The frontispiece is an exact reproduction of Test III.

Part IV measures the accuracy with which the individual has observed the behavior and understood the motives of those around him. This is done by presenting him with thirty generalizations on human behavior, some of which are correct while others are incorrect. The individual taking the test indicates whether, in his judgment, the generalization is true or false by encircling the T or the F in front of each generalization. The following are samples:

T   F   All men are created equal in mental ability.
T   F   We generally like those who bring good news.
T   F   A sure way to keep on friendly terms with two people who are enemies is to attempt to reconcile them.[2]

Part V is devised to measure the extent of a person's social information, the assumption being that the more things with which a person is acquainted and in which he is interested, the more able he will be to appreciate the interests of others and meet them on a common ground. This test consists of fifty statements requiring knowledge of sports, automobiles, theaters, politics, current magazines, science, literature, organizations, travel, art, music, me-

[1] *Social Intelligence Test.* (Center for Psychological Service, Washington, D.C., 1927.)
[2] *Ibid.*

chanics, etiquette and everyday information. The person who is being tested indicates whether a statement is true or false.

Part VI measures the ability to recognize the mental state of the speaker, or the motives back of the spoken word. The person taking the test is given twenty-seven quotations and a list of mental states such as ambition, despair, determination, disgust, fear, hate, jealousy, love, regret, scorn, and suspicion, and is directed to match the quotations with the mental state which prompted the words. The following are examples:

(   ) He has a very ancient and fish-like smell.
(   ) Nay, then, my last hope is gone, I can fight no longer.
(   ) There is something in the way he deals that makes me want to cut the cards.[1]

The norms on the George Washington University Social Intelligence Test will indicate how various industrial and college groups compare.

NORMS ON SOCIAL INTELLIGENCE TEST

SCHOOL GROUPS

GROUP	NUMBER OF CASES	MEDIAN SCORE	Q_1	Q_3	Q
High-school students............	984	81	59	93	17.0
College freshmen................	4840	101	87	113	13.0
Upper-class college..............	1217	111	98	123	12.5
College graduates...............	100	113	99	123	12.0

INDUSTRIAL GROUPS

GROUP	NUMBER OF CASES	MEDIAN SCORE	Q_1	Q_3	Q
Administrative and executive employees......................	100	117	105	126	10.5
Teachers.......................	250	112	99	119	10.0
High-grade secretarial employees..	50	111	94	119	12.5
Salesmen.......................	25	107	89	118	14.5
Engineering employees — draftsmen, electricians, etc..........	45	105	91	119	14.0
Clerical and stenographic employees......................	200	95	81	108	13.5
Lower-grade office workers.......	300	84	74	96	11.0
Nurses........................	75	78	66	90	12.0
Policemen......................	110	74	58	88	15.0
Sales clerks in department store...	35	73	55	97	21.0
Lower-grade industrial workers...	150	65	43	83	20.0

[1] *Social Intelligence Test.* (Center for Psychological Service, Washington, D.C., 1927.)

3. Mechanical intelligence.   Several tests have been devised in the last few years to measure mechanical intelligence.   While a positive relation exists between scores on abstract and social intelligence and scores on mechanical aptitude tests, the scores on the mechanical tests give an additional index of interest and aptitude for mechanical work.

Much diversity of opinion exists regarding mechanical aptitude. Some erroneously hold that those who are high in abstract intelligence are therefore not mechanical, and that others who are not intelligent are therefore mechanically inclined.   That such is not the case is indicated by the fact that positive correlations are found in all groups between the scores on abstract intelligence tests and those on a mechanical test.   The correlations between mechanical, social and abstract intelligence are always positive, but are usually low.

Normal boys come in contact with various mechanical tools and

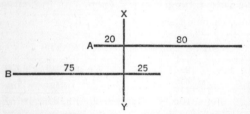

mechanical processes. Those with mechanical aptitude pick up an acquaintance with tools and their uses and with mechanical processes more than do those who are not so inclined. It is to measure this difference that the mechanical aptitude tests have been constructed.   Three of the best-known mechanical tests are those devised by Stenquist, O'Rourke, and McQuarrie.   The test developed by O'Rourke will serve to illustrate the nature of work in this field.

FIGURE 24. THE RELATION BETWEEN SCORES ON A MECHANICAL TEST AND SUCCESS IN TRAINING COURSES IN INDUSTRY

Part I of the test contains pictures of tools, materials, and instruments with which any observing boy with mechanical interest and aptitude might be expected to be familiar.   In taking the test, the boy is required to indicate the tools which are used together or which may be used to accomplish some specific purpose.   Each set of questions is more difficult than the preceding set.

Part II of the test contains questions dealing with mechanical operations. The questions range in difficulty, the first being so simple that any boy who uses a hammer or a screwdriver could answer them, the last demanding considerable insight into mechanical things.

The best indication of the extent to which the tests measure these abilities is found in comparison of test scores with success in training courses and in industrial apprenticeship. Figure 24 is based on mechanist apprentices in industry. The cases represented at the right of line x–y were rated above average in efficiency. Those represented at the left of the line were rated below average. Line A represents the apprentices who made above 240 points on the test. Eighty per cent of this group were rated above average in efficiency and twenty per cent were rated below average. Line B represents those who made 240 points or below on the test. Twenty-five per cent of this group were rated above average in efficiency and seventy-five per cent were rated below average. Note that "below average" does not necessarily indicate inefficiency. It indicates aptitude below the average of the group.

II. THE MORE GENERAL PERSONALITY TRAITS

There are a number of less definite personality traits which are now being studied by psychologists. Very hopeful progress has recently been made in the measurement of these traits, and in all probability within the next few years much more satisfactory tests will be available. We shall briefly consider several of these recent studies, including the investigation of: (1) Introversion-extroversion; (2) Radicalism and conservatism; (3) Character traits —dishonesty, deception; (4) Philosophy of life; and (5) Will-temperament.

1. **Introversion-extroversion.** According to Jung, human beings can be separated roughly into two classes, introverts and extroverts. The introverts are characterized by the "shut-in" personality; they are largely self-sufficient for their emotional outlet. They "sit alone with their thoughts," sharing neither their joys nor sorrows with others. The extroverts, on the contrary, must depend on others for their happiness, consequently they seek society as much as the introverts avoid it. Roosevelt is usually thought of as an

extrovert, while Wilson is classed as an introvert.   They are not perfect examples of these types, for Roosevelt had some of the introvert qualities and Wilson possibly a few extrovert qualities, but on the whole their divergent administrative policies bear out this classification.

Laird [1] has devised an excellent scale for the measurement of introversion-extroversion, and as a result of several years study with this measuring device he has prepared the following list of qualities which, he finds, reveal the introvert or extrovert personality.

How to tell an introvert or extrovert: Personality signs revealed in actions:
1. The introvert blushes easily; the extrovert rarely blushes.
2. The extrovert laughs more readily than the introvert.
3. The introvert is usually outspoken; the extrovert is usually careful not to hurt the feelings of others.
4. The extrovert is a fluent talker; the introvert can prepare a report in writing easier than he can tell it in conversation.
5. The extrovert loans money and possessions more readily than the introvert.
6. The extrovert moves faster than the introvert in the routine actions of the day, such as walking, dressing, talking, etc.
7. The extrovert does not take particular care of his personal property, such as watches, clothes, etc.; the introvert is found continually oiling, polishing and tinkering.
8. Introverts are usually reluctant about making friends with the opposite sex, while extroverts are attracted to them.
9. Introverts are easily embarrassed by having to be in front of a crowd.
10. The extrovert is a more natural public speaker.
11. The introvert likes to argue.
12. The introvert is slow about making friends.
13. The introvert rewrites his letters, inserts interlineations, adds a postscript, and corrects every mistake of the typist.
Personality signs revealed in thinking and attitudes are:
1. The introvert worries; the extrovert has scarcely a care in the world.
2. The feelings of the introvert are easily hurt; the extrovert is not bothered by what is said about him.
3. The introvert deliberates in great detail about everything — what to wear, where to eat, etc., and usually tells one why he decided to do what he did.

[1] Laird, Donald A.: "How Personalities are Found in Industry," *Industrial Psychology*, October, 1926.

4. The introvert rebels when ordered to do a thing; the extrovert accepts them as a matter of course.

5. The introvert is urged to his best efforts by praise; the extrovert is not affected by praise.

6. The introvert is suspicious of the motives of others.

7. The introvert is usually radical in religion and politics; the extrovert — if he entertains any opinions — is usually conservative.

8. The introvert would rather struggle alone to solve a problem than ask for help.

9. The introvert would rather work alone in a room than with others.

10. Extroverts follow athletics; introverts, books and "high-brow" magazines.

11. The introvert is a poor loser.

12. The introvert daydreams a great deal.

13. The introvert prefers fine, delicate work (die-making, accounting), while the extrovert prefers work in which details do not bother.

14. The introvert is inclined to be moody at times.

15. The introvert is very conscientious.

Laird's test for extroversion-introversion is presented on pages 220 to 224.

After giving the test to several thousand individuals both in industry and college, Laird found:

1. Women tend to be more introverted than men.

2. There is no constant racial difference on these traits.

3. Youth is in general extrovert, old age introvert.

4. There is very little relation between intelligence and introversion or extroversion.

5. Introverts get along best with introverts; extroverts best with extroverts.

In industry he found:

6. Foremen and executives whose duties demand the control of others are distinctly extrovert.

7. Office workers, clerks, stenographers, etc., are inclined toward introversion.

8. Bench mechanics show no distinct groupings, being more ambivert.

9. Inspectors, accountants, and research engineers are in general introvert.

Laird's findings support the statement in Chapter V that distinct types do not exist, but that individuals tend to group themselves into a normal distribution curve when measured on any one trait. Introverts may have some extrovert traits, and *vice versa*. The

Make a check mark any place along each dashed line to describe your subject. Consider only how the subject has been the last few months. Read each line through carefully before making a check mark.

1. How steadily has he worked at his job during the day?	continuously until completed	occasional lapse of work	intermittent spurts and lapses	frequent tendency to talk, rest, etc.	stopped with the least excuse
2. How has he considered possible misfortunes?	worried a great deal	sometimes mentioned worries	seemed to suppress worries	rather care-free	not a worry in the world
3. How have his feelings been affected by remarks or actions concerning him?	very easily angered	often aroused	sometimes disturbed	affected in rare instances	unaffected
4. How has he considered the feelings of others?	told truth regardless of feeling	generally outspoken	considerate at times	frank, yet tactful	careful not to hurt others
5. How has he been as a social mixer?	always in the lead	mixes readily	friendly with some	usually retiring	shy and backward
6. How has he been at remembering things to be done?	continually forgetting	occasionally forgetful	forgot minor ones	usually remembered	rarely forgot
7. How has he been in social conversation?	talkative	an easy talker	tended to listen	only answered questions	refrained from talking

Read each line thoroughly before making a check mark. Remember only the past few months are to be considered.

8. Has he usually sought or given reasons for his actions and decisions?	usually went out of way to explain	gave reasons in most cases	explained some significant ones	seldom gave reason	acted impulsively

9. How has he been about making loans?	gave to anyone who asked	rarely hesitates to loan		loaned on rare occasions	never loaned
10. How has he taken to discipline and commands?	obeys unquestioningly	usually obeys willingly	obeys with deliberation	sulked, but obeyed	ignores when possible
11. How has he responded to praise?	did not work so well	worked same as usual	sometimes worked better	usually improved in work	generally worked better
12. How would you describe his actions in general?	generally slow and deliberate	seldom in a hurry	wastes no time	usually rapid	impulsive or quick

Make a check mark any place along each dashed line to describe your subject. Consider only how the subject has been during the last few months. Read each line through carefully before making a check mark.

13. Does he seem to be suspicious of others?	very suspicious	inclined to question actions	tried to unmask important motives	takes interest in others' actions	unconcerned with others
14. How has he talked when with others?	replied only when spoken to	appeared to think more than talk	talked when interested	fluent talker	talked a great deal
15. What is his reaction to questions of politics, religion, social change, etc?	urges some radical changes	thinks many changes needed	has little to say on subject	advocates conservative ideas	very conservative
16. Is he generally inclined to work things out alone?	always works unaided	very rarely asks for aid	sometimes sought assistance	did not hesitate to ask for aid	got aid very often
17. How has he been about dress and personal appearance?	does not seem to care about fashion	appears to dress for comfort	is neat dresser	close attention to dress	dress in extreme style

18.	What care has he taken of tools, personal belongings, etc?	very careful to have them repaired	watches only best ones	gives little time to their care	neglectful at times	very neglectful generally
19.	How have his likes in athletics and intellectual things compared?	likes athletics best	mostly athletic	gives mutual attention to both	mostly reads books in spare time	likes intellectual topics
20.	How has failure affected his actions?	always gloomy and sad	often gloomy	sometimes dull and gloomy	seldom gloomy or sad	not affected at all
21.	How has he been about telling his worries and troubles?	seems to tell all his troubles	often tells worries	once in a while he talks of trouble	seldom speaks of worries	uncommunicative
22.	How has he made friends with the opposite sex?	avoids them	seems uncomfortable with them	does not seek them	happy when with them	always seeks their company
23.	How has he acted in dangerous and embarrassing situations?	cool and self-possessed	uses head to advantage	seems to labor for coolness	nervous and uncertain	loses head completely

Make a check mark any place along each dashed line to describe your subject. Consider only how the subject has been the last few months. Read each line through carefully before making a check mark.

24.	How has he acted when physical courage was needed?	reckless and impulsive	calm but strong	nervous yet unflinching	tried to avoid if possible	shuns all danger
25.	How has he responded to the sufferings of others?	readily moved to tears	sympathetic and kindly	seems blue when others suffer	sad only when near friends are in pain	unmoved by others suffering
26.	How has he acted in front of a crowd of strangers?	awkward and embarrassed	slightly nervous	worked on unperturbed	neglected them most of the time	seemed to ignore them

	seeks opportunity to speak	speaks whenever possible	nervous and hesitant	cannot express self in public	avoids it
27. Has he found it easy to speak in public?					

Read each line through before making a check mark. Remember only the past few months are to be considered.

28. How has he been when mental courage was needed?	cool, calm, and steady	reliable	uncertain yet determined to do his share	nervous and unreliable	breaks down completely
29. How has he been at selling things?	very poor salesman	dislikes selling	sells when necessary	sells when given the opportunity	always selling things
30. What sort of work has he been best at?	coarse, rough work	avoided tedious work		painstaking	exact and delicate
31. How has he been about arguing?	looks for chance	defends own opinions	argues when forced to	dropped argument quickly	avoided all arguments
32. How has he compared with his chosen associates intellectually?	much superior	a little above	about equal	a little below	much inferior
33. How has he been about making friends?	very cautious	must know a long time	somewhat careful in their choice	makes them readily	makes friends with every one

Make a check mark any place along each dashed line to describe your subject. Consider only how the subject has been during the last few months. Read each line through carefully before making a check mark.

34. How does he compare physically with his chosen associates?	much superior	a little better	about equal	a little below average	much inferior

35. How have his moods changed without apparent cause?	often from gloomy to hilarious	somewhat change-able		kept in fairly uniform spirits	moods always the same
36. How have his moods changed with cause.	responded quickly	susceptible to change	must be adequate reason	seldom changes	nothing changes him
37. How high a value does he place upon his own abilities?	underestimates self	very modest value	confident in self	great confidence in own ability	quite conceited
38. How has he been about blushing?	readily, at slight cause	blushed readily	once in a while	on rare occasions	never blushes

Read each line through before making a check mark.   Remember only the past few months are to be considered.

39. Has he expressed himself better in speaking or in writing?	best in writing	preferred writing	in both equally	preferred speaking	best in talk
40. What has he done when things went wrong?	bewails troubles	worries over them (moody)	tries to rectify them	gives them only momentary thought	does not bother him
41. How has he been about sharing things with others?	very rarely does	has, but reluctantly	to friends only	rarely hesitates	does on every occasion

Reprinted by special permission of Donald A. Laird, Colgate University Psychological Laboratory.

most nearly distinct types of introversion or extroversion are found in mental disorders; those suffering from dementia præcox are extreme examples of introverts, while the manics are equally extreme examples of extroverts. If we had distinct types we might expect to find such a distribution as shown at the bottom in Figure 25. In actuality we find a bell-shaped normal distribution.

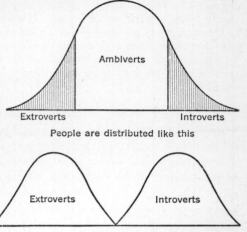

People are distributed like this

Not like this

FIGURE 25. THE DISTRIBUTION OF EXTROVERTS AND INTROVERTS

2. Radicalism and conservatism. Throughout the history of man, two conflicting classes in each age have determined the customs and institutions of that particular period. The first group fights under the banner of conservatism in support of the existing order, and tries to check any deviations from the things that are. The second group, composed of radicals, is continually attempting to break away from the old, well-tried ways of the fathers and to penetrate new and unexplored fields. The conservative defends the institutions and traditions of the past against the radical's challenge of the future.

It is a matter of common observation that some people are apparently born with a predisposition to radicalism, while others are equally predisposed to fight for the status quo. Just how the radical differs from the conservative has never been very well defined. An investigation along this line was carried out by Moore at Dartmouth, who picked out an equal number of the most radical and the most conservative students from a large group of students, on the basis of their answers to a questionnaire. Both groups were subjected to a series of psychological tests, and the following conclusions were obtained:

1. The radicals and conservatives are practically equal in general intelligence.

2. The radicals are more resistant to majority influences as shown by judgments on moral tests.

3. The radicals break habits more easily, as shown by their skill in making a tracing from a mirror (in which they had to make the movements just opposite to their regular ones). In this respect eighty-one per cent of the radicals made fewer errors than did the average conservative.

4. The radicals are about eighteen per cent quicker in their speed of reaction. They are also quicker in making their decisions on judgment tests, seventy-one per cent of the radicals being faster than the average conservative.

3. Character traits — dishonesty, deception, etc:

By taking a number of typical lifelike situations, May and Hartshorne[1] have constructed a measuring device for indicating such character traits as honesty and trustworthiness or dishonesty and deception. Their tests are based on the assumption that a person's tendency to honest or dishonest behavior is indicated by his reactions to certain realistic situations, provided these situations can be presented without arousing his suspicions. The test results seem to bear out the correctness of this assumption.

Their tests include typical situations which occur in the lives of children, giving them the opportunity to cheat, steal, lie, or otherwise deceive. For example, pupils are given a regular classroom examination on three days. On the third day the pupils are given an answer sheet and permitted to score their own papers. They have no reason to suspect that the previous examinations have been so studied that, knowing their honest achievements on the first two, the honest score obtainable on the third can be closely predicted. A marked increase in the score indicates dishonesty. Other tests provide the person tested with opportunity of keeping, without apparent means of being detected, money given him for certain purposes. Other situations provide opportunities to cheat in athletic events.

4. Philosophy of life.

Myerson[2] has penetrated another of the

---

[1] May, M. A., and Hartshorne, H.: *Studies in Deceit.* (The Macmillan Company, 1928.)

[2] Myerson, Abraham: *The Foundation of Personality.* (Little Brown & Co., Boston, 1921.)

more elusive fields of personality. His exploring instrument is a
test consisting of incomplete stories with four possible completions,
one of which reflects the conventional point of view, one the pessimistic, one cynical, and one naturalistic. The completions chosen
are said to indicate the attitude or philosophy of life of the person
taking the test. One story runs as follows:

	Will miss a lot of fun
1. The man who lives a pure life	Will gain the respect of all
2.	Treads a difficult path
	Will be cheated by rogues
	He will regret untasted pleasures
3. As he reaches old age	He will be serene and wise
4.	He will still meet with temptation
	His children will want bread
	His memory will be honored
5. After he is gone	His struggles will be ended
6.	He will be a long time dead
	He will fill a pauper's grave

5. Will-temperament. An investigation of another field of
personality is discussed by June Downey [1] in her book *The Will-
Temperament and Its Testing*. She developed a series of tests designed to show the following characteristics of the examinee: speed
of movement, freedom from load, flexibility, speed of decision,
motor impulsion, reaction to contradiction, resistance, finality of
judgment, motor inhibition, interest in detail, coördination of impulses, and volitional perseveration. All but three of the tests represent writing reactions. While these tests have not measured up to
expectations in dealing with normal individuals, they have been
found to be more helpful in dealing with abnormal cases.

III. PSEUDO-SCIENTIFIC METHODS OF MEASURING
PERSONALITY TRAITS

From the dawn of history people have tried in various ways to
read character and to predict the future behavior of others. Even

---

[1] Downey, J. E.: *The Will-Temperament and Its Testing* (World Book Company,
New York, 1923), 62–63.

to-day astrologers read futures and fortunes in the stars; phrenologists feel the bumps on a person's head and tell his character; and palmists, examining the shape of the hand and the lines in the palm, claim to reveal the character in minute detail. Graphologists study a specimen of handwriting and claim to know the strong and weak points of the writer, and even his pet foibles. Character analysts examine a lock of the hair and the photograph and are supposed to determine for what occupation the individual is best suited. And it is an almost universal requirement that an applicant for a position submit an application in his own handwriting, and a photograph of himself. Even those who scoff at the palmist, astrologist, or phrenologist generally believe that *some* insight into mental characteristics may be gained from the facial contour and expression, or the neatness and style of handwriting.

In recent years many people have concluded that although palmistry may be an interesting parlor game, as a scientific method of determining character it is about as reliable as black magic or hoodoos. And phrenologists have also lost prestige, for it is now definitely known that only the motor and part of the sensory areas in the brain have been discovered, and that bumps on the skull indicate the quality of the brain beneath about as well as the hood of an automobile indicates the condition of the motor. One can predict as successfully whether a motor is good, bad, or absent by examining the hood as he can tell whether the individual is a genius, lunatic, or imbecile by examining his skull.

1. Photographs. A number of studies of the value of photographs in estimating personality traits, notably intelligence, have been made. Laird and Remmers [1] had the photographs of ten college students, five men and five women, arranged in the order of intelligence by nearly four hundred people. An objective measure of the intelligence of the ten whose photographs were used was obtained from the Thorndike Test for High-School Graduates. Laird concluded that the individuals attempting to arrange the pictures of the ten persons according to intelligence could have

[1] Laird, Donald A., and Remmers, Herman: "A Study of Estimates of Intelligence from Photographs," *Journal of Experimental Psychology*, VII, no. 6. (December, 1924.)

done as well with their eyes closed as with them open.   He also found that the age, sex, intelligence and education of the judge had no effect on the accuracy of the estimates of intelligence.

2. **Handwriting.**   Handwriting experts and graphologists claim to determine whether an individual is optimistic or pessimistic, intelligent or stupid, neat or untidy, by examining a specimen of his

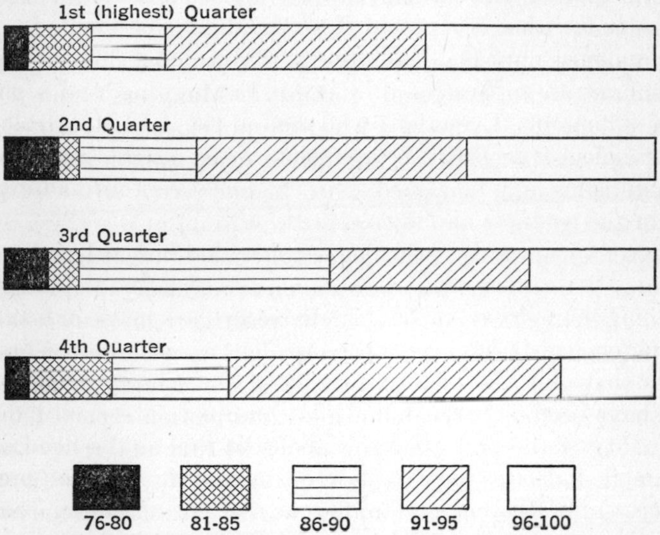

FIGURE 26.   CHART SHOWING THE SPELLING SCORES OF ONE HUNDRED AND FIFTY STUDENTS DIVIDED INTO FOUR GROUPS

The first group consists of the twenty-five per cent making the highest Army scores, Alpha the second group of the twenty-five per cent making the next highest scores, and so on.   (After Omwake.)

handwriting.   In order to discover to what extent people can estimate intelligence from handwriting the following experiment was made by Omwake: [1] Samples of the handwriting of one hundred college students were rated by twenty judges.   Each judge divided the specimens of handwriting into seven groups on the basis of his estimates of the intelligence of the writers.   The Army Alpha Intelligence Test had been given to these students, and their

[1] Omwake, Katharine T.: "The Value of Photographs and Handwriting in Estimating Intelligence," *Public Personnel Studies*, January, 1925.

scores on this test served as the criterion against which to check the estimates of intelligence. From the data obtained it was concluded that a specimen of handwriting is of no value whatever in estimating intelligence, and that there is practically no relation between intelligence and either neatness or quality of handwriting. Several professional graphologists were no more successful in determining intelligence from handwriting than were the amateur judges.

3. **Spelling.** Spelling, too, has been considered almost a fine art, an indication of culture and of ability. Many employers who require merely the writing of a letter of application hold a misspelled word against the applicant, and nearly every one finds his estimate of a friend's ability lowered when he receives a letter from that friend containing several misspelled words. But is spelling really a reliable indication of intelligence? Several investigations have been made to answer this question, and practically all investigators agree that, while there is a slight positive relationship between spelling and intelligence, the correlation is so low as to indicate that spelling ability is useless as an indication of one's judgment and reasoning ability. The following investigation reported by Omwake [1] will illustrate. One hundred and fifty university students who had previously taken the Army Alpha Intelligence Test were given a spelling test of one hundred words. The correlation between intelligence scores and spelling scores was only .173. This is only a little better than a chance relationship. These data are presented graphically in Figure 26. It is interesting to note that all grades of spelling ability are represented in each quarter of the intelligence scores, from the lowest to the highest, and that actually more of the poorest group of spellers made intelligence scores above than below the average for the group as a whole. From such investigations it would appear extremely unsafe to judge a person's intelligence from his ability to spell.

[1] Omwake, Katharine T.: "The Relation of Abstract Intelligence to Ability to Spell," *Public Personnel Studies*, July, 1925.

PART III

THE APPLICATIONS OF PSYCHOLOGY IN PROFESSIONAL AND INDUSTRIAL FIELDS

The man and his capacity for a given job can be analyzed and measured.

DASHIELL

CHAPTER XIII

PSYCHOLOGY AND GENERAL MEDICINE

It is quite as important to know what kind of patient the disease has
as what kind of disease the patient has.

NOWHERE are we confronted more definitely with the problem of
the mind-body relationship than in the applications of psychology
to medicine. As set forth in the preceding chapters, the results of
careful investigations indicate that mind and body are not two
separate entities that play tricks on each other, but that in the
last analysis they are only two aspects of the same thing. The
mind is merely the result or accompaniment of the functioning of
the body as a whole, and particularly of the functioning of the
neurones and glandular apparatus. The mental processes have
just as materialistic a basis as do the digestive processes. And
just as in case of the improper functioning of our digestive system
the smooth functioning of our mental apparatus is considerably
interfered with, even so in case of marked worry or depression the
functioning of our digestive apparatus is likewise disturbed. When
something goes wrong in any part of the body, some effect, however
slight, is produced in the nervous system and consequently in the
mind of the individual. Conversely, definite physical changes in
the different bodily organs can be produced by a stimulus that is
psychical in origin by means of a process technically known as the
"conditioned reflex." Just as the hearing of a bell may cause the
secretion of various bodily fluids that aid in the digestive processes,
it is conceivable that as the result of mental stimuli various bodily
changes may occur that aid in restoring health. In other words,
there is a constant interaction and interdependence of the various
body cells. When the nerve cells are disturbed other cells share in
the disturbance, and when other types of cells are irregular in their
function the neurones are also affected.

The following quotation from Dr. C. Macfie Campbell [1] further
emphasizes the mind-body relationship.

[1] Campbell, C. M.: "The Minimum of Medical Insight required by Social Workers
with Delinquents," *Mental Hygiene*, IV, no. 3, pp. 513–14. (1920.)

It is better to think of the physician as a man whose business it is to treat, not symptoms or diseases, but sick people. . . . The patient is more than a group of symptoms, more than a collection of interesting juices; he is a living individual with a most complicated pattern of reactions, and the physician who overlooks this pattern may find the symptoms intractable, the disease unintelligible. Headache may be a reaction to eye strain, but it may be a reaction to a mother-in-law; pain in the back is sometimes explained by an X-ray plate, but sometimes by unwillingness to work; indigestion may be more closely related to a troubled conscience than to poor cooking; palpitation is not always an indication of organic heart disease — it may be the expression of the romance of life gone astray. Not that the situation is always simple; the patient with organic heart trouble may have romantic longings; a bad cook may conspire with a troubled conscience to ruin the digestion. The extent to which a man is disabled depends partly on the nature of his disease, but perhaps more on the way he reacts to it.

In no sense does the author object to the common belief that mental or nervous experiences may affect one's health. It is his belief that just as so-called bodily conditions may hamper or improve one's mental condition, so mental stimuli acting through the nervous system may change bodily functioning. Myerson [1] is probably correct in his statement that there is "no difference between the experiences taken in through the eyes and ears as words, and those experiences which flow into the organism by the nose or the mouth or the skin, whether as air, food, or toxic product."

The physiological processes on which our mental life rests are as yet only imperfectly understood, but more is being learned about them every day. We know that the mental life can be abolished by all sorts of methods, such as a blow on the head, the inhalation of anæsthetics, and the ingestion of various toxic substances. We know that one's mental efficiency is profoundly affected by the administration of alcohol, and that all such factors as fatigue and loss of sleep play their part in determining the mental state. That one's thinking processes are influenced by his disease processes needs no better proof than the mental apathy which accompanies such diseases as typhoid and malaria. It is universally recognized that, as age creeps on and makes its changes in the physical structure of man, there is a corresponding change in his mental behavior.

[1] Myerson, Abraham: *The Psychology of Mental Disorders* (The Macmillan Company, New York, 1927), 8.

Hardened arteries and stiffened bones are no more characteristic of old age than is the loss of the power to adjust mentally to new situations and experiences.

The relation of psychology to medicine, or the part played by psychology in disease, will be considered under the following heads: (1) Causes of disease; (2) Pathological changes due to psychical stimuli; (3) Symptoms; (4) Diagnosing the case; (5) Prospect of recovery; (6) Treatment.

1. Causes of disease. The part played by the mind in the production of disease is certainly not an insignificant one. An actual count of the causes listed for the thirty-two most common diseases gives some disturbed mental function as one of the contributing causes for over one third of them. Among the diseases in which the psychological agents are of considerable importance are nerve exhaustion, neurasthenia, hyperthyroidism, cardio-vascular renal diseases, diabetes, Bright's disease, cerebral apoplexy, and the large group of so-called functional diseases. Taking Graves's disease as an example, the more usual causes of this disease include business worry, disappointment in love, strong fear, or other intense excitement and prolonged emotional strain.

In many cases when the mental processes are not the exciting causes of the disease they are the predisposing causes. By far the most frequent types of disease produced by mental causes are those types of disease that exist primarily in the mind. Not long ago an orthopedic surgeon confided the information that in going over the records of his cases in a period of two years he found that between fifty and sixty per cent of the patients who consulted him for certain defects of the feet had these defects only in their imagination. In other words, about one half of all the patients who went to this man had not "club feet" but "club minds."

The predisposing effect of bad mental attitudes toward disease will be apparent from the following illustration. Assume that exactly the same kind and amount of food is taken by the individual under two different sets of conditions. In the first place Mr. X has plenty of money and takes his "best girl" to dine at a well-kept dining room where the linen is immaculate, the silver well polished, the china without blemish, and each table made festive by a vase of red roses. The food is served by a well trained and well dressed waiter to the accompaniment of harmonious strains from the orchestra in the corner. Another set of conditions under which Mr. X may dine offers considerable contrast to this picture. As his supply of money is almost exhausted, he goes into a typical "quick and dirty" lunch room, and instead of linen finds bare tables with the remains of spilt coffee and bread crumbs on them. The silver is black and greasy. The dishes are very thick and show the effects of hard usage by dark cracks in their edges. His order for food is yelled by a loud-mouthed waiter through a hole which permits a view of a dark and dingy kitchen, the corners of which are filled with cobwebs. The food is served to the accompaniment of dirty dishes rattling in the hands of the dishwasher, and the most powerful odor which stimulates his olfactory apparatus is that of spoiled cabbage from the kitchen. Under the first set of conditions nearly any kind of food is digestible, while under the second set of conditions even the most powerful stomach succumbs to dyspepsia.

The ease of digestion in the first case and lack of digestion in the second case have, however, a very definite physiological basis. It is definitely known that during depression and anxiety there is a marked decrease or even a total absence in the stomach of the juices necessary to digestion. It is also known that an abundance of these juices accompany pleasant emotional states. The mechanism underlying this is excellently explained by Pavlov's work on the conditioned reflex.

The work of Cannon and other physiologists has definitely established that painful or unpleasant emotions have the effect of inhibiting or suppressing digestive functions in experimental animals. In a series of experiments on cats, Cannon observed the peristaltic movements by means of a fluoroscope. He found that any sign of rage or fear was accompanied by a total abolition of the peristaltic movements. Cannon's observation shows that unpleasant emotions produce a similar effect in human beings. After intense anxiety or marked depression, one usually finds such symptoms as loss of appetite, coated tongue, offensive breath, complaint of discomfort in the stomach, and intestinal disturbances as manifested by either constipation or diarrhœa. A prolonged state of anxiety results in loss of weight, and if the condition is accompanied by sleeplessness and agitation it may lead to what the layman calls a "nervous breakdown."   Thus it is shown that malnutrition and various other disorders may result from the action of "psychic" stimuli on the various bodily organs.   The conditioned reflex explains the mechanism involved in this action.   It operates through a nervous control of these organs.

2. **Pathological changes due to psychical stimuli.**   Most of the pathological effects produced by mental activity are still obscure. Certain things, however, are fairly well demonstrated.   It is generally recognized that any kind of emotional excitement causes changes in blood pressure, the changes being sufficiently marked in some cases to produce a cerebral hemorrhage.   The tragic collapse of President Wilson and the death of President Harding exemplify very well the effect of prolonged mental strain upon the cerebral blood vessels.   The thyroid gland responds to prolonged emotional disturbances with enlargement and oversecretion, and after any very strong excitement there is an increased amount of sugar in the blood.   That emotional strain may cause the hair to turn gray prematurely and to fall out is a common tradition not unsupported by fact.   In the autopsy of animals which had been subjected to intense fear or pain, Crile and other investigators have been able to demonstrate definite pathological changes in microscopic sections of the cerebellum, liver, and adrenal glands.

Acting on the fact that fear, pain, and other unpleasant emotional stimuli will produce definite pathological changes in certain of the body tissues, Crile is convinced that these so-called emotional stimuli are largely responsible for the condition of shock following surgical operations, and he has developed a very fine technique to avoid the shock.   This technique frees the patient from all but the "most beneficent suggestions."   A sedative is given before the operation to calm his nerves and dull his consciousness, only the non-suffocating and odorless inhalation anæsthetics are employed, during the operation no sensitive tissue is cut until it is first made insensitive by a local anæsthetic; this local anæsthetic also serves to cut off the brain from all injurious sensory impulses; after the operation a second local anæsthetic is given to protect the patient against the period of post-operative adjustment. With the above technique Crile has practically eliminated in his patients the surgical shock which so frequently follows a major operation.

3. **Symptoms.** The first question asked by every physician of his new patient is designed to discover the patient's chief complaint or what the patient thinks is the trouble. The patient proceeds to tell about the aches and pains that he feels, and the duration and location of these. In a word, he gives a report dealing almost wholly with his sensations and feelings. Nothing belongs more surely to the province of psychology than one's reactions to his feelings and sensations. A noted French physician has pointed out the fact that frequently the one thing which the physician gets in his examination of the patient which enables him to make a diagnosis is the psychological thing — that is, the sensations that the individual reports. The surgeon also depends on "points of tenderness" to locate a broken bone or deep abscess. Indeed, no matter what the disease may be, the doctor depends to a certain extent upon the psychological factor to help him to make his diagnosis. Psychology also plays a part in the physician's evaluation of what the patient tells him. It is not infrequent that the patient's symptoms are largely imaginary, and are only a plea for sympathy. He complains of terrible pains in order to arouse the sympathy of others. The physician must take all such factors into consideration in evaluating the symptoms reported by the patient.

4. **Diagnosing the case.** In general, the diagnosis of disease is based on the case history, physical examination, symptoms, laboratory findings, and therapeutic tests. For the case history the physician must depend upon the report of the patient or of some one else, and consequently such psychological factors as inaccuracies of memory and the desire, growing out of false modesty, to conceal certain facts, enter to invalidate the history. A record of a venereal disease or of an insane relative is often denied.

In making the physical examination the diagnostician must remember that the heart rate and blood pressure are influenced by the emotional condition of the patient at the time of the examination. The effect of emotional excitement on temperature is shown

in Chart 27. The average temperature of children in a ward at
Lakeside Hospital was
taken under ordinary
conditions. Imme-
diately following a
Fourth of July cele-
bration it was taken
again and found to
have increased an
average of 1⅛ degrees
Fahrenheit.

Temperature	100°	105°
Under Ordinary Conditions		
After Fourth of July Celebration		

FIGURE 27. EFFECT OF EMOTIONAL EXCITEMENT
ON THE TEMPERATURE
(After Crile.)

In a case reported by Crile the effect of fear upon the pulse
is clearly demonstrated:

The patient, a foreigner, was brought into the operating room from the accident ward, pulse and temperature normal. Patient was greatly disturbed
on finding himself in the operating room. It was impossible to make him
understand that his leg was not to be amputated, but only a plaster cast
applied. Under the stimulus of fear his pulse rose to 150 and he soon
developed a temperature of 101.2 degrees.[1]

The part played by the psychical element in the production of
symptoms has already been discussed. Attention has also been
called to the fact that after intense emotional excitement certain
changes are observed in the blood and urine, and due recognition
should be made of these in interpreting the results of laboratory
analysis. The vitiation of laboratory results by emotional excitement frequently occurs in tests for basal metabolism.

5. Prospect of recovery. The patient with the proper attitude
toward life in general and toward his disease in particular, is the
patient the physician considers the best risk. Back in the thirteenth century a medieval physician, Henri de Mondeville, wrote
in a surgical treatise: "Keep up your patient's spirits by music of
viols and ten-stringed psaltery, or by forged letters describing the
death of his enemies, or by telling him that he has been elected to
a bishopric, if a churchman." The striking thing about this is
not the questionable ethics but the depth of insight which it shows.

[1] Crile, George W.: *Man an Adaptive Mechanism* (The Macmillan Company,
New York, 1916), 57. Reprinted by permission of the publishers.

Even though their primary ailment may be equally dangerous, the patient with a "will to live" more often succeeds in doing so than does the patient who "wants to die." One of the leading surgeons in this country refuses to operate, except in an emergency, unless the patient has the proper attitude. He considers the emotional and other elements which go to make up attitude to be of the greatest importance in bringing about the cure of his patient.

Very closely related to this is the effect on the patient of the physician's attitude. What the patient wants is not an undertaker-like expression on the face of the physician, but he wants the physician to recognize the fact that he is not anxious to go into "the grand perhaps," but is planning to stay right here, and is depending upon the physician to coöperate in that endeavor. Confidence in one's physician undoubtedly plays a part in the successful outcome of most therapeutic measures.

6. Treatment. In the treatment of disease "it is quite as important to know what kind of a patient the disease has as what kind of a disease the patient has." According to Clendening, "rest, drugs, diet, and psychotherapy might well be the armamentarium of the modern Galen."

Rest. Rest is considered by some as a panacea, and there are "rest cures" galore for all kinds of ailments. In many cases, however, what the patient needs is not rest, but the things that are incident to rest, such as change of scenery and a relief from the dull monotony of everyday life. The word *neurasthenia*, meaning tired nervous system, is probably a misnomer. If a careful investigation into the history of most neurasthenics is made, it will be found that they are fatigued not because they do so much, but because of the emptiness of their lives. The man who is so deeply absorbed in his work that he spends from twelve to fourteen hours a day immersed in business affairs practically never suffers a nervous breakdown, but nervous breakdowns are much more common with society women who have not even their own homes to care for. Clendening [1] cites the case of an introspective business man who was a constant frequenter of neurologists' offices:

[1] Clendening, L.: *Modern Methods of Treatment* (C. V. Mosby Company, St. Louis, Missouri, 1928), 420.

He was several times psychoanalyzed and was much perturbed over his complexes. During this time his business was getting along perfectly; was prosperous, and needed almost none of his personal attention. But when the wave of business depression of 1920 came along, he found that it was necessary for him to put his shoulder once more to the wheel — to plan, to execute, to assume responsibility, to get to the office early, to stay late. This did more for him than all the neurologists. He lost his complex.

While for many diseases the value of rest is greatly overestimated, and the value of being occupied underestimated, still every one would admit that both mental and physical rest have a very positive value in treating certain diseases. Physical rest conserves our energy and enables us to use the resources of our bodies in combatting the disease instead of in supplying fuel for muscular activity, and mental rest may relieve us from the exhaustive action of worry and anxiety. The chief object of rest, however, is not to eliminate all mental activity, but rather to free the mind from worry and anxiety.

Drugs. In modern therapeutics drugs play a relatively less important part than was the case a few generations ago, but we read of bread pills and other harmless potions that were used even then. Many physicians, realizing that some patients whose ailments exist primarily in the mind come to the physician expecting some kind of "medicine" to be prescribed, always see to it that the patients get medicine, sometimes bread pills, but just as often pepsin or some other harmless remedy. These "medicines" are used because the physician recognizes the importance of imagination, by which a medicine which is taken by the patient with faith overcomes a disease which exists only in the mind. To cure such diseases it is necessary to get the patient in the proper mental attitude. If he has a "club mind," but imagines that he possesses a club foot, the physician must make an impression on his mind through his foot. One way to impress him is by giving him a good deal of pain in the special shoes prescribed, or by strapping up his foot so that he cannot walk, or in the price he is charged for the physician's services. Another way of impressing the patient is by giving him a lot of bitter medicine and keeping him in the house for a few days. Patients are also considerably impressed by the reputation of the physician.   Other things being equal, the same treatment would be much more effective if given by a Mayo than if it were given by some obscure surgeon.

It is interesting in this connection to consider one theory which may explain why we have such a preponderance of unpalatable drugs.   In the olden days men believed that when a person was sick it was because his body was infested by the devil or by evil spirits.   To rid themselves of these parasites they resorted to the use of all kinds of the worst, ill-tasting medicines that the medicine-men could compound, the supposition being that one must take something "nastier than the devil" to drive out the devil.   This probably accounts for the fact that such a large proportion of the drugs in use to-day are so unpalatable.

It must not be concluded, however, that all drugs are worthless; in fact, within the last few years, due to the careful experimental work of some pharmacologists, more has been learned about the actual physiological action of drugs than had been discovered by the trial and error method from the beginning of time.   As a result of these investigations there have been discovered a few "specifics," or drugs that can always be counted on to relieve certain diseases. Quinine, for example, will always relieve malaria, and is consequently a specific for malaria.   Morphine is a specific for pain, and when used correctly is the best friend the patient has.   Few things so completely destroy a patient's vitality and demoralize his fighting strength as pain.   Through morphine we have a sure means of eliminating pain.   There are certain antitoxins which are specifics for some of the infectious diseases.   Most drugs, however, fall into the class of "alteratives" or non-specifics.   Their ultimate action is unknown, but they are given with the hope of producing some beneficial change in the patient.   With the more scientific administration of drugs and investigation of their properties, it is to be expected that the number of "specifics" will steadily increase, and the "alteratives" in use will gradually decrease in number.

Diet.   The effect of food on health is determined in no slight degree by the mental condition of the patient.   As pointed out above, during worry and anxiety, the peristalsis of the stomach is stopped and the digestive processes are seriously disturbed.   In states of mental depression the appetite is absent and even the most attractive foods are not eaten with much avidity. It is accordingly just as necessary to know what is the emotional state of the patient when the diet is taken as it is to know what diet is taken. The way the food is served also has its effect on the patient's appetite.

Psychotherapy. Psychotherapy, or the treatment by mental means, is the oldest form of treatment; all treatment being originally by psychotherapy. Before the discovery of germs it was commonly believed that the patient had incurred the ill-will of the gods and was being punished accordingly. The treatment was therefore designed to correct the spiritual condition of the patient. While it is no longer generally believed that the gods send diseases to torment helpless people, it still often happens that through improper training or bad conditioned reflexes people develop a so-called "functional" disease for themselves. We shall consider the following types of psychotherapy: (1) Suggestion; (2) Auto-suggestion; (3) Hypnotism.

(1) *Suggestion.* From time immemorial man has recognized with a somewhat superstitious reverence certain phenomena produced by suggestion. The trances of the ancient oracles, the magic power of talismans and amulets, the wonders wrought by the medicine man who cured by reciting mysterious words and by performing complicated ceremonies; the healing virtue of the kingly or priestly hand, and the marvelous cures at shrines — all are the result of suggestion. Because of its connection with hypnotism and its use in the treatment of hysteria and allied disturbances suggestion has been looked upon as mysterious and unusual, but, on the contrary, it is a phenomenon of everyday life, and has considerable importance in the control of behavior. It is a method of treatment used by every physician.

Suggestion implies the uncritical acceptance of an idea aroused by the words or actions of another person. It fits very nicely into the S ⟶ R formula, the *Stimulus* coming from another person or object and producing the idea or *Response* in the person thus stimulated. The effect of such external stimuli on behavior is seen by the great difference between the results produced by the positive suggestion contained in the phrasing, "You can come, can't you?" and that resulting from the wording, "You can't come, can you?" The potent effect of suggestion is seen in the contagiousness of yawning or in the immoderate laughter which spreads rapidly through a crowd. Without doubt suggestion plays a very important part in the production of epidemics of suicide or in the spread of the crime waves which sweep the country. It is fairly easy to suggest to a person that he is ill until he believes that it is true, and goes to bed with all the symptoms of illness; and it is equally easy to cure him of his imaginary illness by the same methods of suggestion.

The efficacy of suggestion in curing slight ailments was probably first discovered by a mother. The little child falls down and hurts his knee. When his mother kisses the knee and tells him, "It's all well now," he immediately stops crying, and goes back to his play. But if she says, "Poor little fellow, you hurt your knee badly; I must call the doctor and let him treat it," the child's cries redouble in vigor, and he refuses to be consoled.

The curative value of psychotherapy as used by the physician in his relation to the patient rests very largely on suggestion. The physician has considerably benefited his patient if he is able by suggestion to build up the assurance in the patient that he will get well. This the physician does by a cheerful attitude and by appearing confident that a cure will be effected. He can often increase the beneficial effect of suggestion by seeing that the environment of his patient is the most effective. Changing the surroundings of the sick-room, or bringing optimistic associations into the patient's mind usually aids in his recovery. The physician's task is to eliminate by suggestion those unfavorable factors in the illness of the patient which are due to the state of mind of the suffering individual. When neither drugs nor surgical operations are needed, considerable improvement may result from such suggestive treatment as the administration of doses of flavored and colored water, the application of complicated electrical apparatus with or without current, or by the performance of sham operations.

(2) *Auto-suggestion*. Thus far we have considered suggestion coming directly from an external source. When the suggestion

comes only indirectly from the outside and directly from the mind of the person influenced, it is termed auto-suggestion. Auto-suggestion is a deliberate attempt to influence one's own behavior by keeping an idea constantly in one's mind. The use of auto-suggestion in the treatment of disease is best illustrated by the practice and teachings of the late Emile Coué. Coué attempted to get the idea of improvement and health into the mind of his patient and to keep it there by having the patient repeat at frequent intervals a formula suggestive of improvement. He gave the new patient at his clinic an exercise in auto-suggestion and said to him: "You have come here in search of some one who can cure you. You are on the wrong track. I have never cured any one. I merely teach people to cure themselves, and that is what I am going to teach you." At his clinics the newcomers sat among those who had already been there many times, and who made no secret of their progress to health. The influence of suggestion had already begun to have its effect on the patients before Coué began to treat them, for the fame of the clinic and of the miracle worker had spread abroad, and those who went to his clinic were expecting wonderful results. After the patient had had his lesson in auto-suggestion, he carried on his own treatment according to directions by repeating every morning and evening fifteen or twenty times the remedial phrase, "Day by day in every way I am growing better and better," with special emphasis on "in every way."

There is no doubt that diseases (improper habits of thought) that exist primarily in the mind can be greatly benefited by auto-suggestion, and the service rendered the patient in curing his imaginary ills may be just as great as in curing a definite organic disease, for one's suffering may be just as great and his efficiency just as low as the result of mental ills as it is in the case of the more distinctly physical ills. Auto-suggestion is of most value in the treatment of such diseases as hysteria, insomnia, loss of appetite, and other like ills which may be cured by psychoanalysis, bread pills, a change of climate, a stupendous doctor's bill, or anything that takes the patient's mind from his imaginary troubles. Another class of diseases cured by auto-suggestion consists of the large number of diseases from which the patient would recover anyway.

Only one disease in a person's life proves fatal, and many of the others can be cured by auto-suggestion, or, if given time, by the individual's natural resistance or tendency to get well with no treatment whatever. It is not generally appreciated among the laity how much the human body tends to cure itself, and in many instances the physician cannot render better service to the patient than to keep him quiet and contented while Nature does its work. This is what the old doctor had in mind when he said to his young colleague, "If you can't do any good, be sure you don't do any harm."

(3) *Hypnotism.* Hypnotism is suggestion carried to an extreme degree. In hypnotism we have a state of partial sleep which is not too deep to permit of the functioning of many of the organized habits of the individual. When in this state the normal associative mechanism upon which the individual depends for inhibitory or counter-suggestion is apparently not functioning, hence the soil is prepared for each suggestion to plunge the organism into action.

Several conditions are essential to the production of a hypnotic state. The first condition necessary for the induction of hypnosis is the fixation of attention. The attention of the subject may be fixed on a bright light, on the sound of verbal suggestion, or on the portion of the body over which mesmeric passes are made. Monotony of impressions is the second important factor in hypnosis. Such stimuli as that produced by a dimly lighted room, monotonous and soothing sounds such as the steady flow of running water or the ticking of a clock, and the gentle and monotonous stroking of some part of the body, all tend to produce hypnotic sleep. In all of these the principle is the same; monotonous impressions produce fatigue, and fatigue in turn prepares the mind for sleep. Third, the limitation of voluntary movement is essential. The subject must relax and keep perfectly still.

In hypnotic sleep susceptibility to suggestion is greatly increased. In deep hypnosis sensitivity may be diminished or totally destroyed; anæsthesia frequently appears so that a pin may be stuck through the skin without eliciting any response. Before the use of chloroform and ether to produce anæsthesia, operations were occasionally performed while the patient was in a hypnotic state, but with the discovery of more certain methods of preventing pain, hypnotism was no longer used for producing surgical anæsthesia.

In summary, suggestion, auto-suggestion, and hypnotism are undoubtedly effective in freeing the patient from disturbances of mental origin, and in dulling the recognition of pain, but as methods of treating illnesses of a more distinctly organic nature, they have only an indirect value.   Bacteria are not open to suggestion.

CHAPTER XIV

MENTAL DISORDERS

"MACBETH: How does your patient, doctor?
DOCTOR: Not so sick, my lord,
  As she is troubled with thick-coming fancies
  That keep her from her rest.
MACBETH: Cure her of that.
  Canst thou not minister to a mind diseas'd,
  Pluck from the memory a rooted sorrow,
  Raze out the written troubles of the brain,
  And with some sweet oblivious antidote
  Cleanse the stuff'd bosom of that perilous stuff
  Which weighs upon the heart?
DOCTOR: Therein the patient
  Must minister to himself.
MACBETH: Throw physic to the dogs, I'll none of it."

SHAKESPEARE

THE importance of the problem of mental disorders from a sociological and economic standpoint is not generally realized. At the present time there are more than 300,000 inmates of institutions for the insane, feeble-minded, and epileptic in this country. There are approximately as many in these institutions as there are students in our colleges and universities. There are slightly more in hospitals for the treatment of mental diseases than in all other hospitals combined. It is also probably true that not more than one half of those who are suffering from mental disorders and need institutional care are receiving it. We are paying each year approximately $100,000,000 to care for our institutional cases, and the economic loss due to their being unable to work is estimated at more than $300,000,000. From one third to one sixth of every State's expenditures goes for the support of mental hospitals.

But the financial loss is not all. The amount of crime, degradation, and mental anguish occasioned by mental diseases cannot be reliably estimated. Dr. William J. Mayo of the famous Mayo Clinic is quoted as saying that "Neurasthenia, psychasthenia, hysteria, and allied neuroses are the cause of more human misery than tuberculosis and cancer." The distress caused by mental disorders is not limited to the patients, but extends to their relatives and family as well. Moreover, with the steady increase in the complexity of civilization, the problem is becoming more and more aggravated.

I. CAUSES OF MENTAL DISORDERS

Mental disorders are usually divided into the organic and functional groups. In the organic group the underlying pathology and causes are fairly well known, and the pathological tissue changes can be demonstrated at autopsy. For the functional group no definite pathological changes can be consistently demonstrated, and consequently the causes of these diseases are very imperfectly understood. Some recent work, however, is indicating the great importance of conditioned reactions as causes of mental disorders of a functional nature.

From a historical standpoint it is interesting to note how the field of organic diseases is gradually increasing at the expense of the functional. With the increase of knowledge, and the perfection of technique, it is reasonable to believe that the pathology underlying a very large percentage of the diseases now classed as functional will ultimately be demonstrated and they will be classed as organic diseases. Before it was learned that syphilis is the cause of paresis, all such things as business worry, emotional shocks, and disappointment in love were given as the cause of the disease. Now it is known that these things have nothing at all to do with it, and that the disease has a purely organic basis, resulting from the invasion of the brain tissues by the spirochæta pallida (the microorganism or germ which causes syphilis).

In some instances the pathological changes underlying the disease are known, but the causes that produce these pathological changes are as yet unknown. We know, for example, that brain tumors cause very marked mental disorders, but so far we do not know what causes brain tumors. We know, further, that cerebral arteriosclerosis (hardening of the arteries in the brain) is the chief cause of senile dementia. But we do not know very definitely what causes the hardening.

Among the more specific causes of mental disorders are: (1) Infections of the brain and its membranes; (2) Destruction of brain tissue; (3) Toxins; (4) Glandular disorders; (5) Chronic infections; (6) Other disease processes; (7) Heredity; (8) Training; (9) Emotional shocks; (10) Other predisposing factors.

1. **Infections of the brain and membranes.** Among the more important specific causes for mental disorders are infections of the brain and its membranes. As already pointed out, paresis is caused by an inflammatory process in the brain tissue caused by the germ of syphilis. Mental disorders are also caused by meningitis and encephalitis; the former, an inflammation of the membranes surrounding the brain, and the latter, an inflammation of the brain itself.

2. **Destruction of brain tissue.** Another cause of mental disorder is gross brain injury. All such things as head injuries, brain tumors, and cerebral hemorrhages are important as causal agents in this group.

3. **Toxins.** Among the toxic substances which act as causes of mental disorders, alcohol and drugs are most important. There are also certain toxic substances which develop in the body as the result of improper elimination. An example of this is seen in the uremic coma which follows the breaking-down of kidney function.

4. **Glandular disorders.** Glandular disfunction plays a very important part in producing mental disorders. Typical cases of the mental effects of glandular disturbance are seen in the dull, listless and apathetic behavior of the cretin who lacks the necessary amount of thyroid secretion, and in the highly sensitive, restless, and irritable behavior of the person suffering from an over-secretion from the thyroid gland. Without doubt, many of the cases of abnormal sex conduct are due to some malfunctioning of the endocrine glands.

5. **Chronic infection.** The effect of such low-grade infections as tonsilitis, abscessed teeth, diseased sinuses, and chronic appendicitis on mental efficiency is not generally realized. The excellent work of Dr. Cotton [1] in New Jersey has demonstrated the very close relation between many of the so-called "functional" diseases and chronic infection. He finds that in a large number of cases when the surgeon removes the foci of infection, the accompanying

[1] Cotton, H. A.: "The Etiology and Treatment of the So-Called Functional Psychoses," *American Journal of Psychiatry*, October, 1922.

mental disorder clears up. Dementia præcox is a typical example of a mental disorder which is benefited by the removal of the chronic infection.

6. Other disease processes. Diseases of systems other than the nervous and glandular play their part in producing mental disorders. In heart diseases, due to the disturbed circulation in the cerebral tissues, the mental life is seriously disturbed. And in the exhaustion conditions which follow physical strain, chronic or acute diseases, or the sudden loss of considerable blood, some mental abnormality frequently develops. The delirium which accompanies typhoid fever belongs in this group.

7. Heredity. Heredity is one of the most important predisposing causes of mental disease. In most cases of such important mental disorders as dementia præcox, epilepsy, and feeble-mindedness, the hereditary factor is of major consideration. These disorders seem to run in families, and are passed on from one generation to another. Heredity also apparently plays an important part in producing the group of minor mental disorders generally found in neurotic families. Just how much heredity *per se* is responsible for hysteria, neurasthenia, and psychopathic personalities is difficult to say. The fact that a child is reared by neurotic parents may be more influential in making him neurotic than the fact that he is begotten by neurotic parents.

8. Training. The importance of training in producing or preventing mental disorders is now generally recognized. Watson and the Behaviorists have shown how various anti-social attitudes, phobias, and sex perversions are built up by training. The whole psychoanalytic school proceeds on the assumption that the ills of to-day are the half-forgotten memories of yesterday. They believe that the psychic traumas of childhood are the monkey-wrenches that wreck our adult personalities.

9. Emotional shocks. A sudden emotional shock, such as that resulting from the terrible sights of a railroad accident, may cause a mental disorder. And prolonged worry and anxiety, by acting on the digestive, circulatory, glandular, and nervous systems, may prevent sleep, and throw the body into such a debilitated condition that a mental disorder will appear.

10. Other predisposing factors. The part played by age, sex, race, and external conditions has been discussed in previous chapters. It will be recalled, for example, that age is very important in such disorders as involution melancholia which occurs about the age of forty-five or fifty, and senile dementia, which occurs late in life. Sex also seems to be of some slight importance as indicated by the fact that involution melancholia is more than three times as common in women as in men, while paresis and cerebral arteriosclerosis are more than twice as frequent in men. These conditions may not be due so much to sex as such, as to the different modes of living of the sexes.

II. SYMPTOMS

The popular conception of the behavior of the insane is quite divergent from that which we generally find in persons suffering from those mental disorders known as insanity. People expect the insane to be disrobing, tearing their hair, yelling, and screaming, and attempting to take their own life or the life of another. When an individual who dresses well, talks coherently, and is polite and courteous, is sent to a hospital for mental cases, the layman becomes extremely indignant and feels that an outrage is being committed. To an untrained observer the behavior of patients in an insane asylum presents a conglomerate mixture, incapable of classification. But on closer observation, it is found that the behavior patterns of the insane are extremely limited, and their hallucinations and delusions comparatively easily classified. Men of the most diverse social and intellectual backgrounds develop the same delusions and the same disorders of intelligence when the brain is infected by the germ of syphilis; and we find the same irritability, egotism, and failure of memory in all senile dementia cases who are suffering from cerebral arteriosclerosis. According to Myerson,[1]

Originality and individuality of development disappear with the ravages of mental disease, and the experienced can more easily anticipate the beliefs, motives, and conduct of the insane than of the sane.

[1] Myerson, Abraham: *The Psychology of Mental Disorders* (The Macmillan Company, New York, 1927), 16. Reprinted by permission of the publishers.

Space will not permit a discussion of the many important physical signs of mental disorder. We shall limit the discussion to the behavior symptoms. Among the more common symptoms of mental disorders are: (1) Hallucinations; (2) Delusions; (3) Deterioration of intelligence; (4) Mood alteration; (5) Personality changes.

1. Hallucinations. An hallucination is a response to a situation that has no external reality, as when a delirium tremens patient sees snakes when there is nothing remotely resembling a snake about. Our ideas of the outside world are received through the sense organs, and are interpreted in terms of our previous experience. With the normal these ideas originate in the sensory experiences and flow into the brain, but with the abnormal the process is apparently reversed and inner processes project into the environment ideas of their own creation. The physiology underlying this latter process is not well understood. It is known that diseases of the inner ear or its central connections may cause a person to hear voices or other sounds when none are present; that diseases of the eye or the occipital lobe may make him see snakes and various forms on a bare wall; that chronic diseases of the mucous membrane of the nose are accompanied by annoying olfactory disturbances. A pathological condition anywhere along a nerve tract may be referred to its sensory end organs. A typical case of this is seen in Locomotor Ataxia, when a patient feels as if some one stuck a pin into his leg or was drawing a tight girdle around him; the seat of the disturbance in this case is not in the skin, but in the back part of the spinal cord which is connected with the skin.

Many hallucinations, however, are not satisfactorily explained on the hypothesis of diseased sense-organs or nervous connections. Even a normal person when anxiously expecting the return of a friend at night, frequently hears footsteps where none exist; or when expecting to be called, rather distinctly hears his own name pronounced. Such cases cannot be explained by neural pathology.

Regardless of how they are produced, hallucinations are among the more interesting and constant symptoms of mental disorders. Concerning hallucinations Myerson [1] says:

---

[1] Myerson, Abraham: *The Psychology of Mental Disorders* (The Macmillan Company, New York, 1927), 19. Reprinted by permission of the publishers.

God's voice talks frequently to the insane. He counsels or threatens, and there are enough people who hear the Deity in insane hospitals to furnish the basis for a myriad of new religions. Enemies talk about one, strangers mock and deride, and the walls, if they have not ears, have voices to the mentally sick.

A patient may view his hallucinations with the same detached attitude that a spectator views a motion picture of a scene in which he is not personally concerned. But this is the exception rather than the rule, for patients usually become much excited about their hallucinations. Murders are committed in response to insulting taunts of the imaginary voices, the "eyes make fools of the other senses," and the image, as "a dagger of the mind, a false creation, proceeding from heat-oppressed brain," "doth unfix my hair, and make my seated heart knock at my ribs, against the use of nature." In such cases the patient, cringing with fear, will stop at nothing to rid himself of the horrible sights.

2. Delusions. A delusion is a false belief held in the face of manifest evidence of its absurdity, as when a patient believes that he is president of the United States of the World, or a ditch digger believes that he possesses millions of dollars.

In studying delusions we immediately run into the problem of "what is truth." Truth in one generation is a delusion in another, and what is truth for one religious sect is a false belief for another. To most Protestants, Catholics are deluded; to the Mohammedan all Christians are false believers, and to Christians all agnostics, atheists, and materialists are bound for a devil's hell because of their false beliefs.

In deciding whether an erroneous belief is indicative of insanity, the social background of the individual must be taken into consideration. When the Georgia negro believes in hoodoos, or the Salem Puritans in witchcraft, we do not class them as insane, but if the descendant of these same Puritans who is now teaching at Yale were to believe in hoodoos or witchcraft, the police would certainly hold him for "mental observation." If Al Smith should believe that the K.K.K. or Anti-Saloon League were plotting against his life and happiness, this would not be sufficient reason to place him in an institution, but if an obscure street sweeper believes that the Pope through his Catholic subjects is putting poison into his food, or that the League of Nations is trying to have him assassinated, such a belief is almost *prima-facie* evidence of his insanity.

While there are as many kinds of insane delusions as there are beliefs in the normal world, the delusions which characterize mental disorders tend to fall into three groups: (1) Melancholy delusions; (2) Grandiose delusions; (3) Delusions of persecution.

(1) *Melancholy delusions.* Certain diseases such as involution melancholia are characterized throughout by depression, and all the ideas are of an unhappy nature. The melancholy delusions are monotonous; they are repeated over and over without change. As a rule they are humble and passive, the patient accuses no one but himself, and accepts without resistance the hard fate which he believes himself to have deserved. The more common ideas are: (*a*) Ideas of sin or culpability. The patient considers himself a good-for-nothing, undeserving sinner. He usually thinks that he has committed the unpardonable sin. He, therefore, expects every minute to be arrested, executed, and to burn forever in hell. (*b*) Ideas of poverty. Though the patient may actually be wealthy, he believes himself to be poor, that his clothes will be sold from off his back, and the roof from over his head, and that he will be cast out to starve. (*c*) Hypochondriacal ideas. The patient may believe that his brain has dissolved, or that his heart is paralyzed, or that he has swallowed a snake which is gnawing on his stomach, or that his reason is destroyed and his memory annihilated. (*d*) Ideas of negation. Sometimes these relate to the patient himself, as when he believes that he does not have any head, and that his whole body is but a shadow; and sometimes they relate to the external world, as when he believes that the sun is dead and that the world exists no more.

(2) *Delusions of grandeur.* Grandiose ideas are found in various mental disorders but are seen most typically in paresis. Paretics are immensely wealthy, and there is no limit to their power, either physical, mental, or political. They are gods, popes, kings, sheiks, and creative artists. Often a patient tries to attire himself in harmony with his self-bestowed title, the result being the gaudy

garb affected by so many who suffer from mental disorders. Patients refuse to be annoyed by the flagrant contradiction which may exist between their grandiose claims and their actual state. The author once had a patient who called himself Atlas and claimed to be all-powerful and to hold up the earth, who saw no discrepancy between his great power and begging a mere mortal for a "chew of tobacco."

(3) *Delusions of persecution.* Like the melancholy delusions studied above, the persecutory delusions are of an unhappy nature. But while the melancholiac submits without resistance to the punishment which he thinks he deserves, the subject of persecution protests his innocence, fights back, tries to defend himself, and finally seeks revenge.

Delusions of persecution are frequently associated with false interpretations; any chance occurrence has a hidden meaning. The innocent remarks of acquaintances give undisputable evidence of the conspiracy against him. Some patients do not know the identity of their persecutors, but the majority accuse some particular persons, such as Mussolini, or certain organizations such as the K.K.K. or the Catholic Church. There is a marked tendency for delusions of persecution to remain permanently, and for the patients to grow gradually worse. Delusions of persecution are nearly always the basis of murders committed by the insane.

3. Deterioration of intelligence. Practically all mental disorders with the possible exception of paranoia are characterized by more or less deterioration of intelligence. The memory and thought processes are markedly impaired. The patient may be thoroughly disoriented, may think that the doctor is Christopher Columbus, that the nurse is Queen Elizabeth, that to-day is 800 B.C., and the place a Mohammedan garden. When intelligence tests are given from time to time to patients suffering from mental diseases such as dementia præcox, epilepsy, paresis, and senile dementia, the deterioration is evident in the intelligence scores.

4. Mood alteration. Without doubt the glands of internal secretion are the chief determiners of moods, but the manner of their action is as yet imperfectly understood. According to James, "Some people are born with a bottle of champagne to their credit," and they frolic through life apparently unaware of its burdens. There are others whose moods are always in "the sere and yellow leaf." With the insane there is a more frequent change of mood. Sometimes there is a rhythmical change from one mood to another as is seen in patients suffering from the manic-depressive psychoses.

Among the more important mood types found in mental disorders are the depressed mood, which may reach the depths of despair, and express itself in suicidal attempts; the exalted mood, which is characterized by expansive delusions of grandeur; the maniacal mood, characterized by excitement, furor and incessant activity day and night; the "anxiety" mood, characterized by fear and agitated melancholia; the apathetic mood, characterized by a total loss of interest in life or self. The patient leads a purely vegetative existence, and may appear to have no more mental life than a cabbage.

5. **Personality changes.** One of the first signs of a mental disorder is frequently a change of personality. The honest become swindlers; the virtuous, profligate; the miserly, spendthrifts; the ambitious, apathetic; and the neat, slovenly. The "shut-in," timid personality may become more shut-in, or with the disappearance in cortical control, as in paresis, may embark on an orgy of debaucheries of the wildest type.

III. TREATMENT

Space will not permit an adequate discussion of the physical treatment of mental disorders. The use of such therapeutic measures as drugs, diet, electrotherapy, hydrotherapy, and surgical operations will not be discussed, but consideration will be given to two methods of psychotherapy: (1) Reëducation; (2) Psychoanalysis.

1. **Reëducation.** One of the most recent and most important contacts that psychology has made with medicine is in the field of reëducation. To quote Franz,[1] who is a pioneer in the field of reëducation:

In simple terms, then, the principle of reëducation is that of habit-forma-

[1] Franz, Shepherd: *Nervous and Mental Reëducation* (The Macmillan Company, New York, 1924), 17. Reprinted by permission of the publishers.

tion. It is either a replacement of old, inadequate, or harmful methods of reacting with new habits more like those of the other individuals in his environment, or it is the formation of new habits to take the place of those that have been lost. In other words, reëducation is to the abnormal what education is to the normal — it is a matter of the acquisition of habits that will enable the individual to take his place in the working, playing, social world.

The method of reëducation offers immense promise in the treatment of both physical and mental defectives. To illustrate, if a right-handed individual loses his right arm, by means of reëducation his left arm may in a very large measure take up the functions formerly supplied by his right arm, such as writing, throwing, etc.; or through the reëducation of the shoulder muscles, with a properly constructed artificial forearm, it is possible for him to gain control of the arm even down to the finger movements. Another field in which reëducation can be of considerable service is in treating speech defects. In many cases stammering or stuttering can be cured by proper replacement habits. When these defects are due to nervousness, attention must be given to freeing the individual from his timidity, and when the defect is due to poor control of the muscles of speech, attention should be directed toward showing him the proper placement of his lips and tongue during speech.

As a cause for abnormal behavior the conditioned reflex is being recognized more and more, and the method of treating such cases is by reconditioning them. To illustrate, let us take the case of a patient who came to the writer complaining of a very intense fear of closed places. Her phobia was so intense that she would start to scream when a train on which she was riding entered a tunnel. In all other respects she was apparently normal. After spending some time in trying to discover the cause of her disturbance, and in going over her history it was noticed that the phobia began when she was sixteen years old. It was also discovered that her mother died of heart disease and a brother was killed in an accident about the time the disturbance began. Thus she had a very severe emotional shock which occurred at the time of the phobia. On further investigation it was learned that the patient had a sinking spell when she saw the coffin lid closed over her mother, and another spell when she saw the coffin lowered into the tomb. Almost the same thing occurred a week later at the death of the brother. Having discovered this, it became a comparatively easy matter to establish the causal connection between the emotional shock and the phobia. We thus have a fairly clear case of the conditioned reflex. The closing of the coffin lid, and later of the ground, over her loved ones at first set off the emotional reaction; later any closed place set off the reaction. Having discovered the cause of the trouble, the writer set about her reëducation or reconditioning using the methods of Franz and Watson. In a few weeks she had completely recovered.

Reëducation is also of considerable value in the treatment of the insane. In many cases nervous breakdowns are brought on by the development of habits and attitudes which are socially abnormal. The individual becomes well again when the annoying conflict which produced his nervous breakdown is removed, when he makes the proper adjustment, or when his habits become sufficiently like those of members of his social class or station. According to Franz: [1]

The reëducation of the insane depends entirely, therefore, upon the replacement of bad, perverted, peculiar, slovenly, and unsocial methods of reaction by habits which are social and conventional.

By means of reëducation one should attempt to build up habits which restore sleep and appetite, inasmuch as these are nearly always impaired in mental disorders. According to Myerson, [2]

He who sleeps and eats well faces life well, and can usually handle his own complexes. But when one lies awake at night, little troubles become big ones, and when food tastes like straw it's time to see a doctor.

The advantages of conditioned reflex methods in treating mental disorders are not generally appreciated. While these methods are still in their infancy, sufficient work has already been done to convince the author that no method of psychotherapy has greater promise than these methods.

[1] Franz, Shepherd: *Nervous and Mental Reëducation* (The Macmillan Company, New York, 1924), 17. Reprinted by permission of the publishers.

[2] Myerson, Abraham: *The Psychology of Mental Disorders* (The Macmillan Company, New York, 1927), 71. Reprinted by permission of the publishers.

2. Psychoanalysis. The psychoanalysts agree with Omar that "Yesterday this day's madness did prepare." They believe that our emotional shocks and thwarted desires are not forgotten, but are pushed out of consciousness into the unconscious and there affect our behavior in many devious ways. It is the purpose of the psychoanalyst to discover these suppressed memories or desires and to bring them back to the consciousness of the patient.

The principles of psychoanalysis are well explained by Freud in his lectures delivered at Clark University in which he discussed the steps in psychoanalysis as follows: (1) What our desires are in consciousness; (2) How they are thrust out of consciousness; (3) What they do while they are out; (4) How we get them back; (5) How to treat them when back.

(1) *What our desires are in consciousness.* Freud's doctrine of the libido assumes that the individual possesses a store of energy, sexual in character, derived from the primitive sexual instinct. This energy is supposed to be capable of transference from one set of processes to another. It is further assumed that such a libido is the source of all energy in the individual, though it may be "sublimated" into such highly æsthetic and moral activities that one would not be able to recognize it. According to Freud "complexes" and hysteria are practically without exception the result of sexual repression of some sort, and all wishes are erotic in origin. The desires connected with sex, using sex in a broad sense, are more significant in the life of the individual than any other desires, yet they are the very ones which in civilized society must be most sternly repressed. These repressions, together with the various ideas associated with them, form what is termed a "complex." A complex is a group of related ideas which produce the same emotional effect. For example, a man's fiancée is struck by lightning during a storm. Years later the appearance or even the mention of lightning or of a storm revives in the man a feeling of dread, and he has a sense of impending danger when confronted by a storm or lightning. In other words, he is suffering from a hidden complex.

In many cases the root of the trouble goes back to adolescence and early childhood, for the incompatible, repressed wishes of childhood may lead to the creation of hysterical symptoms later on.

These suppressed wishes or desires of childhood, Freud states, are very generally sexual in nature, although infantile sexuality is entirely disconnected from the function of reproduction which it is later to serve. The desires and complexes of childhood are destined to quick repression, but they still exert a great and lasting effect from the unconscious.

(2) *How the desires are thrust out of consciousness.* Our desires, which, according to Freud, are mainly sexual, cannot always be satisfied because they come in conflict with social barriers, or with the previous training of the individual. There is then a conflict, and the incompatible or unpleasant "wish" is repressed from consciousness and apparently forgotten. The following case cited by Freud [1] illustrates the repression of a disagreeable idea.

The girl grew to feel a peculiar sympathy for her new brother-in-law, which easily passed with her for family tenderness. The sister soon fell ill and died while the patient and her mother were away. The absent ones were hastily recalled, without being told fully of the painful situation. As the girl stood by the bedside of her dead sister for one short moment there surged up in the mind an idea, which might be framed in these words: "Now he is free and can marry me." We may be sure that this idea, which betrayed to her consciousness her intense love for her brother-in-law, of which she had not been conscious, was the next moment consigned to repression "by her revolted feelings." The conflict between desires and resistances leads to pushing the desires from consciousness.

Freud [2] used the following illustration to explain the mechanism of thrusting the desires from consciousness:

Suppose that here in this hall and in this audience . . . there is an individual who is creating a disturbance, and by his ill-bred laughing, talking, by scraping his feet, distracts my attention from my task. I explain that I cannot go on with my lecture under these conditions, and thereupon several strong men among you get up and after a short struggle, eject the disturber of the peace from the hall. He is now "repressed" and I can continue my lecture. But in order that the disturbance may not be repeated, in case the man who has just been thrown out attempts to force his way back into the room, the gentlemen who have executed my suggestion take their chairs to the door and establish themselves there as a "resistance" to

[1] Freud, Sigmund: "The Origin and Development of Psychoanalysis," *American Journal of Psychology,* April, 1910.
[2] *Ibid.,* p. 194.

keep up the repression. Now if you transfer both locations to the psyche, calling this "consciousness" and the outside the "unconscious" you have a tolerably good illustration of the process of repression.

(3) *What the desires do while out.* But the conflict is not necessarily over when the wish or desire is relegated to the unconscious, for, continuing Freud's illustration, the rowdy is not completely suppressed. Although no longer in the lecture hall, by his hammering on the door with his fists, and by his outcries he interferes with the lecture more than ever. While the wishes are outside in the "unconscious" they continue to exist, only waiting for a chance to get back to consciousness. The "censor" prevents them from returning to consciousness in their original form, but they succeed in sending back to consciousness, not the suppressed wish, but a disguised form of it, to which are associated the same painful sensations of which the person thought to rid himself through the repression. These evasions of the censor are frequently brought about by means of a certain amount of dissociation, and may take the form of hallucinations, muscular automatism, or paralysis. Thus are created the symptoms of hysteria. The repressed wishes also appear in symbolic form in dreams, so that dreams are very significant to the psychoanalyst.

(4) *How we get the desires back into consciousness.* The problem of the psychoanalyst in curing patients suffering from hysteria is to bring these incompletely suppressed wishes back into consciousness. In other words, the psychoanalyst acts as the peacemaker in Freud's illustration who speaks to the rowdy outside, and returns with the recommendation that the latter be let in again provided he agrees to behave himself. The repression is then stopped, and peace and quiet reign again. When the patient recognizes the cause of his disorder, and when the emotion associated with the suppressed idea is allowed expression, the symptoms of hysteria disappear.

There are three methods of getting the repressed ideas back into consciousness: (a) Word association tests; (b) Interpretation of dreams, and (c) Slips in everyday life. There are two forms of word association tests, the method of free association and that of controlled association. In the free association tests the patient is told to say any words that he may think of just as they come to his mind. It is found that at certain points there is a blockage to the even flow of his words. This blockage is supposed to be caused by the stream of words leading into a mental sore spot or complex, which the patient does not wish to reveal. By noticing where these blockings occur one is able to locate the "complex." Freud describes the method of discovering the complex by free association as follows:

> So we let the patient speak along any line that he desires, and cling to the hypothesis that nothing can occur to him except what has some indirect bearing on the complex we are seeking.

In the method of controlled association the patient is given a list of words and is told to reply to each word with the first word that comes into his mind. The list contains many words that have no relation to his complexes but it also has some significant words that refer directly to it. By noting the time that elapses between the giving of the stimulus word and the response, and by also noting the nature of the response it is possible to discover the significant words and by means of them to locate the complex. It is found, for example, that the patient takes a longer time to respond to the significant words, and is much more likely to give far-fetched or peculiar responses to the significant words.

A second method by which complexes may be discovered and unraveled is by the interpretation of dreams, day dreams and night dreams, which reveal the complex in disguised form. All dreams, according to Freud, are of the "wish fulfillment" type; that is, the person dreams in a disguised form of the fulfillment of wishes which he suppresses during waking life. The dreams are often couched in "symbols," whose meaning only those versed in psychoanalysis are able to interpret.

A third method of discovering complexes is by noting and interpreting certain everyday mental phenomena. Quoting Freud [1]:

> These are the bungling of acts among normal men as well as among neurotics, to which no significance is ordinarily attached; the forgetting of things which one is supposed to know and at other times really does know

---

[2] Freud, Sigmund: "The Origin and Development of Psychoanalysis," *American Journal of Psychology*, April, 1910, p. 194.

(for example, the temporary forgetting of proper names); mistakes in speaking which occur so frequently; and analogous mistakes in writing and in reading, the automatic execution of purposive acts in wrong situations, and the loss or breaking of objects. . . . It follows that they deserve the rank of symptoms, and their observation, like that of dreams, can lead to the discovery of the hidden complexes of the psychic life.

(5) *How to treat the desires when they are back.* After getting the desire back into consciousness, the important thing is to give expression to the emotion which has been repressed. The emotion is expressed by the process of "transference," which is explained by Freud [1] as follows:

Every time that we treat a neurotic psychoanalytically there occurs in him the so-called phenomena of transfer, that is, he applies to the person of the physician a great amount of tender emotion often mixed with enmity, which has no foundation in any real relation, and must be derived in every respect from the old wish fancies of the patient which have become unconscious. Every fragment of his emotional life, which can no longer be called back into memory, is accordingly lived over by the patient in his relation to the physician, and only by such living of them over in the "transfer" is he convinced of the existence and the power of these unconscious sexual excitations.

The dangers and possible embarrassments that may result from this "transfer" are obvious. Where conditions are such that a normal expression cannot be secured for the desires, the desire is sublimated and its energy is supposed to be drained off in a socially approved channel.

Criticisms of psychoanalysis: (a) *The contributions made by Freud's work.* Although many objections can be made to Freud's work, it is only fair to say that he has made a number of significant contributions to the understanding of human nature. In the first place, he deals with the dynamic side of life rather than with the empty speculations of medieval philosophy. His emphasis on the "why" is certainly to be commended. Secondly, he recognizes the effect on behavior of little things which are ordinarily passed over unnoticed. Psychoanalysis emphasizes the fact that nothing happens without a cause — a point of view which is valuable in any scientific work. Thirdly, Freud was one of the first to emphasize

[1] Freud, Sigmund: "The Origin and Development of Psychoanalysis," *American Journal of Psychology*, April, 1910, p. 194.

the part played by emotional thwartings in the production of disease.

(b) *Objections to Freud's work.* In the first place, the Freudians greatly overemphasize sex. While Freud and his followers have made a very positive contribution to the understanding of certain phases of human behavior, their attention has been so occupied with a few things that they have entirely overlooked or ignored certain very important elements in the explanation of behavior. Only a small proportion of our desires are erotic in origin. The fact that sex is not the strongest motivating force in life is brought out clearly in animal experiments. When rats were allowed to choose between satisfaction of the hunger drive and satisfaction of the sex drive, four out of five chose the food. Among humans the situation is not very different; many people marry for money or for social position rather than love; others do not marry because they would not be able to maintain a home in the style they wish. Sex behavior itself is controlled to a great extent by fear of blame and desire for approval, which shows that with the average person these are more powerful motivating forces than is the sex drive.

The psychoanalyst is led to place so much emphasis on sex because he sees only the abnormal cases. The prolonged thwarting of any desire in susceptible individuals may produce a nervous breakdown, but the other drives, as the food drive, are usually not thwarted. In the present social state the sex drive is very often thwarted; therefore those in asylums as the result of mental conflict are chiefly cases of the thwarting of the sex drive. Examples of wholesale breakdowns as the result of conflicting drives in which sex is not involved are not uncommon. The widespread epidemic of "shell-shock" which occurred during the war is an excellent example of nervous breakdowns from causes other than thwarted sex desires. In shell-shock the chief element was the soldier's desire to save his life. We also see many cases of nervous breakdowns brought on by failure in business or by defeat in politics. There are many drives the thwarting of which are conducive to nervous breakdowns, but the Freudians tend to ignore all the drives except the sex drive.

Second, in the life of every individual thousands of desires which cannot be fulfilled are laid aside and forgotten without causing complexes. In general the thwarting of a desire is sufficient cause for a mental breakdown only in the case of neurotic individuals. If every disappointed lover whose former sweetheart married another man were to develop a complex, there would not be enough normal people left to take the names and case histories of those entering hospitals for mental patients.

Third, dreams, instead of always being due to thwarted desires which lie stagnating in the unconscious, are generally due to quite different causes. They are very often caused by such stimuli as cold, an uncomfortable position, or by over-eating, or they may be caused by the leftovers from the excitement of the day before. Nothing could be farther from wish-fulfillment than the dream of dying and going to Hades, a dream which is by no means uncommon.

Fourth, forgetting is not satisfactorily explained by the Freudian contention that the unpleasant and painful memories are forced into the unconscious and apparently forgotten. The things one forgets are not in themselves necessarily painful, but the forgetting of them is sometimes the painful part, as any one who takes examinations knows. Nor does losing a wedding ring always indicate eagerness for a divorce; it may merely mean that the ring was too large for the finger on which it was worn. Remembering and forgetting depend very largely upon interest. We remember the painful things as well as the pleasant things in which we are interested, and we tend to forget those events which hold no particular interest for us.

CHAPTER XV

PSYCHOLOGY AND LAW

"Causes for an act always exist, but causes are not excuses."
JOHN DEWEY

SOME people commit crime and get caught; more people commit crimes with impunity; but most people are in general law-abiding citizens. As little or nothing is known about that group whose criminal careers are never discovered, we shall limit our attention to the group of criminals who by accident or otherwise are apprehended and find themselves in the toils of the law. From a psychological standpoint the major problems relating to this group are: I. Causes of crime; II. Methods of detecting crime; III. Preparation of the case for trial; IV. The trial; V. Corrective measures.

I. CAUSES OF CRIME

No one is a "born criminal," but many are born with tendencies which predispose to a criminal career. All laws grow out of certain drives in human nature. Because most people want to live, we have laws protecting human life. Because the average individual desires to own a certain amount of property, we have laws protecting property. But law is not more surely rooted in human nature than is crime; and so long as human nature remains what it is, so long will crimes be committed. So long as it is human nature to desire what belongs to another, just so long will certain individuals commit murder or burglary to get it.

The causes of crimes are of two general kinds, predisposing causes and motivating causes. By predisposing causes are meant those factors which operate in the background and set the stage as it were for a scene of criminal behavior. By motivating causes are meant the immediate impelling forces, or emotional drives, which serve as the spark to set this behavior in action. For example, one of the predisposing causes of the criminal career of Macbeth was his psychopathic personality, which made him especially susceptible to outside influences, as evidenced by his superstitious acceptance of the prophecy of the witches; while the chief motivating cause was his "vaulting ambition" which was spurred on by the taunting of his wife.

The following causes of crime will be considered: (1) Insanity; (2) Feeble-mindedness; (3) Environmental factors; (4) Use of drugs; (5) Laws which conflict with well-established habits; (6) Emotional drives.

1. Insanity. Insanity has long been recognized as a cause of crime, and is being more and more frequently offered as a defense in criminal procedure. The most obvious types of insanity, such as those accompanied by convulsions, delirium, or marked hallucinations, are generally recognized; but there are certain types of insanity which are likely to lead to serious crimes which are practically never recognized except by an expert in mental diseases. The person suffering from paranoia is usually able to reason logically and to conduct most of his affairs with average judgment, yet when it comes to the question of his fixed delusion he hesitates at nothing that would further his revenge on those who, he imagines, are persecuting him.

The following types of insanity are of importance as a cause of crime: (a) epilepsy; (b) paranoia; (c) paresis; (d) dementia præcox; (e) senile dementia; (f) impulsive obsessions; (g) psychopathic personality.

(a) *Epilepsy.* Epilepsy is a common form of mental disease characterized by attacks which occur at varying intervals and are accompanied by loss of consciousness. Preceding or immediately following the attack the person may be considerably excited, showing undue irritability, and sometimes a condition known as epileptic furor. In this condition he is totally unaware of his acts, and due to his excitement, is liable to kill any one with whom he comes in contact, even though it be his best friend or his dearest relative. A short time ago the writer examined a young man who, when in a state of epileptic furor, had killed his mother. He was practically normal except about the time of an attack, but at that time he had apparently no control over his acts.

(b) *Paranoia.* Paranoia is a mental disease characterized by well-systematized delusions of persecution or grandeur, and accompanied by no apparent mental deterioration. The person suffering from paranoia is by nature suspicious: he tends to attribute his failures in life to the persecutions of his enemies. In the early stages of the disease he usually looks on some powerful organization as his persecutor. Some paranoiacs find their persecution in the Catholic Church, others in the Ku Klux Klan, and others in the League of Nations or some other organization. As the disease progresses, he tends to pick out some particular individual in these organizations and to attribute his persecutions to him. At first he runs away from his imaginary persecutors; later he designs all sorts of schemes to protect himself, and in the end he frequently turns and attacks his supposed enemy. It often happens that the unfortunate victim of this attack was totally unacquainted with the paranoiac, and had never harmed him in the least. Conklin cites the case of the owner of a small farm who was apprehended after a neighbor of his had been seriously injured by an explosion which occurred when he placed in his kitchen stove a stick of wood in which dynamite had been concealed. Another stick of wood exactly like that used by the injured man was found in the home of the farmer, and this stick was also loaded with dynamite. An examination of the farmer showed the typical paranoid history, including a long series of imaginary persecutions from which he sought to escape by killing his neighbor as indicated above.

(c) *Paresis.* Paresis is a type of insanity caused by syphilitic infection of the brain. The disease usually begins insidiously: the energetic become lazy; the ambitious, slothful; the virtuous, dissolute; the miserly, extravagant; the timid, aggressive; and the truthful, false. There is no consistency of purpose. As the judgment fails, marked egotism and grandiose ideas develop. The patient becomes boastful and delights in telling of his wonderful powers. A previously respected citizen, probably one of the pillars of society, suddenly begins to associate with dissolute characters, and to sink into drunkenness and debauchery. During this time he may commit various types of crimes, especially those of a sex nature, or due to his grandiose delusions, he may imagine himself to be immensely wealthy and attempt to pass bad checks.

(d) *Dementia præcox.* Dementia præcox is a mental disease which usually occurs in the late teens or early twenties and is characterized by the appearance of delusions and hallucinations early in the course of the disease. It progresses with a rapid mental deterioration, ending in complete dementia. It is one of the most frequent types of insanity. Like paranoia, it is very frequently accompanied by delusions of persecution, and by a belief on the part of the patient that his life is in danger. He hears imaginary voices speaking to him, and these voices often incite him to acts of violence. As this disease is accompanied by such marked mental deterioration that the judgment is seriously impaired, all sorts of anti-social conduct may be manifested.

(e) *Senile dementia.* Due to the anatomical changes which accompany senility, old age is not infrequently accompanied by dementia. The normal inhibitions become greatly weakened, resulting in the manifestations of anti-social conduct, particularly vagrancy and sex crimes. Paranoid delusions are often developed and occasionally lead to such serious crimes as murder or arson.

(f) *Impulsive obsessions.* Some persons seem to be possessed of an inner urge to one particular line of anti-social behavior. Among the most common impulsive obsessions are: kleptomania — an uncontrollable impulse to steal without any real desire or use for the stolen articles; dipsomania — the uncontrollable craving for drink; and pyromania, a morbid desire to start fires. In a recent case in Washington, D.C., a pyromaniac was apprehended who admitted that during his life he had set fire to several hundred buildings. In one night he started so many fires in Washington that the fire departments from Baltimore and other surrounding places were called on to lend aid in fighting the fire.

(g) *Psychopathic personality.* An individual with a psychopathic personality usually manifests great emotional instability, and is unable to withstand an average amount of emotional stress and strain. His inhibitory mechanisms are very weak, and as a consequence he becomes easily involved in criminal behavior. This is one of the most difficult types of mental abnormality to detect. In it are included pathological liars, various degenerates, and the group of "moral imbeciles." Psychopaths are very frequently involved in medico-legal cases. During the last two years several notorious crimes which have attracted the attention of the whole nation have been committed by psychopaths.

The part played by mental abnormality in crime is indicated in the following table:

PER CENT DISTRIBUTION OF CRIMES AMONG CLINICAL GROUPS
(646 PATIENTS) [1]

CRIMES	PER CENT OF TOTAL CRIMES						
	SENILE	GENERAL PARALYSIS (PARESIS)	ALCO-HOLIC	MANIC-DE-PRESSIVE	DEMENTIA PRÆCOX	C.P.I.[2]	WITH MENTAL DEFI-CIENCY
Homicide......	..	2.9	17.6	2.9	32.4	14.7	17.6
Assault........	..	3.8	24.1	7.6	25.3	17.7	6.3
Burglary......	..	13.2	..	7.9	39.5	23.7	5.3
Larceny.......	1.3	22.8	5.1	6.3	24.1	15.2	7.6
Public Intoxication..	2.9	2.9	70.6	..	5.9	5.9	..
Disorderly Conduct.....	2.4	13.4	17.1	12.2	17.1	17.1	7.3
Vagrancy or Prostitution..	8.5	15.4	13.8	4.3	35.1	6.9	7.4
All crimes.....	3.6	11.5	16.9	7.3	25.5	14.7	7.4

Without doubt psychopathic trends play an important part in crime, and it should be the immediate object of the psychiatrists to develop more objective methods of demonstrating the existence of these trends. Instead of talking so much about the emotional dullness of the psychopath, his pathological inconsistency and deformity of character, his high degree of impressionability and suggestibility, his instability and weakness of will, psychiatrists should discover some means of measuring emotional dullness, just as we now measure intellectual dullness. The determination of the moral stability of the criminal ought to rest on more than an opinion basis.

2. **Feeble-mindedness.** The feeble-minded differ, in general, from the insane in that the feeble-minded have never possessed intelligence, whereas the insane may have once had it; or, to state it more crudely, the feeble-minded have never arrived; the insane have ar-

[1] Table from Glueck, S. S. *Mental Disorders and the Criminal Law* (Little, Brown Company, Boston, 1925), 326.

[2] Constitutional Psychopathic Inferior.

rived and departed. One of the chief forces contributing to criminal behavior is the inability to foresee the consequences of an act. The more lacking in intelligence an individual is, the less able he is to judge in advance the results of his behavior. Since the development of standardized intelligence tests, many studies of the intelligence of criminals and delinquents have been made. In some groups as many as ninety per cent were found to be feeble-minded; in others as few as seven per cent were feeble-minded. After analyzing a thousand cases of repeaters from the Juvenile Court of Chicago, Healy concluded that about ten per cent were definitely feeble-minded, and that the percentage of feeble-mindedness increased with the age of the group tested. Concerning feeble-mindedness among criminals generally, Healy states that various reformatory or prison populations, if properly tested, would show from ten to thirty per cent or even more to be feeble-minded.

Kuhlmann [1] recently reported a comparison of the intelligence levels of inmates of penal and corrective institutions with those of the general population on the basis of school surveys in twenty-three towns. The prisoners were consistently inferior to the general population. Kuhlmann reports the relationship of the proportion of individuals of different I.Q. levels in a State prison group of 969 inmates as compared with the proportion in the general population (on the basis of school surveys). The following table indicates for each I.Q. level, the number of times greater the proportion is in the prison group than in the general population. For example, 8.32 times as many prisoners as members of the general population had I.Q.'s below 75; 1.54 times as many prisoners as members of the general population had I.Q.'s between 75 and 84; .61 or about six tenths as many prisoners as members of the general population had I.Q.'s between 85 and 94; etc.

I.Q.	0–74	75–84	85–94	95–104	105–114	115–124	125 up
RELATIONSHIP	8.32	1.54	.61	.40	.28	.25	.20

An average of a large number of recent investigations would place the per cent of apprehended criminals who are feeble-minded at

[1] Kuhlmann, F.: *Biennial Report. Division of Research of the State Board of Control, Minnesota, for period ending June 30, 1926.*

about 25. The following studies will give some idea of the extent of feeble-mindedness in different penal institutions. Spaulding found 44 per cent of 400 prisoners he tested feeble-minded. In another group of 300, Rossy found only 22 per cent feeble-minded. Gilliland found 33 per cent of the 100 inmates of a workhouse feeble-minded, and Terman and Knollin found only 17 per cent of 155 tested in a penitentiary feeble-minded.

While feeble-mindedness is in general a cause of crime, there are certain crimes which feeble-mindedness prevents the individual from committing. Inasmuch as the feeble-minded can seldom read or write, they are practically never guilty of forgery; they neither originate "get rich quick" schemes nor sell fake oil stock. On the other hand, there are certain crimes to which feeble-mindedness especially predisposes. Being of low mentality, the feeble-minded frequently find it difficult to keep a job, and as a result, are especially prone to vagrancy. They rank particularly high in petty thievery, and in the use of violence in connection with robbery. Defectives are about twice as common among murderers as the law of chance would lead one to expect.

After an intensive study of native white, colored, and foreign-born criminals, Murchison concludes that crimes against property are consistently committed by groups in general superior to the groups committing crimes against the person, and that the more abstract crimes against property are consistently committed by still more superior persons.

From the above studies it is apparent that while feeble-mindedness predisposes to crime, its importance is markedly influenced by the type of crime.

3. **Environmental factors.** If an individual were living alone on a totally isolated island, he would be unable to commit crime; for crime exists only when the rights of others are violated. Among the environmental factors which contribute to crime are; (*a*) Bad neighborhoods; (*b*) Economic conditions; (*c*) Defective social machinery; (*d*) Publicity given crime; (*e*) External conditions.

(*a*) *Bad neighborhoods.* It is natural for one to long for the approval of his associates, and to do whatever is necessary to secure this approval. So long as one acts as his associates do, they can find little fault with his conduct. We generally judge the rightness or wrongness of our own conduct by the way our immediate acquaintances react to it.

Every city has its vicious neighborhoods where all types of crimes and delinquency are generally practiced. Criminal gangs flourish in such communities, because the force of community opinion favors rather than opposes criminal behavior. Burgess found that in the same city delinquency in some neighborhoods was eight times as frequent as in others. Spot maps which locate the scene of crimes indicate these neighborhoods with unerring accuracy.

(b) *Economic conditions.* There is a close relation between the economic status and the probability of criminal behavior. Most convicted criminals belong to the poorer classes. In Italy it has been found that while sixty per cent of the Italian population belong to the poorer classes, they furnish from eighty-five to ninety per cent of the convicted persons. This condition may be due in part to the fact that the richer criminals have sufficient money to escape conviction, but it is also due to the fact that the poor man has more cause for crime than the rich man, for the poor need food, clothing, and shelter, and sometimes do not have the money to provide these things. Sutherland [1] summarizes the relation of crime and poverty as follows:

Poverty generally means a low status, with little to lose, little to respect, little to be proud of, little to sustain efforts to improve. It generally means bad housing conditions, lack of sanitation in the vicinity, and lack of attractive community institutions. It generally means both parents away from home for long hours with the fatigue, lack of control of children, and irritation that go with these. It generally means withdrawal of the child from school at an early age, and the beginning of mechanical labor with weakening of the home control, the development of anti-social grudges, and a lack of cultural contacts. Poverty, together with the display of wealth in shop windows, streets, and picture shows, generally means envy and hatred of the rich and the feeling of missing much in life because of the lack of satisfaction of the fundamental drives. Poverty seldom forces people to steal or to become prostitutes in order to escape starvation. It produces its effects most frequently on the attitudes rather than on the organism.

[1] Sutherland, E. H.: *Criminology* (Lippincott, 1924), 168.

(c) *Defective social machinery.* In the medical field, preventive medicine is considered to be much more important than curative medicine: but in the legal field, preventive law is a term practically unknown. Most of our penal institutions, instead of tending to prevent crime, are the chief promoters of the very conditions which they seek to prevent. Boys go into our reformatories with one vice and come out with a knowledge of all the vices. Girls are sent to our training schools for some minor violation, and there receive a liberal education in "delinquency — its methods and practices." Concerning the demoralizing influence of prison life Oscar Wilde, who had served a term in prison, said:

"The vilest deeds like poison weeds
Bloom well in prison-air:
It is only what is good in man
That wastes and withers there."

(d) *Publicity given crime.* That most people are open to suggestion is generally conceded. The box-car headlines announcing the sensational facts of each new murder and the tabloid presentations of the more intriguing criminal scenes seem to cry to their million readers "go thou and do likewise." For an individual of a psychopathic personality the description of some lurid crime may be the exciting force necessary to induce him to the commission of a similar crime. The front-page descriptions of the act of some unfortunate who has ended his sorrows by taking his own life, point the remedy to many others who find their heartaches and burdens difficult to bear. The widespread publicity given to crime, vice, and profligacy tend to make these things attractive. From the evidence brought out in the Hickman case, the publicity given to the Remus case, and to the Loeb and Leopold case, played no small part in preparing Hickman for the commission of his crime.

(e) *External conditions.* As pointed out in Chapter IV such factors as climate, season, and weather have their influence on human behavior. As these factors have been discussed in some detail in that chapter, only the more important facts will be summarized at this point: (1) In warm climates crimes against persons are more prevalent than crimes against property. (2) There is a seasonal variation in crime; crimes against property being more numerous in winter and those against persons more numerous in summer. (3) More drunkenness occurs during the winter months and on cold days. (4) More cases of insanity develop during the hot days of summer.

4. Use of drugs. Drugs exert a double effect in contributing to the causation of crime. In the first place, an individual under the influence of drugs very often has his reasoning ability paralyzed, and in that condition he is totally unable to distinguish between right and wrong. This is particularly true in the case of chronic alcoholics. In the second place, most drugs are habit-forming, and build up so strong a desire for the drug that the addict will resort to any behavior, criminal or otherwise, to secure it. This is well illustrated in the case of the dope fiend, who frequently resorts to robbery or even murder in order to secure his drug. For a more complete discussion of the effect of drugs, the reader is referred to Chapter III.

5. Laws which conflict with well-established habits. Without law there can be no crime, for crime is by definition a "violation of law." Thus an act which is considered as criminal at one time is condoned a century later, and as new laws are made, new violations, or crimes, arise. Since crime is a violation of law, it is obvious that if a law comes into existence which conflicts very radically with the habits of a large percentage of people, this law will be violated to a large extent as the result of habit. Such an instance was seen in the passage of the Eighteenth Amendment to the Constitution. Very many of our citizens were in the habit of taking alcoholic beverages consequently, when this law was enacted, many were unwilling to change their habits; the result being the wholesale violation of the prohibition law which is seen to-day. No such widespread violation would have occurred if a law had been passed to prevent the drinking of absinthe, for few people in America have ever formed that habit. When a law was passed preventing the smoking of opium, it was violated by relatively few native Americans, for they have never built up habits of smoking opium, but if a law were passed preventing the smoking of tobacco, a radically different reaction would be met with; not that the tobacco habit is stronger than the opium habit, but because so many more people in America use tobacco than use opium.

Society's attitude toward breaking laws has a considerable influence upon the extent to which they are broken. Society does not take seriously such petty thievery as that involved in stealing apples from a neighbor's orchard. Even the bootlegger is not regarded as a criminal by many people. Instead, his crime is laughed at, and he is patronized by many of those who should prosecute him. Society refuses to treat bootlegging seriously because the Eighteenth Amendment does not have its full approval, and the breaking of an unpopular law is easily condoned.

6. Emotional drives. In the last analysis, the real basis for crime is found in the nature of those who commit crimes. As long as it is human nature to become jealous, and to long for revenge, just so long will murders be committed; and as long as the tendency to become angry is an essential part of the make-up of man, so long will we have crimes of assault and battery. As long as men and women are prone to love not wisely but too well, so long will the eternal triangle exist; and as long as the possession of property can give to its possessor so many of the pleasures of life, so long will there be injunctions like the following: "Get money, my son, get money. Honestly if you can, dishonestly if you can't, but get money."

As pointed out in Chapter I, the behavior of any one is the resultant of his drives to action and the opposing resistances. The same emotional drives which cause criminal acts also motivate the normal acts of normal people. One individual is hungry and steals, the immediate cause of the theft growing out of the normal hunger drive; another individual becomes involved in a love affair and commits murder, the basis of the murder being the thwarting of the love drive. No one would seriously claim that it is pathological to desire either food or affection, yet these desires resulted in the commission of anti-social acts. Thus it is seen that the immediate cause of crime usually lies in the thwarting of a normal impulse of the individual.

On analyzing several hundred murder cases, Arthur Train[1] found that about seventy-five per cent of the killings were due to quarrels

[1] Train, Arthur C.: *Courts, Criminals and the Camorra*, Scribner's, New York, 1912.

over small sums or other matters, drink, and women; over fifty per cent to petty quarrels, and about thirty per cent to quarrels over more significant things. The disproportion between the causes of the crimes and the seriousness of the crimes is shown by the fact that in three of these particular cases tried in a single week, the total amount involved in the disputes was only eighty-five cents, an average of less than thirty cents per life. In the days of our forefathers many murders grew out of quarrels about dogs or pigs, and to-day we read of murders growing out of quarrels concerning insignificant automobile accidents.

II. METHODS OF DETECTING CRIME

From time immemorial, man has devised methods of differentiating the guilty from the innocent. In the days when anti-social and criminal persons were thought to be possessed of the devil or inhabited by demons, a person's guilt was determined by a "trial by water," in which the accused was thrown into a river. If he drowned, he was pronounced innocent, and immediately forgiven; if he survived, he was considered guilty, and punished accordingly. Another method based on superstition was the "trial by fire." The accused was forced to thrust his hand into a fire. If he was burned his guilt was established, but if he was innocent Divine Providence was supposed to protect him just as the Hebrew children were protected in the fiery furnace.

The following methods are used for the detection of crime: (1) Third-Degree Methods; (2) Study of Criminal Habits; (3) Analysis of Motives; (4) Experimental Methods.

1. **Third-degree methods.** Although not an orthodox or ethically approved method, the third degree is one of the methods most commonly used by police officers for wringing a confession from the accused. To bring about the confession, it is often necessary to keep the accused without food or sleep for hours, to exhaust him physically and mentally by continuous questioning, to nag him, to threaten him, sometimes even to torture him. In the more important cases the accused is put through some sort of a stiff line of questioning by the captain at the station-house. If the prisoner fails to respond to this line of treatment he is turned over to a sergeant and

two privates, who can use more drastic methods. If the bullying and inquisitorial methods fail to make the prisoner break down and "give up what he knows," he may be placed in a cell with a "stool-pigeon" who will try to worm a confession out of him, or he may be subjected to a heart-to-heart talk in some isolated room with an officer.

Using this method for the detection of crime, the measure of endurance becomes in no small part the direct measure of guilt. The evils of the system are obvious. Innocent men sometimes find it easier to confess an uncommitted crime, and in some instances to describe in detail an act they did not commit, than to bear up under the continual torture of their examiners.

2. Study of criminal habits. The study of criminal habits, when supplemented by such data as finger-prints and other objective data, is one of the methods most generally used in the detection and apprehension of criminals. Criminals, like others, develop certain habits of procedure. The professional criminal usually commits more than one crime of a given type. By familiarizing themselves with the methods commonly used by certain habitual criminals in the commission of their crimes, the police officers are often able to find certain common elements in any new crime which point directly to the man who committed it. For example, in Washington a series of burglaries were committed by a man who specialized in robbing certain types of houses in a rather circumscribed locality. He gained admission to all the houses in practically the same way, and the things he stole at the various houses were quite similar. The various burglaries had so many common elements that the study of any given crime led rather easily to placing the responsibility for the crime. Most of our detective bureaus have in their files a fairly complete record of the criminal habits of the more notorious criminals. These records are exchanged by detective bureaus in different cities, and aid very materially in the detection and apprehension of criminals.

3. Analysis of motives. The method which has been used throughout the ages, and which still offers the most certain results in detecting wrongdoers is based on the assumption that certain motives underlie conduct. When a crime is committed, the first thing to do is to discover the motives that produced the crime; and the second thing to do is to discover which individuals would be most likely to possess such motives. Take for an example the case of a married man and a woman other than his wife who were found murdered on a lonely road. The reputation of both had been above reproach. No witnesses to the murder could be found, and the task of solving it depended upon discovering the motives of the murderer. The following motives for the crime were suggested. First, robbery — but neither the money nor the jewelry had been taken from the bodies; second, accident — but the woman was shot several times and the print of a sharp heel was seen on her face; third, jealousy. This last theory was borne out by the facts. It was next necessary to decide what person would have jealousy as a motive for committing the crime. In this instance the evidence seemed unmistakable; the man had been shot once, and after death his hands had been folded gently over his breast; the woman had been shot four times and after death the murderer had stamped on her face. In view of these facts there could be little doubt that the murderer was very bitter toward the woman, but still retained a feeling of tenderness toward the man. Recognition of the motive for the murder considerably limits the number suspected, and points toward the guilty individual.

4. Experimental methods. Since the advent of experimental psychology, numerous attempts have been made to find a short and sure road to the detection of crime. All the methods experimented with are based on the assumption that when examined the guilty suspect will show more emotional disturbance than would an innocent person. Accordingly, means of measuring emotional disturbances are devised. The word association test offers a promising method of determining emotional responses. This test consists of a list of one hundred words, most of which bear no relation to the crime, but some of which are peculiarly significant to one who knows all the details of the crime. As each word is pronounced to the suspect he is asked to respond with the first word that comes into his mind. It is assumed that the guilty man will give abnormal responses to significant words, or hesitate an unusually long time in responding to words closely related to the crime. Deviations from the normal response indicate that closer examination of the suspect is desirable.   This method is discussed in more detail in Chapter XIV.

Another experimental method to which Larson and Marsden have given considerable attention is based on the measurement of bodily changes which accompany emotional disturbances.   Larson attempted to detect lying or deception by changes in the heart and respiratory rates.   He secured continuous blood-pressure and respiratory curves while the suspect was replying to a number of questions answerable by "yes" or "no."   He found that when an individual gave false answers the curves differed from the normal curves for the same individual.   Larson claims that using this method it is possible to select the guilty from the innocent before confession in about ninety per cent of the cases, and that the records of experienced offenders can be as easily interpreted as those of first offenders.   He believes that blood-pressure and breathing curves can be made sufficiently reliable to be introduced into court as evidence of guilt or innocence.   At present little practical use is made of the experimental methods.

III. GETTING THE CASE READY FOR TRIAL

Just as in war victory is usually on the side of the army with the most reserves, so in criminal procedure guilt or innocence is determined in no small part by the amount of money or influence the defendant can marshal to his cause.   According to Hobhouse the modern criminal trial is a "battle by purse instead of a battle by person."   Let us consider a hypothetical case.   Two murders are committed; one by the friendless son of a ne'er-do-well; the other by the frolicsome son of a millionaire.   Both murders are equally atrocious and cruel.   Theoretically, both murderers should receive the same punishment, but such is not the case.   Murderer No. 1, being without friends or money, is unable to hire a lawyer to defend him, and after the trial has actually begun, a young, inexperienced lawyer is drafted by the judge to defend him.   Neither time permits nor is there sufficient money available with which to prepare a plausible defense.   The trial is hastened through with such celerity that murderer No. 1 is buried and forgotten three months after the commission of the crime. Murderer No. 2 has on his side all the aids and legal technicalities which wealth and influential friends can provide. Long before the case is called, the counsel for the defense has mapped out a line of procedure. The scene of the murder is studied, and the witnesses are interviewed. Special detectives and investigators are employed to "get something on" or to remove the more damaging witnesses of the prosecution; and it occasionally happens that through the influence of money, witnesses are found who are willing to perjure themselves to establish an alibi for the accused or in some other way to further his cause. Various expert witnesses are brought from afar to examine the defendant and to prepare to testify in his behalf. In so far as possible the press is controlled, and public opinion is influenced in behalf of the accused. Realizing that the sympathy of the public for the murdered man tends to die out with time, and the resentment against the murderer to become less, numerous technicalities will be resorted to in order to postpone the trial. A case is sometimes postponed through one technicality or another, for as long as eight or ten years, by which time many of the witnesses for the prosecution have either died or moved away, and public feeling is no longer hostile to the defendant. When it is not possible to postpone the trial, the defense frequently asks for a "change of venue"; i.e., it is asked that the case be tried in another community where the victim was not known, and where consequently there is much less resentment against the murderer. The inequality of murderer No. 1 and murderer No. 2 before the law is apparent to all. The part that money may play in criminal cases is well illustrated by the Thaw case, in which it is estimated that the defense spent over $300,000.

In the preparation of the case, three factors stand out as of paramount importance: the lawyers, the jury, and the witnesses.

1. **Selecting the lawyers and preparing the case.** In the olden days, when it was customary for legal disputes to be settled by trial by combat, the custom was introduced of substituting a defender to fight instead of the accused. Thus began the custom of employing attorneys to represent the interests of the accused, and as in the olden days the fate of the accused depended upon the skillful thrusts of his defender, so in modern trials the accused's release or

conviction is largely determined by the skill with which his attorney conducts the case. The State's attorney is selected by the people, and is supposed to see that all concerned receive justice. In practice, it usually works out that the State's attorney conceives his job to be the securing of conviction at any price. Being the officer duly elected to represent the State, he receives his cases automatically. The lawyer for the defense, on the other hand, is chosen by the accused for the express purpose of looking after the interests of the accused. His selection is therefore determined by the type of case involved, and his reputed skill in handling such cases. Many times the defense is not content with employing one lawyer, but employs different ones for the diverse features of the case. Besides these, additional attorneys, various so-called experts, are employed and paid by the accused to testify in his behalf. If the accused can command the money necessary to pay the fee, he can secure lawyers to defend him who are much more brilliant than the State's attorney who will oppose him. But if the accused has not the fee, he is represented by a lawyer far inferior to the State's attorney.

2. **Selecting the jury.** A famous criminal lawyer once said: "Get your jury and the case will take care of itself." Selecting the jury represents a conflict of interests; the prosecution, seeking conviction, desires twelve men who will not hesitate to convict; and the defense, desiring an acquittal, is especially anxious for a similar number with leanings toward acquittal.

For some time before the case is called, every member of a panel is subjected to an unseen inquisitorial process. The prosecutor, by the aid of his private investigators, studies with minute care the political and social affiliations, the family connections, the economic status, the personal habits, and the past performances of every potential juryman, so that he may know exactly whom to accept and whom to refuse when the case is called. The extent of the preliminary investigations made by the defense is determined very largely by the amount of money he can provide. In the case of the wealthy defendant the inquisitorial process is much more thorough than is that made by the prosecution, whereas in the case of a poverty-stricken defendant, no preliminary investigation of the jury is made. When the case has actually been called, days, weeks, or even months are expended in finding twelve jurymen acceptable to both the defense and the prosecution. In a case cited by Sutherland, 4821 were examined and the jury fees amounted to thirteen thousand dollars before twelve men acceptable for jury duty were found. In a recent case in Washington, D.C., six hundred talesmen were called before twelve jurymen were accepted.

In selecting the jury advantage is taken of race, sex, age, religion, politics, fraternal organizations, social status, occupation, and other factors which tend to prejudice the minds of the prospective jurymen. Other things being equal, it is recognized that individuals are more tolerant of crimes committed by one of their race against an individual of another race. Nationality, religion, and the other factors mentioned above play the same rôle. That being true, the proper thing would be to get a jury in no way connected with the defense or prosecution. For example, if a Protestant had killed a Catholic, the logical jury would be composed of Jews. But unfortunately neither the prosecution nor the defense would agree to such an arrangement. Both sides are looking for sympathetic ears into which to pour their pleadings.

3. Selecting and preparing the witnesses. While the jury may be impartial, the witnesses practically never are. Both the prosecution and the defense select their witnesses for a specific end; the prosecution, to produce conviction; the defense, to produce acquittal. If, in the preliminary examination of witnesses before the case begins, it is found that a proposed witness will give testimony injurious to his side of the case, neither the prosecution nor the defense will hesitate to dispense with his services. Practically without exception, all the witnesses in criminal cases are interviewed by the side that proposes to offer them as witnesses before the case is brought to trial in order to "get a line on" their testimony. As the memory of the average witness is extremely unreliable, by using suggestion the lawyers are frequently able to make him think he remembers events which have never occurred. In that way, one side is frequently able to build a chain of evidence which, although untrue, can be made to appear thoroughly reliable and impregnable.

IV. THE TRIAL

1. Setting the stage. Since most people are controlled by sympathy, and have their sympathy considerably aroused by things they see, no skillful attorney overlooks the question of stage-setting in the more important trials. No detail is so small that it can be neglected. The aged mother of the defendant, wearing a black bonnet, with a shawl draped over her bent shoulders, sits sobbing in the courtroom, apparently broken by grief. The wife and small children of the defendant are brought into the courtroom looking the picture of woe, and are used effectively to produce a sympathetic feeling in the minds of the jury. Parsons [1] cites the case of two men who were indicted for the killing of a railroad detective who caught them in the act of robbing a freight car. They were both arrested at the home of one of them, and part of the loot of previous robberies was discovered. They were tried separately. The first to be tried was a single man, and he was convicted. His partner, whose wife and small child were constantly in the courtroom, was acquitted, in spite of the fact that exactly the same evidence and witnesses were presented against him. In his case the defense decided to stake everything on an emotional appeal, and won by so doing. The prosecuting attorney is not willing to be outdone in this important matter of stage-setting. The desolate widow of the murdered man is given prominence, and her now "fatherless" children are usually present in the courtroom.

Having thus set the stage, attention is paid by the defendant's lawyers to the appearance of their client. He is taught how to assume the sad appearance of one who is deeply wronged, for it is realized that such things do not pass unnoticed by the average juryman. When the case is called, the defendant comes in "looking like an early Christian martyr."

2. Presenting the evidence. Through the aid of witnesses, chosen as indicated above, the testimony is presented. In many cases the witnesses are honest, but their testimony is unreliable; in others, due to bias, or deliberate perjury, the evidence is vitiated.

(*a*) *Unreliability of evidence.* Time and again it has been demonstrated that the most honest and intelligent eye-witnesses to

[1] Parsons, P. A.: *Crime and the Criminal* (Alfred A. Knopf, 1926), p. 212.

an act are unable to testify about it with any degree of accuracy or unanimity. There are two main sources of unreliability of evidence: (1) faulty observation, and (2) imperfect memory.

(1) *Unreliability due to faulty observation.* Faulty observation may be due to defective judgment, to poor sense organs, or to lack of training in the thing to be observed. Weber demonstrated this lack of observation in a very clever experiment. At a meeting of the Association of Legal Psychology and Psychiatry in the Grand Duchy of Hesse at Göttingen, during one of the sessions, a clown and negro rushed in, and after an excited altercation, rushed out. No one in the audience had expected the occurrence, nor was aware that it was only an experiment. Each one present was asked to write an account of it. Forty reports were handed in, and of these there was only one whose omissions of important details amounted to less than 20 per cent. Fourteen omitted 20 to 40 per cent of the important details, twelve omitted 40 to 50 per cent, and thirteen more than 50 per cent. In only six papers were there no absolute misstatements of facts; in twenty-four reports, 10 per cent of the statements were purely imaginary, and in ten, more than 10 per cent of the statements were absolutely false.

The effect of lack of training in a specific line of observation is illustrated by the following experiment which was conducted by the author: A class of two hundred college students were asked to estimate the time which elapsed between two signals, thirteen seconds apart. The average estimate was approximately forty seconds, and the range of estimates was from seven seconds to as high as four and a half minutes. This shows the unreliability of estimates of time; yet conviction or acquittal often depends on just such testimony.

Defective sensory apparatus is another cause of faulty observation. When two witnesses see the same dress, and one swears that it is red, whereas the other is equally certain that it is not red, are we to infer that one of them is deliberately lying or that he is colorblind? If a witness sees an automobile under one type of illumination it may appear blue, whereas with a different illumination the color is reported as black. One witness swears the motorist sounded his horn before rounding the corner; another that he did not. In such cases the failure of witnesses to agree may be due, not to dishonesty on the part of either, but to defective sense organs.

(2) *Unreliability due to imperfect memory.* The defects of memory are more detrimental to the reliability of evidence than are those of faulty observation. Few events are remembered with very much accuracy four days after they occur; yet the witnesses are expected to recall in great detail the happenings of four years ago. The following case from Swift [1] is an excellent illustration of the part played in evidence by treacherous memory.

In 1871 Alexander Jester started east from Kansas in a light spring wagon with canvas top, drawn by two small pony horses. While fording a stream near Emporia, as the horses were drinking, he fell into conversation with Gilbert Gates, a young man who was returning from homesteading land in Kansas. Young Gates was traveling in what was then known as a prairie-schooner drawn by a pair of heavy horses. Jester had three young deer in his wagon, and Gates a buffalo calf. They decided to travel together, and give exhibitions with their animals to meet expenses. When they reached Paris, Missouri, Gates had disappeared. Jester's explanation, at the preliminary hearing, was that he became homesick and sold his outfit to him that he might hasten home by rail. Jester was seen leaving Paris driving Gates' heavy team with his own lighter team tied behind. Later he sold the heavy horses and various other articles known to have belonged to Gates, but which he claimed were purchased. It is not the purpose of the writer to decide the merits of the case, but rather to call attention to certain exceedingly interesting psychological features.

Jester was soon arrested but escaped, and was not brought to trial until 1901. Thirty years had therefore passed since the events concerning which witnesses were called upon to testify. Besides, there was a blinding snowstorm at the time when the crime was supposed to have been committed; and of course, this would have interfered with accurate observation. Further, when the witnesses "saw" the things which they related, they were not aware that a crime had been committed. Two preliminary questions thus suggest themselves: First, would any one note, as carefully as the subsequent testimony indicated, the peculiarities of a chance traveler on the road, especially in a blinding snowstorm, and at a time when no reason existed, so far as is known, for unusual observation? Second, would observers, under these circumstances, be likely to remember, after the lapse of thirty years, the minute details of what they had seen?

[1] Swift, E. J.: *Psychology and the Day's Work* (Scribner's, New York, 1918), pp. 273–77.

The incidents were of the unimportant, uninteresting sort that were frequently experienced at that time. Even the prairie-schooner could hardly have been exceptional enough to attract special attention, since, as will be seen later on, one of the witnesses was taking his wedding trip on horseback, with his wife behind him on the same horse. But let us turn to the testimony.

When the trial was held, two women described the size and color of all the horses, the harness of the heavy team, the figure and appearance of Jester — height, a little over six feet; weight, about one hundred and eighty pounds, with a hook-nose, grey eyes, powerful physique, and large hands. They further testified that, looking into the first wagon as it approached, they saw lying in the bottom the outlines of a human form with a buffalo-robe thrown over it; and they gave this testimony confidently, thirty years after the crime, notwithstanding they were twelve and fourteen years of age, respectively, when the events transpired, and though they were riding at a canter in the face of a heavy snowstorm, with veils tied over their faces, and the horses which they met were traveling at a fast trot when they passed in the storm. A farmer swore that the buffalo-robe was covered with blood, and still another witness that, while helping Jester start his wagon, the canvas blew back and he saw the body of a man with his throat cut. The description of the body was that of young Gates.

A man who had just been married, and was taking his wife behind him on his horse to their new home, described the horses attached to each wagon, the wagons, and the dog; and this in spite of the fact that his own horse was going at the "single-foot" gait, that Jester's horses were trotting fast, that it was snowing hard, and that, being on his honeymoon, other thoughts and interests would seem to be occupying his mind.

A man of thirty-six, who consequently was six years of age at the time of the crime, testified that later, during the thaw and heavy rains of spring, he and his father saw the body of a young man of eighteen or twenty years of age floating down the stream. He described the color of his hair and complexion, and said that he had on a blue-checked shirt and blue overalls. His description of the shirt agreed with that of Mrs. Gates of a shirt which she had made for her son. It is interesting to note, in this connection, that neither the father of the six-year-old boy nor the girls who saw the outline of a human form in the wagon, nor the man who helped start Jester off, said anything about their observations until Gates' disappearance and Jester's arrest had been published.

The witnesses in the foregoing case were people of good reputation, who honestly believed they were telling the truth. But it seems obvious that no casual witness could testify so accurately after thirty years. Swift explains how it happened as follows:

The key to the mystery lies in the way in which the case was worked up, in the publicity which it received, and in human psychology. After Jester's final arrest, Pinkerton detectives were employed and seven or eight leading criminal lawyers of Missouri and Chicago were engaged to assist the prosecution. The detectives, as they secured one fact after another, cultivated the information by suggestive questions and statements to those with whom they conversed. When, for example, a prospective witness said that there was a buffalo-robe in the wagon the detectives would ask if it covered the outlines of a human form. The man would think it likely, and soon that it did. Of course the case was featured in the county newspapers. It was a first-class news story. Pictures were published, pictures of Jester and Gates, pictures of the horses and wagons, pictures of the dog, and pictures of scenes in the chain of events leading to the alleged crime. The pictures were based on what witnesses said they saw, and what the detectives said they must have seen, and reportorial imagination supplied whatever was lacking. The clothing of Gates was described, the articles he had with him were enumerated, the facts to which certain witnesses would swear were told to other witnesses and reported in the newspapers. Indeed, all the events of the crime as it was conceived by witnesses, reporters, and detectives were portrayed and described with much the effect of a moving-picture representation, until fact and fiction were indistinguishable. It is a well-known principle of psychology that if you tell a man something often enough he finally accepts it; and as he continually repeats it, even as a possible fact, it ends by becoming firmly fixed. Then he believes that he saw or heard it.

The amount remembered with the lapse of time is graphically shown in Chart 28. Over half of the details are forgotten during the first half-day; by the end of the fourth day, less than twenty per cent of the details are remembered; and by the close of the first week approximately ninety per cent of the details have been forgotten.

(b) *Vitiation of evidence.* In trying the case an effort is made to get damaging evidence into the minds of the jurymen concerning the opposite side, by introducing leading questions as to the previous bad conduct or reputation of some of them. Insinuations which have no bearing whatever on the case are made, and suggestions about facts, situations and events that have never occurred are slipped into the examination of the witnesses. Of course, the questions by which the damaging suggestions are introduced are promptly objected to by the opposition, and are ruled out by the court as not pertaining to the case; but while the suggestions are stricken out of the testimony they are far from being wiped out of the minds of the jurymen, and their effect in determining the decision of the jury is often of paramount importance.

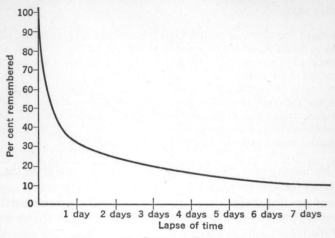

FIGURE 28. CURVE OF FORGETTING

Much of the straightforward evidence on which the decision should logically be based is distorted and camouflaged by the opposing side. Certain well-known tricks are used. For example, to offset the well-considered evidence of an expert witness, the opposing side may attempt to show that the expert is a theoretical rather than a practical man, and hence that "the practical men of the jury should not believe him." Another insidious way of weakening expert testimony is to show that the witness is receiving remuneration for the time he is giving. While it is just as logical that an expert engineer should be paid for testifying as to the cause of a bridge's collapse as it is that he should be paid for building another bridge, the average juryman does not think so.

3. **Pleading the case.** Just as the acts of the opposing attorneys throughout the case have been controlled by the thing which they wished to accomplish, so are their pleas at the close of the case influenced by the same objective. The defense attorney plays

on such epithets as "the youthful offender," the "man who risked his life for his country," "loving father of seven children," the man "hounded by police." He also tries to get in some damaging suggestions about members of the opposition. In discussing the pleas of the defense attorneys in the famous White murder case, Daniel Webster says:

A tone of complaint so peculiar has been indulged in, as would almost lead us to doubt whether the prisoner at the bar, or the managers of this prosecution, are now on trial. Great pains have been taken to complain of the manner of the prosecution. We hear of getting up a case; of setting in motion trains of machinery; of foul testimony; of combinations to overwhelm the prisoner; of private prosecutors; that the prisoner is hunted, persecuted, driven to his trial; that everybody is against him; and various other complaints, as if those who would bring to punishment the authors of this murder were almost as bad as they who committed it.

In his closing plea the attorney takes full advantage of the susceptibility of the jurymen to emotions, and proceeds to use all types of emotional appeals, some subtle, some otherwise; and it not infrequently happens that the non-subtle appeals are the ones that yield the best results. The tears of some attorneys are very much in evidence at each of their murder trials, and it sometimes happens that many of the jurymen show by their tears that they also feel "the dint of pity."

Not only are jury trials vitiated by emotional appeals, but there are certain tricks employed by the very best of lawyers which would not be tolerated in a scientific proceeding. In spite of the fact that Daniel Webster stands in the first rank of the legal profession, we see him stooping to such tricks in his closing argument against John J. Knapp for the alleged murder of Captain White. The only evidence against Knapp, as was freely admitted by Webster, was circumstantial evidence. The prisoner was not present when the crime was committed, but the prosecution contended that he was in a street back of the house of the victim waiting for the real murderer to come out, and in that way he became a principal in the crime and if convicted could be punished by death. To meet this contention the defense attempted to prove that Knapp was not in the street or near the scene of the crime at the time it was

committed.   Knapp's father, who was one of the best citizens of
the community, and whose veracity was above reproach, testified
that his son was at home when the State contended he was in the
street aiding in the crime.   Recognizing that the jury would be
considerably influenced by the testimony of the father, Webster
took the following very effective means to discredit his testimony.

I come to the testimony of the father.   I find myself incapable of speaking of him or his testimony with severity.   Unfortunate old man!   Another Lear, in the conduct of his children; another Lear, I apprehend, in
the effect of his distress upon his mind and understanding.   He is brought
here to testify, under circumstances that disarm severity, and call loudly for
sympathy.   Though it is impossible not to see that his story cannot be
credited, yet I am unable to speak of him otherwise than in sorrow and
grief.   Unhappy father!   He strives to remember, perhaps persuades himself that he does remember, that on the evening of the murder he was himself at home at ten o'clock.   He thinks, or seems to think, that his son came
in at about five minutes past ten.   He fancies that he remembers his conversation; he thinks he spoke of bolting the door; he thinks he asked the
time of night; he seems to remember his then going to his bed.   Alas! these
are but the swimming fancies of an agitated and distressed mind.   Alas!
they are but the dreams of hope, its uncertain lights, flickering on the thick
darkness of parental distress.   Alas! the miserable father knows nothing, in
reality, of all these things.

Such tactics as those above show the urgent need for a trained
jury.   Parsons was probably right in saying that the jury has out-
lived its usefulness, and should be replaced by a small group who
have been especially trained to consider evidence and make scientific deductions from it.   With such a group the cheap tactics of
lawyers for confusing jurors would soon be abandoned, for such a
group of experts could not be "taken in" by such tricks.

4. Determining responsibility.   Responsibility is determined
not on the basis of what is done, but on the basis of the person who
does it, and the degree of responsibility equals the measure of the
amount of guilt.   If a gun is accidentally discharged and kills some
one, the person who discharged it may be in no way held responsible for the death of the victim, because the occurrence was purely
an accident.   We accordingly have our first instance in the case of
non-responsibility for our acts; i.e., in general, we are not held

responsible for those acts which are produced without intention. There has been a tendency in recent years to make an exception to this in the case of criminal negligence. For example, if an individual is killed as a result of being run down by an automobile, the brakes of which are in poor condition, the driver of the automobile may be found guilty of manslaughter. A second instance in which the law does not recognize responsibility is in the case of a crime committed by a child, for up until a certain age regardless of how disastrous the act of a child may be, he may not be punished for it. A third exception recognized by law is insanity. About the year 1800 the so-called "right and wrong" test was applied to determine the responsibility of individuals for crime. It was ruled that when an individual could not differentiate between right and wrong he was not responsible for his acts. A fourth type of defense on the ground of non-responsibility for crime was first accepted in 1843 when the McNaughten case was decided in England, and on the basis of this a precedent was established whereby insane delusions or partial insanity could be offered as a defense in crime. In this case it was shown that the defendant was laboring under an insane delusion that the victim was trying to murder him, and while laboring under this delusion the defendant killed the other man. Since then numerous cases have been decided on this ground.

Once insanity has been accepted as an excuse for crime it is only natural that hundreds of criminals should enter this plea. Our newspapers are constantly citing cases of criminals excused on this ground. The Remus case which was tried in Cincinnati in 1927 shows that with some juries a man may deliberately kill another person in cold blood and be excused on the ground of insanity, even though he is sufficiently sane to appear as chief counsel for himself in his defense at the trial. Such cases as the one just cited show the danger of accepting insanity as an excuse for crime.

v. CORRECTIVE MEASURES

1. **Theory underlying punishment.** Society's verdict of what should be done with the criminal, or to what extent he should be punished, has been influenced by three distinct considerations. One of the oldest motives underlying punishment was that of re-

venge. The criminal was regarded as a deliberate wrongdoer, who maliciously injured society; and society saw to it that he was punished. He had sinned against society and society must get even with him. While the revenge motive is not so generally admitted at the present time, it is still much more powerful than is generally recognized. While the old Mosaic law of "an eye for an eye" and "a tooth for a tooth" is not generally applied, most States still practice capital punishment and take the life of one man because he has taken the life of another.

At the present time the most widely accepted motive underlying punishment is protection. It is felt that society, to protect itself, must prevent a recurrence of crime by placing the criminal in an institution and depriving him of the opportunity to commit crime.

At the present time a new attitude is developing toward the criminal. The keynote of this attitude is neither revenge nor protection of society, but the reformation and rehabilitation of the criminal himself. This reformation is brought about by reëducation, which is designed to give the criminal a new set of motives. It is obvious that this is feasible only in the case of the normal, and does not apply to feeble-minded or insane criminals. Those who favor reëducation of the criminals are inclined to look upon criminal acts as the result of wrong habits. They would replace these wrong habits with others more acceptable to society.

While the scientific study and education of the criminal are to be encouraged, still the protection of society must not be overlooked; and to protect society it may be necessary to injure some of those whose behavior leads them sufficiently afar from normal that they are unable to fit into an organized society. Society is built on the assumption of a normal functioning of the individual, and when he slips so far away from this normal behavior that his acts become a menace to the rights of others, society has to resort to force to protect itself.

It is now recognized by most scientists that nothing happens without a cause. In the case of the criminal, the man's own nature and the influences of his environment are generally recognized as the determiners of his crime. But the mere fact that society accepts as a basic principle the natural causation of behavior, is no reason to argue that punishment should not be meted out to those found guilty of crime. What an individual does in life is without doubt the result of certain laws or forces which are acting upon him; and one of the forces that certainly acts on potential criminals and serves as a deterrent from crime is the knowledge that if they commit the crime they will be punished.

2. The nature of punishment. All methods of punishment, either current or past, have been based upon the thwarting of certain drives or desires. Capital punishment thwarts the natural desire to live. Banishment thwarts the desire to be with the old familiar scenes and places. Physical punishment thwarts the desire to escape pain. Financial loss blocks the desire for possession. Solitary confinement thwarts the desire to be with others. Disgrace or humiliation thwarts the desire for the social approval of one's fellow men.

3. Tendencies in legal reform. During the last few years some very significant reforms have been introduced in our dealings with the criminal. Among the more outstanding of these are: (*a*) Special prisons; (*b*) Suspended sentence; (*c*) Indeterminate sentence; (*d*) Parole system; (*e*) Continued detention of certain classes; (*f*) Juvenile courts.

(*a*) *Special prisons.* Recognizing that criminals differ as much as do law-abiding citizens, a number of penal institutions have made provision for grouping them in so far as possible in fairly homogeneous classes. In New York, separate prisons are provided for the following classes; normal young adults, normal old adults, mental defectives, criminal insane, and the emotionally unstable. Such a classification of prisoners has much to recommend it, for it is not well to bring the young person of normal mentality in too close contact with hardened criminals or with mental defectives; nor is it well to mix adult prisoners of normal mentality with the insane or feeble-minded.

(*b*) *Suspended sentence.* Because of the demoralizing effect of our penal institutions, the ends of society are better served by refraining from punishment of first offenders even though their guilt is obvious. Instead of sending him to prison, a suspended sentence is given, and the offender is released for the duration of good behavior, with the understanding that an additional sentence will be given if he commits another crime. Frequently the shock of being arrested and of having the shadow of a prison over him is sufficient to turn the first offender back into socially approved paths.

(c) *Indeterminate sentence.* Unlike the suspended sentence, the indeterminate sentence places the offender in prison, but releases him after he has served a sufficient amount of time so that some idea may be secured of his behavior and fitness to be released. This plan has two objections not found in the case of the suspended sentence, for the disgrace of having gone to prison is attached to the offender, and the bad influences of other prisoners leave their effect upon him.

(d) *Parole system.* Closely akin to the indeterminate sentence is the parole system. Here the prisoner is given a fairly long sentence, but he may be released from prison upon the recommendation of the prison authorities. Before he can be paroled, most States require that he shall have served a specified part of his sentence. The chief difficulty of the parole system is that of determining what prisoners are fit for parole. At present this is based purely on the opinion of people who have no reliable way of judging such things; and as long as we have no objective measures of character, it is doubtful if any one would be able to give a very reliable prediction of how a man would act if released on parole. From Warner's study of the successes and failures of parole in Massachusetts it would appear that the present methods of choosing those who will be given parole are little more reliable than a purely chance selection.

(e) *Continued detention of certain classes.* So long as feeble-mindedness cannot be corrected or improved, it appears wise that a feeble-minded person who has once started on a criminal career should be detained permanently in an institution. This serves two purposes: in the first place, the feeble-minded will be unable to commit further crimes, and in the second place, they will be unable to beget others of the kind to be a burden upon society.

The Baumes Law which was recently passed in New York provides for the permanent retention of the chronic or habitual criminal. When a criminal has been convicted for the third time of committing a major crime he is put in prison for life.

(f) *Juvenile court.* One of the most hopeful signs in legal procedure that has developed in a number of years is the juvenile court. In the juvenile court we have none of the contentiousness of partisan lawyers, none of the inefficiency of an ignorant jury, and none of the sensational publicity which characterizes the proceedings of our formal courts. Instead, the proceeding is characterized by privacy and informality. The more delicate family affairs are not dragged into the view of the public eye. Groups of trained workers investigate the case and scientific studies of the offender are made before the case is called to trial. All the data accumulated from these studies are taken into consideration by the judge in disposing of the case.

4. Treatment of ex-prisoners. One of the causes of repeaters in crime is society's attitude toward those who have been found guilty of crime. Few employers will willingly give employment to an ex-convict, and in those cases where employment is given it is generally only at menial tasks calling primarily for physical strength. The more intelligent whose previous training fits them for mental rather than physical labor find it especially hard to adjust to such a condition, and accordingly drift back into crime as their only way out.

CHAPTER XVI

PSYCHOLOGY AND BUSINESS

"The dollar is an adventurer's barque that may come home from the market with colors flying, or may be wrecked on a hidden reef."

CHASE AND SCHLINK [1]

I. THE STRUGGLE FOR THE CONSUMER'S DOLLAR

THE chief objective of modern business is to secure the consumer's dollar before the other fellow gets it. To accomplish this end floods of the most seductive advertising and thousands of high-pressure salesmen are poured on an unsuspecting public. When one dealer spends a thousand dollars for advertising, his rival, in order not to be outdone, spends five thousand dollars, forcing the first dealer to spend even more, until in the end both firms are spending so much in trying to sell that, although the goods are sold at a high price, the net profits from selling are small. Automobile manufacturers and dealers in 1929 are planning to spend more than one hundred million dollars trying to inveigle the debt-burdened public into further taxing itself to buy the latest models. Retail clothiers find it necessary or profitable to spend six per cent of their receipts for advertising, trying to persuade the wage-earner to put his earnings into clothes instead of food, automobiles, jewelry, and other commodities. The bewildered consumer finds it difficult to escape from those who would get his money. Cigarette manufacturers shriek at him from billboards, cry at him from the housetops, literally bellow at him from the sky itself that "there's not a cough in a carload." Even in his own home the consumer cannot escape, for the dealer goes on the air, and by playlet, song, and jazz band extols the merits of this or that article. No age or emotional state is wholly free from the onslaught of organized business. When a child is born, the dealers in baby carriages and go-carts besiege the parents to purchase their vehicles, and when a man dies, his relatives are urged to provide a bigger and better

---

[1] Chase, Stuart, and Schlink, F. J.: *Your Money's Worth* (The Macmillan Company, 1927), 77.

funeral. Even the slow and smooth-running process of love-making is constantly being speeded up by such advertisements as "you furnish the girl, we'll furnish the home."

In the struggle to get the consumer's dollar, powerful industries are expending vast sums for nation-wide advertising campaigns to bring their products before the consumer — to make him radio-active, fur-coat-active, automobile-active, cigarette-active, cough-drop-active, anything-active — before his bank account becomes inactive.

Most writers on advertising and salesmanship deal primarily with the weak points in the defense of the consumer, and outline the steps by which the advertiser can break through this defense. Nearly everything is written from the standpoint of the business man and his interests. Little attention is paid to the consumer's interests; with the result that the consumer frequently pays high prices for inferior goods or is persuaded to buy goods for which he has no need whatever. Two factors make this condition pos-sible: (1) The consumer's ignorance; (2) The consumer's weakness for emotional appeals.

1. **The consumer's ignorance.** Other things being equal, the more ignorant the consumer, the easier it is to sell him a worthless or injurious article. This is illustrated in the way the laity flock to the sale of patent medicines, practically all of which are valueless and a large number of which are actually injurious. Although many illustrations of this might be cited, the fat-reducers are sufficiently typical to serve as an example for the whole patent-medicine field.

As an example of methods of quack fat-reducers, let us consider in some detail the "Texas Guinan, Inc." fraud, which was exposed by the American Medical Association. The manager of this con-cern, which was located in Los Angeles, was Walter C. Cunning-ham. Previous to his connection with "Texas Guinan, Inc.," he had controlled the following enterprises:

North American Company: fraudulent real estate
Evelyn Burlingame: mail-order beauty treatment
Evelyn Cunningham: mail-order bust developer and wrinkle eradicator

Della Carsen: mail-order bust developer and wrinkle erad-
icator and fat-reducer
Marjorie Hamilton: mail-order fat-reducer
Princess Tokio: mail-order beauty treatment

After he had worked the above frauds until they became un-
profitable due to unfavorable publicity in connection with the
exposure by the American Medical Association, he cast about for
another lead. He happened to read that Texas Guinan, an actress,
had at one time been very stout and was now much less so. He
immediately set out to induce her to sell him the use of her name
for advertising the "Texas Guinan Obesity Cure." For the use of
her name she received five hundred dollars down and fifty dollars
per week as long as her name was used. A study of the advertising
campaign which followed is an education in quackery. Space will
not permit discussion of the advertising copy, booklets, pictures
of Texas in tights and many other ingenious devices for catching
the attention, but the follow-up letters are so enlightening that the
whole correspondence as described by Dr. Cramp,[1] Director of the
Bureau of Investigation, A.M.A., is reproduced below:

Being desirous of finding out all that could be found out about Mr.
Cunningham's latest venture, the member of the *Journal* Staff in charge of
this department wrote the following letter to Texas Guinan:

DEAR MADAM: Please send me your book that is free, and oblige.

The name signed was one of several assumed in writing for quack literature; no prefix "Miss" or "Mrs." was put before the signature. This
point is mentioned because, as will be seen later, this short, non-committal,
uninforming, unemotional, strictly business-like note from a lean man was
to bring a series of heart-to-heart letters from Texas Guinan. "My dear
friend," wrote Texas — but let her speak for herself:

"I am sincerely glad to get personally acquainted with you through your
reply to my advertisement. I am positive it is going to prove a friendship
that will result in a world of boundless happiness for you, of a deep, sincere
and unforgetting gratitude on your part for the great, glorious, precious
new liberty that will be yours after you have been forever released from the
cruel prison of Fat that has so long held you captive; when you will arise
in the morning and greet each beautiful new-born day with a glad song

---

[1] Cramp, Arthur, J.: *Nostrums and Quackery* (American Medical Association
Press, Chicago, 1921), 660–65.

upon your lips instead of a sigh; when you will glow from head to foot with a thrilling exultation of becoming slender day by day, actually seeing with your own eyes the superfluous flesh melt away; and instead of the flabby, ungainly lines, the new and bewildering grace of youth will steal as if by magic over your entire form."

The "bewildering grace of youth" was an appealing promise — to a lean man of forty — and the enthusiasm of Texas was contagious:

"Listen, dear friend: I am so wildly enthusiastic over my world-thrilling, perfect and positive fat-reducer that I am madly impatient for every fat human being in the universe to get the wonderful benefits of it right away!"

"Madly impatient" is good. Why this mad impatience, may be explained by the following paragraph that occurs a little further along in the letter:

"I am a woman, and in this thing heart and soul, out of the great joy it has brought me both to be slender and to see all others slender, so if you will fill out the enclosed guarantee order blank and send it at once, with $20.00, there will be sent you immediately under plain cover the complete guaranteed Texas Guinan positive fat-reducing treatment, of which you have never dreamed, and which the world has never before seen advertised in America."

For a paltry $20.00 Texas was "madly impatient" to send her unfailing treatment! And how simple and harmless it was to prove!

"With this absolutely unfailing fat-reducer, let me firmly impress upon you that you have no internal medicine to take, no nauseous pills, tablets, or powders, no exercise of any kind — not one, no tortuous massage, no masks or apparatus, no rollers, none of the old, moth-eaten, worn-out, silly, senseless, daily self-denial, or third-degree methods. I guarantee all this, and on the day you receive the treatment you will yourself be happily aware that you have at last found the only real and rational treatment known to the world's science."

And after dilating on the evils and tortures of fatness:

"After the dark hours, dear friend, comes the dawn. The dawn is now for *you!*"

Then came the peroration and the letter closed:

"Hoping to receive your $20.00 order as soon as possible, I am, Your Deeply Sincere and Sympathetic Friend, Texas Guinan."

THE SECOND LETTER COMES

Four days after the first letter was received, Letter No. 2 arrived, in which Texas says:

"I am puzzled! More puzzled than disappointed at failing to get a warmly enthusiastic response from you before now."

She need not have been puzzled, as she failed to allow sufficient time to elapse between the first and second letters for an answer to her first letter to reach Los Angeles from Chicago, even had it been written at the earliest possible moment. Possibly Miss Guinan expected a telegram:

"Well knowing your inmost yearning, burning desire to be slender and feeling sure you fully realize my positive treatment will make you so, I even expected your Rush Reply by Special Delivery."

Evidently the trouble lay in the letter sent from *The Journal* office. It was too confiding, too personal, for Texas says:

"Truly, from the way you answered my advertisement, I felt positive you were Intensely in Earnest in your great longing to be rid of your fat."

Apparently, too, the once obese actress had read into the letter that was sent her, something that was certainly never intended, for we read:

"You know there's sometimes a Wireless System of Sympathetic Understanding between human beings. Your letter, strangely enough, filled me with the almost uncontrollable desire to Rush this Positive Reducer to you at Once; to even take it to you myself; to get on the train and go to you with it and remain with you for several days. . . ."

Evidently, on thinking over the matter more carefully, Texas Guinan controlled her "almost uncontrollable desire," and instead of coming to Chicago in person, sent the letter — which was probably just as well. Yet there surely is no doubt that the lady is much in earnest.

"When I electrified my friends and admirers and all the theatrical world by my quick transformation from fat-girl to thin-girl: when I stunned to speechless Surprise and Satisfaction that Great Manager, Mr. Shubert (whose former criticism of my overweight had stung me to the soul) — when I Dazzled him with my fresh, new, fairy slenderness of figure, my lithe-limbed, small-waisted winsomeness from head to heal [spelling original with Texas. — *Ed.*] — why, dear friend, the Happy Scene it made when I presented myself before him, a New-Born, Superbly Sculptured Being and — Presto, I Stepped Across the Thrilling Threshold of 'Stardom.' Ah, my friend, no change, no scene, can e'er efface my mind's impression of that time and place."

All of this preliminary to the great "offer"; to the "one chance to save $10 on the Texas Guinan Positive Fat-Reducer." For a mere $10 it was possible for the more or less cadaverous male who received this letter to get a preparation that "from the very moment you receive it, There is No Power on Earth That Can Keep You from Losing Flesh Rapidly. . . ." The change that he would undergo would be remarkable:

"Your chin — throat — arms — abdomen — hips — thighs and lower limbs are immediately destined for almost unbelievable alteration; your enchanting, new graceful willowness more noticeable every blessed day. . . ."

LETTER NUMBER THREE

And with this wonderful promise, Texas closes her letter, from "Yours for New Youth and a New Deal with Destiny." With man-like perversity, even this letter remained unanswered, and as a result, Letter No. 3 came in due time, and in this Miss Guinan became even more personal:

"Pardon me, dear, you may think me awfully conceited, but I AM a bit proud of what great critics have said in the press about me and my newly made-over form. You, too, would be — for we are only women after all — and Beauty and Admiration are a part of our very lives, aren't they dear!"

Almost uncanny are the powers of Texas:

"But I can see you in my mind's eye to-day, Dear Friend, as you really are."

Here we are afraid Texas is mistaken. If she really could see her "dear friend" as he is she would have instructed her corps of typists to remove his name from the mailing-list and charge up to profit and loss the stationery and postage already expended. Still it was hard to refrain from sending the $10 when for this small sum such a product would be sent.

"Behold! I believe I have right in my hand a treatment designed to make you Beautifully Sinuous, Fascinatingly Slender and Adorable! I believe I have right in my hand the power to give you back the Glory of Youth's Lithesome Grace, a pliant, peerless, reedlike form."

"Reedlike form" seems particularly good as applied to the recipient of this letter; the only criticism offered is that it should have been applied to the present instead of the future. Nevertheless and notwithstanding the fact that Texas closed her letter "with sincere, Sisterly Solicitude," the $10 was not sent.

THEN THE FOURTH LETTER

One might have imagined that after three such pleading epistles, Miss Guinan would feel that she was indeed casting her pearls before swine. But no, Letter No. 4 came strictly on time, with the explanation:

"As long as you are still among the Piteous Prisoners of Fat, fat-girded, fat-manacled, fat-menaced, I cannot find it in my heart to forget you! Really, truly, sincerely, dear, I cannot for the life of me, blot out of my mind the awful unrest, the dull, desperate unhappiness you must feel!"

As has been surmised, the letter that brought this flood of correspondence from Miss Guinan was not sufficiently impersonal.

"Your answer to my advertisement was, in itself, full of pathos to me, for I understood it through and through!"

Unlike the lady in Mr. Kipling's poem, Texas, it seems, did understand, and having understood, exhibits an "all-conquering sympathy for you that makes me forget the sordid money part of it all." She has a "great surprise" that will "make it Doubly Easy and Even Profitable for you to grow slender with lightening [more original spelling. — Ed.] speed." This is it:

"Here, my dear, I am making you a most Sisterly Proposition! I could not be more liberal if I were your own flesh and blood!"

The "sisterly proposition" is an offer of the Texas Guinan $20 "obesity cure" for the "small price of $5." All that she asks is that you send her "the names and addresses of five fat men or women," which Miss Guinan considers "worth $15." This, the fourth letter, begins to exhibit a spirit of doubtfulness, as though Texas was slowly becoming convinced that the person to whom it was addressed did not think much of her "obesity cure." To dispel any growing skepticism, we are told that should we stop a moment and reason we must inevitably conclude that every statement Texas Guinan has made regarding her cure "must be true, because my reputation is at stake. I am traveling the country starring in 'the Passing Show of 1912,' backed by Mr. Shubert, America's greatest theatrical manager." And yet we receive signed letters from Texas Guinan from Los Angeles!

"I would expect to be mobbed at the stage door as I finished my performance, if I deceived the fat-burdened folks of America by selling them anything but a high-class proven fat-reducer."

And whatever you do, do not confuse Texas Guinan's only original fat-reducer with anything else of which you may have heard or dreamed!

"All the wafers, pills, powders, miracle dope, rubber jackets, rollers, weakening baths and willy-nilly what nots, are a hilarious joke to you the moment you begin this treatment and behold with grateful, astonished eyes, the marvelous, quick effects."

LETTER NUMBER FIVE

In spite of all this, and much more; in spite of the fact that Texas inscribes herself "Your fond and faithful friend"; in spite of the promise of the "exuberant happiness" that would follow "the magic of this world-bewildering treatment"; in spite of everything, Letter No. 4 fell on deaf ears. Thus it became necessary for Texas to send Letter No. 5. This epistle lacked the fiery enthusiasm of the previous ones, whether because it was signed "Texas Guinan, per H. D. T., Manager," or because in this letter the price of the treatment is reduced to the ridiculously small sum of $3, it is hard to say. "This offer," you are told, "expires twenty days after you receive this letter." Moreover, "this is the last offer that will be made you; after that date the original price will be $20." To get it at this low price it is necessary to "send the names and addresses of ten fat men or women"; further, "it is understood that you will keep sacredly confidential the special $3 offer made you."

THE CURE IS PURCHASED

Finally the money was sent and in due time a package came by express containing "Texas Guinan's World-Famed Treatment for Corpulency." This $20 treatment consisted of a quart bottle filled with a muddy liquid which on standing separated into a pinkish sediment and an almost colorless liquid. The stuff was analyzed in the Association's laboratory, and as a result of the examination, the chemists' report might be summarized as follows:

To make a mixture having essentially the same composition as the "Texas Guinan World-Famed Treatment for Corpulency," take a quart-sized fruit jar and put into it:

Powdered alum..................	1 pound
Alcohol........................	10 ounces
Water, sufficient to make..........	1 quart

The approximate cost of these materials is 30 cents; selling price from $20 to $3 according to the ease with which one parts with his money.

Day after day in almost all papers and magazines miraculous means of reducing weight are advertised. On analysis these remedies are seen to fall into two classes, those that are pure hokum and have no effect whatever on weight, and those that reduce the weight but are harmful to health. Practically without exception, the fat-reducers now on the market that will actually reduce a person contain thyroid extract in quantities harmful to him. Most of the widely advertised fat-reducers contain no thyroid and would be just as efficacious in reducing the distance from New York to Paris as in reducing the girth line of the moron who takes them. In the latter type of fat-reducers, two are especially interesting: one is sold as a reducing soap, which according to the advertisement accomplishes its results through the simple means of taking a nice, pleasant bath using this particular brand of soap. The other is a brand of chewing gum, for which it is claimed that, by chewing daily two or three pieces of this delightful, refreshing gum, one can remove all his unsightly rolls of fat.

The following experiment quoted from Starch [1] illustrates the dense ignorance and gullibility of the consumer and the ease with which he can be exploited:

GLORIOUS OPPORTUNITY TO GET RICH QUICK

INVEST IN

THE CALIFORNIA RANCHING COMPANY

Now being organized to start a cat ranch in California

We are starting a cat ranch in California with 100,000 cats. Each cat will average 12 kittens a year. The cat skins will sell for 30 cents each. One hundred men can skin 5000 cats a day. We figure a daily net profit of over $10,000.

[1] Starch, D.: *Principles of Advertising.* (A. W. Shaw Company, Chicago, 1923.)

Now What Shall We Feed The Cats?

We will start a rat ranch next door with 1,000,000 rats. The rats will breed twelve times faster than the cats, so, we'll have rats to feed each day to each cat. Now what shall we feed the rats? We will feed the rats the carcasses of the cats after they have been skinned.

Now Get This

We feed the rats to the cats, and the cats to the rats, and get the cat skins for nothing. Shares are selling at 5¢ each, but the prices will go up soon. Invest while opportunity knocks at your door.

The California Ranching Company

The above advertisement was placed in the window of a savings bank in its campaign to promote thrift. The advertisement was accompanied by the warning in large letters:

Some gullible people will try to buy this stock. It is a foolish fake, of course, but no more foolish than many "wild cat" schemes being promoted to-day. Investigate before investing. Don't hand your money over to any unknown glib-tongued salesman.

Large crowds gathered to read the advertisement, and so many inquiries for the stock were received, both in mail and in person, that the advertisement had to be removed.

Being ignorant of the intrinsic merits of nine tenths of the material they buy, the rank and file of consumers are totally unable to differentiate between a superior and an inferior material, to tell a genuine from an imitation article, or a pure from an adulterated product. Theoretically, the price should be a criterion of quality, but in actual practice, there is little relation between price and quality. Chase and Schlink cite the case of a maker of flashlight batteries who sold two grades of batteries, one the highly advertised grade, the other identical in make and quality, but bearing a different label. The highly advertised battery sold for twice the price of the other. By having two prices, it was possible to cater to different classes of the buying public.

One thing can always be expected — that is, that the seller will charge all the traffic will bear, regardless of cost of manufacturing or of the quality of the goods. This is illustrated by the Listerine advertising offensive. Concerning the cost and value of Listerine,

Sollmann,[1] who is one of the most eminent pharmacologists in America, makes the following statement:

Thymol, plus small quantities of boric and benzoic acid, under the name of Listerine, sells at a dollar a bottle. It is really too bad that bacteria cannot recognize a superior antiseptic as well as the nose — for, according to the bacteriologic test, as quoted by Wood, four hundred and ninety-five dollars' worth of Listerine has the antiseptic action of a cent's worth of corrosive sublimate; or fifteen dollars' worth of Listerine equals a cent's worth of carbolic acid.

It is interesting to note that Listerine advertising has recently gone through four stages: at first it was advertised as a more or less general remedy; next came the powerful halitosis campaign; then the deodorant appeal; and lastly, the promise to remove dandruff. Judging from the way Listerine has sold, Barnum was probably right.

As the consumer is unable to differentiate between various grades of a material, he is forced to rely upon price as a measure of quality. The consumer has come to believe that a higher price insures a better product. Unfortunately for him, this belief is generally ill-founded. Results of scientific tests of the quality of products on the market would be an eye-opener for the consumer. Examples given by Chase and Schlink illustrate the lack of standards of quality, or price. Laboratory analyses of nine makes of sheeting determined the relative quality of each. These qualities were then compared with the market price. The make of sheeting ranking eighth in quality ranked second in price; of two makes of identical quality, one sold for two and one-half times as much as the other. Engineers testing oils found that the oil which produced most carbon in all tests was that which sold at the highest price, and yet the more carbon there is, the less is the efficiency of the machine. Sales of a certain French perfume, imported into this country, were very small. But when the price was deliberately marked up above that of most other perfumes, and it was supported by the slogan "it costs a little more, but Milady deserves the best," it became exceedingly profitable. Two pairs of shoes of identical quality were displayed in a shop window; one pair was marked six

[1] Sollmann, T.: *Journal of American Medical Association*, July 4, 1925.

dollars and the other twelve dollars.　More people asked for the twelve dollar pair.　An advertiser can sell almost anything to a certain class of people by saying "it costs more, but it's worth it."

2. Consumer's weakness to emotional appeals.　Ignorance is not the only weakness in the consumer's line of defense, for his extreme susceptibility to emotional appeals is even more inimical to his prosperity than is his ignorance.　In the world of business, for every sale that is made as a result of logical or scientific appeal, there are at least ten sales made as the result of emotional appeals. Because of the extreme importance of emotional appeals, the advertising copy-writer must rack his brain to connect some emotional drive with all sorts of uninteresting things.　He must tie up mother-love with the inferior concoction of baby food which he is called upon to advertise; or he must give advertisements a "kick" by connecting such mundane things as safety-razors, automobiles, furniture, and clothes with the love-drive.　An example is the glove advertisement showing the picture of a beautiful girl with her cheek resting on her hand and the caption: "See how she leans her cheek upon her hand!　Oh, that I were a glove upon her hand that I might touch her cheek."　No wonder copy-writers become cynical.　Who could work year after year without becoming cynical when one day he is called upon to picture the disastrous consequences of halitosis; the next day he must tell of the effect of a certain mixture of hog-grease and potash on "the skin you love to touch," and the next day he must find an emotional appeal for a worthless hair-restorer.

In advertising a product, it is best for the vivid imagination of the copy-writer not to be hampered by too much real knowledge of the thing he is advertising.　It is usually better for him never to see the factory in which the product is made nor to know the true ingredients of it.　The advertiser should know the appearance of the finished article and some of the merits that are claimed for it, and above all, the conditions under which it is to be sold — the buying group to whom the appeal must be made.　But when too much of the inner truth about an article is known it is difficult to wax enthusiastic in the copy which sells it.

Few things are advertised on their intrinsic merits, but the appeal is usually of an emotional nature. Millions of dollars are spent each year for no other purpose than to "keep up with the Joneses." Certain classes spend more money on beautifying agents than on food. For every dollar given by the alumnus to improve the scientific laboratories of his Alma Mater, ten dollars are given to improve her athletic teams. Man is supposed to be a rational animal, but the surest way to separate him from his money is through an appeal to his emotions rather than to his reason.

Such being the nature of the consumer, we will now consider some of the problems involved in advertising and selling.

II. ADVERTISING

The present state of skill in the art of advertising is a recent acquisition, but the game of advertising had its beginnings in remote antiquity. Griffith has pointed out that numerous walls and sign boards upon which were legends and drawings, some of them in color, were found in the excavations at Pompeii. These apparently served the same purpose as our outdoor advertising does to-day. The ballyhoo which informs the rabble that one Jack Dempsey is going to fight fifteen rounds with Gene Tunney for the "Heavyweight Championship of the World" had its counterpart in advertisements announcing the gladiatorial combats in Rome. Our alluring posters telling of some seashore resort "where ocean breezes blow" had its forerunner in the advertisements of baths with warm sea and fresh water as seen in the following advertisement.[1]

THERMÆ
M. CRASSI FRUGII
AQUA. MARINA. ET. BALN.
AQUA. DULCI. JANUARIUS. L.

Advertising consists of presenting a commodity to the public in such a way as to induce the public to buy it. The advertisement itself is a group of stimuli designed to produce in the public the response of purchasing the goods advertised. The advertise-

[1] Sampson, H.: *A History of Advertising from the Earliest Times* (Chatto and Windus, London, 1874), 38.

ments must be of various kinds to appeal to the different types of people purchasing different commodities; but most of them must appeal to the average person, for advertising is mass selling.

According to the things advertised, advertising can be subdivided into four groups: (1) Advertising a community; (2) Advertising a firm or organization; (3) Advertising an individual; (4) Advertising goods.   The latter has received most attention from psychologists, and is also more in accord with the commonly accepted conception of advertising.

1. **Advertising a community.**   In the olden times each community stood on its merits; no artificial booms were brought about by the magic wand of advertising.   But times have changed.   Each community has its Chamber of Commerce and several business clubs whose purpose it is to tell an uninterested world just how fine this particular community is.   Every little town must try to impress those who pass through it with the fact that it is "surpassed by none, equalled by not any," and that there is no better place to rear a family than in Podunk or some of the thousand other insignificant places.   It may be the home of the "sunkist raisins" or only the home of the bachelor's buttons, but the world must know that it is the home of something.   The extent of such advertising of the community is a fair indication of the energy and financial ability of the local chamber of commerce.   The number who know that Ashville is in "the land of the sky" is commensurate with the extent of advertising this slogan has received.

Due to skillful advertising, certain communities together with their land values suddenly go uphill.   As a result of the advertising boom, Florida land sold for more than six times as much as it did one year before the boom.   In advertising, the bad qualities of a community are skillfully suppressed.   It is claimed, for example, that the Red Cross was seriously handicapped in its efforts to secure aid for the victims of the tornado which swept over Florida in 1926.   The Florida business interests, recognizing that storms and tornadoes are poor advertising for the "land of perpetual youth" are alleged to have minimized reports of the actual extent of the damage.

2. **Advertising an organization.**   The purpose of advertising an

organization is generally somewhat different from the purpose of advertising goods. The motive in gaining favorable publicity for an organization is to secure the good-will of the public or to mold public opinion. Thus churches, business concerns, charitable organizations, colleges, professions, and fraternal organizations advertise, at times subtly, yet in reality all their publicity campaigns are advertising campaigns. An organization can advertise with telling effect by contributing generously and publicly to some worthy charity; or by holding a "charity ball" or other striking social event. Newspaper publicity recounting the activities and successes of the organization aids in gaining public confidence and good-will. Well-known firms advertise to have their names kept before the public as a reminder of the service offered by the firm. The proposal of a large jewelry concern to place a wrist-watch on the Statue of Liberty is an excellent case of advertising the firm.

The result of advertising is shown in the recognized value of the good-will of the firm. No owners of a business establishment which is well advertised would sell out without demanding an amount of money over and above that for the actual goods possessed by the establishment. This additional money is supposed to pay for the good-will of the firm. As a result of skillful direct and indirect advertising, the Ford Motor Company has an inestimable amount of intangible assets in the form of good-will of the public. As a result of this good-will, any product offered for sale by the Ford Company finds a ready market. An identical machine could be produced by an unknown company and sold for the same price as the Ford car, but for every sale made by the new company hundreds of sales would be made by Ford. This good-will or confidence accounts for the enormous sale of new Fords before a single one had been manufactured, and even in spite of the fact that no purchaser knew what the new car would be like.

3. **Advertising an individual.** The use of advertising is not confined to communities and organizations. Individuals also advertise in order to sell themselves to the public. The individual advertises to make himself known by the public for some purpose. The politician skillfully keeps his name before the people in order to get their votes. The part played by advertising in politics is indi-

cated by the fact that in the presidential campaign of 1928 the
two major parties spent more than $8,000,000 trying to sell
their candidates to the voters. The prize fighter wants a crowd
and sees to it that he gets the proper publicity. Jack Dempsey
in no small way achieved his popularity through the publicity
work of the ballyhoo. The actress likewise must have a crowd,
and her publicity manager or advertiser secures the coveted prominence by circulating rumors of flirtations and indiscretions, and
stories of her great success and popularity. A tiger cub as a
pet on Fifth Avenue, an unusual and original costume, or a "near
scandal" also serve as effective mediums for personal advertising.
Giving time or money to some worthy and well-known cause is an
excellent method of securing publicity. Not less conducive to the
desired results, though less open, is the subtle publicity adopted by
the clergyman, lawyer and débutante. Billy Sunday is a shining
example of what advertising can do for a preacher.

Probably the most skillful self-advertiser the world has ever
seen was P. T. Barnum. He lost no opportunity for gaining publicity for himself and incidentally for his "greatest show on earth."
Notoriety, for Barnum, was the very breath of life, and the newspapers on every occasion supplied it without scruple. They might
call him fraud or faker, but Barnum gained regardless of what was
said. Barnum is quoted as saying, "I don't care what you say
about me just so you say something." C. J. Finger tells how at
the height of the show Barnum used to drive into the arena in an
open carriage drawn by a beautiful team and attended by liveried
footmen. At his approach the trumpets sounded and the show was
stopped as if he were a king arriving. Acrobats ceased their stunts,
and horsemen dismounted, while the band played "See the Conquering Hero Comes." Then Barnum proceeded, stopping his carriage before each tier of cheering admirers with the jovial greeting:
"This is Barnum, P. T. Barnum, glad to see you." And thus he
moved around the large arena touching the hearts of his hearers
and driving them wild with enthusiasm. Nothing shows more
clearly Barnum's skill in advertising than the fact that during his
old age hundreds of thousands would pay their hard-earned money
merely to look at him. As an advertising achievement his success
is practically without an equal.

4. Advertising goods. The purpose of advertising a commodity is to condition the public so that when a need arises the brand advertised will be thought of to fulfill the need. Sometimes, where the need does not naturally arise, advertising a commodity takes on an additional purpose of creating a need in the minds of the buyers.

A. STEPS IN ADVERTISING. Since the successful advertising of goods is dependent essentially upon emotional appeals, it is necessary to analyze the appeals. They can best be divided into four steps or stages, as follows: (1) Getting the attention; (2) Holding the attention; (3) Arousing desire; (4) Getting the response.

1. Getting the attention. The matter of attracting attention has its instinctive basis and its emotional tone. According to Thorndike,[1] "Man is by original nature attentive to (1) *sudden change and sharp contrasts* and (2) to *all the situations to which he has further tendencies to respond*, as by flight, pursuit, repulsion, play, and the like." Some of the more important factors in gaining attention are: (a) Intensity; (b) Size; (c) Movement; (d) Color; (e) Contrast; (f) The unusual.

(a) *Intensity.* Under normal conditions the mind is very sensitive to intense stimuli, whether they be loud noises, bright lights, bright colors or pungent odors. In advertising, then, the attention of the prospective buyer is best arrested by presenting a stimulus stronger than any of the objects surrounding him. The town crier used to ring a bell to catch attention; the fishmonger used a horn. To-day the advertiser uses shrieking bill-boards. Brightly lighted signs attract the attention from the darker surroundings, and brilliant electric signs seldom fail to gain attention.

(b) *Size.* A second factor in gaining attention is size. The huge bill-board looming up at the curve in the road strikes the eye of the motorist; the monstrous electric sign flashes its message into the mind of the spectator while the small signs receive scant notice. Wrigley's huge electric sign, which for many years was displayed in Times Square, New York, cost $104,000 a year to maintain, but every one passing was reminded of Wrigley's gum.

[1] Thorndike, Edward L.: *Educational Psychology, Briefer Course* (Teachers College, Columbia University, 1924), 14.

(c) *Movement*. Men instinctively give attention to moving objects. This fact is taken advantage of in arranging advertisements. The moving electric sign is particularly effective; of a number of signs, other conditions being equal, the moving one is invariably noticed first. The sign which flashes on and off is more effective than the stationary sign. Even the suggestion of movement produces much of the response produced by actual movement. In a display, the reader's eye follows a succession of spots, an arrow, the undulating pattern of a rug or wallpaper. Motion is also suggested by the action of the figures of people, and the observer's attention is directed in the direction of a rolling ball, a running man, or a pointing finger.

(d) *Color*. Colored illustrations or advertisements are found to be more effective in gaining the attention than those in black-and-white. Much of the value of color in advertising is due to the emotional tones of different colors. Color has an emotional effect which excites, invites, repels, depresses or saddens. It is said to be a symbolic language, each tone having a specific value. Yellow suggests light, cheer and pleasure; red is aggressive, irritating, capable of stirring human action; blue soothes, restrains, even repels; green is light and cool; purple suggests gloom and depression.

(e) *Contrast*. An important factor in attracting attention to the advertisement is the skillful use of contrast. When a dark shade and a light shade appear close together, the contrast tends to make the dark appear even darker, the light even lighter than it would appear alone. One of the most common forms of contrast is that of black and white. In colored advertisements the background should always be less intense than objects thrown upon it, so that the objects may stand out by contrast. Moreover, the larger the colored area in any design, the less intense the color should be, and conversely, the smaller the area, the more intense the color may be.

(f) *The unusual*. The unusual catches the eye quickly. Advertisements featuring bizarre type, unusual combinations of words, catchy phrases, striking colors, or original and unusual illustrations gain the attention. Such directions as "do not read what is behind this," or those that make the reader turn the page upside down to read them, arouse attention and curiosity. Anything novel appeals to man's curiosity, and is a strong incentive to closer attention and interest. Any novel device, however, if too frequently used, loses its novelty and becomes commonplace.

2. Holding the attention. After the attention is caught it must be held long enough for the message carried by the advertisement to be received, otherwise the advertisement fails in its purpose. The successful advertisement holds the attention through: (a) Complexity; (b) Unity; (c) Feeling tone.

(a) *Complexity.* The picture or the copy of the advertisement must be fairly complex in order to hold the attention. No one looks long at a picture which is perceived, analyzed and interpreted all in a single glance. The complexity must be sufficient to arouse interest as well as attention. The one thing that needs to be guarded against is the sacrifice of unity for complexity, for complexity fails in its purpose when it is carried so far as to produce confusion.

(b) *Unity.* To be attractive and retain attention, the arrangement of the parts of the advertisement into an agreeable composition within the given space is extremely important. In the first place, the advertisement should have unity: everything should be subordinated to one main feature. The illustration and the verbal appeal should emphasize the same thing, and should be attractively placed. The illustration must be so placed in the space that the effect is a general balance of display, not an effect of top-heaviness, or weakness at the base. The optical center of the space, or the point which appears to be located at the center, is above the mathematical center. Therefore to give the impression of stability and sufficient support it is necessary to make the lower section of the advertisement slightly larger. The best position for the prominent display feature of the advertisement is at the optical center, with everything else subordinated to it.

(c) *Feeling tone.* In retaining the attention, the feeling tone of the advertisement is of the utmost importance. Advertising depends almost entirely upon emotional appeal for its success, and every care must be taken to make the emotional appeal pleasant. The large proportion of the people in advertisements who are pictured as smiling as compared with the proportion of smiling people in real life indicates an effort to secure the proper feeling tone for the advertisement. Pleasant names add to the attractiveness of a commodity. Just from the name, who would not prefer "Cheri-cola" to "Wah-wah Sauce"? In using direct appeals to the senses care must be taken not to give offense by making repulsive statements as "Click go the teeth. Out trickles the juice of —— gum," or "Make your breath as sweet as a cow's breath." The advertisement showing a package of breakfast food with vermin creeping over it and the caption "vermin cannot enter" produces just the wrong feeling tone, for though vermin cannot enter the package, the idea of them enters the mind. Most people like meat, but few enjoy being reminded that the luscious ham had its origin in the lowly hog. The picture of the ham as an appetizing dish, daintily arranged, on the other hand, may be very effective. "The skin you love to touch" makes a powerful appeal, but the statement that the soap is made from pure hog grease would not give the same emotional effect.

Since the feeling tone of the advertisement must be pleasant, symbolism is used when unpleasant or sorrowful things must be mentioned. Death is spoken of as a sleep, or a departure, and is symbolized by a burnt-out candle, a ship, or a setting sun. Even in dealing with the sorrowful, an effort is made to avoid a sad feeling tone.

Hotchkiss [1] gives a list of word families, each group of which carries a certain feeling tone due to the similarity of sound to other words of the same family whose meanings are either pleasant or unpleasant.

A word acquires suggestion from the meaning of other words which it resembles, just as the reputation of a person is affected by the character of his brothers. And, as in families, a single black sheep often does more harm than a dozen respectable citizens can redeem.

Words beginning with "sn" such as sneer, sniff, snip, snake, sneak, snare, snore, snob, snub, snide, snipe, snoop, snitch, have an unpleasant feeling tone because the sound itself is unpleasant — to pronounce them involves a distortion of the lips and nose that is unpleasant to see or to feel — and

[1] Hotchkiss, G. B.: *Advertising Copy.* (Harper and Brothers, New York, 1924.)

incidentally is a kind of contemptuous gesture. And some of the words like snipe and snide have a very unpleasant meaning.

There is the unpleasant "gr" family, with greed, grab, grate, grasp, grip, grim, gross, groan, grudge, graft, grub, grind. The "sq" family is equally unpleasant. Among them are squint, squirt, squirm, squat, squeeze, squib, squeak, squab. Other unpleasant word-families are those ending in "um" like glum, grum, scum, slum, gum, rum, numb; the "ump" family, such as bump, dump, hump, lump, rump, slump; the "imp" family, such as skimp, scrimp, crimp, limp, pimp, shrimp; and the "unk" family such as bunk, hunk, flunk, punk, junk.

3. Arousing desire. Catching and holding the attention are not sufficient. The effective advertisement arouses the desire to buy the thing advertised. This is accomplished by (a) The use of various types of appeals; (b) By creating confidence.

(a) *Types of appeals.* One of the best places to study the psychology of advertising appeals is in the appeals capitalized by the quack. According to Chase and Schlink [1] there are five human desires which the quack plays on to his own profit. By skillfully working the gullible public, millions have been "raked in" as a result of each. These five desires are:

(1) *Desire for wealth.* This desire furnishes the motive-force used by various get-rich-quick operators. The promise of large returns nearly always succeeds in separating a fool and his money. Nothing better shows how little the average man knows about human nature than the fact that he will believe a total stranger who promises in six months' time to double his money for him. A moment's reflection should teach the prospective "sucker" that if such profits were possible, the stranger would keep them for himself and his friends instead of lavishing them on a total stranger. The numerous swindlers in fake oil stock, "salted gold mines," and inflated land values are examples of such schemes.

(2) *Desire to be sexually attractive.* Millions of dollars are spent each year on the various beautifiers, including wrinkle-removers, hair-restorers, fat-reducers, cross-eye straighteners, and bad-breath eliminators. The money spent for the popular agents designed for these purposes might just as well be thrown into the ocean for all

[1] Chase, S., and Schlink, F. J.: *Your Money's Worth.* (The Macmillan Company, New York, 1927.)

the good it will do. One might just as well hope to restore life to the mummy of King Tut, as to restore hair on a bald head by the remedies now widely advertised.

(3) *Desire for health.* No group of swindlers deserve a sentence in the penitentiary more than the group who seek their profit by selling worthless or even injurious remedies to sick people. Many widely advertised cures for cancer, tuberculosis, rheumatism, epilepsy, and high blood pressure operate on this desire. To read the advertisements in the newspapers one would conclude that all the more serious ailments "that flesh is heir to" can easily be cured by a trifling investment in the advertised "cure." As a matter of fact the only cure for cancer is the early application of radium or the surgeon's knife, and at present no drug is known which will cure tuberculosis, epilepsy, rheumatism, heart disease, or high blood pressure. To cause a cancer victim to waste on a worthless remedy the valuable early period during which he might have been cured by the proper treatment is nothing less than murder.

(4) *Desire for power.* Many quacks capitalize man's desire for fame and power over his fellow men. It is almost impossible to pick up a magazine without reading of some magical scheme whereby one can develop his "hidden powers," and "latent energies" in ten lessons. According to these advertisements "concentration" may be taught over night and a wonderful memory had for the paltry sum of fifty dollars. By spending two evenings a week on a correspondence course one is promised to double his salary in three months; and by taking a home course in scenario writing he is led to expect that millions will fall in his lap from the movie industry. Various sucker-lists have been prepared, containing the names of those who are willing to pay their good money for any worthless remedy promising to give them a "commanding and seductive personality." What will the newly rich not pay for the chance of getting their names on the social register!

(a) *Desire for worship.* No promises are so impossible but that some one will believe them. Whether we promise a thousand per-cent profit in this world or a golden harp in the next makes little difference in the number who will believe the promise. We accordingly read such advertisements as the following which appeared during the Middle Ages:

> "As the money in the coffer rings,
> The soul from purgatory springs."

While certain desires as those mentioned above are common to all men, the same type of appeal is not equally effective with all persons, nor with all commodities, otherwise advertising would be less varied and colorful. The appeals used in arousing desire vary with the commodity advertised. Food advertisements frequently emphasize the qualities of purity, healthfulness, and deliciousness; women's clothes are represented as fashionable and of good quality, but children's play clothes are described as durable and cheap; furniture is represented as comfortable, elegant and durable.

The type of appeal also varies with the character of those to whom the advertisement is directed. The poor are interested in the durability and cheapness of an article; the wealthy in its exclusiveness and elegance. Men are more interested in tobacco and sporting goods; women in cosmetics and beautiful clothes. In regard to clothes, the adolescent and the young adult are interested primarily in style, the old in durability and price. All these characteristics of the user and many others must be taken into consideration in framing the advertisement.

(b) *Creating confidence.* Before the advertisement can result in the purchase of the article, the public must have confidence in the desirability of the article. Various devices are used to create confidence in the commodity and in the firm advertising it.

Repetition. The constant dropping of the water of publicity gradually wears away the stone of doubt; and the article which is well known through repeated advertisements seems like a familiar friend. It was correctly said that "repetition is reputation." Why do we believe that the Prudential is as "strong as the rock of Gibraltar"? Simply because we are told so every time we pick up a magazine.

The fact that the frequent repetition of an advertisement is of more importance than its size is brought out by the results of an investigation conducted by Munsterberg. He judged effectiveness by the memory of thirty persons for advertisements seen in a sixty-page series, containing six full-page advertisements, each of which occurred once, two half-page, each occurring twice; four fourth-page, each occurring four times; eight eighth-page, occurring eight times each; and twelve twelfth-page advertisements, each occurring twelve times. He found that in order of memory value, the four times repeated quarter-page advertisement was the best, having about one and one half as much value as a single repetition of a full-page or two repetitions of a half-page. The eight eighth-page advertisements were not so good as the four quarter-page advertisements.

Length of time in business   A second method of creating confidence is by emphasizing the length of time the firm has been in business.   People have more confidence in old, long-established firms than in new, untried ones, hence the appeal in "Gloves since 1854," or the brokerage concern which says "in business for more than 100 years without the loss of a single cent for a customer."

Prestige of users.   A third method of creating confidence in an article is by saying that it is recommended by people of prestige. "Ask Dad — he knows" or the fact that "the most beautiful Queen in Europe recommends Pond's Cold and Vanishing Creams," or that Cleopatra used Palmolive soap, carries conviction of the quality of the goods.

Certain prominent people sell to commercial concerns the right to use their names in advertising.   When Jess Willard whipped Jack Johnson the advertisements claimed that it was Nuxated Iron which did it; and when the same Willard was knocked out by Dempsey four years later the victory was again awarded to Nuxated Iron.   In 1915 Willard wrote, "Without Nuxated Iron I am sure that I would never have been able to whip Jack Johnson so completely and easily as I did."   In 1919 Dempsey wrote, "Nuxated Iron put added power behind my punch and helped to accomplish what I did at Toledo."   Nor are the prominent names limited to the field of sports; for we read that "Former United States Senator Moran, pioneer in pure Food and Drug Legislation, Father of the Rural Free Delivery System, takes Nuxated Iron to obtain renewed Strength, Power and Endurance."

In this connection we should note some of the methods employed to get the endorsements of various products by famous people. Regardless of how worthless or harmful the commodity may be it is possible to purchase testimonials and the exclusive use of photographs of certain famous personalities for advertising the commodity. There is an organization known as "Famous Names, Inc.," with its main office in Chicago and branch offices in New York and Hollywood, that makes a business of selling to commercial concerns signed endorsements from movie stars, athletes, society people, and other "famous personalities." According to their circular advertising this service, "The fee for the exclusive use of a star is between $150 and $2500, depending upon the standing of the star and the length of time the exclusive use is desired. This fee includes the special posing and signed endorsements." The methods used are indicated in a form letter which was sent to a large New York advertising agency about the time of the recent visit of Her Highness Queen Marie. Mr. H. C. Klemfuss, the writer of the letter, stated that he would be glad to "consider arranging for endorsements of commodities or products of national reputation from Her Majesty, the Queen of Roumania." Such being the methods by which testimonies and endorsements are secured, it is readily apparent that we can put little confidence in the sincerity of such endorsements.

Testimonials of users. Almost without exception, patent medicine advertisements depend on testimonials for creating confidence. An investigation of the American Medical Association has revealed how little such endorsements mean. In that investigation it was learned that some of the testimonials are purchased, others are faked outright by the agencies handling the advertising. Most testimonials, however, were genuine, being written by those who thought they were benefited. The benefits, however, were in most instances imaginary. In the case of those who endorsed "cancer cures" and "consumption cures," it was only necessary to wait a few months and the death certificates of these same endorsers would be available showing that they had died from the same disease from which they had been cured according to their testimonials. It was found in some instances that the testimonials of those who had already died from the disease the medicine was claimed to cure, were still being printed to create confidence in the drug.

Sometimes newspapers carrying testimonials also carry the refutation of these testimonials. Such an instance occurred in the *Holyoke Daily Transcript* of May 11, 1917, which carried a testimonial from Mr. Fred Wick telling how Tanlac, "The National Tonic" had relieved him of stomach trouble and caused him to gain ten pounds. The funeral notices of the same issue of the paper told of the death two days before of the same Mr. Fred Wick from cancer of the stomach.

People write testimonials for the following reasons: (1) Money. If the advertiser is willing to pay the price, it is easy to get testimonials. (2) Desire to see name in print. Some people long to see their names in print, and will go to any extent to accomplish this end. A writer in the *Toronto Star* once gave the following advice to such people: "If your brains won't get you into the papers, sign a patent medicine testimonial, maybe your kidneys will." (3) Ignorance. Many people like the Mr. Wick described above, think they are cured when in reality they are not in the least benefited. There are many others who attribute to a patent medicine a cure which was in fact due to the natural resistance of the body. Only one disease in a lifetime proves fatal.

Success. A fourth method of creating confidence is by referring to former success. It is particularly true in advertising that "nothing succeeds like success." Such advertisements as the following are based on this appeal. "Steadfast, unfailing quality has earned for the Chesterfield the confidence of men everywhere. Such popularity must be deserved." Advantage is also taken of any prizes won, such for example as "First prize at the St. Louis Exposition," or "Blue Ribbon at the World's Fair."

4. **Getting the response.** No hard and fast rule can be set down as to what advertising appeals will be most effective in getting the desired response. Two chief types of appeals are used with about equal success. These appeals are made by (*a*) Suggestion, and (*b*) Argument. The type of appeal most effective in any individual case depends upon the article to be sold. In general, articles of a

personal and intimate character as ornamental clothing, flowers, candies, or perfume can be best sold by a direct appeal to the emotions through suggestion. If the article is impersonal, utilitarian, and not to be enjoyed for its own sake, logical argument is a better mode of advertising.

(*a*) *Suggestion.* Suggestion is more or less subtle persuasion to buy through an appeal to the emotions. Indirect suggestion is ordinarily more successful than direct suggestion, for it arouses in the mind of the consumer no opposition. Appeals to love of family are effectively used in such suggestions as the following: "Do you love them enough to give them a .... for Christmas?" A direct suggestion appealing to the parental love is used in the advertisement, "Give your boy a Corona for Christmas." A forceful suggestion is more likely to bring results than is a weak suggestion. "I want you to choose between two shapes" is more dynamic than the weak and ineffectual, "Here are two favorites — take your choice." A positive suggestion is more effective than a negative suggestion. "A shoe that does not pinch" is poor, for the association in the mind of the prospective buyer is between shoe and pinch. "A shoe that insures comfort" is much better. A suggestion of quality combined with low price is successfully made in the advertisement of an automobile "built for the man who could pay more — priced for the man who shouldn't."

The dynamic effect of a suggestion varies directly in proportion to the prestige of its source. A certain prestige which aids in getting the desired response is given by the past success of the article or the prestige of patronage by the recommendation of the article by some person of note. The name may lend prestige through suggestion. A "Yale" jack-knife or "Yale" motorboat borrows significance from the dependability of Yale locks or the success of Yale's football team. In general it may be stated that the value of a suggestion in advertising depends upon its source and its emotional appeals.

(*b*) *Argument.* The "reason why" type of appeal is the most effective means of getting the response with some commodities and with some persons. The "reason why" appeal is valuable because we like to believe that we think. Therefore an advertisement that describes in detail the method of manufacture of the article, or that appears to present all facts impartially, flatters our vanity by allowing us to feel that we act on reason. Advertising, however, seldom uses the reasoning type of appeal exclusively, as indicated by the fact that over ninety per cent of contemporary non-classified advertisements use pictures and contain practically no reasoning material. Not more than ten per cent of advertisements rely upon reasoning exclusively, and in many cases where reasoning is involved it plays only a secondary rôle. The individual may use the argumentative part of the advertisement to justify his decisions which are based on feeling.

The purpose of argumentative advertising is to produce action by rational persuasion. Argument or persuasion is most effective in selling things which in themselves offer very little basis for emotional appeals, such as automobile tires, machinery, roofing materials, boilers, and similar articles. Banking and investments are likewise best advertised by "reason why" appeals. In such fields it is the argumentative advertisement that usually gets results.

B. Choosing the Medium for Advertising. After the copy has been prepared the next problem is that of placing the advertisement in the proper medium. It should be placed where it will reach the particular class of persons who are the actual or potential consumers of that commodity. In choosing the medium a number of factors must be taken into consideration. The value of any publication for advertising purposes depends upon four things:

1. **Circulation.** Other things being equal, the more people who see the advertisement the more sales will occur as a result of it.

2. **Class of readers.** The people who read the *Atlantic Monthly* are not usually the people who read *Liberty Weekly*, and accordingly the two publications carry different types of advertising matter.

3. **Time and frequency of appearance.** In general, advertisements designed for men should appear in the afternoon papers, those for house-wives in morning papers.

4. **Territory in which distributed.** Advertisements concerning farm implements should appear in papers distributed in farming sections; school furniture in school journals, etc.

The more important agencies for advertising are: (1) Newspapers; (2) Magazines; (3) Street-car cards; (4) Outdoor advertising; (5) Window displays. There are advantages in the use of each medium for advertising certain articles, and each has certain limitations.

(1) *Newspapers.* More money is expended for newspaper advertising than for any other type of advertising. The expenditure for newspaper advertising is approximately forty-seven per cent of the total expenditure for advertising. The expenditure for magazine advertising is approximately twelve per cent; and the other mediums are of less importance. The newspaper must therefore be considered an important advertising medium. In an investigation reported by Starch [1] a study was made of the extent to which advertisements are read, comparing newspaper and magazine advertisements. In this investigation 603 persons were interviewed, including business men, house-wives, and students. He found that the great proportion of men (54.5 per cent) see advertisements in a newspaper only incidentally. Only 7 per cent always look for them, and only 7.7 per cent usually look for them. With women the case is somewhat different. The proportion of women who always look for the advertisements (18 per cent) or who usually look (18.9 per cent) is about two and one half times as great as the corresponding proportions for men. As newspaper readers are busy people, and as they as a rule do not read the advertisements for their own sake, an advertisement which is going to catch the attention at all must do so quickly. Newspaper advertisements do not depend for their appeal upon artistic make-up. They are often based on human appeal, or contemporary events of public interest, or on reason. The similar investigations in regard to advertisements in magazines show more nearly equal interest by the men and women with a somewhat larger percentage purposely looking for advertisements.

(2) *Magazines.* Magazine copy must be quite different from that used in newspaper advertisements. In Starch's investigation it was found that approximately one third of the men and women always look through a magazine to see what advertisements it contains; nearly a fourth usually do so; and not quite a fourth occa-

[1] Starch, D.: *Principles of Advertising.* (A. W. Shaw Company, Chicago, 1923.)

sionally do so. This is a considerably larger per cent than see newspaper advertisements. Moreover, the magazine reader looks through the advertisements in a leisurely fashion. The types of appeals used are therefore different. Magazine advertisements depend much more upon artistic and colorful effects, and upon emotional appeals, and feature price less than those in the newspapers. Moreover, magazines reach a different class of people whose buying habits and needs are different. Magazines are better mediums for advertising some commodities, newspapers for others. The two should not be antagonistic, for they supplement each other. Magazines carry the general publicity, presenting the strongest arguments and strongest appeals in favor of the general proposition. The newspapers, sending a reminder of the article daily into the homes of the people, keep up the campaign.

(3) *Street-car cards.* Street-car cards as a medium for advertising have a number of particular advantages. All cards have practically an equally advantageous position as far as being seen is concerned, and none are placed in close juxtaposition to fraudulent advertisements, for the latter are supposed to be barred. The street-car cards reach all classes of people who live in cities, for nearly every one rides on the street cars at one time or another. Street-car cards are an especially good medium for the advertisement of foods, household articles, toilet articles, wearing apparel, and many local commodities.

(4) *Outdoor advertising.* There are three general types of outdoor advertising; panel posters, painted signs, and electrical signs. Most of the posters are controlled by the Poster Advertising Association, and are governed by its regulations. These regulations determine the number of panel posters which shall be erected in a community, and fix the number of these which shall be illuminated. There are a number of objections to the widespread use of posters. They frequently detract from the beauty of the surroundings, and when placed at the curves of highways, they tend to cause accidents by taking the attention of the motorist from the road. In many communities public opinion is against the use of outdoor advertising posters, and laws are being proposed to prevent their use. The same objections apply equally well to the use of advertisements

painted on barns and fences. These are generally unattractive, and mar the appearance of the country-side, particularly as the paint is seldom renewed frequently enough to be in good condition.

(5) *Window displays.* The window display is an important advertising medium, particularly for food and drink products and toilet articles. An attractive window trim gains the attention of passers-by as well as those who are entering the store. It therefore serves as a reminder of the product advertised and helps the retailer to dispose of his goods. It is not necessary for the window trim to be expensive. It should be inexpensive so that it can be frequently replaced by a new one. Realizing the advertising value of window trims, manufacturers seldom charge the retail dealer for them. The Association of National Advertisers has found that approximately eighty-one per cent of manufacturers do not charge their customers for window trims.

C. PREFERRED POSITIONS. The greater value of one position over another consists largely of greater attention value, due to the fact that a greater number of people are likely to see the advertisements in these positions. Experiments have shown the outside cover page to be worth twice as much in attention as an inside page. The inside cover pages have approximately two thirds the attention value of the outside cover, and the positions adjacent to reading matter are next in value. Other

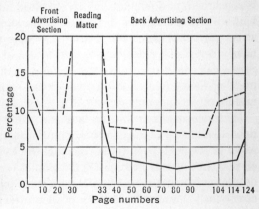

FIGURE 29. ATTENTION VALUES OF VARIOUS POSITIONS IN A STANDARD MAGAZINE

Dotted lines represent men; solid lines, women. (The breaks in the lines for the front advertising section are caused by the absence of any full-time advertisements at that point.) (After Starch.)

things being equal, after the first three or four pages are passed, the value of a position for advertising purposes is markedly decreased until the reading matter is approached, and after the first three or four pages following the reading matter the attention value of a position again declines until the back pages are approached. This was demonstrated by Strong, whose results (in terms of the percentage of persons recognizing the advertisements in different positions in the magazine) are shown in Figure 29.

In addition to these "preferred positions" in the magazine it has been experimentally determined that the right-hand page is slightly superior to the left-hand page in advertising value. The attention value of the upper half of the page is about ten per cent greater than the attention value of the lower half of the page. Nor are the four quarter-pages equal in value as advertising space. The upper right quarter has the greatest attention value and the lower right quarter next. The lower left quarter of the page is of least value as advertising space.

Obviously all positions in a magazine are not equally favorable for advertising. There is unquestionably a difference in the advertising value of positions on a page, yet there is seldom a difference in the rate for different positions on the page, and except for the cover pages, there is seldom a difference in the rates for different pages.

D. TRADE MARKS. The value of a trade mark, whether it consists of a symbol, design, or word, is almost wholly psychological, depending chiefly on its value as a means of identifying the product. Advertisers give the answer, "Everything" to the question, "What's in a name?" The trade mark or name derives its value from the good-will in the minds of the people toward the produce or firm for which it stands. The value to the firm of a popular trade name is immense. In numerous instances its worth to the user is more than one third of the total value of the firm.

But its value depends to a large extent on the original selection of the trade name. Only very good trade names and those which are widely advertised attain the maximum value. A good trade name must be simple and short, easy to pronounce and remember. It must be unique so as to avoid danger of imitation and infringement. The name should be fanciful, yet suggestive or descriptive of the article to which it refers.

Trade marks and trade names are only about a generation old, having come into prominence as transportation facilities improved, and the market for goods became more than local. Every year a greater number of trade marks are registered. There are at present considerably over 175,000 trade marks registered. With so large a number there are naturally frequent resemblances and confusions. The successful trade marks are frequently imitated by less successful competitors. The trade mark "Uneeda" of the National Biscuit Company has been imitated over four hundred times. Many of these imitations have been judged by the courts to be infringements and hence declared invalid. Much litigation is constantly in process over infringements of trade names.

The question as to whether two trade marks are sufficiently similar to cause confusion in the minds of the people is primarily a psychological problem. Yet psychological effect has been very little considered by the courts dealing with infringement cases. A careful study of the factors involved was made by Paynter.[1] In this investigation he used sixty pairs of litigated trade marks. One series of sixty trade marks was shown to the observer, one at a time. The observer was then asked to tell whether the trade marks in the second list, seen under the same circumstances, were identical with the trade marks which had been seen before. Some of the trade marks in the second list were identical with those in the first, others were imitations, infringements, or similar names. In some cases legal decisions had already been passed, ranking the names as either infringements, or non-infringements. In this investigation the degree of confusion between the names was measured in terms of the number of cases in which the imitation was mistaken for the original. The following table presents the court decisions and the amount of confusion determined by psychological experiment in nine pairs of trade names.

ORIGINAL	IMITATION	PER CENT CONFUSION	LEGAL DECISION
Sozodont	Kalodont	28	Non-infringement
Nox-all	Non-X-Ell	28	Infringement
Club	Chancellor Club	35	Infringement
Bestyette	Veribest	35	Non-infringement
Mother's	Grandma's	38	Non-infringement
Au-to-do	Autola	40	Infringement
Peptenzyme	Pinozyme	43	Non-infringement
Green River	Green Ribbon	50	Infringement
Ceresota	Cressota	53	Infringement

[1] Paynter, Richard H.: "A Psychological Study of Confusion Between Word Trade-Marks," *Bulletin of United States Trade-Mark Association*, May, 1915.

Some of the imitations declared to be legal confused more people than some of those which were declared to be illegal. Court decisions on infringements would be more reliable and would more often mean what they are supposed to mean if an attempt were made to get at the psychological basis of confusing one name with another.

III. SALESMANSHIP

Salesmanship, though having some points in common with advertising, and having the same general aim, is quite different from advertising. The materials of advertising are concrete and tangible, consisting of printed posters, colored illustrations, or electric signs. These materials can be studied and analyzed over a period of months and years if desired. The sales talk is much less tangible. It involves the individual relation between salesman and buyer, with all the complexity and variableness of the "personal equation." The appeal of the advertisement is fixed, and once presented, its effectiveness is determined and cannot be improved. But the appeals in salesmanship can be modified or changed according to the circumstances. The salesman may repeat his best selling points, and most convincing arguments, change his line of attack, supplement it with additional arguments, and in many other ways adapt his sales talk to the immediate situation and to the prospective buyer. Salesmanship is so largely dependent upon personal conditions that it is impossible to standardize selling, or to study accurately the process by laboratory experimentation. Advertising is of a general nature, directed at the masses; salesmanship is individual, with direct contact between the purchaser and the salesman.

1. **Personality traits of the salesman.** Since selling depends fundamentally upon personal relations, the personality of the salesman is of vital importance. All agree that the salesman should possess a pleasing personality, but few agree as to just what a pleasing personality is. Still less is known about how to measure it. Certain traits which go to make up a pleasing personality, and which a successful salesman must possess, have been given considerable attention. The more important qualities are health, good personal appearance, enthusiasm, confidence, sincerity, tact, courtesy, cheerfulness, initiative, and memory.

While health is not strictly a trait of personality, it is nevertheless the basis of many other important traits. Vigor, vitality, alertness and aggressiveness depend largely upon general health. The
healthy man is the one people like to deal with. The psychological
effect of health and vigor is strongly in favor of the success of the
sales interview. The dress of the salesman is a second important
factor in making a good impression. The salesman should be well
dressed, avoiding extreme fashions and flashy clothes. An ill-kept
or untidy appearance prejudices the prospective customer from the
very outset. Poor clothes suggest poor wares, and few expert salesmen are willing to incur this handicap.

Certain more specific traits are of vast importance in making the
sale. Cheerfulness, courtesy, and tact are indispensable, as in other
personal relations. The tactful salesman increases his chance of
making a sale, while the man who is rude kills any chance that he
might have had. The salesman with initiative plans new modes of
attack and wins the customer while the one with no initiative makes
no particular impression, and the too aggressive salesman only
offends.

The salesman with an air of confidence in his goods inspires confidence in the prospective buyer, while a lack of this confidence
arouses the distrust of the customer. Enthusiasm and confidence
on the part of the salesman tend to inspire equal confidence in the
prospective customer. The salesman who does not sincerely believe in the quality of the goods he is selling is likely to bluster to
hide his lack of confidence. The average man cannot make a success selling an article he believes to be worthless.

The attitude of the salesman toward people is important. In
order to deal with people effectively one must enjoy contacts with
people. The recluse, or the taciturn or introverted individual is
not adapted to selling. The successful salesman is chiefly interested, not in his own thoughts, but in people and events outside
himself. A friendly attitude toward the prospective customer is
generally responded to, but coldness or lack of interest creates an
attitude of indifference or hostility.

2. **Methods of selecting salespeople.** The work of the salesgirl
at the notions counter and that of the automobile salesman have

certain points in common, yet there are also important differences between them.   The one is the salesperson who makes many sales, each involving only a few cents, while the other is the salesman who makes relatively few sales, but each one involving several hundred dollars.   There are likewise differences between the problems and practices of the traveling salesman and those of the stationary salesman.   These differences must be taken into consideration in the selection of salespeople.   The tests used in the selection of salespeople must be adapted to measure the particular type of selling ability required for the job.

The older methods of selecting salespeople have proved too wasteful and inefficient for the present day.   A few years ago when an employer needed a new salesperson he interviewed the applicants, and tried out the most promising among them by observing his work on the job.   But concerns employing hundreds or thousands of salespeople cannot afford to "try out" prospective employees on the job.   The necessity for some easily administered tests which would predict with a high degree of accuracy success or failure in selling was keenly felt.   Thus tests for salespeople began to be devised.

The first of these tests had nothing to do with the work to be performed.   They consisted chiefly of purely academic tasks, such as the following: underlining the adjacent letters forming a word in a series of several hundred unspaced letters; completing sentences in which words are omitted; completing words when the first and last letters are given; rearranging the mixed-up letters of a word which when properly arranged spells the name of an animal; or crossing out specified numbers in a series.   As would be expected, many of these tests failed to differentiate between good salespeople and poor salespeople, and so proved of little value.   Such tests have the additional disadvantage of lacking a practical appeal to those taking them.   A salesman resents being asked to rearrange "rdcioleoc" to spell "crocodile," or to make a word out of "c——p."

A new type of test for salespeople is seriously needed to replace the academic tests described above.   A movement is now on foot to construct tests in terms of the work actually to be performed.   These tests would measure the factors necessary for success as a salesperson and have the additional advantage of appealing to those taking the tests as practical and fair.

The test outlined below will serve as an example of a practical test for salespeople. The test consists of four parts, each of which measures an important element or factor in selling ability.

Test 1. *Judgment in dealing with selling situations.* This test consists of a number of sales problems in which the situation is described and four possible means of meeting the situation are suggested, of which the person taking the test is to choose the best. These questions deal with selling situations involving judgment and tact in dealing with the public, and in relations with other employees. A salesman who can deal successfully with a certain difficult customer can almost always pick out the best method of dealing with the customer when the situation is described on paper. The applicant who consistently picks out tactless or ineffectual methods of meeting the situation in the test could hardly be expected to choose the best means in actual work.

The following questions [1] from a test for salespeople will serve as examples:

3. Assume that you are a saleslady and in trying a coat on a small child, candy is smeared on it. It would be best to:
   —— Insist that the coat be bought.
   —— Call the mother's attention to it and ask her what she will do about it.
   —— Say nothing, but send the coat to the cleaning room.
   —— Tell the child to be more careful about soiling things.
4. A charge customer who has over-run her account asks to have a dress charged. The office reports "no credit." You should:
   —— Tell her you are sorry but that you can't sell her anything on credit.
   —— Inform her that she must go to the office first.
   —— Ask her why she had not paid her past bills, and if she gives a satisfactory explanation, let her have the dress.
   —— Explain that you cannot charge the dress, but that if she will make a small deposit you will be glad to reserve it for her.
20. Suppose you are selling an expensive piece of silk to a woman. After you have cut three yards from the bolt she tells you that she called for three and a half yards. It would be best to:

[1] Reprinted by special permission of Center for Psychological Service, Washington, D.C.

—— Cut three and a half yards from the bolt and keep the three yards.

—— Tell her that you will cut one-half yard more, but that she must take the three yards.

—— Ask her to take the three yards, and if that is not enough to come back for more.

—— Insist that inasmuch as she called for three yards, it is her duty to take it.

The best results are obtained by first letting the prospective salesperson take the test and then during the personal interview asking his reason for each answer. In that way considerable light is thrown on his habits of thinking. In the third question, for example, a person with a nagging reformer type of disposition would take the fourth answer. The second and third answers are usually made by a person who looks to the immediate sale regardless of making friends for the future. The first answer creates no enemies, and builds up good will for future sales.

Test 2. *Accuracy of observation of human nature.* The successful salesman must know the motives that govern human behavior, and the ways in which the different emotions find expression. He must be able to understand facial expressions well enough to know the reactions of the prospective buyer to the sales talk. The salesman's knowledge of human nature is tested by presenting to him a large number of generalizations on human nature, some of which are true, others false. He is told to indicate whether each generalization is true or false.

The following questions from the test referred to above will serve to illustrate:

If a statement is true, encircle the T; if false, encircle the F.

T F   5   Bargain sales have to offer real bargains to attract customers.
T F 12   Most people will pay more liberally to be made to laugh than to be made to think.
T F 18   It is better to talk the good points of one article than the bad points of another.
T F 20   Pretense and sham are often inspired by the desire for social admiration.
T F 22   What will please one person can safely be assumed to please another.

T F 30 All people who become wealthy or famous must be either
bright or hardworking.

Test 3. *Memory for names and faces.* Ability to recognize a
customer whom he has seen before and to call him by name is a
valuable asset for a salesman. It tickles one's vanity to be remembered, and puts him in a mood to buy. Memory for names and
faces is tested by giving the applicant a sheet of twelve photographs,
each with a name under it. The applicant studies the faces and
names for several minutes. Later he is required to select the faces
he has seen before from another sheet of twenty-five, and to put the
proper name with it. It is found that salesmen recognize faces
much more frequently than they remember names.

Test 4. *Arithmetical reasoning.* This test has two main purposes; first, to see whether the applicant has sufficient knowledge of
arithmetic to make the necessary sales calculations quickly and accurately, and second, to measure the mental alertness of the applicant. There is a high correlation between arithmetical reasoning
(reasoning problems in arithmetic) and mental alertness.

The written test is designed to supplement the interview, not to
supplant it. An interview is essential to determine the personal appearance, poise, dress, and other personality traits of the prospective salesman. The interview reveals whether the applicant has the
power to create a favorable impression, essential in salesmanship.
A quiet, conversational tone makes the buyer feel that he is talking
to a friend. Carriage and posture are also noted in the interview.
An erect carriage helps to create a favorable impression. It seems
to inspire confidence as also does a straightforward glance. These
factors cannot be measured by a written test. Their importance
thus makes the interview a very fundamental part of the program of
selecting salespeople.

3. **Steps in selling.** In studying salesmanship, it is customary to
analyze the selling process into certain divisions or steps. The
names assigned by various authors to these steps are not always
uniform, but the ideas underlying the names are more constant. A
number of authorities recognize the following eight steps in the selling process: (*a*) Pre-approach; (*b*) Winning the interview; (*c*) Presentation or demonstration; (*d*) Creating desire; (*e*) Creating confi-

dence; (f) Meeting objections; (g) Closing the sale; (h) Closing the interview.

(a) *Pre-approach.* The salesman, like the military genius, must plan his attack if he expects to succeed. No general would willingly go into battle without knowing as much as possible about the resources of his enemy, nor will the salesman approach a customer without first getting certain important information. The pre-approach is a scheme for securing such information and investigating such facts as will aid the salesman in making the sale. If the salesman knows the name of the customer or prospect, knows his prejudices and understands his ambitions, likes and dislikes, financial resources and the requirements of his business, it enables him to present his proposition in such a way as to interest the customer directly. Without this information he must find these things out from the prospect by presenting different propositions more or less aimlessly, and noting his reactions. By making such a preparation, and formulating a plan of attack before approaching the prospective buyer, the salesman can surprise him with an unexpected knowledge of his business, and with an unexpected interest in his affairs, thereby inclining him more favorably toward buying.

(b) *Winning the interview.* One of the most difficult points in the selling process of the traveling salesman is securing an interview, for if the salesman fails to win the interview, that of course ends it. The approach is of great relative importance in the process of making a sale, for if the salesman makes a bad start, he very greatly lessens the possibility of making the sale. The object of the approach is to make a favorable impression on the customer, and thus secure his attention, at the same time to size him up so that the salesman may better adapt himself to the man. The approach is greatly facilitated by a prosperous appearance, attractive personality, pleasant voice and courteous manners. In his approach the salesman conveys the impression that he realizes the value of time, his customer's and his own, and that he does not intend to waste any. A long introductory talk with a busy man may do far more harm than good.

(c) *Presentation or demonstration.* After introducing himself and getting the attention of the customer, the salesman proceeds to make known to the customer the services he proposes to render in satisfying his needs. The goods or propositions offered by the salesman are described and explained at this point. He displays his samples in attractive form so as to bring out their utility, beauty, superiority over competing goods, and other advantages. Sharp, clear-cut ideas about the goods or propositions are essential since they are much more effective than superlatives and generalities. In order to make a successful presentation the salesman must be thoroughly familiar with his goods, so that there will be no hesitancy or doubt in any of his statements, and so that he may meet objections fully and convincingly.

An effort should be made to focus the attention of the prospective buyer on the thing to be sold. This is best accomplished by presenting some material portion of the exhibit. When we see things our attention is caught. The skillful life-insurance salesman in picturing the effect of an initial investment in a ten-year policy, does the computation before the eyes of a prospective customer. In that way, the attention of the customer is held through the whole demonstration.

(d) *Creating a desire for the goods.* Showing the samples and describing the benefits to be derived from possession are designed to create in the customer a desire to possess the thing described. In making the presentation and creating desire the points are made in the order of increasing importance, since the last point made tends to be most effective. In order to create in the prospective customer the desire to possess the article, the salesman must know human nature and the motives that govern human behavior. The principal motives with which a salesman has to reckon are profit, pleasure, caution, utility, pride and desire for social approval. The salesman must determine which ones are most important in any particular case, and adapt his sales talk accordingly.

(e) *Creating confidence.* The salesman not only must make the prospective customer want the article he has to sell, but also must convince him that it would be a good thing for him to have. He must inspire confidence in the value and utility of the article. One method of developing confidence is by showing that many other people are purchasing the article. He must give an impression of sincerity on his part, since the confidence and sincerity of the sales-man are powerful factors in inspiring confidence in his goods.

In this connection it should be remembered that we will believe anything if it is told to us often enough. There are usually several attractive features that will be valuable for the salesman to focus upon. By repeating these points their hold is rendered more permanent. The form of the repetition, however, should be varied, but a good selling point may be repeated in different form a number of times.

(f) *Meeting objections.* No matter what his line may be the sales-man has to meet certain types of objections over and over. He soon learns these objections and has his answer prepared in ad-vance. If the salesman knows his goods thoroughly he usually has little difficulty in answering objections, and in preparing the way for closing the deal.

If the buyer mentions some good point in a rival company's merchandise, the salesman should not respond by knocking the competing line, but he should readily admit all the desirable points in the goods of others, and end by showing that when all things are considered, his own goods have superior advantages and should therefore be purchased. If, for example, an automobile salesman is trying to induce a customer to buy a Chevrolet car and the customer raises the objection that the Ford costs less, the Chevrolet salesman can meet the objection by admitting that the initial cost of the Ford car is less, but claim that the upkeep of the Chevrolet is much less, and that the Chevrolet is more comfortable and luxurious. He should not, like some Chevrolet salesmen, tell how the gasoline tanks on the new Fords are liable to catch on fire since they are close to the motor, and how the Ford differential shakes to pieces in a few hundred miles. Most prospective customers have seen thousands of Fords but have never seen either of these things hap-pen. Consequently such stories kill confidence in the sales talk.

The psychology of this point is clear. By emphasizing the bad points in the Ford you clutter up the mind of the customer with dis-tracting thoughts and may prejudice him against buying any auto-mobile. Moreover, we all know how we rebel when we are told not to do something. Negative ideas should never be advanced except as indirect points to serve as contrast to the final positive points. No one loves a "knocker." It is best to avoid all reference to competitors unless the mention is first made by the prospective customer. Objections should never be suggested to the prospect, even if they can be answered easily.

(*g*) *Closing the sale.* The crucial test of a salesman's ability is closing the sale. He should be ready to close at any time during the sales talk when the interest of the prospect seems to indicate the "psychological moment." When the critical moment arrives, the salesman must act. He often accomplishes his purpose by assuming that the order has already been given, and by talking as though the deal has been closed, so that signing the order becomes a mere formality. Or the effective appeal in closing the sale may be that which puts the proposition up to the prospect as an opportunity to be accepted within a certain time or lost forever. But in whatever way it is done, the important thing is to get the buyer to sign on the dotted line.

(*h*) *Closing the interview.* After the sale has been consummated, it is bad policy for the salesman to linger. He should take his leave as promptly and as courteously as he can. Further talk merely wastes the time of his customer and his own time, and often endangers the sale by giving the buyer time to change his mind. Hugh Chalmers recognized the value of a proper get-away in the following words: "A salesman, like a railroad, must have terminal facilities."

CHAPTER XVII

SELECTION AND CONTROL OF PERSONNEL

A careful survey of almost any large plant would reveal many a workman with slow reaction time vainly trying to keep up with a rapidly operating machine, or a man with poor powers of attention attempting to concentrate on a task that is too complex for him, or with intelligence too low to grasp the problems and make the decisions necessary in his work.

HAROLD BURTT [1]

PEOPLE differ as much in ability as in wages, but ability is seldom the determining factor in the amount of wages. Men of equal ability working in the same concern often differ more than four hundred per cent in the wages they receive, and it not infrequently happens that one employee with more than four times the ability of another receives the same wage as the inferior employee.

Some people are "born" mechanics and can manipulate the most intricate machinery with ease and dexterity; most individuals can learn to perform the simpler mechanical jobs with a fair degree of efficiency, but there are some so devoid of mechanical sense that no amount of teaching will equip them to do mechanical work. Some make friends without effort and seem to have an uncanny insight into the motives of others, while some have such thorny dispositions that their mere presence tends to irritate us. The first group should be hired as foremen and executives; the second group should be hired only for positions where they will not have to deal with others. Some, who can succeed at one operation, make dismal failures at another, and some, who fail at the former operation, when placed in the latter position, make for smooth running. It is the job of the personnel officer to discover these individual differences and to select and place his employees accordingly. It has been estimated that an average investment of $4888 capital must be made for each worker. This comprises the machinery, land, and buildings. With this expensive outlay, it is only logical that more attention should be paid to the selection and control of these workers.

[1] Burtt, Harold: *Employment Psychology.* Houghton Mifflin Company, Boston, 1926.

I. SELECTION OF PERSONNEL

In the olden times, when each man carried on the vocation of his father or that of some neighbor to whom he was apprenticed, the problem of selection was not very serious. But with the coming of the Industrial Revolution all this was changed, and instead of the close personal relation of the employer to the employee, and his consequent knowledge of the ability of the employee to perform the work, men by the thousands were in a short time mobilized for various jobs about which many of them knew nothing, nor did their employers know anything about their ability to do the work. Progress in the selection of workers did not keep pace with progress in the mechanical elements in industry. Machines were early perfected and standardized, but for years the operators of these machines were very largely selected on a trial-and-error basis. Generally the "boss" or foreman was given the job of hiring and firing the employees for his particular unit, but the foreman had little time to devote to the selection of men, and less knowledge on which to base a decision as to the man's fitness.

The selection of employees by a foreman instead of a trained personnel officer is just as archaic as is the use of horses instead of motor vehicles for transportation purposes. Personnel methods have developed more in the last two decades than in all the time previously. The most important problems involved in selection are: (1) Job analysis and specification; (2) Attracting applicants; (3) Interviewing applicants; (4) Testing applicants; (5) Methods of measuring vocational success.

1. **Job analysis and specification.** With the coming of the machine age and the development of mass production, the duties of the various employees became much more specialized and restricted. Thousands of new jobs were created and hundreds of old ones broken up; the result being that we now have a multiplicity of jobs to fill and such a diversity of training and ability in those with whom to fill the jobs that the problem of selection has become very complicated. As a result of this specialization, the number who receive a general training is becoming fewer and fewer. Instead of general automobile mechanics, we have "ignition experts," and instead of all-round plumbers, we have experts in the cutting of

sewer pipes. But the "ignition expert" is often unable to repair the differential of the automobile, and the expert pipe-cutter is unable to install a set of bathroom fixtures. Therefore, in selection, it is necessary to learn what duties we want the employees to fulfill, and then to devise methods of discovering a person qualified for these duties.

The first step in this procedure is *Job Analysis*. Kitson [1] has defined job analysis as "a process of dissecting a job and describing its component elements." Such jobs as plumbing are broken up into the various operations which must be performed by a plumber, such as cutting pipes, threading pipes, wiping joints, etc., and the steps necessary for the proper execution of each of the operations are described in detail. Job analysis not only gives the duties to be performed by the employee, but the working conditions, psychology, and qualifications for the job are usually given. The analysis often includes various mental traits such as are usually embodied in rating scales. Specifications for certain jobs may contain critical scores in intelligence. For example, people with scores less than 60 on Army Alpha are practically never able to render efficient service as stenographers. Recognizing 60 as a "critical score for stenographers," the specifications would require a score of at least 60 to qualify for consideration for the position. With the larger concerns tests for special ability are sometimes developed for the various jobs and certain critical scores on these tests stated as a part of the job requirements.

2. Attracting applicants. Having analyzed the job and having laid down specifications for the type of employee desired, it next becomes necessary to find the person with these qualifications to fill the job. Unless competent people can be induced to apply for the positions, no system of selecting personnel, however thorough it may be, will secure qualified persons for the position. Other things being equal, if we have one hundred persons to choose from, we have ten times as good a chance of getting an employee qualified for the job as if we have only ten to choose from. In getting the better people to apply, the problem of advertising enters, and

---

[1] Kitson, H. D.: "Scientific Method in Job Analysis," *Journal of Political Economy* (1921), xxix, 508. Courtesy of University of Chicago Press.

in the opinion of the writer, here is where personnel officers, especially Civil Service administrators, have done their least satisfactory work. In the past, a few mimeographed announcements were made stating when and where examinations would be held. These mimeographed sheets were posted on some inconspicuous bulletin board along with many announcements of events that had long since occurred. This tended to call the examination to the attention of only the chronic job-seekers, and in many instances, the better qualified did not compete for the position simply because they did not know about it.

That such ineffective methods of advertising are being recognized and remedied by personnel officers is shown by the 1925 report of the Chief Examiner of the United States Civil Service Commission, in which he mentioned the following methods for announcing examinations used in 1925; radio broadcasting of announcements; announcements in trade journals; announcements through technical, professional, and scientific societies; posters in public libraries, Y.M.C.A., and other organizations; and announcements by means of specially prepared mailing lists. In other words, each announcement is given individual treatment according to its peculiar needs.

3. **Interviewing applicants.** Having got the applicants to apply, the actual job of selection begins. At first there was no effort to make a scientific approach to the employment problem, but as time went on and competition became more fierce, necessitating more adequate methods of selecting personnel, a central employment office where all the employees of the firm were selected was established. In this office, as a rule, the personnel officers were better trained for their job of selecting workers than were the foremen under the old system. But while for years most of their selections were determined by purely subjective estimates and opinions, still, the opinions of men who had considerable experience in selecting employees are usually of more value than the haphazard judgment of a foreman whose experience in picking personnel is much more limited. In arriving at a decision as to the relative fitness of applicants, personnel officers have depended very largely on the personal interview.

(a) *Purposes of interview.* As pointed out by Burtt [1] the interview serves three very distinct purposes. In the first place, it gives the executive an opportunity to discover certain traits not revealed in any other procedure. The personal appearance and many other personality traits cannot be measured in a written test. For those positions in which the employee must have considerable contact with others, an interview is very important, for if an applicant's personality affects his interviewers unfavorably, there is some reason to suspect that he would affect others accordingly. This, of course, is not always true; for some reason the applicant may affect only the interviewers adversely. The reliability of the interview is always increased with the number of judges.

In the second place, the interview gives the applicant an opportunity to secure certain information about the job and the company, so that he need not begin work with the wrong impression about the position. A third advantage claimed for the interview is that it affords the opportunity to make a friend for the company; to hire an applicant who will have a more coöperative interest in working for the company.

(b) *Factors making for unreliability.* As pointed out above, while an interview is often indispensable, the data secured from it are not very reliable. There are three chief causes for this unreliability. In the first place, an interviewer tends to generalize on too few experiences. If the interviewer has had an unfortunate experience with a red-headed person, he tends to regard all red-headed people with suspicion; if he has been swindled by some one with a hooked nose, he feels that no persons with hooked noses should be trusted; and if a man of the Jewish race has double-crossed him in the past, he tends to place less confidence in other members of that race.

Another cause for unreliability of the interview is the widespread assumption that habits are general rather than specific. It is assumed that neatness in one situation will carry over into other situations. Clean hands may be taken to indicate clean morals, and dirty hands, dirty conduct. It may be assumed that a person

[1] Burtt, Harold: *Employment Psychology.* Houghton Mifflin Company, Boston, 1926.

who talks rapidly will be a rapid typist, and that a person with slow speech will work slowly. The fallacy of such assumptions has been demonstrated time and again. All habits are specific and involve certain definite reactions to equally definite situations. Nervousness on the part of the applicant is sometimes a third cause for unreliability. In the excitement of an interview, the applicant not infrequently fails to do himself justice.

(c) *Experimental measurement of the reliability of the interview.* During the last few years employment methods have been subjected to a series of investigations which have brought to light the fallacy of a number of time-honored practices and led to the substitution of more adequate methods. No method of employment has lost so much prestige as a result of these investigations as has the method of determining the relative fitness of men solely on the basis of a personal interview. The following investigation is typical of those which have shaken our confidence in the reliability of the interview as a basis for employment.

Hollingworth [1] reports a study of ratings of fifty-seven applicants for sales positions, each of whom was interviewed by twelve different sales managers. Each applicant was assigned a rank from 1 to 57 by each judge, a rating of 1 meaning that the applicant was considered the best in the group, a rating of 57 that he was considered poorest. Figure 30 shows graphically the range of ratings given by the twelve sales managers to the first three applicants. It will be noticed that applicant A is judged 6 by one judge and 56 by another, one sales manager placing him in the upper eighth of the group and another placing him next to the lowest. For all the applicants there is marked disagreement even though the ratings were made by men supposed to know the qualifications necessary in the applicant and by men who had had considerable experience in such ratings. Such experiments as these indicate that the personal "sizing-up" of applicants by interviewers is only a little more reliable than determining their fitness by an alphabetical arrangement or a chance shuffling of the names of the applicants.

(d) *Increasing the reliability of interviews.* It is obvious that if

[1] Hollingworth, H. L.: *Judging Human Character* (D. Appleton and Company, New York, 1923), 65.

Graphic Rating Scale [1]

1. It is requested that you indicate by check (√) your opinion of the applicant in each of the qualities specified. Place only one check after each quality. For example, on the specimen scale below the check mark indicates that the supposed applicant is in the class which "learns and adapts slowly" but is more nearly average than dull, because the check is placed nearer the "average" group than the "dull."

Specimen — Do not mark here.

ABILITY TO LEARN.

Consider ease and rapidity of understanding new instructions and adapting to new situations.

Dull and unadaptable.	Learns and adapts slowly.	Average in learning and adapting.	Learns and adapts readily.	Learns with exceptional ease and rapidity.

ANSWER ALL OF THE FOLLOWING.

In giving your opinion on a particular trait, disregard for the moment every trait but that one, as specifically defined, and consider the applicant's ability in this trait from the point of view of GENERAL CLERICAL WORK only.

(a) ABILITY TO LEARN.

Consider ease and rapidity of understanding new instructions and adapting to new situations.

Dull and unadaptable.	Learns and adapts slowly.	Average in learning and adapting.	Learns and adapts readily.	Learns with exceptional ease and rapidity.

(b) INDUSTRY.

Consider energy, and application to duties, day in and day out.

Lazy.	Indifferent.	Average application.	Industrious.	Unusually energetic.

(c) INITIATIVE.

Consider ability to go ahead with work without being told every detail, and to make practical suggestions for doing work in a better way.

Needs constant direction.	No originality.	Minor constructive ability.	Considerable constructive ability.	Highly constructive.

[1] Filer, Herbert A., and O'Rourke, L. J.: "Progress in Civil Service Tests," Journal of Personnel Research (vol. I, no. 11, March, 1923), 519. Courtesy of University of Chicago Press.

(d) COOPERATIVENESS. Consider ability to maintain good working relations with co-workers.	Trouble maker.	Causes slight friction.	Indifferent.	Coöperative.	Exceptionally coöperative.
(e) ATTITUDE TOWARD WORK. Consider voluntary interest and effort in work.	Unconcerned and no voluntary effort.	Interest and effort below average.	Average interest and effort.	Interest and effort above average.	Shows keen interest and whole-hearted effort.
(f) SPEED. Consider rate at which applicant is able to work.	Very slow.	Slow.	Average rate.	Fast.	Exceptionally rapid.
(g) ACCURACY. Consider ability to do work without errors.	Unsatisfactory.	Makes many errors.	Average accuracy.	Seldom makes errors.	Exceptionally accurate.
(h) DISPOSITION. Consider natural temper of mind.	Decidedly ill natured; uncivil.	Easily vexed; moody.	Average self-restraint.	Rarely vexed.	Exceptional self-control.
(i) NEATNESS. Consider orderliness in work.	Disorderly.	Somewhat below average in orderliness.	Average orderliness.	Somewhat above average orderliness.	Exceptionally orderly.
(j) ABILITY TO SUPERVISE. Consider ability to direct work of others effectively.	Unable to direct work of others.	Somewhat below average ability in directing others.	Shows average ability in directing others.	Somewhat above average ability in directing others.	Maintains loyal and effective working force.

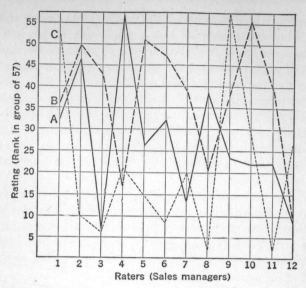

FIGURE 30. THE RATINGS OF THREE APPLICANTS FOR
POSITIONS AS SALESMEN BY TWELVE SALES MANAGERS

personal interviews cannot be made more reliable than is indicated
by these studies of reliability, the results cannot be trusted. But,
seeing certain advantages of the interview for measuring some
traits not measurable in the written test, and for supplementing
other measurements, various personnel administrators are making
attempts to improve the reliability of the interview. First of all,
where interviews are necessary or desirable, an effort is being made
to have more than one person do the interviewing, thus increasing
the reliability by pooling the judgments of several judges. Other
efforts to improve the interview are directed largely toward a
standardization of the interview procedure. The interviewer himself may be given special training in the technique of his job, or the
questions which he asks the applicant may be standardized on the
basis of objectivity or importance and value as indicative of fitness
for the job. Rating scales for the use of interviewers also add to
the reliability of the interview.

The latter of these — the rating scale — is the most important contribution which psychology has made to improving the interview. When the interviewer uses a rating scale, he has before him a standardized list of traits which he is to notice in the applicant. This list of traits has been selected because of the importance of the traits in making an individual qualified for the job. They are usually arranged on a sheet in such a way that the rater can easily assign a quantitative rating to each trait. For most purposes the most satisfactory way of arranging the qualities to be rated has been found to be in the form of a graphic rating scale. A reference to the scale used by O'Rourke in rating clerical applicants will illustrate the form.

Scales like this are interpreted numerically by using a stencil which is the length of the rating line and which is marked in convenient numerical divisions usually from 1 to 10. Each trait rated is given a value corresponding to the position which the check for that trait occupies on the stencil. A total rating may be obtained by adding the separate values for all the traits.

There are several purposes which such graphic rating scales may serve. First of all, when properly used, they give a means of measuring some apparently non-measurable traits. By placing before the interviewer or rater the traits to be considered, they reduce the likelihood of ratings being based on "general impressions," perhaps arrived at by noticing only one trait. They offer a uniform method of expressing opinion, especially desirable when several raters are to rate the same group of men.

Aside from their use in rating applicants for positions, graphic rating-scale methods have also been found useful in rating for promotion, in indicating progress of employees during periods of employment, and in comparing efficiency of various employees. In fact in any problem where objective ratings of personal traits are necessary the rating-scale method has been found the most reliable available.

4. Testing applicants. Considering the unreliability of the interview method, it was only natural that some other method of selection should be sought. To get away from the difficulty of selection on a purely subjective basis, personnel officers began to give written examinations to assist them in their task of choosing employees. At first the chief use of written examinations was by personnel officers in the public service. When the supporters of the merit system succeeded in routing the spoilsmen and in establishing civil service commissions empowered to select the public personnel, the change was so abrupt that it found those empowered with the task of selecting employees ill-prepared for their task. At that time intelligence tests were as yet unborn and standardized trade tests totally non-existent.

It is obvious that tests for selecting applicants have passed through considerable development. It is accordingly of interest to note the rapid evolution of our present system of testing applicants. Five stages stand out in this development, represented by the following types of tests: (a) Examination in terms of school subjects; (b) Essays in terms of the job; (c) General intelligence tests; (d) Special aptitude tests in terms of the job; (e) Achievement or trade tests in short answer form.

(a) *Examinations in terms of school subjects.* When Civil Service commissioners were confronted with the task of selecting employees on the basis of relative merit, they cast about for some system of determining merit; and the only place where they found any attempt to gauge relative merit was in the academic examination used by school teachers as a basis for assigning grades. No other examining method being available, personnel officers began using these academic tests for all kinds of positions. No matter what position was to be filled, they used such tests as spelling, handwriting, and arithmetic to determine the relative fitness of the various applicants for the position. Strange as it may seem, exactly the same type of examination in spelling was used to fill such diverse positions as patrolman, prison guard, assistant librarian, plumber, matron, fireman and carpenter. It is obvious that ability to spell, in and of itself, has no relation to the successful performance of these jobs. And experiments show that ability to spell is one of the poorest indications of one's general intelligence. There was little reason, therefore, for including such subjects as part of the civil service examinations, except that it was necessary to have something more than personal opinion on which to select employees, and spelling was the thing available. Penmanship was also used in almost all types of positions, regardless of whether the employee would have to use his penmanship any more extensively than to sign the monthly payroll. Handwriting, like spelling, has also been demonstrated to have little or no relation to mental alertness or general ability. In fact, it would be just as effective in most positions to select personnel according to height or weight as according to their penmanship or spelling ability.

(b) *Essays on various phases of the job.* It is obvious that methods of selecting personnel, no more closely related to the job than those just discussed, would of necessity be replaced by more adequate methods. We accordingly find civil service examiners asking the competitors to write an essay about some particular phase of the job for which they were competing. The following question from an examination for plumber is typical of the kind of questions used in this stage of development. "Discuss plumbing sanitation." Similar questions were made for all the skilled and unskilled positions. The chief advantage of this type of examination was that the questions had some bearing on the job to be filled and appealed to the competitors as being practical.

The disadvantages, however, were very serious, because in the first place the type of person who applied for such a position was not as a rule accustomed to doing much writing, and accordingly, the competitor's poor rating on the test was often due to his inability to express himself in writing, rather than to his lack of practical knowledge of the job. It had the further disadvantage of being very difficult to grade, for examiners were always either consciously or unconsciously influenced by such extraneous things as handwriting, spelling, and facility of expression. This method of selecting employees continued for several years in various jurisdictions, and in fact is still used in some places, but it is fast yielding place to the methods which will be discussed in the following paragraphs.

(c) *General intelligence tests.* The feasibility of using general intelligence tests as a quick and fairly reliable method of determining one's general ability or mental alertness was demonstrated during the World War. After the wide use of intelligence tests in classifying the army personnel, many civilian personnel officers began using these tests indiscriminately in selecting personnel for all types of positions.   In fact, these tests were used entirely too extensively, and without due regard to the traits they were designed to measure. In the first place, in the lower range of the industrial field, intelligence beyond a very low minimum has little or nothing to do with success, and in fact in some positions, it may even mitigate against a successful performance on the job, owing to the fact that the duties of the job are decidedly menial and are of such a monotonous character as to demand very little intelligence for their successful performance.   In the second place, the intelligence levels of most of the unskilled and semi-skilled trades are practically the same, and so an intelligence score would not differentiate between an expert horseshoer and an expert bricklayer, or cook, or barber. This overlapping of intelligence scores is seen in Figure 31, based on 18,000 cases in the army.

In spite of the great overlapping between the various groups, there is a selective factor at work, barring those of low intelligence from certain positions, and favoring those of higher intelligence for the better positions.   Yet, as brought out by Thorndike, many men capable of a high grade of work, are performing menial tasks much below their ability.   The middle 50 per cent of the scores made by the members of each occupational group is indicated by the horizontal line following the name of the occupation.   The left end of the line indicates the point where the lowest quarter ends and the second quarter begins; the little vertical line indicates the dividing point between the upper and lower halves of the scores, and the right end of the line indicates the point where the third quarter ends and the highest quarter begins.   As brought out by Thorndike,[1]

No less significant is the variability within each occupational group. Taking the measurements as they stand, the 75 percentile unskilled laborer is up to the level of the median general mechanic, tool-room expert, or automobile mechanic, and up to the level of the 25 percentile mechanical engineer.   The 75 percentile railroad clerk is at the level of the average accountant or civil engineer.   The 75 percentile receiving or shipping clerk is at the level of the 25 percentile physician.

[1] Thorndike, E. L.: *The Selection of Military Aviators, United States Air Service*, vol. i, no. 5.

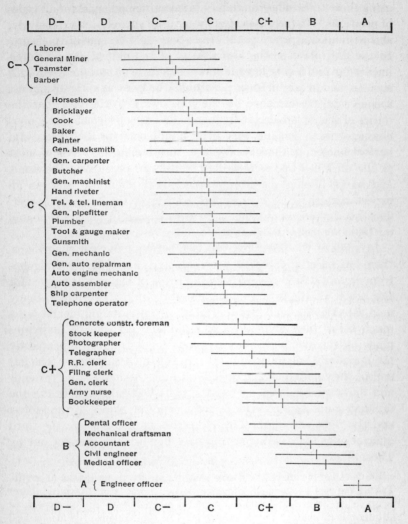

FIGURE 31. OVERLAPPING OF INTELLIGENCE SCORES FOR DIFFERENT OCCUPATIONS

The length of each bar represents the range of the middle fifty per cent; the median is shown by a cross-line.

The use of intelligence tests in selecting employees in industry, however, may be of value in differentiating between the man who should remain at a low grade of work all his life, and the man who can profit from training, and who is capable of assuming a more important position later on. The advantage of the use of tests of intelligence in employment with this end in view is stated by Carney [1] as follows:

The modern employment manager is not satisfied when he has merely introduced the applicant to his first job in the organization. He feels that he must follow up this first placement by such transfers and promotions as are necessary to bring out all the best that the man is capable of attaining. To do less than this is not only unfair to the individual, it is also poor business. For nothing makes for a loyal force of enthusiastic workers so much as a vigorous educational or promotional program. The fact that those in high places have risen from the ranks is the strongest argument that there is a future for men of ability in the organization and men of ability cannot be held long at any wage where they feel they are working in a blind alley.

(d) *Tests for special aptitude.* The use of intelligence tests was a distinct advance over the old subjective methods of selecting personnel, for these tests yielded a definite numerical result, that was free from the personal bias of the examiner. But the abilities measured by these were so general and the scores so coarse that for most positions they were not so useful in selecting employees. To overcome these difficulties, a number of tests have recently been designed to indicate one's special aptitude for a certain position. The tests are constructed specifically for the position for which they are to be used, and are specialized intelligence tests in terms of the job. The specialized tests may measure the same kind of ability as the general tests, but this ability is exercised on more relevant material. In testing practical judgment, for example, the applicant for a clerical position is more likely to be asked why files are useful than why stoves are useful.

Specialized tests appeal to administrators as being practical; they appeal to the applicant as being a fair test of the ability he thinks is required of him. By making a greater appeal to appli-

[1] Carney, C. S.: "Some Experiments with Mental Tests as an Aid in the Selection and Placement of Clerical Workers in a Large Factory," *Bulletin of the Extension Division*, Indiana University, vol. v., no. 1, pp. 60–74.

cants, thus creating greater interest and calling forth better efforts, the specialized tests often actually have a considerably better selecting value than any general test so far as the relation of scores to ability is concerned.

A specialized intelligence test constructed by Telford and Moss [1] and used by various State and city civil service commissions for selecting policemen is a good example of this type of test.   Their analysis shows several general abilities essential for success as a policeman.   These abilities include observation, memory, comprehension, and judgment.   Taking material directly from what the policeman may be required to observe, the applicant's power of observation is tested by giving him a picture of a collision between a street car and an automobile to study for a limited time, and requiring him to answer later (without looking at the picture) a number of questions about it, all answerable by one or two words. Memory is tested by requiring the candidate to pick from a large number of photographs certain faces that he has seen before, much as he would be required to recognize a person to be apprehended. Comprehension in terms of the job consists in understanding sufficiently well to answer questions about them, printed selections from laws, ordinances or police regulations.   Judgment in terms of patrolman duties is illustrated by the following question from the test.   The applicant is instructed to check the correct answer.

If a policeman considers himself unfairly treated by his Sergeant, and gets no satisfaction when he explains to the Sergeant that he is not treated fairly, he should:
—— Refuse to obey any orders given by the Sergeant
—— Invite the Sergeant to meet him when both are off duty so that they can settle the matter themselves
—— At the first opportunity report the matter to his Lieutenant or Captain
—— Immediately hand in his resignation

In the Federal Civil Service, the first special intelligence test to be developed was one for selecting clerical workers, developed under the direction of L. J. O'Rourke, Research Director of the United

[1] Telford, Fred, and Moss, F. A.: "Suggested Tests for Patrolman," *Public Personnel Studies* (1924), II, 112–25.

States Civil Service Commission. In this field a thorough investigation of the best method of selection was much needed since several thousand applicants for positions in the clerical service are tested each year. The new tests developed replaced the old examination of spelling, arithmetic, penmanship, letter-writing, and copying and correcting manuscript. With the old examination it was practically impossible to secure uniformity and fairness of scoring, but this difficulty was absent from the new tests. The new clerical test consisted of questions testing practical information, range of vocabulary, ability to read figures, letters, and words accurately, ability to alphabetize, ability to see simple relations, and ability to classify various items.

The greater value of these tests over the ones previously used is indicated by a quotation from a report of the tests by O'Rourke.[1]

It was believed that a test of this kind would be more interesting as well as fair to the applicants, as it would be an index of their ability to do the actual work to be required of them if employed. The material selected was such as could be duplicated readily, in order to make it possible to present similar problems of equal difficulty in subsequent examinations.

In the field of education as well as in that of personnel management, the question is being constantly asked about the relation of speed to accuracy. This question was very largely answered by the results of O'Rourke's tests. As used in the examinations, the clerical test is a "speed test" the time being so limited that relatively few are able to complete the test in the time allowed. People are often inclined to say that this is unfair since the slow workers and rapid workers may not have obtained the same relative position if the slow workers had had time to finish. But study of results of this test by its author proved that the slow workers, or those who made the lowest scores when speed was a factor, were also least accurate when measured in terms of the percentage of questions that they got right compared to the number attempted. This shows conclusively that the time element has little effect on one's relative standing. The following charts from O'Rourke's report indicate how high is the relation between speed and accuracy.

[1] Filer, Herbert A., and O'Rourke, L. J.: "Progress in Civil Service Tests," *Journal of Personnel Research* (vol. i, no. 11, March, 1923), 484.

Figure 32 shows the accuracy of the 125 most rapid workers as compared with that of the 125 slowest workers. The percentage of accuracy of each individual was based on the relation between the number of items in the test answered correctly, and the number of items tried. The relative number of items answered correctly, as well as the relative time required by slow and rapid workers are shown in Figure 33. In accordance with the rates of

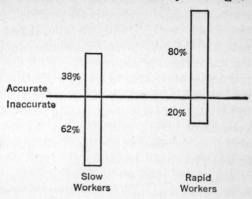

FIGURE 32. THE ACCURACY OF SLOW AND RAPID WORKERS
(After O'Rourke.)

speed at which they worked, the slow group would have taken 110 minutes to answer 200 items correctly, as compared with 20 minutes

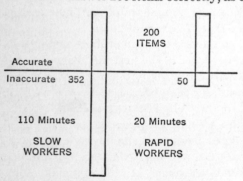

FIGURE 33. INACCURACY OF SLOW AND RAPID WORKERS
(After O'Rourke.)

required by the rapid workers. In order to answer these 200 items correctly the slow group would have answered 352 items incorrectly, as compared with 50 answered incorrectly by the rapid group.

During 1925 a specialized examination to select employees for positions in the Post Offices was also developed by the Federal Civil Service Commission under the direction of O'Rourke. The general test which comprises a part of this examination, consists of typical test questions of intelligence — vocabulary tests, but with words common in Post Office usage;

arithmetical reasoning, but with problems confronted by the Post Office clerk; comprehension, but of reading matter pertaining to postal work, etc. With this specialized intelligence test are used two tests of aptitudes necessary in sorting and routing mail matter. The relation between scores on these tests and the efficiency of the workers on whom they were tried, demonstrated clearly their value as means of selecting qualified employees; and the reduced time required for giving and scoring showed their value as time-savers.

(e) *Short answer duties tests.* There are certain types of positions where high intelligence or special aptitude alone will not suffice, but where the employee must have definite information and technical training for the job itself. The employing officer must be certain that the applicant for these positions has acquired by training this technical knowledge or skill. This necessitates the use of a specific content examination. In the past, employees for these positions were selected very largely on this trial and error basis or by means of the essay type of examination discussed above. For the reasons pointed out, both methods of selecting employees are unsatisfactory, and personnel administrators are now casting about for more satisfactory types of examinations.

The solution seems to be in the development of short answer tests in terms of the work to be done. The test for Bacteriologist developed by Hunter and Moss [1] will serve to illustrate the nature of this type of test. These tests have been used by several state employment agencies and by the United States Civil Service Commission for testing persons seeking positions in bacteriological laboratories of the health department or in similar work in government departments. The test contains approximately two hundred questions which can be given in one hour. A wide sampling is thus secured of the applicant's knowledge in the field of bacteriology. The tests are of such a nature that the scoring is purely objective and can be done with stencils by any person of average intelligence regardless of whether or not he is familiar with the subject matter of bacteriology. This conserves the costly time of highly paid ex-

[1] Hunter, O. B., and Moss, F. A.: "Standardized Tests in Bacteriology," *Public Personnel Studies* (1925), III, 52–66.

aminers for more important tasks.   Moreover, the scoring is of such a nature that regardless of who scores it, a given paper will always receive the same rating, and a score of seventy-five on one examination paper will mean exactly the same as a score of seventy-five on another examination paper.   The tests consist of various types of problems involving reasoning, information, technical procedures, and the identification of organisms.   The tests are easily administered and appeal to the competitors as being fair and to the point

This type of test is not limited to such high-grade positions as bacteriologist, but tests to determine knowledge and skill in the various trades have been employed.   Such trades as plumber, painter, and automobile mechanic have been analyzed and tests devised to measure information and skill in the trade.   Trade tests were first developed and used extensively in the army during the World War.   Trade tests are primarily achievement tests, and are to industry what educational achievement tests are to the schools. Unlike intelligence tests or aptitude tests, they are not designed to indicate ability to learn to do a job, but measure the amount the individual knows about it at the time the test is taken.

5. Methods of measuring vocational success.   In constructing tests for the purpose of selecting and placing industrial employees, it is first necessary to test the validity of the test to see whether those who make high scores on the test succeed in industry, and those who make low scores on the test have a comparatively low degree of success in industry.   The test must first be given to a sufficient number whose success is known, before employers can safely give it to new applicants and use the results to predict their success.   In order to do this, some method of measuring the occupational success of those tested must be devised.   With this in view W. V. Bingham [1] has suggested thirteen criteria of occupational success.   In some instances one criterion may be available, in other instances several criteria may be used.   In general the more criteria employed the more reliable will be the results. His suggested criteria follow:

[1] Bingham, W. V.: "Measures of Occupational Success," *Harvard Business Review*, October, 1926.

a. Time required to train employees. In occupations where preliminary training is given to each new employee, if the records of the time required to train the employees are available, they may be used as criteria of occupational success. Other things being equal, the value of the employee to his organization varies inversely in proportion to the time that must be spent in preparing him to begin productive work for the organization.

b. Standing in corporation schools. When the preliminary training has been given in the plant's school, the relative standing of the students at the end of the training period will be available, and constitute a measure of future success on the job.

c. Quantity and quality of output. The best criterion of all is how much work of a standard quality the employee can do in a given time. In industry, the number of products completed; and in salesmanship, the amount sold are examples of such criteria. The other conditions must of course be kept constant in preparing such criteria. The methods used by O'Rourke to secure criteria of the vocational success of post office clerks and railway mail clerks will illustrate this. He took a representative group of 124 employees in the Chicago Post Office and studied their performance over a six months' period. The average number of pounds of first-class mail distributed by each clerk, together with the time required to do it, was used as his first criterion. As a second criterion he used the score on a monthly test of the accuracy and speed with which each clerk could sort a definite quantity of mail. These criteria are purely objective and are very reliable indices of each employee's value.

d. Performance in standardized examinations. The success of a typist may be indicated by his performance on a standardized test for typists; the success of a file clerk by his speed and accuracy on a filing test, and the success of the pathologist by his ability to diagnose pathological conditions with a microscope in a standard set of slides of diseased tissues.

e. Accidents and loss due to breakage or claims. Other things being equal, the more the employee costs his organization, the less valuable he is to it. The amount of breakage or accident claims which the company has to bear for the employees is an indirect measure of the success of those employees. This method of measuring success is particularly useful in vocations such as that of taxicab drivers and street-car motormen.

f. Salary. The relative amount an organization pays its employees gives a fair indication of the occupational value of these employees. The reliability of such a criterion is of course decreased by the extent to which salary is determined by such variables as length of service, and the family relationship of the employee to some of the high executives. But, despite the fact that such factors enter into salary determination, there is probably a rough correspondence between salary and success.

g. Commission and bonuses. This criterion is closely related to *c* above, for most commissions and bonuses are paid on the quantity and quality of output, over a prescribed minimum.

h. Length of service or stability on the job. Since the cost of training and initiating new employees into service is an item of considerable expense, and since, up to a certain point, experience adds to efficiency, if other factors are kept the same, the length of service is a fair index of occupational success.

i. Advancement in the firm. If promotions were based purely on merit rather than on such mechanical factors as seniority, the rapidity of promotion would be the best index of occupational success. While there are many other factors than merit which determine promotion, still, advancement in the firm is probably of some value as a criterion of success.

j. Degree of responsibility. The degree of responsibility is indicated by the number of subordinates, or the value of the product handled, or the nature of the supervisory duties performed. Other things being equal, the greater responsibilities which a man carries in the firm, the greater his success.

k. Membership in professional societies. Where entrance into professional societies is based on merit, the number of memberships one holds in such societies is indicative of his occupational success.

l. Trade status. Workers in certain trade groups are classed as novices, apprentices, journeymen, or experts. In general, the further up the scale one has progressed, from the status of novice, the higher his occupational success.

m. Ratings. Ratings by superior officers or by fellow workers are widely used as criteria of vocational success. The wide use of this method of measuring vocational success in checking the validity of tests is probably due to the relative ease of obtaining such a criterion. Ratings are necessarily subjective, and where they are used as measures of success, great effort should be made to increase their reliability by careful selection of raters, training them in the technique of rating, and use of reliable rating scales.

II. CONTROL IN THE SERVICE

Having secured the worker, the personnel department is next confronted with the problem of so arranging his work that he may give the most efficient returns. The problem of working efficiency is a two-sided thing, involving the worker and his happiness as well as the management and net profits. Poffenberger gives an excellent definition of human efficiency as the production of the maximum output of the highest quality in the shortest time with the least expenditure of energy and with the maximum satisfaction.

In attempting to reach this ideal of efficiency, the following problems are among the most important confronting the personnel manager: (1) The proper placement of employees; (2) Organizing the path of work; (3) Reduction of time and motion in industrial processes; (4) The utilization of mental set and avoidance of habit interference; (5) The economical distribution of effort; (6) Minimizing the undesirable effects of noise on efficiency; (7) The use of shop incentives; (8) Building morale; (9) Teamwork in management; (10) Promotion; (11) Separation of the employee from his job.

1. **The proper placement of employees.** Some of the largest industrial concerns, including the Ford Motor Company, are taking all who apply for a job and are paying little or no attention to the problem of selection. They are able to do this by having several thousand kinds of jobs, in some of which almost any man, regardless of how defective he is, can be used to advantage. In 1925 the Ford Motor Company, for example, had 7882 different jobs indexed, and had among its 158,000 employees 9563 physically defective men. There were 207 with only one eye, 37 deaf, 234 with only one leg, and so on with various other defects. There were even jobs where the totally blind could earn a minimum salary of six dollars per day.

The problem with this company and others like it, accordingly, shifts from that of the initial selection of the men to that of the proper placement after employment. And although the problems are somewhat different, the methods of solving them are very similar. For in both instances, the solution lies in a thorough job analysis, and in a careful inventory of the employee's capabilities. When this is done, it is a simple task to match the man with the proper job. For example, in the Ford plant, if a certain operation can be accomplished in twenty seconds, and if an employee is found to be slow in reaction time so that he cannot finish the operation in the time allowed, he is shifted to a job which requires less speed of movement. By such a system, all types of employees can be utilized to the mutual advantage of employer and employee, for the individual employee is recognized as the unit and provided for accordingly.

Another thing which makes it possible to take indiscriminately all who apply, is the fact that the various jobs are analyzed into their basic movements. By reducing each job to a few operations, it is possible for some of the operations to be performed by workmen who are endowed with a relatively low grade of mental ability. With a few hours' training, they are able to learn the few movements necessary for the job and their work is so organized that they perform the same simple job over and over again and do not have to learn any other. This seems an ideal solution for the problem of the moron, for here the moron can do the job just as well or better than the person with superior intelligence. By such an arrangement, the persons of higher mentality are released for the more complicated tasks.

But some sentimentalists, closing their eyes to the fact that in most cases this type of work is all the employee is either capable of doing or desirous of mastering, bewail the deadening influence of such work on the "creative impulse" and mental life of the employee. The proof of the pudding is in the eating, and only those who do the eating can tell whether they have pains afterwards. But in this case the complaints do not come from the employees, but instead from armchair sociologists or impractical dreamers, most of whom have never been inside a large industrial plant. Ford's answer to their complaints is very convincing.

It is true that repetitive work would almost kill some men, but others prefer it to anything else. Several years ago, an executive order that every man change his job every three months was put into effect. To the surprise of everybody, this order was fiercely resisted by the majority of the men on these monotonous jobs. As a matter of cold fact, the majority of the men on these jobs dislike working their brains more than is absolutely necessary, and if they find that a job can be done almost automatically, a surprisingly large proportion prefer sticking to it than to learning something new. One branch of the employment department does nothing but attend to transfers, and if a man finds the monotony of his job getting on his nerves, he asks to be transferred, and this is done as soon as there is an opening. When they find an able and ambitious man who wants to work in as many departments as possible in order to learn the business, he gets enthusuastic coöperation.[1]

2. Organizing the path of work. Organizing the path of work in industry amounts to planning such elements of the work ahead and adopting a sequence of tasks or arrangement of equipment which

[1] *The Ford Industries,* Ford Motor Company (1925), 45.

will best conserve the human energy which is to be expended. Taking so simple a task as assembling ten pages of a pamphlet, it is obvious that less energy will be expended if the pages are arranged in order from one to ten than if they are arranged indiscriminately so that perhaps the first page must be picked up at one end of the table and the second page at the other.   To take another example, the shopper who carefully prepares a shopping list so that each department in a large store will have to be visited only once, and the other departments will be visited in the order of contiguity, is using the principle of organizing the path of work.   In a similar way, large industrial concerns benefit by a well-planned routing of the operations to be performed by its employees.   Two important phases of the problem present themselves for study: First, is the arrangement of the shop so as to eliminate useless expenditure of energy in moving from one machine to another, or from supplies to machine.   Second, is the planning of the order of doing tasks or performing separate operations so as to reach the final product or finish the total number of operations to be performed by each worker in the least time and with least effort.

In some of the larger concerns, including the Ford Motor Company, this problem has been met by the conveyor system, whereby a system of mechanical conveyors carry the materials from place to place within the factory and enable the men to remain at one place.   This system is described by Ford [1] as follows:

Conveyors are carefully timed and synchronized to insure an even output and govern the rate of production.   Careful time study of each operation is required so that the conveyors do not move too slowly, wasting time, nor too fast, crowding the men or machines beyond their efficient capacity.   Order, cleanliness, and system are insisted upon.   Everybody is busy, yet nobody rushed.   Consecutive operations are placed adjacent to one another.   The machines being placed in sequence makes it possible for each succeeding operation to be passed on to the next with a minimum of handling and delay.

3. Reduction of time and motion in industrial processes.   Industrial managers in their attempt to increase the efficiency of employees have used various principles contributed by the human

[1] *The Ford Industries*, Ford Motor Company (1925), 9.

engineer in his study of the time and movements required in work processes. Time and motion study consists in accurately analyzing each activity of the worker into its separate parts, studying each part as to time required to perform it, the movements required to complete it, and its relation to other parts, with a view to eliminating useless steps, wasted time, faulty coördination, or poorly planned order of procedure. The facts obtained from a careful study are made the basis of planning and control by the manager.

By means of the motion-picture machines, taking a hundred pictures every second, and by the use of very accurate timing and recording devices, any movement can be analyzed into its stages, and its route clearly indicated. In that way all unnecessary motions and inaccuracies at any stage can be detected. These can then be either eliminated or corrected.

The most extensive work in this field has been done by the Gilbreths. Their first contribution in the field was a perfection of methods of measurement far beyond the old stop-watch methods, so that even the swiftest and most delicate movements such as those made by the typist or musician could be accurately recorded. They replaced old instruments and methods of measuring by sensitive micromotion apparatus, and by stereoptical and motion-picture machines for recording each movement of the worker.

F. G. Gilbreth's work in connection with the bricklaying trade will illustrate the results of his methods. Each movement in the process of bricklaying was studied, and as a result, changes were made in the disposition of material and in the routing of work, so that all useless movements could be eliminated. The change reduced the number of movements used in laying bricks from 18 to 4, and increased the output in bricks laid per hour from 120 per man to 350 per man.

Closely related to time and motion study of the individual is the problem of machine speeds in relation to output. Considerable study has been made of this subject by the Industrial Fatigue Research Board in England.[1] Their investigations show that in

---

[1] Wyatt, S.: "Machine Speeds and Output," *Journal of the National Institute of Industrial Psychology*, London, October, 1927.

most instances industrial employees are unable to attain their maximum rate of output because of the limitations imposed by the speed of the machines.   By increasing the speed of the machine it was found to be possible to exceed the original rate of output by approximately 18 per cent, and in the case of some of the more efficient workers by an even greater percentage.

Marked individual differences were found, some of the men being able to work from 40 to 50 per cent faster than others.   Under the present conditions, in most factories operators of superior ability are reduced to the level of the least efficient workers.   The obvious remedy is to arrange a series of machines with progressive speeds. The novices and slow workers would be assigned to the slowest machines, and as their efficiency increased they would be promoted to the faster running machines, until they eventually arrive at machines having a speed which harmonizes with their final rate of working.   In that way individual differences in ability would be adequately provided for, and each employee would be comfortably and efficiently employed.

4. The utilization of mental set and avoidance of habit interference.   When a task consists of separate elements which are to be accomplished, to shift from one element to another, working continuously for only a short time on any one element, is a rather inefficient way of proceeding with the work.   Shop managers have not always realized this, and have often arranged the work of their employees in such a way that the worker hardly gets "warmed up" to one operation before he shifts to another to work on it for such a short time that the former operation does not cease to be an interfering factor.   To take a simple illustration, it would be no more foolish for the typist to shift continuously from one make of typewriter to another than for the shop worker to perform a dozen different kinds of work within the same hour.

Every performance of a task, other things being equal, facilitates the next performance of the same task, and the performance of one task often establishes habits that interfere with the performance of other tasks although they aid in the future performance of that particular task.

The inefficiency due to shifting operations was clearly demon-

strated in Culler's [1] experiment with card sorting. His experiment
in part consisted in having two groups of persons sort a pack of
eighty cards into a box divided into ten compartments numbered
from one to ten. The cards were also numbered from one to ten.
Two boxes with the compartments labeled differently provided
two entirely different sorting arrangements. The first group sorted
eight times per day for six days always using the same sorting arrangement, while group two sorted sixteen times per day for six
days, alternating the two arrangements. In that way group one
did not shift its operations, but group two shifted fifteen times each
day. Their results are indicated graphically in Figure 34. The

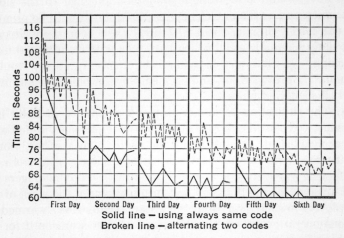

FIGURE 34. THE EFFECT OF SHIFTING OCCUPATION ON OUTPUT
(After Culler.)

solid line indicates group one with no change of arrangement, and
the dotted line indicates group two. The curve shows clearly that
the group that did the shifting consistently took longer than the
group that did not shift.

These principles of mental set and habit interference are provided for in industry by giving each employee a unit operation to

---

[1] Culler, A. J.: "Interference and Adaptability," *Archives of Psychology*, no. 24,
New York, 1912.

perform and keeping him at it.   When it is not possible to install such a system, efficiency demands that it be approximated.   For example, if a carpenter is making twenty window screens, he should first saw all the pieces for the frames, then make all the frames, then stretch the wire on all the frames, and as a final operation, paint all the frames, rather than do the various operations necessary to finish one screen before beginning another.

5. The economical distribution of effort.   One of the biggest problems with which the industrial psychologist must deal is that of fatigue.   As pointed out in Chapter II, fatigue of the worker can be lessened or delayed in onset by a scientific study and adjustment of working conditions such as noise, light, space, ventilation, temperature, or arrangement of equipment, and all of these are important considerations.   But with perfect working conditions, the shop manager would still be faced with the problem of fatigue, and the only remedy now available is the use of rest periods to overcome fatigue.   His problem then becomes one of selecting the most efficient length of work period, and most efficient length of rest periods, or of bringing about the most efficient distribution of these. Work periods should not be so long that the effects of fatigue greatly reduce output, nor should they be so short that all advantages of being started or warmed up to the job are lost.   In general, the frequency of rest periods conducive to greatest efficiency is somewhat greater than popular opinion would suppose.   It is seldom in industrial work that very long work periods followed by very long rest periods have any advantage over short and more frequent rest periods.

By an ingenious arrangement, Shepard [1] has been able to establish the optimum relation between work and rest for "light-heavy" muscular work by measuring the foot-pounds of work per hour with varying periods of work.   His results are shown in the accompanying table.

The best results are not obtained from a program that allows either the shortest or longest work periods, but from those which avoid both extremes.   It would thus appear that in muscular work

[1] Shepard, G. A.: *Fatigue Experiments at Purdue University, Industrial Management*, 1921.

Length of Work Period in Minutes	Length of Rest Period in Minutes	Average Foot-Pounds of Work per Hour
25	8	88,232
30	8	96,880*
35	8	98,237
40	8	97,600*
45	8	98,712
50	8	96,600*
55	8	95,730
60	8	94,823

* Low temperature and high humidity.

about one sixth of the time should be spent at rest. It should, of course, not be concluded that this proportion of work and rest time is best for all types of work. Some types may require a smaller proportion of rest and others a larger proportion.

6. Minimizing the undesirable effects of noise on efficiency. The human engineer in industry should be concerned with the problem of distractions in the factory or office. The employee's efficiency is seriously affected by the conditions under which he works. One of the most disturbing factors and one which is very injurious to efficiency is noise. In order to measure the effect of noise on working efficiency, Laird [1] constructed a "noise machine." The machine was driven by electricity, and produced such sounds as would be produced by an electric motor; ball-bearings rotated in a hexagonal sheet-iron drum; an auto siren and a telephone bell intermittently and automatically. The subjects were tested at typing and at maintaining the position used when typing but without actually typing. During one series of tests, the walls of the test chamber were left bare so that by reverberations, the sounds tended to increase in effect. During another series of tests the walls were covered with demountable panels which reduced the sound about fifty per cent.

The effect of the noise was measured in terms of the amount of energy consumed as indicated by metabolism tests. It was found that when the noise was at full blast there was an average increase of 71 per cent of the working metabolism over the resting metabolism; and that when the panels were used to deaden the sound the

[1] Laird, Donald A.: "The Measurement of the Effects of Noise on Working Efficiency," *Journal of Industrial Hygiene*, October, 1927.

increase in metabolism was only 52 per cent. Thus 19 per cent saving in energy consumption can be attributed to the quieter conditions: that is, the typist consumed 19 per cent more energy when working under the noisy conditions than under the reduced noise condition. An average gain of 4.3 per cent in speed on the part of the typists was found when the noise was reduced. It is of interest to note also that the more skilled typists were more affected by the adverse conditions than were those with less skill. Gains in efficiency and decreases in energy consumption such as indicated in this experiment may be expected to take place in actual working situations when effort is given to reduce the effect of distracting factors.

7. The use of shop incentives. If one would secure the highest efficiency in a group of workers, some incentive to high attainment must be provided. Those in the higher type of positions have this in their desire to climb the heights of fame or to gain the approving recognition of their friends. But for the lower grade worker, it is the task of the management to provide incentives. The incentive may be provided in the form of reward for effort by promotion, increased salary, bonuses, special privileges, or provision for ownership in the concern.

Various traits of human nature may be made the basis of devices for creating a desire for better work. One of the greatest joys of life is to stand well in the eyes of one's fellow workers. Hence, it is often effective to bring forth maximum effort by rewarding the worker with honors, titles, privileges, or anything that will gain for him social recognition. Another trait of human nature on which the manager may play in creating incentives to work is the spirit of rivalry. His use of this incentive consists in keeping accurate records of attainments, publishing or posting these so as to create competition between various groups of workers in the shop, between individual workers, or competition of the worker with his own record. The posting of records not only serves as a stimulus to make the employee wish to excel his fellow workers, but it often spurs him on to beat his own record. The effects of practice in whatever kind of work the worker may be engaged are greater if he can know the results of his effort.

One of the most effective incentives with industrial employees is ownership in the concern.   About this incentive, Charles Schwab,[1] Chairman of the Bethlehem Steel Corporation, said:

But even with good wages and steady employment, the working man is likely to lack one factor essential to his fullest efficiency and greatest interest in the company in which he is employed.   This factor is ownership. A sense of proprietorship affords a powerful incentive to arouse interest in the performance of work.   This principle has been the motivating influence of those who have been willing to take the risk incident to the building of new business.   Its application to the wage earner in industry is relatively new, yet nowhere is the whole-hearted interest of human beings so necessary and vital to successful accomplishment.

Under this plan the mutuality of interest which should exist in industry finds its greatest expression.   On the one hand the company prospers because the employees strive for the elimination of waste and the better doing of their jobs, and on the other hand the employees themselves profit as the company prospers.

8. The building of morale.   Closely related to the question of incentives is the problem of morale.   The most important factor in determining morale is wages.   Industrial welfare organizations very often are best known to the employees for providing a summer picnic or an inexpensive and useless Christmas present as a substitute for decent wages and working conditions.   To self-respecting employees, all activities savoring of charity and "uplift" are disgusting.   What they desire is a fair compensation for their labor and reasonable working conditions.   Back of every industrial dispute is the desire for higher wages and better working conditions. That employees are not as some people seem to think, natural trouble-makers, provoking strikes and lock-outs, is well illustrated by the history of the Ford Motor Company.   For more than twenty years the company has been in operation without the least dispute of the "labor vs. capital" nature.   The war came and went bringing with it floods of industrial unrest, but still we saw no ripple in the wholesome relations existing between Ford and his employees.

One reason why Ford has had no labor disputes is that he has paid his men a living wage.   No one in his shops, no matter what his

---

[1] Schwab, Charles: "Trained Men," *Human Engineering*, Spring, 1928.   Scranton, Pennsylvania.   Courtesy of International Correspondence School.

work may be, gets less than $6 per day. Over 60 per cent of his employees earn more than this minimum wage. It was said of old that "man cannot live by bread alone," but Ford has learned what few other industrial leaders seem able to understand, that he cannot live at all without sufficient wages to buy the bread. The first essential in producing happy relations is the payment of adequate wages.

The second essential in producing pleasant relations is the establishment of fair working hours. Under the pressure of modern conditions the twelve-hour working day will soon be a thing of the past. Actual experiment shows that capitalists are in error in thinking that extra-long hours mean increased production. In fact, the opposite seems to be true. In a series of well-controlled experiments in the Ford Company, it was found that for every hundred motors that were put out in a nine-hour day, one hundred and twenty could be built in an eight-hour day. Even greater increases were found in making some of the other parts of the machine. And in no single case was it found that the total amount of production was decreased by reducing the working period from nine to eight hours.

A third thing which often causes labor troubles is the failure of employers to provide for the health, comfort, and safety of their employees. All such matters as lighting, ventilation, suitable locker accommodations, and clean and sanitary toilets are important in this connection. Employees naturally prefer to work in a plant which is well kept. It is only natural that uncomfortable and slovenly conditions within the plant should produce slovenly work and poor morale on the part of the employees. Conditions in many plants are being remedied, due in no small part to the discovery by capitalists that keeping workers healthy and contented is economically profitable. No man who is worried or anxious about his safety can do his best work.

Leaders in industry are providing for the recreation and leisure of their employees. What lines these recreational activities will take is determined by local conditions. In some cases athletic fields have been provided for employees, in others theaters and moving-picture houses and various other recreational facilities. The general tendency is to provide the facilities and interfere as little as possible with the way in which the employees use these facilities. Employees resent paternalism.

9. Teamwork in management. The ability to secure teamwork is the most valuable one an executive can possess, for nowhere is teamwork more important than in an industrial organization. To secure teamwork one must organize with this end in view. Positions of responsibility should be filled by chiefs and foremen who are able to organize their departments into efficient, contented groups. For that reason it is usually better to select executives from within the organization, for their personality traits are better known. The man who has an exaggerated ego is not fitted for executive positions, for, overrating his own ability, he injects himself into everything, and attends to details which should be left to others. Such individuals belong to a small business where they can dominate the whole situation. The "star" performer is equally ineffective in a position of responsibility. Just as the individual star is useless on a football team unless he can get the support and coöperation of the other members of the team, so the brilliant solo workers can accomplish little as executives in an industrial department.

10. Promotion. Promotion is the chief reward for the consistent efficiency of an employee. Promotion may be of two kinds, promotion in rank, or increase in salary. Not infrequently the professional man or the executive prefers a change of title to an advance in salary. In most cases the two go together, and an increase in rank carries with it a salary increase. As stated above, promotion can be made one of the greatest incentives to endeavor. But unless there is some reliable and fair basis for promotion, the morale of the service is lowered rather than improved by promotions.

Merit, or ability to do the job, should be the chief basis for promotion. Many departments do not reward promotions on the basis of merit but on seniority. Granting promotions according to seniority, that is, according to the length of time the employee has been on the job, is the oldest system of promotion. But it has many serious disadvantages for it wholly overlooks the efficiency of employees while in the service, or their relative ability to handle the job to which they are being promoted.

In any great emergency, promotion is based more on merit and less often on seniority. During the World War, relatively little attention was paid to seniority in determining promotions, but no sooner was the emergency passed and the demand for real efficiency gone, than the old seniority system was restored. The seniority system of promotion is extremely deadening to efficiency, for when a man sees the "incompetent waiter" promoted over many others who are much better qualified, it kills his initiative and makes him ask "why work when you get no recognition for working?"

The chief reason for the use of a seniority list as a basis for promotion is inertia and lack of courage on the part of the promoting authorities. It is easy to understand why personnel administrators object to making promotions on the basis of the kind of efficiency ratings that have been obtainable in most organizations. But for many positions it is now possible to obtain efficiency ratings on the basis of objective tests with the same degree of accuracy with which the employees were selected in the first place. As these objective test methods are perfected, they will gradually replace the antiquated seniority system of promotion, and employees will be promoted on the basis of what they can do rather than on how long they have been trying to learn how to do it.

11. Separation of the employee from his job. In industry, as in other lines of human endeavor, it is sometimes necessary for men and their jobs to part. Aside from promotion, the chief causes of this parting are: (a) Inefficiency on the part of the employee, resulting in his being "fired" or demoted; (b) Dull business, which necessitates the laying-off of a number of employees; (c) Old age, with its accompanying inability to "carry on."

An effective system of retiring the incompetent is fully as important as an efficient system of selection and promotion of the competent. Progress demands the retirement of inefficient workers, and of the aged employees who have passed the age of usefulness. For this purpose, relative efficiency should be determined by a purely objective measuring device. Objective tests offer considerable promise as a means for determining the relative efficiency. But regardless of what method is used to measure efficiency, retirement should be on a merit basis, the less efficient being those retired.

The problem of the old employee in an organization is a serious one. When an employee who has spent his best years in an organization has reached the time when he is no longer able to do his work, the employer is confronted with the task of replacing him, and making provision for his future. Justice and industrial morale will not permit the cold cutting-off of an old employee without providing for his future. More and more concerns are making this provision in the form of an old-age pension. This is particularly true in the public service. The efficiency of the employee throughout his working period is increased with the knowledge that his old age is provided for.

Moreover, the retirement of the aged employee is a benefit to the rest of the working force. Decrepit and superannuated employees among younger ones lower the morale of the whole group and often set an example for killing time and drawing the salary. Old employees frequently retard the wheels of progress by opposing the adoption of new methods and procedures, and by refusing to adopt new policies and attitudes. Osler was working along the right line in saying that it would be of incalculable benefit in commercial, political, and professional life, if all were automatically retired at sixty. Sixty is probably too early for the retirement of most employees, but there are very few whose efficiency has not undergone a marked decline by the age of sixty-five.

CHAPTER XVIII

THE RELATION OF PSYCHOLOGY TO STREET AND HIGHWAY TRAFFIC

The most difficult problem in the successful prosecution of war is that of transporting men and supplies.

HANNIBAL

SINCE the days of ancient Pompeii highway transportation has been a problem. Long before the birth of Christ one-way streets were inaugurated, and restricted parking spaces were resorted to in the more congested districts in an effort to alleviate the traffic conditions. But the traffic problems of the ancients were as child's play as compared with the traffic problems confronting the modern city. More people are killed in highway accidents on one Sunday in America than were killed in such accidents in a whole month in ancient Rome. And more traffic passes along Broadway in one day than passed along the Appian Way in one year. The chief cause for the increase both in the amount of traffic and in the number of fatalities is the widespread use of the automobile as a means of transportation. The importance of the automobile in vehicular traffic is evidenced by the fact that in the United States to-day there are approximately 22,000,000 machines in operation, and each year by these machines the lives of more than 24,000 people are snuffed out.

There are two main elements in the traffic problem — the purely inanimate, including the machine and the highway on which it operates, and the animate or human element that controls the operation. The first of these elements has been given much consideration by the traffic engineers, while the second is practically an untouched field. The civil engineer has done a great deal to make the highways, as such, safer. He has removed the more dangerous curves, widened the road bed, reduced the number of grade crossings and generally increased the road capacity. The mechanical engineer has likewise contributed his quota to making the world a safer place in which to drive. He has standardized requirements for such important mechanical elements as brakes, lights, and steering apparatus.   He has developed all kinds of safety devices that make sure that accidents will not be due to some defect in the machinery.   In making his machine, lock washers and cotter pins are used freely to insure that the nuts will stay where he puts them.   Unfortunately the human engineer has no lock washers or cotter pins to hold the human "nuts" in their proper position, the result being the fatal accidents that we read about daily.

Both the civil engineer and the mechanical engineer have done a fairly good job; their work at the present stage is at least 80 per cent perfect, which means that in these fields further progress will be slow and expensive, and before long the stage of diminishing returns will be reached.   Not so with the human engineer; except in a few isolated instances, little attention has been given to the human side of the traffic problem, the result being that the traffic increases, and the problem remains unsolved.

It is no longer a matter of opinion whether a steel beam can withstand the stress and strain that follows its being placed in a highway bridge over which the floods of traffic must pass, but it has not been determined whether the automobile driver can stand up under the stress and strain of steering his machine through this same flood of traffic.   The construction engineer has arrived at his knowledge of the steel beam by substituting mechanical facts for opinions, reliable units of measure for mere guesswork, and when the human engineer places the selection and licensing of drivers on other than subjective guesses, he will be able to state with a fair degree of accuracy the probable competency or lack of competency of prospective drivers.

Each year several million new automobiles are put on the streets and at the end of the year we find that the accident fatalities have increased by several thousand.   Approximately three fourths as many were killed in traffic accidents in the United States in 1927 as were killed in battle in the American Army in the World War. All students of the problem are agreed that something must be done to meet the situation.   The psychologist can assist in solving the problem in four ways: I. By devising competency tests for operators which will remove the more incompetent drivers and thus increase the capacity of our streets.   II. By studying the direct and contributing causes of accidents and as a result of the study suggesting ways of prevention.   III. By aiding in the selection of street-car motormen.   IV. By aiding in the selection of traffic officers.

I. EXAMINATIONS OF OPERATORS

Since the highway capacity is limited and one incompetent driver is often able to disrupt the even flow of a whole stream of traffic, placing himself and others in peril, it is obvious that some means must be found for removing these incompetent drivers from the highways.   This means will probably be found in the use of adequate examinations of operators so that incompetency in its various forms may be detected.   This part of the problem will be discussed briefly under the following heads: 1. Methods of examining applicants for licenses.   2. Special examinations of repeaters. 3. Special examinations for professional drivers.   4. Special examinations for the physically handicapped.

1. **Methods of examining applicants for licenses.**   The First National Conference on Street and Highway Safety,[1] convened by Secretary Hoover in 1924, recommended the following:

Before granting an operator's license, the department or division should determine the applicant's ability to operate a motor vehicle safely by ascertaining his physical and mental fitness and his knowledge of the laws, and by requiring an actual demonstration of his ability to operate a motor vehicle.

Most authorities on the traffic problem agree that a very large proportion of all accidents is caused by a group of drivers who compose a relatively small percentage of the total number of drivers.   The first concern of all traffic directors should be the detection and elimination of these few incompetent drivers.

A survey of the present conditions shows that practically nothing is being done on this phase of the problem.   Only about one fourth of the States require a driver's license of any kind, and several of

[1] *Report of National Conference on Street and Highway Safety.*   Washington, D.C., 1926.

those that do require a license make no pretense of examining those who apply for license, but issue licenses as a routine procedure to all who purchase number plates for their machines. In many of the States where examinations are required the questions are of such a superficial character as to indicate little or nothing of the applicant's fitness to operate an automobile. Moreover, these same superficial questions are asked over and over again so that they soon become known to all automobile dealers, and any applicant with the intelligence of a low-grade moron can easily secure a license by memorizing the answers to a dozen questions.

Perhaps the chief cause of the superficiality of the tests for driver's license is the fact that administering an adequate examination to the large number who apply for licenses is extremely time-consuming. Inasmuch as the number who apply for licenses is so large it is obvious that if an examination is to be given it must be very brief and easily administered. Such a measuring device has been found in short-answer type examinations, by which a large number of applicants can be examined at once on a test of information and judgment on driving problems. And by casting the questions in the short-answer form it is possible to give twenty-five or more questions on driving problems in not more than fifteen minutes. This information and judgment test should consist of questions designed to measure the applicant's knowledge of the traffic regulations which he is expected to obey, his judgment in dealing with typical driving problems, and his ability to recognize dangerous situations. The following questions will give some idea of the type of question to be used.

If you are driving along beside a street car which stops to unload passengers at a station without a loading platform or safety zone, and if you have already passed the rear door but not the front door when the car stops, you should:
—— Back up ten feet behind the rear door and stop.
—— Stop immediately and remain at rest until the car moves on.
—— Pass on slowly, exercising great caution.
—— Step on the accelerator.
The one of the following vehicles which would have the right of way at a street intersection is:
—— A large truck.

—— A wagon.
—— A taxicab.
—— An ambulance.

These samples were taken from a test which was tried out on several hundred university students, and are very similar to ones used by the writer in testing the Motor Transport Corps at Camp Holabird, the chauffeurs of the Philadelphia Automobile Club, and a number of taxicab drivers.

In addition to testing judgment it is well to test the applicant's ability to recognize dangerous situations. This can be done by using prints or pictures showing situations which are generally admitted to be dangerous, as one machine passing another on the crest of a hill, parking on a curve, or passing a street car loading or unloading passengers. The applicant is asked to indicate the danger in each situation presented. Samples of the situations used by the writer are shown in Plate I.

How well examinations of this kind indicate driving ability is shown by the results obtained at Camp Holabird where the tests were given to 53 enlisted men and 20 officers of known ability. The 73 men were divided into four groups by the instructors who were familiar with the driving ability of each. The first group consisted of five men who could not be trusted to operate a machine under any circumstances, the so-called unteachable group.

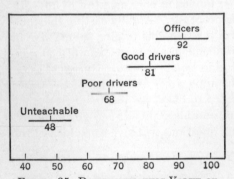

FIGURE 35. DIFFERENTIATING VALUE OF SCORES ON AUTOMOBILE TEST

The length of the bar indicates the range of the middle fifty per cent; the cross-line the median.

The average score for this group on the tests was 48. The second group was composed of eleven men who were allowed to operate a machine provided some one was along to direct them. The average score of this group was 68. The third group consisted of 37 good drivers who could be trusted to operate a machine under the most

Number 2: Automobile parked

ANSWER:...........................

....

Number 3: Both Automobiles in motion

ANSWER:...........................

....

Number 4: Automobile in motion

ANSWER:...........................

....

Number 5: Automobile in motion

ANSWER:...........................

....

Number 6: Truck in motion — Automobile stopped.

ANSWER:...........................

....

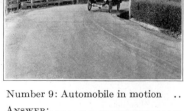

Number 9: Automobile in motion ..

ANSWER:...........................

....

PLATE I. RECOGNITION OF DANGEROUS SITUATIONS
Courtesy of Bureau of Public Personnel Administration

METHOD OF MOUNTING PISTOLS UNDER RUNNING-BOARD

The first is fired by the experimenter, the second by the person under test, in applying the brake-pedal. Shells loaded with red lead make bright red spots on the road.

SPOTS ON THE ROAD MADE BY DISCHARGING THE PISTOLS

The distance between the spots could be measured to .01 feet. The ratio of this distance to the speed of the car, in feet per second, is the reaction-time of the person under test.

PLATE II.

Courtesy of the Journal of the Society of Automotive Engineers difficult conditions. The average score of this group was 81. The fourth group consisted of the 20 officers who were of such high grade ability that they could be entrusted with the actual command and responsibility for the movement of a large motor caravan. The average score of this group was 92. How well these groups were differentiated by the tests is shown graphically in Figure 35, which gives the range of the middle fifty per cent of the scores for each group.

It is generally agreed that an actual operating test is essential to determine the ability of the applicant to drive a car. And this should be more than merely driving around the block, with no traffic; or driving straight ahead for a few hundred yards, neither of which would indicate much of the competency of an applicant. A thorough driving test consists of the most common operations performed by drivers. The following five operations are now a part of the driving test in the District of Columbia:

(1) Parking parallel to the curb between two machines in a space which is only ten feet longer than the car.
(2) Starting and stopping on a hill in traffic.
(3) Making a left-hand turn in traffic.
(4) Making a right-hand turn in traffic.
(5) Reading road signs while driving.

2. Special examination of repeaters. One of the most important groups of drivers from the standpoint of safety is made up of those who have several times been involved in accidents, or who have been guilty of repeated violations of the traffic laws. Any one may have one unavoidable accident or even two, but if a driver has more than two or three serious accidents his driving qualifications should be looked into very carefully. Any driver may park too long at some time or other, or may exceed the speed limit, but the cause of numerous repetitions of the offense should be investigated. The importance of the repeater in traffic violations or in traffic accidents is readily apparent when it is recognized that a very large proportion of all accidents is caused by a relatively small number of repeaters. If these few drivers are eliminated the number of accidents could be considerably reduced.

The first problem in dealing with repeaters is to determine the cause of the repeated violations or accidents. The next problem is to determine how to deal with the repeater. Whenever a driver has more than one accident resulting in personal injury or in property damage of over one hundred dollars he should be required to submit to an examination to determine the psychological or physical factors which led to the accidents. These examinations should be conducted by specially trained examiners in a laboratory equipped for the purpose. The test should consist of a thorough physical and mental examination to determine what traits are especially conducive to accidents. Certain physical or psychological conditions may be found to be typical of repeaters in traffic accidents. A very low grade of intelligence might easily cause an individual to be a repeater. Defective vision or hearing, or the tendency to lose one's head in an emergency are also frequent causes of accidents.

Ability to react quickly in an emergency is another qualification which is very important. A safe driver must not only know when and how to apply the brakes to avoid an impending tragedy, but he must also be able to apply them quickly. Nearly all jurisdictions require the brakes to be capable of stopping a machine going at a speed of twenty miles an hour in a distance of fifty feet. But in no jurisdiction is there the requirement that in order to qualify to operate a machine an individual must be able to move his foot from the accelerator to the brake within such a time that the brakes will have a fair opportunity to act in the required time. Yet standardizing the human element is fully as important as standardizing the mechanical element.

In order to determine how much time it takes for the average automobile driver to move his foot from the accelerator to the brake and to begin to apply it, a series of experiments were conducted by the writer in coöperation with H. H. Allen [1] of the United States Bureau of Standards.

The apparatus used in the test consisted of an automobile with two revolvers mounted on the under side of the running-board. See Plate II. The revolvers were loaded with red lead, so that when either was fired, a bright red spot was made on the road.

[1] Moss, F. A., and Allen, H. H.: "The Personal Equation in Automobile Driving," *Journal of the Society of Automotive Engineers*, April, 1925.

One revolver was fired by the examiner as a signal for the person taking the test to move his foot from the accelerator and to apply the brake just as if to avoid an accident. The second revolver was fired automatically when the person taking the test first touched the brake pedal and began to apply it. In order to make the results as accurate as possible a chronometric tachometer was used instead of the ordinary speedometer to indicate the speed at which the machine was traveling when the two revolvers were fired. By measuring the distance between the two red spots on the road, and by dividing it by the speed at which the driver was going when the shots were fired, it was possible to determine how much time elapsed between the hearing of the signal and the initial motion toward applying the brake.

The average reaction time of those tested was slightly more than one half second. If a driver with a reaction time of one half second were traveling at the rate of 30 miles per hour, he would go approximately 22 feet after hearing the signal before beginning to apply the brake, whereas a driver with as slow a reaction time as one and one half seconds would go 66 feet before beginning to apply the brake. It should be borne in mind that this time does not represent the time required for the brake to stop the machine, but is the time that elapses before the driver even puts his foot on the brake. From the foregoing it will be seen that, even though a machine had the finest set of brakes possible, the driver could not begin to stop it in the 50 feet allowed at a speed of 20 miles per hour if he happened to have a one and one half seconds' reaction time.

One of the most frequent causes of accidents is emotional instability. Working with the Yellow Cab Company in Chicago, Snow [1] devised some very ingenious tests to measure one's emotional control in an emergency. By these tests he was able to pick out those who would lose their heads in an emergency and those who retained perfect control under such conditions. His tests require too much time and apparatus for their use with all automobile operators, but tests along this line could very profitably be given to all repeatedly involved in accidents.

[1] Snow, A. J.: "It Will Take More than Education to Stem Traffic Accidents," *Industrial Psychology Monthly* (July, 1927), 360.

In such a series of examinations and tests one might expect to find certain constant characteristics among those involved in accidents. Having discovered these characteristics it will be possible in the future to take the necessary precautions for protection either by refusing licenses to drive to individuals possessing such characteristics or by granting them limited licenses such as would prohibit them from driving in cities or from driving at night. In the case of those guilty of repeated serious offenses, the license should be revoked to protect the public.

3. **Special examinations for professional drivers.** This class includes drivers of taxicabs, buses, and trucks; chauffeurs in public or private service; drivers of school buses and cars; and drivers of emergency vehicles such as hospital ambulances, police wagons, and fire patrols. The question of tests for licensing of these professional drivers is of the utmost importance. All of these operators make more continuous use of streets and roads than other drivers; some of them have the right of way over all other traffic; for some of them the speed limit is waived; and many of them are operating more unwieldy machines requiring greater skill for driving or capable of doing more serious damage than the ordinary automobile.

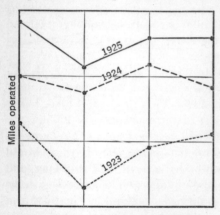

FIGURE 36. COMPARATIVE TAXICAB MILES IN CHICAGO

A comparison of this chart with Figure 37 shows that, although the cab mileage showed a large increase, a proportionately much greater decrease in the number of accidents, particularly between 1924 and 1925, occurred. (After Snow.)

The need for a more severe examination for these drivers than for private operators is therefore apparent. Their qualifications for driving must be exceptionally high to make them safe drivers. There is little doubt but that it would be desirable from the standpoint of safety to require professional drivers to undergo special examinations of their knowledge of the laws and regulations and of their ability to meet difficult situations in traffic. Such special examinations should include tests of visual and auditory acuity, color discrimination, mental alertness, quickness and accuracy of muscular control, and presence of mind in an emergency. Those drivers with physical or mental defects, unless extremely slight, should not be granted licenses to operate commercial or emergency vehicles. Public safety makes it necessary to examine carefully the qualifications of those desiring to operate these vehicles and to refuse licenses to all except those who meet strict requirements.

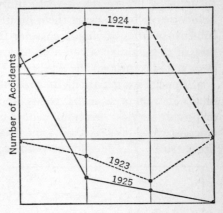

FIGURE 37. TAXICAB ACCIDENT RATE DURING FIRST FOUR MONTHS OF THREE YEARS, SHOWING DECREASE IN 1925 AFTER USE OF PSYCHOLOGICAL TESTS
(After Snow.)

Several of the larger taxicab concerns are finding it good economy to select their drivers on a basis of psychological tests. A. J. Snow [1] has done some work along these lines for the Yellow Cab Company in Chicago. As a result of tests on 311 applicants he predicted that 258 of these would make "satisfactory" drivers, and that 19 would not stay long, and that 34 would be "unsatisfactory." How well he succeeded in his prediction is shown in the table on page 386, and in Figure 36 and Figure 37.

4. **Special examinations for the handicapped.** This group includes those who are deficient in the physical or mental traits important in driving. Deficiencies to be considered would include defective eyesight, hearing, low intelligence, poor physical condition, senility, and record of insanity. The attitude toward the licensing of the handicapped varies markedly in different localities. In many States no mention is made of the handicapped. In certain jurisdictions a license to operate a motor vehicle is not granted to

[1] Snow, A. J.: "Tests for Chauffeurs," *Industrial Psychology* (January, 1926), 30.

COMPARATIVE ACCIDENT RECORD OF DESIRABLE AND UNDESIRABLE DRIVERS AS DETERMINED BY THE TESTS

	NUMBER OF MEN EMPLOYED	MEN NEVER STARTED TO WORK	MEN THAT DROPPED OUT	MEN STILL WORKING	ACCIDENTS			MEN WHO HAD ACCIDENTS	MEN WHO HAD MORE THAN TWO ACCIDENTS	AVERAGE NUMBER OF ACCIDENTS PER MAN *	PERCENTAGE OF MEN WHO HAD ACCIDENTS *	PERCENTAGE OF MEN WHO HAD MORE THAN TWO ACCIDENTS *	PERCENTAGE OF MEN WHO QUIT *
					CARELESSNESS GROSS NEGLIGENCE	QUESTIONABLE	NO LIABILITY						
Unsatisfactory group.........	34	8	5	21	26	7	9	17	10	1.00	64	38	19
Group that will not stay long......	19	1	6	12	3	0	2	6	0	0.16	33	0	33
Satisfactory group......	258	10	50	198	50	19	24	84	32	0.20	33	12	20

* This tabulation does not include accidents which are "Questionable" or "No liability."

any one who has lost a limb or an eye. In others those who are deaf cannot be licensed, or the mentally handicapped are debarred from driving. None of these individuals who are handicapped either physically or mentally should be granted a license to operate an automobile without being given special tests.

Licensing those who are discovered to have such handicaps should be based first upon thorough mental and physical examination with special emphasis on the sense organs and reaction time. The results of the various tests should be combined or weighted, and the applicant granted or refused a license as the result of his combined score. The combined score should be determined in such a way that it is possible for a deficiency in one requirement to be offset by high qualifications in other requirements. Thus an individual who has defective hearing could be licensed provided his car is well equipped with mirrors, his eyesight is keen, his general intelligence satisfactory, and his speed of reaction quick. A high rating in these might compensate for a low rating on hearing. But if in addition to having poor hearing his eyesight is found to be defective, his general intelligence low, or his reaction time abnormally slow, he would be refused a license. An individual with an artificial limb may safely be granted a driving license after demonstrating his ability to drive his car in spite of his handicap. Mechanical devices may take the place of the missing limb.

Distinctions, however, must be made within the handicapped group. There are certain handicaps which would automatically debar the individual from receiving a license, and which cannot be compensated for by high ratings in other qualifications. Total blindness, feeble-mindedness, and insanity are examples of defects which would automatically debar from driving. By differentiating carefully between those handicapped individuals who are capable of being safe drivers, and the handicapped who under no conditions should be allowed to drive, it is possible to grant the privilege of driving to those capable of driving with safety, without unfair discrimination against any class of drivers.

II. CAUSES OF ACCIDENTS

As pointed out above, there are two main elements to be considered in accident prevention, the purely inanimate, or physical, including the machine and the highway on which it operates, and the animate or human element that controls the operation. The first of these has been given a great deal of consideration by the traffic engineer, while practically no attention has been paid the second. The highways have been greatly improved and the automobile so perfected that the word "unavoidable" has practically been eliminated from the category of accidents. But the human engineer has contributed little to the other side of the problem. And yet the human has always been just as important from the standpoint of safety as the mechanical side. In fact, at the present time, it is by far the most important factor to be considered.

An analysis of the causes of accidents shows that about ninety per cent of all accidents are due to the human factor, and only about ten per cent to purely physical factors. The work of the mechanical and civil engineer has progressed to such a state of perfection that the point of diminishing returns has in all probability been reached, and we can expect little further improvement from this source. It is obvious, therefore, that the traffic engineer must shift his emphasis and begin paying attention to the element that offers the greatest possibility of improvement — the human element. The following table shows the distribution of blame among factors involved in accidents according to different compilations of statistics.

DISTRIBUTION OF BLAME AMONG FACTORS INVOLVED IN ACCIDENTS

FACTOR CAUSING ACCIDENT	ALL ACCIDENTS		FATAL ACCIDENTS			AVERAGE FIVE SOURCES
	Conn. 1924	Ore. Wash. 1924	Mass. 1924	N.A.C.C. Jan. '24 May '25	St. Louis 1924	
Operator..............	77.7	63.5	62.0	40.0	59.2	60.6
Non-operator..........	15.4	11.9	26.3	46.7	36.7	27.4
Total, human factor...	93.1	75.4	88.3	87.1	95.9	88.0
Vehicle...............	5.6	11.3	11.2	5.8	3.1	7.4
Highway..............	1.3	13.3	0.5	7.1	1.0	4.6
Total, physical conditions.........	6.9	24.6	11.7	12.6	4.1	12.0

From the above table it will be seen that the human element is responsible for from seventy-five to ninety-six per cent of all traffic accidents. Under the human element is included both the driver of the car and the persons other than the driver who may be responsible for the accident. Various statistics place the per cent of accidents due to persons other than the operator at from twelve per cent to about fifty per cent. Physical factors, such as the condition of the machine and of the highway, play a decidedly minor part in causing highway accidents. Accidents are caused by such things as loose brakes or worn steering apparatus, but in such accidents, the real cause is not in the poor brakes or steering apparatus but in the driver who knew that his brakes were loose or his steering apparatus in bad condition and failed to have it repaired.

Thoughtlessness and poor judgment on the part of drivers, adult pedestrians, and children cause from thirty to fifty-five per cent of the recorded accidents. It is only in rare cases that jay-walking, inattention, carelessness, confusion, and inexperience are intentional violations of the laws of safety, and such violators either are not aware of the risks they run, or they do not know how to be careful.

The twelve most frequent causes of all accidents, as listed by the State of Connecticut for the year 1924 are as follows:

Cause	Percentage of total accidents due to cause
1. Inattention of driver	20.6
2. Failure to grant right of way	17.3
3. Skidding	8.7
4. Pedestrian crossing street carelessly	6.4
5. Driving on wrong side of road	5.7
6. Careless backing	3.2
7. Inexperience	3.0
8. Careless motorman	3.0
9. Failure to signal	3.0
10. Pedestrian stepping from behind other objects without looking	3.0
11. Carelessness of unknown operator	2.3
12. Following too closely	2.3

Figure 38 shows a more detailed analysis of the accident problem.

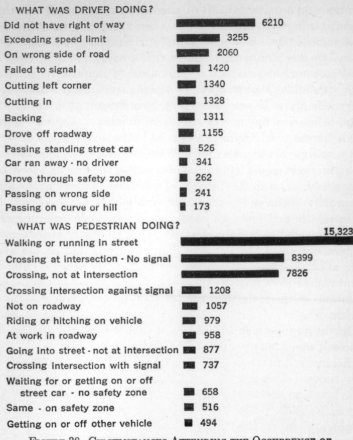

WHAT WAS DRIVER DOING?

Did not have right of way	6210
Exceeding speed limit	3255
On wrong side of road	2060
Failed to signal	1420
Cutting left corner	1340
Cutting in	1328
Backing	1311
Drove off roadway	1155
Passing standing street car	526
Car ran away - no driver	341
Drove through safety zone	262
Passing on wrong side	241
Passing on curve or hill	173

WHAT WAS PEDESTRIAN DOING?

Walking or running in street	15,323
Crossing at intersection - No signal	8399
Crossing, not at intersection	7826
Crossing intersection against signal	1208
Not on roadway	1057
Riding or hitching on vehicle	979
At work in roadway	958
Going into street - not at intersection	877
Crossing intersection with signal	737
Waiting for or getting on or off street car - no safety zone	658
Same - on safety zone	516
Getting on or off other vehicle	494

FIGURE 38. CIRCUMSTANCES ATTENDING THE OCCURRENCE OF ACCIDENTS AS REPORTED BY POLICE DEPARTMENTS

Certain human causes can be more easily reduced by directing efforts toward something besides the driver. Those causes due to violations of rules and regulations are not wholly to be blamed on the motorist.

Traffic safety very largely depends on one's ability to predict the behavior of others, and the more the behavior of all concerned is controlled by uniform habits, the easier it is to predict what they will do under a given set of conditions. In the United States we have built up a uniform habit of passing on the right all cars that are going in the opposite direction. But think how the accidents would increase if we had no such uniform method of passing. Unfortunately this is only one of the very few rules that apply equally in all communities. There is such lack of uniformity in most traffic regulations that an operator whose driving habits make him a very safe driver in one State, may be a dangerous driver in another State where the driving habits are different. Consider hand signals, for example. Some States require the driver to signal for a right turn by extending his arm with the forearm extending upward at a right angle, and a left turn by extending the arm and forearm horizontally. But in the District of Columbia, extending the arm horizontally indicates either a right or a left turn. It is easy to understand how drivers who are accustomed to interpreting the horizontal signal as indicating a left turn, frequently misinterpret the hand signals of District of Columbia drivers and collide with them when they are attempting to make right turns. Lack of

uniformity of laws and regulations confuses the motorist who is making a long trip, during which he must change his driving habits a dozen or more times. Uniform traffic laws and uniform signs and signals make the observation of the law much easier for the motorist.

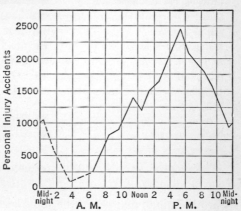

Fatigue is undoubtedly another human factor which enters into the causation of accidents,

FIGURE 39. DISTRIBUTION OF 28,000 ACCIDENTS ACCORDING TO TIME OF DAY IN NEW YORK STATE FROM JANUARY TO JULY, 1925

although the extent of its influence is hard to determine directly. As indicated in Figure 39, a disproportionately large number of accidents occur at the peak hour of traffic in the late afternoon, between five and six, as compared with the number at the peak hour in the morning. How far the fatigue of the driver after a long period at the wheel, or of the pedestrian after a day's work causes an increase in accidents at the close of the afternoon is not fully determined. Some idea may be secured of the part played by fatigue in causing accidents by a study of accidents at various hours of the day. The indication is, however, not wholly reliable, for we do not know the relative number driving at the various hours.

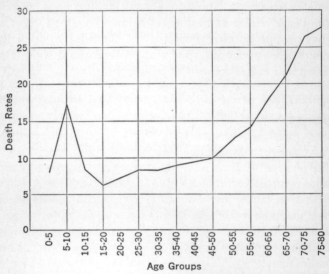

FIGURE 40. AUTOMOBILE DEATHS PER 100,000 POPULATION IN THE SUCCESSIVE FIVE-YEAR AGE GROUPS

The use of alcohol is another frequent cause of serious accidents. Even small amounts, insufficient to intoxicate, tend to decrease the higher forms of skill and lessen the sense of responsibility. Yet a driver is seldom charged with driving while under the influence of liquor unless he is actually drunk. It is, therefore, highly probable that alcohol has contributed to many accidents charged to other causes.

Of the persons other than the motorist who are responsible for accidents, the pedestrian needs most consideration. He is just as likely to be careless as is the motorist, and he is the one who receives the damage if there is an accident. Of the accidents which result fatally, the most frequent cause is adult jay-walking. Children playing in the streets constitute the next most important cause. While the number of collisions between vehicles has decreased in the past few years, the number of pedestrian accidents has about doubled.

The part played by age and age-groups is indicated in Figure 40.

From the above it will be seen that the greatest hope for reducing the number of accidents lies in: (1) A more thorough examination of drivers before granting licenses; (2) A careful study of the repeaters; (3) A strict examination of professional drivers; (4) The education and regulation of the pedestrian.

III. METHODS OF SELECTING STREET-CAR MOTORMEN

Before the advent of the automobile the psychologist was devising tests for street-car motormen, for even in the days of horse-drawn vehicles, the problem of safety was an important one. The number of street-railway accidents involving the public (excluding collisions with motor vehicles) is decreasing steadily. But collisions between trolley car and motor vehicles on the streets in the last few years have complicated the job of the motorman. The fact that the street car is confined to the tracks limits the means by which the motorman may avoid an impending accident, and necessitates quick action on his part. The motorman cannot get out of the way, he can only speed up or apply the brakes in an emergency. Careful and competent driving on the part of the motorman is particularly important because of the large number of lives entrusted to him.

Realizing the importance of the securing of competent motormen in solving the traffic problem where street cars are concerned, investigators all over the world have devised tests for the selection of motormen. Some pioneer work in the scientific selection of motormen was conducted by Münsterberg in 1912. In avoiding accidents he found the following abilities to be of greatest importance: the ability to keep attention constant, the ability to resist distraction by chance happenings on the street, and the ability to foresee the possible movements of pedestrians and vehicles. He tested these mental abilities by cards shown through a window in a moving belt. Each card had lines through the center representing street-car tracks; and pedestrians, horse-drawn vehicles and motor cars were scattered unevenly over the space representing the street. The speed and direction in which each was moving was given, and the person taking the test indicated the points in the track where a collision was imminent. The window slowly moved over the card, and the person taking the test followed the lines representing the street-car tracks with his eyes as if he were actually operating the car.

Later tests measured the ability to react correctly to quick and unexpected happenings as well as the power of attention. In order to see how a prospective street-car motorman will behave in the event of a danger, whether he will lose his wits to the extent of letting go the controller handle and brake and passively stand by, or whether he will promptly take measures required for the safety of all concerned, the man is placed before a controller handle and while he is practicing with it, he is frightened by a sudden loud noise, a short-circuit flash passing before his eyes, or the floors yielding below his feet. If he loses his presence of mind in these circumstances, the company knows that he should not be entrusted with the care of a car.

Speed of reaction is another important element in safe operation of a street car. The motorman who can move quickly to apply the brake, may avoid an accident in a situation in which an accident could not be avoided by a man who had a long reaction time. A difference of half a second may mean the difference between an accident and safety.

IV. METHODS OF SELECTING TRAFFIC POLICEMEN

The part played by the traffic policeman in keeping the wheels of traffic running smoothly is of paramount importance, and yet little attention has been given to selecting men for this work. In many jurisdictions those members of the regular police force who indicate a preference for traffic work are transferred to traffic. In other places those in charge prefer, for traffic work, men who have had no general police experience, for the reason that the aggressiveness

and repressive attitude exercised in general police duties enter unconsciously into traffic direction and control if these men are transferred to the traffic division. And in a few places the newly
appointed recruits to the general police force are looked over carefully, and those who are intelligent, and who have a pleasing personality, mental poise, and good appearance are assigned to the
traffic division.

The work of the traffic policeman varies in different places. The
chief duties of the "traffic cop" at a busy corner are as follows:
His most important duty and the one to which he devotes the
major portion of his time is directing the flow of traffic. Second
in importance among his duties is that of enforcing traffic regulations, correcting offenders, and making arrests if necessary. It is
his duty to investigate every traffic accident which comes to his
attention and to make a complete report of each to headquarters.
The "traffic cop" at the corner must direct people to all parts of
the city, and must give these directions clearly and accurately.
He must administer first aid when necessary; and must see to it
that the handicapped, as the blind, the lame, and the old people
are able to cross the street. Each of these duties involves direct
personal relations between the "traffic cop" and the public. The
courtesy, poise, and firmness with which he deals with each individual motorist and pedestrian largely determine his efficiency.
Antagonizing the public by "bawling out" every one fosters dis-
respect for the law and makes the control of traffic more difficult.

In order to secure the men best fitted for the job, the qualifications necessary for the efficient performance of these duties of traffic
policemen should be measured in the examination for the position.
No longer should the applicant be required to take the regular
patrolman examination, but traffic officers should be selected for
that distinct purpose by means of an examination covering the
following points:

Test 1. Special intelligence test. A special intelligence test
should be used, and only those applicants who are considerably
above the average of the population in intelligence should be
considered for the position. The intelligence test may be in terms
of the job. This test should be very largely of the nature of a social

intelligence test, that is, it should measure one's ability to deal with others.

Test 2. Duties test. The test of knowledge and abilities requisite for the efficient performance of the duties assigned should include a number of separate parts. (*a*) Accuracy of observation: A picture of an automobile wreck, or of a traffic violation might be given the applicant for study. After several minutes, without looking at the picture, he might be required to answer questions designed to test his observation and memory of important things he saw in the picture. (*b*) Knowledge of traffic laws and regulations: This test should be thorough, and should stress the application of the regulations to individual cases as well as actual knowledge of the law itself. (*c*) City information: The location of the chief public buildings, highways, and hotels should be asked. The applicant should be able to give directions for reaching these from any point specified. (*d*) Knowledge of first aid: A traffic policeman should be capable of rendering first aid to any one injured at his corner. (*e*) Judgment in relations with motorists, pedestrians, and fellow officers: This test should measure his ability to choose the best method of dealing with people. Questions such as the following might be used, giving the situation with four possible means of handling it, of which the person taking the test must choose the best one.

If you were a traffic officer at a busy corner, and a motorist in a car bearing the tags of a distant state failed to give the proper hand signal as he turned the corner, you should:
—— Order him to report to the nearest police station.
—— Tell him the fine for failing to signal, and warn him that next time he will have to pay it.
—— Tell him the local regulations as to hand signals and let him go.
—— Pay no attention to him as he is a stranger, and let him go on without stopping.

Test 3. Physical examination. A thorough physical examination should be given to each applicant for the position of traffic policeman. He should have good health, a good physique, good sensory apparatus, and quiet nerves.

Test 4. Interview. An interview is necessary to determine the poise, manner, courtesy, and personality of the applicant.   The man of pleasing personality gets the coöperation of the public, and maintains respect for the law.   He should be even-tempered, and able to keep his head in an emergency, otherwise he may jam traffic and cause accidents.   An irritable, loud-mouthed traffic officer is considerably worse than no officer.

CHAPTER XIX
THE RELATION OF PSYCHOLOGY TO POLITICS

When the poor hath cried, Cæsar hath wept.

SHAKESPEARE

In politics, as in all other affairs of life, nothing happens without cause. Why a voter is a Republican rather than a Democrat is not a mere matter of chance. The defeat of a candidate to-day and his election by a "landslide" two years from now is produced by certain very definite factors. Why the politician enters the political arena, how he conducts his campaign, his actions when elected or defeated, are controlled by forces no more mysterious than are the forces which control the rest of the universe.

The more important items in the problem of politics are: I. The Voter; II. The Politician; III. Political Strategy.

I. THE VOTER

The most important single factor in the science of politics is the voter. As indicated above, the behavior of the voter is not a chance affair. He acts in accordance with certain habits of thought which have been built up by contact with the environment to which he has been exposed. His behavior is easily influenced by suggestion, and his emotions are extremely responsive to the seductive words of the politician and his campaign managers.

Concerning the voter we shall consider: (1) The general nature of the voter; (2) His party attachments.

1. **The nature of the voter.** The general characteristics of the voter will be considered under the following headings: (a) The voter's ignorance; (b) The voter's emotionality; (c) The voter's tendency to follow the herd.

(a) *The voter's ignorance.* The average voter knows little about the issues for which he votes or about the candidates whose cause he supports. The candidate may stand on a good platform of sound principles, but the voter seldom knows much more about these good principles than is contained in a few vague, ringing phrases that have been used as speech keynotes or party slogans. Not one in a thousand of the voting public is so informed on national or state problems and needs that he could logically select the best candidate for dealing with these needs. As a rule voters run through the list of candidates on a party ticket and find only a few candidates that they have heard of before. Yet none of these considerations keep the average voter from voting. His vote, though cast in political ignorance, counts just as much as the vote of the best-informed citizen.

In order to discover how much young people of voting age know about politics, the author tried an experiment with about 300 upper-class college students. These students were given a test designed to measure knowledge of politics. The test consisted of 63 true-false questions on current national affairs and contemporary personalities in the political field. The following will serve as examples of the questions:

T F 1 Prohibition is one of the chief campaign issues in the presidential election of 1928.

T F 2 Senator Borah is inclined toward more violent action against Mexico.

T F 3 Demands for Senatorial investigation of the Nicaraguan situation indicate that there is considerable opposition to the administration's foreign policy.

T F 9 Most of the insurgent Republicans are from the New England States.

T F 24 The interests of the East and the West in farm legislation are essentially the same.

T F 34 Senator Hiram Johnson is the leader of the group that is opposing the passage of the Boulder Dam Bill.

T F 55 The McNary-Haugen Bill met much opposition on its equalization fee clause.

Among the students, the men were on the average able to answer 32 questions, while the women could answer only 25. This shows the dearth of knowledge of political problems even in a group that because of its superior education, culture, and interests we should expect to be perhaps better informed than the general public. Approximately 25 per cent of the group were close relatives of politicians in high office. A large majority of these university students expressed definite political party adherences, 93 per cent stating that they were attached to some party, 29 per cent signifying a strong attachment to their party.

In an effort to analyze the lack of knowledge of politics, these same students were asked to state whether they were "greatly interested in politics," "somewhat interested," or "not at all interested." Only 12 per cent were greatly interested in politics, 68 per cent were somewhat interested, and 20 per cent were not at all interested. Lack of interest perhaps accounts very largely for ignorance in regard to politics, for the average person has plenty of opportunity through newspapers, magazines, radios, and speeches to become informed.

Closely related to the voter's ignorance, or perhaps a part of his ignorance, are the delusions under which he often works. One of these delusions which a great many American voters have is that politicians and political leaders are very superior personages. One of the popular misconceptions is that political leaders are of necessity very astute and possess great shrewdness and subtlety. This misconception is indicated in the tendency to make heroes of the successful politician and to idolize him in a vague sort of way. That the average politician shows no marked superiority in wisdom and intelligence will be demonstrated in a later section which deals with the personal characteristics of the politician. In politics as in anything else, "distance lends enchantment to the view." The voters in the remote communities who are sufficiently far removed from their United States senators and congressmen, tend to look on them with awe and reverence. But the inhabitants of Washington, who know them better, recognize the fact that they are only men and are subject to the same frailties as the rest of humanity.

Another delusion into which the public's ignorance may lead it is the belief that in a big campaign, the national headquarters are manned by able men whose main idea is to elect the ticket and who are inspired by the utmost devotion to the cause and the candidate.

The extreme ignorance of the voting public both in regard to political events and in regard to methods and characteristics of politicians makes the voter much more susceptible to the methods of appeal used by the politician.

(b) *The voter's emotionality.* People find it much easier to be led or influenced by the emotional appeals of the campaigner, speech writer, or press agent than by the rational analysis of the real motives and aims of a candidate. As in all other affairs, in winning a vote it is easier to win the man through his feelings than through his intellect. It takes facts to stir the man's intellect, but a very trivial catchword will stir his emotions. The great emotionality of the voter is the reason for home-town speeches which stress the boyhood haunts and ties of the candidate rather than his views on world affairs. This is why Hoover's visit to his old swimming hole in Iowa received more press comment than the speech he made on the same visit. Al Smith's refusal to have his picture made laying bricks and Hoover's refusal to kiss the baby produced ten times as much discussion as their statements on foreign affairs. The emotionality of the voters demands a shouting, band-playing, torch-waving campaign. It accounts for the use of such lowbrow tactics as those used in the famous "hard-cider" campaign of William Henry Harrison, and the "whispering" campaign waged against Smith in the last presidential election.

The successful politician knows he can sway his followers by playing on their emotions and arousing their prejudices, whereas rational appeals would either strike a blank wall, or fall on unappreciative ears. This lack of reasoning gives the opportunity for exploitation of the many by a few. It enables the man who knows mob psychology to utilize the herd to his own or his party's advantage.

In politics as in love-making there is a tendency for the wooed to have certain rises and falls of emotional ardor. If any one thing is definitely known about the emotions of the voters, it is that the emotions change. The successful politician must recognize when they are going to change and act accordingly. There is a tide in the emotionality of the voters "which, taken at its flood leads on to fortune." The politician must "take the current when it serves," or lose his ventures. When the emotional flood is against one's party as it was against the Democrats in 1920, to venture forth is fatal. The tide of the voter's emotionality seems to ebb and flow with a fairly rhythmical periodicity, and the efforts of the campaigner must be ready to take advantage of this. If the election in Bryan's first presidential campaign had occurred a few weeks earlier he would easily have won, and if the election in 1916 had occurred a few weeks earlier Wilson would have lost.

(c) *The voter's tendency to follow the herd.* People like to be with the rest of the group and they like to be on the winning side. If the politician can convince the voting public that his is the winning side, he will have little difficulty in piling up the votes.

When the idea once became widespread that Hoover had a majority of the delegates at Kansas City, his previous opponents went to him in droves. This tendency of the herd to climb on the bandwagon of the successful candidate is seen in the haste of the mob shift from Pompey to Cæsar when Cæsar's victory became apparent. Marullus denounces the fickleness of that mob as follows:

> Wherefore rejoice? What conquest brings he home?
> What tributaries follow him to Rome,
> To grace in captive bonds his chariot wheels?
> You blocks, you stones, you worse than senseless things!
> O, you hard hearts, you cruel men of Rome,
> Knew you not Pompey? Many a time and oft
> Have you climbed up to walls and battlements,
> To towers and windows, yea, to chimney-tops,
> Your infants in your arms, and there have sat
> The livelong day, with patient expectation,
> To see great Pompey pass the streets of Rome;
> And, when you saw his chariot but appear,
> Have you not made an universal shout,
> That Tiber trembled underneath her banks,
> To hear the replication of your sounds
> Made in her concave shores?
> And do you now put on your best attire?
> And do you now cull out a holiday?
> And do you now strew flowers in his way
> That comes in triumph over Pompey's blood?
> Be gone!
> Run to your houses, fall upon your knees,
> Pray to the gods to intermit the plague
> That needs must light on this ingratitude.
>
> SHAKESPEARE, *Julius Cæsar*, I, 1.

The campaigner makes constant use of the tendency of people to follow the herd. Rallies, torch-light parades, stump speeches, distribution of buttons — all appeal to the mob spirit. Modern campaigners are making use of the radio; but the radio will probably never replace the actual meeting because it lacks the element of personal touch. We see very excellent exhibitions of the mob spirit in action at our big National Conventions. A demonstration for a candidate as he is nominated may become contagious and result in his nomination. This is particularly true if the demonstration is spontaneous and not a mere hollow, unenthusiastic parade, as is most often the case. In these conventions, "mob appeal" sometimes secures the nomination of a dark horse that most delegates would never have thought of voting for two weeks previously. Bryan's first nomination was accomplished in that way.

The advantage of name plates on automobiles and of many political slogans, depends on this widespread tendency of the voters to try to vote for the candidate that they think will be successful. "All for Al and Al for All" is an example of such a slogan in the 1928 presidential campaign.

2. **The voter's party.** While most voters belong to a party, they are not immovably attached to this party as is indicated by the fact that the same constituency may give a Republican victory one year and a Democratic victory the next. The extent of this swing in the party vote over a period of more than fifty years is shown in the table on page 404. The figures are not yet available for the 1928 election, but the present indications are that more votes were changed in this election than in any that has gone before.

Bertrand Russell has pointed out that many people really believe that the ills from which they suffer would be cured if a certain party were in power. They accordingly shift from party to party. They vote for one party without getting any improvement in their hard lot. They then conclude that it was the other party that was to bring the millennium. By the time that the voter is thoroughly disillusioned with all parties, he is ready to die with old age. His children, in turn, retain the belief of his youth, and the political pendulum swings on.

Presidential Elections [1]	Change in Percentage of Vote Polled by Republican Party
1856–1860	6.8
1860–1864	15.2
1864–1868	2.4
1868–1872	2.7
1872–1876	8.1
1876–1880	1.0
1880–1884	0.1
1884–1888	0.4
1888–1892	5.2
1892–1896	8.3
1896–1900	0.8
1900–1904	4.7
1904–1908	4.8
1908–1912	1.0
1912–1916	1.0
1916–1920	14.2
1920–1924	6.5

There is, however, a very large group, constituting in all probability the large percentage of voters, who vote for the same party always, no matter who the candidate may be. Many of them are like the old Georgia Democrat who when asked his opinion of Hoover said: "I think Hoover is right and Smith is wrong; but you know Hoover is a Republican, and that is enough to damn anybody."

In the study of 300 university students mentioned above, 93 per cent signified attachment to a political party. This attachment was analyzable from the data into further differentiations as shown in the following table:

Party	Strength of Attachment	
	Slightly Attached	Strongly Attached
Republican	72%	28%
Democratic	64	36
Third Parties	74	26

The question which arises in the mind of the psychologist in connection with attachment to political party is: What causes the

[1] Rice, Stuart A.: *Quantitative Methods in Politics* (Alfred A. Knopf, 1928), 304.

voter to belong to a particular party? Certain of the factors behind this have been analyzed. The influence of the following will be considered in turn: (a) The party of one's father; (b) The location of one's birthplace and residence; (c) Sex; (d) Age; (e) Nationality; (f) Race; (g) Vocation; (h) Education; (i) Intelligence; (j) Religion.

(a) *The party of one's father.* It requires little argument to demonstrate the importance of family relationship in determining the party for which one votes. When the politician can count on the vote of the head of the family, he can usually count on the eligible votes of the rest of his family. The young man coming into his rights of citizenship, selects, except in rare instances, the party of his father; and enfranchising the woman has in most instances only doubled the vote without changing the final result.

In the investigation of the 300 university students, each student was asked to answer the question: "Do you belong to the same party to which your father belongs?" The analysis of the replies shows the following to be true: Seventy-one per cent of the group are of the same party as their father. Seventy-three per cent of the Republicans follow in the footsteps of their fathers, and eighty-one per cent of the Democrats. Those adhering to third parties, however, show only ten per cent of the same party as the father.

(b) *The location of one's birthplace and residence.* The place in which one is born, reared, and lives undoubtedly has an effect upon his party adherence. The importance of tradition and social inheritance can be seen in the differences according to State. Originally the differences in most instances really stood for something — a particular State was solidly Democratic for a particular reason; now often the differences stand for little more than a handed-down social habit.

There are three different aspects of the residence influence which may be considered: (1) State differences; (2) Regional differences; (3) Urban and rural differences.

(1) *State differences.* In the college study already mentioned, there were sufficient students from five different States to make an analysis in regard to State in which born. The District of Co-

lumbia showed 67 per cent Republicans, 29 per cent Democrats; New York, 55 per cent Republicans, 45 per cent Democrats; Virginia, 6 per cent Republicans, 94 per cent Democrats; Maryland, 45 per cent Republicans, 40 per cent Democrats; Pennsylvania, 76 per cent Republicans, 12 per cent Democrats. In at least three of these States the differences are large enough to show a distinct trend.

Rice, in his quantitative study of politics, has also analyzed state influence. He has attempted to show that simply the State itself, aside from any regional or commercial connection, has its influence. To demonstrate his point, he compared adjacent counties of the Northwestern States in their LaFollette votes in the presidential election of 1924. He first compared adjacent counties within the same State, then adjacent counties across state borders.

He found [1] that the differences of votes of adjacent counties was much more where state boundaries intervened than where this was not the case. The average difference in adjacent counties of adjoining States was approximately fifty per cent greater than that of adjacent counties of the same State.

(2) *Regional differences.* This refers to the part which regional influences other than state boundaries, such as trading-centers, communications, etc., play in determining party votes. Rice again in his analysis of the distribution of the LaFollette vote of 1924, found that the influence of state boundaries is greatly reduced within areas with a common retail trading-center. He also found some indication that diffusion may be furthered by the presence of regular lines of rail or mail communication.

(3) *Urban and rural differences.* Wherever statistical analysis has been made, votes show decided differences according to population of the district. Facts do not indicate conclusively whether these differences are stable differences or whether they are fluctuating. But decided urban and rural differences practically always exist in an important election. Voters in the variously populated areas are undoubtedly influenced by the factors which cause these differences; in the city there may be a greater uncertainty and fluctuation of party because of the greater possibility of newspaper-

[1] Rice, Stuart A.: *Quantitative Methods in Politics* (Alfred A. Knopf, 1928), 144.

headline appeal and crowd sentiment.   A clear example of urban
and rural differences is seen in the Smith vote in the New York
governor's election of
1920.   This is shown
graphically in Figure
41.[1]

(c) *Sex.* This is
not a very important
factor in determin-
ing party or vote.
Women are usually
somewhat less in-
formed on politics,
and somewhat less
interested in politics
than are men, which

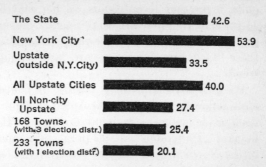

The State	42.6
New York City	53.9
Upstate (outside N.Y.City)	33.5
All Upstate Cities	40.0
All Non-city Upstate	27.4
168 Towns (with 3 election distr.)	25.4
233 Towns (with 1 election distr.)	20.1

FIGURE 41. PERCENTAGE OF TOTAL VOTES FOR
GOVERNOR RECEIVED BY SMITH IN VARIOUS
POPULATION UNITS
(Adapted from Rice.)

may give rise to a more constant tendency on their part to "vote
the party." Women often lean more strongly to the so-called
"civic" and "moral" side of issues and react more vigorously
against the radical; and these tendencies have a bearing upon
their vote. Women tended to vote against Smith in the 1928 election on account of his stand on prohibition.

(d) *Age.* Age probably has something to do with the party to
which one belongs, although no quantitative studies have demonstrated to just what extent it is a determining factor. The younger
people of the voting public are somewhat less inclined to be "set"
in their party adherences, so that more shifting from party to party
with succeeding elections will usually be found among them than
among the older voters. Younger citizens are somewhat more
inclined to be on the radical side, so that they usually have a larger
percentage represented on the third-party tickets.

(e) *Nationality.* Within one country where voting privileges are
granted to all, nationality groups tend to vote together. On certain types of issues which bear directly upon the characteristics or
welfare of a national group this is particularly true. The German-
Americans in regions where distinct groups of these people live,

[1] Rice, Stuart A.: *Quantitative Methods in Politics* (Alfred A. Knopf, 1928), 173.

furnish examples. Upon the question of prohibition, as a general rule the rural dwellers voted for prohibition, while the city dwellers tended to vote against it. Although on most issues the German-American farmers voted with the rural voters, nevertheless, on the prohibition issue, they tended to unite with the voters of the city. In the 1928 election there was a tendency for the so-called "foreign vote" to support Smith.

(f) *Race.* In American politics, the negro has, ever since his enfranchisement, offered a group problem. "Negro voter" has usually meant Republican in the past. The solid south has remained solid largely because of the race question. Race plays its part not only in determining certain habits of party affiliation but also in causing wholesale desertion of a party by the members of a particular race. This is particularly true of the negro in some of the northern districts of the country. In the election of 1926, the Nineteenth Assembly District of New York County which includes a large part of the great colored district in Harlem, cast 6435 votes for Alfred Smith, the Democratic candidate for governor, as compared with 4758 for Ogden L. Mills, the Republican. The main reason that the negro vote of the north is beginning to go into the Democratic column is the dislike of negroes for the Ku Klux Klan. The Klan in the north generally supports the Republican candidates. The Klan was particularly opposed to Smith because he is a Catholic. The Klan is also traditionally an enemy of the negro. Thus as a result of a common enemy the negroes could easily become friendly to the cause of Smith. Voting habits of colored citizens have been in the past quite fixed, but indications are that the future will witness much change in the colored vote.

(g) *Vocation.* Does one's occupation have any bearing upon the selection of or adherence to a political party? Occupation on a large scale may be important, when we consider that farming interests may line up with one party, "big business" with another, and "labor" with still another. But considering individuals, specific occupations probably do not have a great deal of influence. As an indication of the bearing that individual occupations have, the records of 1000 individuals selected at random from *Who's*

Who were analyzed according to party adherence. The following table shows the results for the various occupations included.

OCCUPATION	PERCENTAGE OF EACH PARTY		
	REPUBLICAN	DEMOCRATIC	NO PARTY GIVEN
Congressmen or Statesmen.............	69	31	0
Lawyers............................	41	36	23
Business Men.......................	43	14	43
Engineers..........................	46	11	43
Newspaper Men.....................	·40	6	54
Doctors............................	29	10	61
Clergymen and Church Workers........	26	11	63
Teachers and Educators..............	19	11	70
Musicians..........................	22	0	78
Scientists..........................	13	8	79
Writers............................	13	7	80
Artists............................	16	4	80

The table is given in order of tendency to align with some party. It is interesting to note which occupations least often express an attachment to a party. These occupations represent, on the whole, ones which would probably be less interested in politics and which would have little or nothing to gain from an adherence to one or the other party. There is a tendency for business men, engineers, and newspaper men to line up with the Republicans, but there are many exceptions, as seen in the 1928 campaign, in which the Democratic campaign manager and several of his lieutenants were drawn from the ranks of big business.

(*h*) *Education.* The relation between party and extent of education of prominent men (*Who's Who* group) does not show anything very significant. The percentages with college degree are about the same for the two major parties. Sixty-nine per cent of the Republicans included have college degrees, sixty-six per cent of the Democrats — very nearly the same.

It is rather hard to find a direct measure of the relation between education and party belonged to. Statistics on 111 college students show some degree of relationship, a correlation of .25, between college grades and knowledge of politics; indicating in an indirect way a definite relationship, though not a very close one.

Perhaps of more significance is the fact that the percentages belonging to each of the political parties for university students is quite different from those for the population at large. The percentage of third-party adherents is very much larger, which indicates that the better educated are more likely to have liberal tendencies.

(i) *Religion.* According to the Constitution of the United States, religion and politics are not to be mixed. But as Rice points out, the religious factor is continually involved as an underground influence, and as such has perhaps been more important than if it had constituted a formal basis of party alignments. The fact that Smith is a Catholic lost him thousands of votes in 1928. The part played by religion in politics is indicated by the fact that it is well-nigh impossible to get a Jew nominated, regardless of how good his qualifications may be.

II. THE POLITICIAN

Politics is organized effort guided by the personal touch. It is the politician who furnishes this last element; because of the politician, politics becomes largely a game of personal appeal. The politician is at the same time the standard-bearer of a party, a gambler in the fortunes of a profession, and a wooer of popular favor.

A psychological study of the politician should include a consideration of why men become politicians, a study of the personality of the politician, and a statistical analysis of the characteristics of the politician. These aspects of the study will be discussed in the order given above.

1. **Why a man becomes a politician.** Politics, like other vocations, has various types of appeals to replenish its ranks. The most important of these will be considered.

(a) *Liking for the political game and enjoyment in playing it.* To some people politics is a most fascinating game, and they enjoy manipulating other people just as the card-shark enjoys manipulating the cards. This group enters politics for the love of the profession itself. They are the "born politicians." The typical politician who can be classed here would not trade his job for another though he were assured of more money or of even greater fame. He enjoys the element of chance and uncertainty in winning the people and trying to keep up with the changing tides of political activity. It pleases him as much to court a difficult electorate as it pleases the proverbial "sheik" to teach a maiden to love.

(b) *Desire to produce some reform.* Some enter politics because they have a desire to help humanity, and deem political life the most direct way of accomplishing this end. Many people are born with an artificial feeling of paternity, often of an egotistical type. If these individuals become politicians they are likely to make their platforms full of reform planks, they are likely to win votes by promises of making the world better, they are likely to bewail the terrible conditions brought on by previous administrations. There are several types of reformers distinguishable among politicians. There is the money grafter who uses the reform appeal because it is the best or the most convenient way of securing easy money. Another type is the "gentleman" of independent means who becomes a political reformer to occupy some of his time and give him an excuse for living. And there is the reformer type who enters politics for revenge. He may enter with a grudge engendered by some old business feud which he thinks was started by some financial ring in politics, and he desires to beat them at their own game.

(c) *Desire for fame.* All politicians desire fame to a certain extent, and some are in the game for that alone. For those who have the natural qualities of a successful leader, political fame is more easily obtained than fame along other lines. For that reason we have many attempts with a relatively high proportion of failures in the cases of those who cannot climb the high steps.

(d) *Desire for social advancement.* Social allurement not infrequently leads a man to enter public life. In most civilized countries, the high government officials, representing the highest types of political attainment, are of a distinctly superior social class. They enjoy privileges which appeal to the eyes of their fellow citizens, they are in the social limelight as well as in the political limelight. Social advancement is an element in most professional struggles, but in the political struggle it seems to play a more important part than in any other profession.

(e) *Money.* The desire for money is another reason why men enter politics. High political officials receive fairly good salaries, with certainly not an undue standard of excellency of performance necessary after the man is elected. This motive offers opportunity for the dishonest, grafting politician. Looseness of campaign organizations, and personal assignment of jobs in campaign headquarters, means that there are an untold number of political jobs for which money is lavishly spent for no returns whatever in service.

(f) *Accident.* Lastly, some people apparently just fall into politics. Just as chance starts some in jobs as engineers, teachers, or preachers, it starts others on a political career. This is the group referred to by House when he said: "Comparatively few men get into politics deliberately. Most of them are pitchforked in."

2. The personality of the politician. Since the politician is in a sense selling himself to the voters, it would seem that an important part of the selling appeal should be based on the man himself. It is hard for a man with no leadership qualities and with no personal appeal to sell himself. In such a case, about the only way in which he could enter politics would be as the mouthpiece or spokesman of a strong political machine. Politicians should have a pleasing personality, but not necessarily a very strong personality. There have been several men whose prominence and length of service in politics should have rewarded them with the highest political office — the Presidency — but whose strong personalities were forced to give way to lesser personalities or dark horses. We need no better illustrations of this than Webster, Calhoun, Clay, and in more recent times, LaFollette.

We shall now consider some of the more important personality traits of the politician.

(a) *Leadership qualities.* Before they became politicians many of our great public men demonstrated their qualities of leadership. Some were orators, some great journalists, some industrial magnets, and some famous military leaders. The public eye was upon them before they became candidates; and sometimes they were elected to office on previous leadership qualities which did not at all fit them for such a thing as the high office of presidency.

Bartlett [1] defines three types of political leaders: The *Dominant*

---

[1] Bartlett, F. C.: "The Social Psychology of Leadership," *Journal of the National Institute of Industrial Psychology,* London, October, 1926.

Type, the *Institutional* Type, and the *Persuasive* Type. The first of these, the Dominant type, is the Napoleonic or Mussolini sort of leader. He holds his constituency through a sort of unseen force. He is dominating in his ideas and in his actions. So long as he is in the public eye as their hero, his wishes are carried out like magic. Political leaders of this type are the most active, and are likely to accomplish more things, and to make more changes than any other type of leader. From their own standpoint they must always be on guard, however, for their very characteristic of domination which makes them leaders, often causes their downfall when something turns against them. The same qualities which made Napoleon a dominant political figure for so long, made him a fallen man finally. Andrew Jackson was an example of a dominant type of leader; Roosevelt would also probably come in this class.

The *Institutional* type is the organization politician who is serving as the standard-bearer of his party or of the organization which is backing him. He is usually quite conservative in his official acts. His measures are the expressions of his party or his organization, and he hesitates to introduce any which could not be sanctioned by them. The institutional type of leader is often put forth by an organization when their logical leader, though a man with real leadership qualities, has some characteristic about him which would lessen the universality of his appeal to the people. The institutional type often represents a compromise of qualities in an attempt to find a leader acceptable to all, the hope being that the people will vote for the party, if not for the leader. Having been elected by the institution, this type of leader depends upon the institution for his tenure of office. With the party backing him he may be reëlected; without the party he has no hope whatever of reëlection. A good example of the institutional leader in American politics was President Harding.

The third type of leader, the *Persuasive* type, is the one who wins his office through his powers of appeal to the people. He is the politician who wins by carefully analyzing the trend of public opinion and public sentiment, and adjusts his appeals and promises to what he finds. He is less likely to accomplish great things of startling nature than is the dominant leader, but he is also less likely to go down in defeat. He makes his own decisions and feels the responsibility for his acts much more than is the case with the institutional leader. Lincoln was a leader of this type and Smith is probably the best recent example.

(b) *Ability to get along with other people.* This is what might be called the social intelligence requirement of the politician, and it is an important qualification. The man who does not know how to deal with people has little chance of becoming a great politician. He must be able to enter with a whole-hearted appearance into the activities of his voters, he must know how to enter into conversation which would interest them, he must know about their interests in the community, he must know their motives for various actions; in other words, he must have a keen knowledge of human behavior. The skillful politician knows his constituency as the bridge player knows the cards. He knows whom he can rely on and who will sell out to the opposition. He knows how much power each man yields in a given community. As evidence of the quality of social intelligence in the politician, we usually find him a ready handshaker, a good mixer, an interesting talker, and a person showing a sympathetic understanding of the problems of others.

(c) *Persistence.* Persistence in the game of politics seems to be characteristic of most politicians. "Once a politician, always a politician" seems to be very generally true. Few politicians admit that they are defeated. A defeat is only a call for another battle.

3. Statistical analysis of characteristics of politicians. A few attempts have been made to analyze in a definite statistical way some of the factors pertaining to the politician. Such factors as the age of entering politics, the education of the politician, and the amount of experience it takes to reach the heights of political achievement, lend themselves to definite analysis. Study of some of these characteristics may give an additional insight into the "why" and "how" of politicians. Analysis of the following will be given in turn: (a) Previous occupations of politicians; (b) Age of politicians, both at time of entering politics and at time of reaching the height of fame; (c) Education and intellectual qualities; (d) Experience.

(a) *Previous occupations of politicians.* Here an attempt was made to find out whether those in any particular occupation have an advantage over others when it comes to entering politics. The previous occupations of the Senators of the Sixty-Ninth Congress, whose names appeared in *Who's Who* in 1926–27, 94 in all, were studied. Occupation seems to have an important significance. The lawyers lead all others in breaking into politics. Of the Senators, 57 per cent had been lawyers, 30 per cent business men, 13 per cent teachers, 7 per cent in the Army or Navy, 6 per cent newspaper men, 3 per cent farmers, 2 per cent clergymen or church workers, and one per cent each of public-service men, explorers, dentists, and physicians. (The percentages are not absolutely exclusive, since a few men were classed in more than one group.)

(b) *Age.* In connection with age, two questions naturally arise. First, at what age does the politician enter politics; and second, how old is the average politician before he has attained a high position in politics?

1. *Age on entering politics.* The politician as a rule enters politics young. An analysis of this factor was made for the group of Senators referred to above. Age at entering politics was taken as the age at which first office of a political nature was held, or age at which record is made of actively engaging in a political campaign. The youngest age at which any entered politics was 19, the oldest 63. The median age was 32. Thirteen per cent entered politics by 25 years of age, 65 per cent by 35, and 75 per cent by 40 years.

2. *Age on reaching height of political career.* Taking the election to a seat in Congress as typical of a political height, figures are available showing the average age of politicians holding such an office. Rice [1] has calculated the average age of American Congressmen from the First to Sixty-Eighth Congresses. Figure 42 has been taken from his data. This chart shows that from 1790 to the present time there has been a gradual increase in the age at which politicians reach this height of attainment. At the present time the average man does not reach the height of Congressman much younger than 45 or 50 years of age. This would indicate that for most Congressmen there has been considerable political experience before their election to the Federal Legislative office.

[1] Rice, Stuart A.: *Quantitative Methods in Politics* (Alfred A. Knopf, 1928), 300.

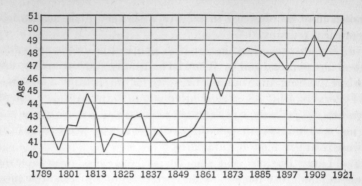

FIGURE 42. MEDIAN AGE OF CONGRESSMEN, 1ST TO 68TH CONGRESS
(After Rice.)

(c) *Education and intellectual qualities.* High abstract intelligence and high academic attainment do not seem to be closely correlated with political success.

No actual measure is available on the intelligence of politicians. There is reason to believe, however, that very high abstract intelligence is not essential for the politician. Some of our outstanding politicians are given credit for very high intellectual ability, some for very little. Beyond a certain limit, higher intelligence probably adds very little to possibilities of success as a politician. Social intelligence or ability to deal with people is much more important than abstract intelligence or ability to deal with abstract ideas.

An analysis of the academic education of the 94 Senators studied in terms of school achievement is as follows:

No college education.............................. 26 per cent
Attended college but did not obtain degree........... 17 "   "
Academic degree.................................. 36 "   "
Law degree...................................... 36 "   "
Medical degree.................................. 2 "   "
(Some had more than one degree)

The results show nothing very distinctive. It might be noted that the percentage graduating from college is less than for famous men in most other professions represented in *Who's Who*, forty-three per cent not being college graduates. Long periods of academic preparation are required for renown in some professions, but equal renown may be obtained in politics with very little academic or theoretical training.

(*d*) *Experience.* Men in our high political positions are seldom new at the political game. They have usually started farther down the line, holding some minor local office before securing a high State or Federal office. Rice has pointed out that the average Congress member has had an experience in Congress of approximately 2.5 terms, which means that in any Congress a large percentage of the members are reëlection candidates.

4. **"Lame Ducks."** "Lame Ducks" are those who have had their day as great politicians and are unwillingly relegated to the class of the "has-beens." Let us consider how they become "Lame Ducks." The biggest and most general reason is because they *fail to play the game* properly. They may have played it with too much duplicity. The politician who straddles issues and plays both ends against the middle, must eventually meet his Waterloo.

Too much *pretentiousness* and *overconfidence* is another reason why politicians crack. Nothing alienates more former supporters than for the politician to loose the "common touch." It is too often the case, as pointed out by Cassius:

> "That lowliness is young ambition's ladder,
> Whereto the climber upward turns his face;
> But when he once attains the utmost round
> He then unto the ladder turns his back,
> Looks into the clouds, scorning the base degrees
> By which he did ascend."
>
> SHAKESPEARE, *Julius Cæsar*

Closely related to pretentiousness is overconfidence. After winning a few times the politician gets the idea that his position in the good will of the voters is impregnable. Such men are headed for the shock of their lives for they fail to take proper precautions to prevent their overthrow.

Too much *suspicion* of those on whom he has to depend often causes the downfall of the politician. The fortunes of any leader are dependent upon the loyalty and support of his lieutenants. If he cannot trust his subordinates, the morale of his political machine is soon broken and the machine wrecked.

The part played by *physical condition* in breaking the politician should not be overlooked. The "high-up" official cannot expect to last long if five dinners out of seven are of the "State" dinner variety and at each one he indulges to the fullest extent. He cannot enjoy for long the luxury of social overindulgence of every sort. His health cannot stand the strain.

III. POLITICAL STRATEGY

In the daily papers we often read of "playing politics." The office-holder introduces a bill, thinking not about what its effects will be upon the prosperity and progress of the country but about what its effects will be upon the variously interested groups of political constituents or upon the public mind. That is "playing politics." The political organization proposes its candidate, not because he is believed to be the man who can do the most good for the country, but because he is believed to be the one who can best carry the party standard to a majority vote with the people. That is again "playing politics." The remainder of this chapter will consider the methods of "playing politics."

To get the candidate elected one must first sell him to the people. Since the first step in selling the candidate to the voting public is introducing him or making him known, the first part of this discussion will deal with that problem and the methods used.

1. **Getting the candidate known.** The candidate may have been known to some of the voters as a possibility before his nomination, but after his nomination it becomes the first problem of his party or his campaign organization to put him before the public as a candidate for election. Even before actual selection as a candidate takes place, the big nominees are given a rousing introduction in a nominating speech, which is heard not only by those at the convention but by thousands of radio listeners among the voters. Very shortly after nomination we see photographic posters along the highways, on public bulletin boards, and in merchants' store windows. The first issues of newspapers and magazines after the nomination of a candidate for an important office carry photographs of the new nominee, often showing him at various stages of his life. They also often carry photographs of his family and perhaps of his

home; and contain detailed accounts of the candidate's former accomplishments. Through legitimate means or questionable ones, the partisan and machine-supported newspapers, about this time, begin to make a big subscription drive with many sample copies of the newspaper sent out to prospective subscribers (or prospective voters). Moving pictures also introduce the candidate to the "movie-going" portion of the voters.

The importance of the initial speeches made by the candidate should not be overlooked in considering the means of introducing him. The interested portion of the public is looking to the first speech for an indication of what the candidate is going to stand for and what line of attack he is going to use. Acceptance speeches of presidential nominees serve this purpose. In fact that is what they serve rather than any function of acceptance, for the candidate has accepted his nomination long before the nominating speech was made.

After the candidate has been introduced comes the real campaigning. Campaigning is the process of "Goose-stuffing"; and the one who profits is the stuffer rather than the stuffed. The extent to which campaigning is "Goose-stuffing" will depend upon the extent to which the candidate lacks real qualities of leadership, and upon the extent to which the campaign lacks real issues.

Campaigning may be done through headquarters or it may be done simply through the candidate himself. Though the two sources overlap, sometimes considerably, the campaign activities have been considered in this chapter with the division into: (1) Headquarters campaigning; (2) Campaigning by the candidate.

2. **Campaigning from headquarters.** (a) *Feelers for gauging opinion.* The first thing those at headquarters are interested in knowing is how the people feel about the candidate. They are also interested in learning how the people feel about the opponent. When they know this, they have an indication of how strenuous the campaign must be. There are various ways in which opinion may be gauged. The candidate's popularity with the people both before nomination and after are noticed, the candidate is mentioned and talked-up in casual conversations, reactions to introductory meetings and speeches are carefully watched. Straw ballots

are extensively used to give popular opinion, and various "feelers" are put out by the "spokesman" of the candidate.

(b) *Slogans and songs.* Men have undoubtedly been elected on such yells as "The Full Dinner Pail," "Prosperity's Advance Agent," or "He Kept Us Out of War," even though the sayings mean very little and though the little meaning they have is incorrect. It is hard to realize just how important the cries and slogans of a campaign are when they are employed as an intimate and constant part of a campaign. The slogans and campaign songs are pasted on billboards, worn on buttons and badges, passed around in literature, shouted in meetings, and displayed on automobiles. It is said that a National Headquarters paid four thousand dollars for a campaign song — rather expensive campaigning, but who knows how many votes the song produced.

There seems to be nothing that can take the place of a slogan. There are the party platforms — but who reads them? They are for the academic politician; but for the rank and file of people there must be something they will really listen to. There are the meetings — but what is a meeting without a good slogan to set the people going, a good catchy phrase for them to carry away and repeat to their friends and neighbors? There is the campaign literature — but it must attract by big slogan headlines and must be dotted with alliterative phrases.

What constitutes a good slogan? "Alliteration's Artful Aid" goes a long way toward making a good one. A slogan must go like the chorus of a popular song, it must have a musical swing which moves with the greatest ease. It must have punch and pep. Notice the snappy alliterative effect of some slogans that have constituted an important part of bygone campaigns: "Tippecanoe and Tyler Too," "Van, Van, Is a Used Up Man," and "Coolidge or Chaos." The slogan must be short; the best ones have usually been only phrases. A slogan must mean something — at least to the people — but not too much. It must not be so meaningful that people will get suspicious of it and begin to analyze to see what it really means; nor so shallow that they will not feel that it means a great deal. In meaning, slogans often hinge upon something which is uppermost in the public mind. The old slogan "Fifty-four Forty or Fight" used in the Polk campaign was supposed to express Democratic sentiment on a real issue. It is interesting to note, however, that the argument was settled with forty-nine not fifty-four and that there was no fighting. "Sixteen to One," reiterated in the Bryan campaign, was another having a meaning based on a real issue. Slogans during the Wilson campaign had much opportunity to draw from problems uppermost in the minds of the people. "He Kept Us Out of War" seemed to have a significant meaning in terms of current affairs. But the phrase rang to another tune soon after election. Good slogans sometimes draw their appeal from quite a different thing, they often turn from current problems to a sentimental appeal. Such are numerous ones of the slogans attaching to Lincoln, such as, "Old Abe," "The Rail Splitter," "From Log Cabin to White House," or the one applying to Roosevelt, "Our Teddy."

The effect of slogans from a psychological point of view rests on their ease of repetition, their sentimental appeals, and their contagiousness in groups of people. They constitute one of the best means of appealing to the mass of voters in a rather subtle way.

(c) *Favors and buttons.* Badges and buttons are apparently an essential part of every political campaign. Almost as soon as the presidential candidate is chosen, there appear celluloid buttons bearing his picture, his name, or something for which he stands. There are distributed from headquarters, and at every mass meeting various badges and signs of party support to be worn, placarded on the automobile, or passed on to another person. There are in every novelty store, various types of novelties stamped with the presidential candidate's mottoes, or adorned with his photograph. Badges and buttons serve their purpose of repetitive advertising, through showing in a more definite way the support of those who wear them, and through making the wearers feel that they are an important element in pushing forward the campaign.

(d) *Canvassing and visiting.* In certain kinds of political campaigns, canvassing voters is an important way of rounding up the votes. It also serves the purpose of indicating to headquarters just how much support can be counted on. This makes the obtaining of votes like selling on a salesmanship basis rather than selling on an advertising basis. Canvassing may be done either by representatives from headquarters or by the candidate himself.

Very much can be done to build up the right attitude toward a candidate by skillful visiting long before the nomination is even made. The local politician who has at some time or other paid almost every voter in the community a visit, has conversed with each on his hobby, whether it be radios, stamp-collecting, or rabbit-raising, if he has done it skillfully, stands a much better chance with the people than his opponent who has not.

Canvassing can be done in various meeting-places for large numbers of people. Eating-places offer considerable possibilities, and a cheap eating-place is more profitable than a fashionable restaurant. Numerous places of sport and amusement can be visited with the hope of stirring up votes. The candidate or campaign manager who can be seen at county fairs, baseball games, religious meetings, club meetings, etc., usually gets a majority of the votes.

Canvassing is a local and personal form of campaigning, and for that reason must usually be used in coöperation with the local political organizations. This is perhaps one reason why it is more often utilized as a means of gaining votes in local elections than in the more important national elections. Canvassing done by a person who knows his candidate, and makes friends easily, can be important in securing many votes which would otherwise have gone unvoted through apathy of the voters, or which would have been won by the other side.

(e) *Campaigning through the press.* Newspaper sale in America is enormous. One large city newspaper may have a circulation of a million or more. When the extent of newspaper appeal is so great, it would be foolish for politicians to neglect so universal a source of advertising its candidate. Newspapers are lined up in partisan array for one candidate or the other. Near election time the news columns are largely reports of political activities; the editorial columns are full of tributes to the candidate; and when a presidential candidate and his party on a speaking tour occupy a single coach on a special train, three coaches are occupied by newspaper reporters, photographers, and press agents.

The partisan newspaper illustrates in the most extreme degree the use of the newspaper for campaigning. Such newspaper campaigning sometimes becomes very bitter, especially if there are two opposing newspapers in the same city or same community. As soon as the candidate has put his hat into the ring, his newspaper appears with photographs in as many different poses as it is judged the public can stand. In a partisan newspaper there are no pictures of the opponent; he is presented in grotesque cartoons rather than in pleasing photographs. There are recounts of the great public benefits wrought by the paper's candidate, but the misdeeds rather than the public services of the opponent are stressed. The reception given the candidate in a small town is reported as a large turnout of the whole town; an equally large crowd to meet the opponent is reported as a small group of farmers "who happened to be in town for the Saturday marketing."

Much so-called "dirty politics" goes on in connection with newspaper support and abuse of candidates. A newspaper may be paid to ignore rather than abuse the candidate and such tactics are absolutely closed to investigation and refutation. A good example of such tactics was reported recently in a large city newspaper. A man high in the political life was booked for a speech on the public ownership of power plants. Most people naturally expected that the views he expressed would be published and commented on in the local paper. But a private utility company (Electric Light and Power Company) which opposed government ownership had been doing a little "public relations" advertising, and had caused the newspaper to keep quiet for fear of losing a nice little sum of advertising money. The following letter commenting on the situation and quoted in the discussion of the affair shows what happened:

Dear Mr. ——:

I am much interested in the very handsome little ad which the —— Electric Light and Power Company is running in the —— newspapers.

When all is said and done it is the advertising that counts.

The fact that —— has received practically no notice in the —— newspapers, is, I believe, due to the fact that the electric light and power companies are good customers of the newspapers.

It is not very easy for anybody to bite the hand of a good customer.

Very sincerely yours,

(f) *The whispering campaign.*   Campaign attacks of the "whispering" type are much more widely used than is generally believed. No candidate for a prominent office fails to get those pinpricks of individual attack on his character.   In a quiet underground way scandal is diligently spread about most prominent candidates.   An editorial in *The Washington Post* [1] has the following to say concerning this:

Does any candidate for presidency escape abuse and calumny?   No candidate has ever escaped.   Washington was accused of padding his expense account and embezzling public moneys.   Jefferson was whispered against as an infidel, Jackson was denounced by a preacher for gambling, and assigned to perdition.   Lincoln was "confidentially" described during his first campaign as a boor, an ape, a baboon, and a jackleg lawyer.   Cleveland and Wilson were subjected to whispering charges of immorality.

The whispering attack on Smith in the 1928 campaign probably surpassed all others.

(g) *Political propaganda.*   Propaganda is an indirect type of appeal through suggestion, which makes possible the management of people.   Propaganda may sell a commodity, an idea, or a man — not on the basis of merit but through emotional or suggestive appeals which strike a sympathetic chord in the imagination of the public.   The public responds without recognizing the falsity or insincerity of the appeals.   And, as one man put it: "God help those who manipulate this propaganda hypodermic if the world ever discovers what is being stuck into its arm." [2]   Judging from the past the world probably won't find out, but will go on selecting candidates who have been sold to them purely on propaganda.

Some who know the tricks claim that through skillful propaganda they can lead the people to any line of action.   One of our politicians who has had an opportunity to see many a candidate and policy slipped over to the people through insidious propaganda, gives the following satirical illustration of the power of propaganda:

If the Toothbrush Holder Manufacturers' Organization wanted to start a Brush-Em-Thrice-a-Day-from-Left-to-Right movement and have it put into platforms and came to me to take the job on a contingency fee, I would

[1] *The Washington Post*, September 14, 1928.
[2] *Behind the Scenes in Politics*, Anonymous, E. P. Dutton & Company.

do it. I'd begin by the phrase "Cleanliness is next to Godliness." I'd get a few preachers. I'd have college presidents on my honorary committee. I'd make life insurance companies buy space for me. I'd have movie close-ups showing a tooth in various stages, after having been brushed in the wrong direction. I'd defy an opposition Congressman to open his mouth. He wouldn't dare because the public would look in. A personal liberty league might challenge me. If they did I'd say they were bought up by the National Dentists Union because of the fear that my movement would spoil the filling and pulling business. I'd accuse them. I'd say that they were against the Church and religion and progress. I'd have the legislation passed. If people did not brush their teeth from left to right I'd have the law on them. They'd be my own personal slaves. I'd see 'em brushing their teeth and I'd say: "I made 'em do that! Me! I'm a benefactor! I am! I'm a benevolent, I am! and I've had my way and made 'em do it whether they wanted to or not! I've got their conscience and free-will. I'm a lover of mankind. My name is in the papers. I'm a crusader. I'm a divine agent." That's what I'd be able to say, all because of goose-stuffing.[1]

So powerful is political propaganda when skillfully manipulated that the mass of voters can be made to believe one thing to-day, a quite different thing next week, and its opposite a month hence. The public elected a president on the plea that "He Kept Us Out of War"; then they immediately were won over to the belief that we must "fight to save democracy." And while we were fighting to save democracy we were led to undergo many sacrifices and to buy many undesirable kinds of food to "win the war." By skillful propaganda the idea was first sold to the masses that we were "too proud to fight"; a later group of propaganda built up the idea of "peace without victory"; and in the end we had a flood of propaganda preparing the people for "force without limit."

Propaganda is nothing but advertising. Martin [2] says:

We should always look for what the propagandist has to sell and should not be taken in by his big words. Professions of faith in ideals on the part of propagandists are only screens which hide their real intent. If you can get a number of people to agree to anything, true or false, you may turn that belief into a platitude, an abstraction, treat it as something final, something to be accepted uncritically. Then identify it with your own

---

[1] *Behind the Scenes in Politics*, Anonymous, E. P. Dutton & Company.
[2] Martin, Everett Dean: *Psychology* (W. W. Norton & Co., Inc., New York, 1924), 201.

ulterior purpose, smear it all about your purpose like the sugar coating about a dose of quinine, and in swallowing the sugar men will swallow your quinine also.

3. Campaigning by the candidate. Although the candidate's friends may assist him and propaganda be skillfully spread in his behalf, his political fight cannot attain the maximum success unless he can add the personal touch to the campaign. This is best achieved through the speaking-tour by the candidate. Since the earliest political history, speaking has been an important method of winning the people.

Drawing the crowd is the first step toward a successful campaign meeting. To get the crowd one must depend upon advertising. The candidate usually starts out on a speaking-tour with a definite schedule sent ahead several weeks. The dates and times of speaking are chosen with a view to getting the biggest crowd most easily. Small towns are invariably addressed in open-air meetings on Saturday when everybody is in town anyway. Announcements of the meeting are posted in conspicuous places; the meeting is announced through the churches, clubs, and labor unions. Careful management of the ticket distribution often swells the crowd. A sense of personal privilege given to those who can give the tickets to their friends makes them campaign workers for the candidate. Thirty thousand tickets "not good after 8 P.M.," printed for a 5000-seating-capacity hall emphasizes the importance of the meeting. One of the best recommendations for the candidate is an "angry" mob attempting to get in a packed house.

Finally, if all the efforts at drawing a crowd have failed, the campaign speaker, especially in an outdoor meeting, should go ahead with a handful, resting on the assurance that others will stop to see what is going on. Crowds are like snowballs and tend to increase with manipulation. It doesn't take long for a crowd of five to attract a crowd of five hundred.

In a big campaign meeting there are many details to be managed. One of the most important of these, from the standpoint of winning the approval, is the management of platform seats. Every big meeting has a platform audience. If necessary, to include all those who deserve platform seats and who must have them for fear of losing a vote, the candidate must make his platform a large part of his audience. The job is so important that one writer on campaigning has urged all candidates to have an official platform seater among his helpers.

Another official which the candidate might include in his list of subordinates is a "grand master of introduction of the great." This man's duty would be to select the man who would do the introducing and make arrangements for the details of the introduction. The job of introducing the candidate requires a skillful man, one who will extol the candidate, but will not steal his thunder, one who realizes that he is not the principal speaker, and one who himself is not so great that he outshines the candidate.

Having thus set the stage, it remains for the candidate to make his appeal. He may do it through the keynote or theme of his speech, he may do it through personal magnetism, or he may do it through convincing argument or subtle suggestion; usually he does it through a combination of all these. In the next section will be discussed some of the types of appeals the candidate makes, and some of the types of activities he engages in to win the people.

Appeals and activities for winning votes. One of the most important questions which arises in campaigning is: How will the candidate treat his opponent? Will he ignore him, will he attack his personal characteristics, will he dwell on the corruption of his opponent's official administration, or will he indirectly drop suggestions as to his opponent's unfitness? Open attack on the opponent is the method often used, and it often fails entirely in its purpose. One of the surest ways to kill off an opponent is to ignore him. Concerning such tactics, a shrewd observer of the 1916 Wilson-Hughes campaign said: "Hughes talked about Wilson, Taft came out and talked about Wilson, Roosevelt came forth and made attacks on Wilson. They were all in a sweat and talked about Wilson and Wilsonism. And now and then in calm pauses Wilson would come out onto the porch at Shadow Lane and talk about Taft and Roosevelt — and Wilson. Nobody talked about Hughes."[1] Consequently Hughes was left in the background, apparently not worthy of attention.

[1] *Behind the Scenes in Politics,* Anonymous, E. P. Dutton & Company.

A campaign based essentially on the corruption of an opposing administration is likely to be lost. Corruption seems to be all right as one campaign cry, but corruption in government is not by itself a winning issue for the party out of power. After too much dogging on the corruption issue the voters are likely to lose their indignation and get tired of the corruption cry. The voters finally arrive at an indifferent attitude and a belief that there is no real party guilt so far as the accused party is concerned, and even if there is, the accusers were in it too, or would have been if they had had the chance. As an example, notice the flattening out of the corruption charges against the Republicans in the Davis-Coolidge campaign, although the facts show that the charges had a real foundation.

The candidate must be careful in the promises which he makes. Promises are an accepted means of appeal to a constantly dissatisfied voting public. The skillful candidate, however, protects himself by making his promises general. He promises a high tariff, but not a twenty per cent tariff on corn, or he promises to increase the legal alcoholic content of our beverages.

Another appeal which the campaigner not infrequently makes is the group appeal. He tries to win over, and have vote as a group, all the labor voters, all the women voters, etc. If skillfully manipulated, this is good strategy; but if the candidate overworks it, the voters become sick of being branded "labor voters," or "women voters" and support his opponent for spite.

In recent times, candidates have used a rather unique type of appeal in the form of putting themselves on the level of the common voters. The hope has been that this will create a "one-of-the-people" atmosphere. The ridiculousness and danger of such appeals is brought out very well in the following quotation from Arthur Corning White: [1]

In this year of our Lord a political candidate to secure general approbation at the polls must stump the country in shirtsleeves and suspenders. He must do this literally. Which is unfortunate. He must also do it figuratively. Which is worse than unfortunate. For it is fatal!

[1] White, Arthur Corning: "Politics and Suspenders," *Forum Magazine*, January, 1925.

The increasingly recurrent pictures in the popular press are what disturb me. Mr. Calvin Coolidge, in shirtsleeves and suspenders, driving a mowing machine on the old New England farm. Memorials of the late Warren G. Harding, in shirtsleeves and suspenders, setting up type in the pressroom of the *Marion Star*. Senator Magnus Johnson, in shirtsleeves and suspenders, his copious buttocks precariously balancing on a three-legged milking stool in his own cow barn, a heap of manure in the background for local flavor and the true Tolstoyan naturalistic touch. And that egregious photograph of Mayor John H. Hylan's dear old mother hanging out the family wash in her Brooklyn back yard. As individual instances, all these are harmless enough, but considered together and augmented by the hundreds of similar pictures in general circulation, they are significant. To me they suggest the beginning of the end of the United States Constitution as a going concern.

Just which of the various campaign methods and types of appeal discussed will be adopted by a particular candidate will depend upon the candidate himself, upon his constituency, and upon the place in which he must campaign. Most candidates make use of all of them at one time or other.

4. **The election.** The day of election is a busy one for the politician and his allies. The indifferent voters must be brought to the polls and the tickets for the ignorant voters prepared. Thousands of dollars are spent in every election to furnish free transportation to voters, and literally millions are spent in every big election for "watchers" at the polls. These "watchers" are supposed to assist ignorant voters in marking their tickets in the proper way and to perform other such functions. As a matter of fact, paying "watchers" is generally only a legalized method of buying the votes and influence of certain unscrupulous individuals.

Ballot-stuffing is another device occasionally employed to win an election. This consists in getting into the ballot box more votes than are legitimately cast. This is frequently done by voting in the name of some qualified voter who has no intentions of voting, and has no idea that others are voting in his name. In a few instances votes may be cast under names of people long since dead. In a recent election in Pennsylvania, votes were cast under the name of William Penn.

In machine politics a common method of fraud is to fail to count the votes cast for the opposition. This method was in evidence in some of the questionable elections recently investigated by the committee from the United States Senate. In some instances three fourths of the votes cast for a candidate in a given ward are not counted in the final returns.

5. "Nursing the constituency." When the politician is elected to office his job of playing politics has just begun. If he wishes to retain the favor of his constituents, these constituents must be nursed along in various ways. Take, for example, some of the methods used by United States Congressmen to hold the favor of their constituents. Free garden seeds are sent to the farmers. Disabled or hypochondriacal veterans who want more compensation must be cared for. Job-seekers of various types must be appeased, and their disgruntled voices hushed. When an influential constituent comes to Washington, he must be entertained. Moreover, the people back home must be constantly remembered and properly impressed with what their representative is doing for them. His wordy speeches are printed by the government and sent to his many constituents in a government envelope free of postage. His secretary must also see that the press back home is supplied with the proper news.

Nor is the congressman oblivious to the happenings back home. When he learns that a new school or church is to be built in his district, he writes and compliments the trustees on their undertaking, and he may even send his check. When he learns of a death in an influential family, he sends his condolence. If a new baby is born, the parents should receive a letter of congratulation from their congressman. In short, the successful politician must never miss an opportunity to make a friend or to prevent an enemy.

CHAPTER XX
PSYCHOLOGY AND EDUCATION
The art of education depends on the science of psychology.

FROM the earliest times educational theory and method have depended upon the current theories of the way the mind works. When the current psychological belief maintains that nature is inherently wrong, it is followed by the tyrannical educational system of the Puritans; but when a preponderance of psychological opinion holds that "nature is right," we see the educational theory and practice swerve to the Rousseau *laissez-faire* system. When people believed that the mind was divided into various compartments or faculties, disciplinary education to train the faculties was provided. But when experiments showed that the so-called faculties were nothing more than gratuitous assumptions, a great change in educational theories, content, and methods was brought about. And so, in various ways, as scientific experiment has demonstrated the fallacy of some pet conception of mental behavior, our educational process has experienced a corresponding change as the result thereof.

In a single chapter it is impossible to discuss the many points of contact and interdependency of education and psychology. We must be content with the consideration of a few of the major contributions of psychology to education. We shall accordingly consider the relation of psychology to I. The curriculum; II. The learning process; III. The measurement of pupils; IV. The measurement of teachers.

I. THE RELATION OF PSYCHOLOGY TO THE CURRICULUM

The content of the curriculum as well as teaching methods have changed with the recent progress in psychology. A large part of the change both in curriculum and methods has been brought about by change in the attitude toward the doctrine of the "transfer of training." At an early period education had a unit purpose, which was "training the mind," "molding character," or "giving culture." At that time the mind itself was thought of as a unit. A few years later the mind was analyzed into its component parts, the "faculties" of memory, reason, and judgment; then faculty psychology held the center of the stage. Education was directed toward developing the different "faculties" of the mind; and the chief emphasis was placed upon the classical languages, mathematics, and logic as disciplinary subjects to train the "faculties." The "faculties" of memory and reason were held to be of particular importance. Training in disciplinary subjects was considered valuable because it was thought that training in the activities involved would give a general power or ability which would be useful and available in any situation, even in those entirely unrelated to the original activity. For example, it was thought that learning to remember Latin declensions would increase one's ability to remember names and faces. This was the doctrine of "transfer of training," which dominated education for many years and the influence of which has not yet wholly died out in our schools.

The experiments of Thorndike, Woodworth, and various other investigators demonstrated the fallacy in regard to the transfer of training. It was then learned that instead of developing a general mental power applicable in any subject, practice in one activity is of value in another only if there are identical elements in the two subjects. Knowledge of Latin makes it easier to learn Greek, not because of any general transfer of knowledge, but because Latin and Greek have certain elements in common. There is a transfer of training only in identical elements, such as, habits of learning the vocabulary of a foreign language, and knowledge of grammar and sentence structure.

Following the discovery of the fallacy of the disciplinary conception of education came a still greater threat of the demolition of long-cherished theories. This threat was contained in the statement that the difference between various studies, ranging from arithmetic to sewing and stenography, in ability to bring about the power to think, was "almost negligible." This led logically to the point of view that since any school subject trains the mind, the criterion of a valuable subject in the curriculum is the practical value it will be to the student.

After a very extensive experimental study of the relative disciplinary values of the various high-school subjects, Thorndike says: [1]

By any reasonable interpretation of the results, the intellectual values of studies should be determined largely by the special information, habits, interests, attitudes, and ideals which they demonstrably produce. The expectation of any large differences in general improvement of the mind from one study rather than another seems doomed to disappointment. The chief reason why good thinkers seem superficially to have been made such by having taken certain school studies, is that good thinkers have taken such studies, becoming better by the inherent tendency of the good to gain more than the poor from any study. When the good thinkers studied Greek and Latin, these studies seemed to make good thinkers. Now that the good thinkers study Physics and Trigonometry, these seem to make good thinkers. If the abler pupils should all study Physical Education and Dramatic Art, these subjects would seem to make good thinkers. These were, indeed, a large fraction of the program of studies for the best thinkers the world has produced, the Athenian Greeks.

The present tendency in education is to enable the student to acquire habits, attitudes, knowledge, and skills which will be of use to him in life. The curriculum is growing steadily more practical. The biological sciences, social sciences, and manual arts are taking the place of higher mathematics and the classical languages. The latter are still retained in the curriculum of many schools, but their defenders are attempting to justify them on some other basis than their disciplinary value. If the signs of the time are correctly interpreted, twenty years from now such subjects as typewriting, physiology, psychology, and household science will be found in the school curriculum with as much constancy as Latin and Greek were found twenty years ago.

II. THE LEARNING PROCESS

It is recognized that all learning is conditioned by the original make-up of the organism, or, as Cattell put it: "What a man can do is determined by heredity, what he will do is determined by circumstances." It is the function of education to bring such cir-

---

[1] Thorndike, E. L.: "Mental Discipline in High School Subjects," *Journal of Educational Psychology*, xv, 1 and 2 (January and February, 1924), 1–22, 83–89.

cumstances to bear on the original nature of the individual as to produce in him the changes requisite for life in a civilized society. In discussing this section, we shall consider: 1. The nature of animal learning; 2. Laws of learning; 3. Rate of learning and forgetting.

1. **The nature of animal learning.**   How circumstances would produce certain changes in the individual, whether it be a man or lower animal, is illustrated in the following experiments in animal learning, which were conducted by the writer.[1]

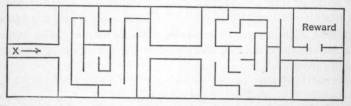

FIGURE 43. MAZE USED TO MEASURE THE LEARNING ABILITY OF RATS

a. *Teaching rats to find their way through a complicated maze.* The rats were placed at "X" in a maze the floor plan of which is indicated in Figure 43.   In the compartment marked "reward" was placed the food or the female while trying the first two parts of the experiment; when working on the third section of this experiment, the "reward" box was the only part of the maze which did not contain ice.   Fifteen rats were used, five for each part of the experiment.   They were about the same age and special care was taken to get the groups as similar as possible.

The five animals in the first group were kept without food for 48 hours and then placed in the maze one at a time.   The time required to go from "X" to the food and the number of errors were recorded for each.   The average time taken by the five in this group to find the food on the first trial was 38 minutes with 29 errors.   They were permitted to eat for fifteen minutes and were then removed from the maze.   They were given another trial the next day.   This time they threaded the maze in 21 minutes with only 17 errors.   They were again permitted to eat for fifteen min-

[1] Moss, F. A.: "A Study of Animal Drives," *Journal of Experimental Psychology.* June, 1924.

utes and removed. This procedure was repeated for the next three days. The average time for the rats on the third, fourth, and fifth trials was 3 minutes, 50 seconds and the average number of errors was 7.

In the second part of the experiment in which the sex stimulus was used, five males were placed in the cage one at a time and a female in heat was placed in the "reward" box. The time and errors were recorded as in the first part. When the male reached the reward box, he was left in it with the female for 15 minutes. The average time of the first trial for the rats to find the reward box was 49 minutes with 31 errors. On the second trial the average time was 22 minutes, 14 seconds, with 19 errors. The average time for the third, fourth, and fifth trials was 3 minutes, 5 seconds, with 8 errors.

In the third part of the experiment in which punishment was used as the incentive, the floor of all parts of the maze except that of the "reward" box was covered with crushed ice. The only way the rats could escape from the cold was to go to the reward box. The average time on the first trial was 36 minutes with 29 errors. On the second trial, the average time was 28 minutes with 18 errors. The average time for the third, fourth, and fifth trials was 5 minutes and 20 seconds with 12 errors.

The results of the three parts of the experiment are combined in the following table:

TIME TABLE

TRIAL	FOOD	SEX	PUNISHMENT
1st	38 min.	49 min.	36 min.
2nd	21 min.	22 min. 14 sec.	28 min.
3, 4, 5	3 min. 50 sec.	3 min. 5 sec.	5 min. 20 sec.

ERRORS TABLE

TRIAL	FOOD	SEX	PUNISHMENT
1st	29	31	29
2nd	17	19	18
3, 4, 5	7	8	12

Thirty days later these tests were repeated to measure the permanency of learning. Each rat was given two trials. The average results of these two trials are shown in the following table:

	[Food	Sex	Punishment
Average Time	6 min. 40 sec.	5 min. 12 sec.	10 min. 18 sec.
Average Errors	16	13	17

b. Teaching rats not to eat cheese. In one corner of a rat cage was placed a block of cheese three inches long and one inch in width and thickness. The approach to the cheese was so guarded by brass plates that every time the rat tried to nibble the cheese, he got an electric shock of 60 volts.

In this experiment five rats were used. The rats were kept supplied with a liberal amount of food, other than cheese, so that they would not become very hungry. The animals were left in the cage with the cheese thus protected for a week. When the protecting electrical apparatus was removed, none of the animals disturbed the cheese, although it was left in the cage unprotected for a week. These results show that by punishment we can build up in an animal a permanent inhibition of a desire for a particular kind of food.

The different experiments which have just been described illustrate very well the characteristics of the learning process. It may be noted that learning proceeds by a reduction in the time required and in the number of errors made in the thing learned. The tables also indicate, as is characteristic of practically all learning, that improvement takes place more rapidly at the beginning of the learning period than at later stages. In most instances the improvement from the first to the second trial is almost as great as the improvement from the second trial all the way through the fifth. One other factor should be noticed — that rate of improvement bears some relationship to the incentive used.

2. The laws of learning. In the experiments described above, the three laws of learning as first stated by Thorndike are illustrated. These laws are known as the laws of Readiness, Exercise, and Effect.

a. The law of readiness. Thorndike states the law of readiness as follows: [1] *"When a conduction unit is ready to conduct, conduction by it is satisfying, nothing being done to alter its action; for a conduction unit ready to conduct not to conduct is annoying, and provokes whatever responses nature provides in connection with that particular annoying lack; and when a conduction unit unready for conduction is forced to conduct, conduction by it is annoying."* Sandiford [2] states the law more briefly as follows: "When a bond is ready to act, to act gives satisfaction, and not to act gives annoyance. When a bond which is not ready to act is made to act, annoyance is caused." The law of readiness may be illustrated from the above experiment as follows: Having been deprived of food for 48 hours, the rats were hungry when placed in the maze. Their hunger produced in them a tendency toward activity which resulted in their learning the maze. In other words their hunger produced in their neurones a state especially susceptible to learning. Had the rats not been hungry, they would in all probability have lain down near the X end of the maze, and made no effort to find the food at the other end of the maze, for their neurones would not have been "ready" to act. Thus it is seen that the law of readiness depends on the physiological condition of the animal. With one physiological condition the neurones are ready to act, but with a different physiological condition the neurones are unready to act.

b. The law of exercise. The law of exercise consists of two parts: the laws of use and disuse. According to the law of use, the more times a given response is made to a certain situation, the stronger the connection becomes between that situation and the response, and the more likely is the response to be made when the situation arises again. The law of disuse holds that the longer the period of time which elapses after the making of a response to a given situation, the weaker the connection between the situation and response becomes. In other words, the thing becomes partially forgotten.

The tables given above for maze-learning by rats illustrate this law. The law of use is illustrated by the tables of time and error

[1] Thorndike, Edward L.: *The Original Nature of Man,* Teachers College, Columbia University, New York (1924), 128.

[2] Sandiford, Peter: *Educational Psychology,* Longmans Green and Company (1928), 201.

over five trials. It will be noticed that so long as the animal received practice each day in the maze, both his time for making the trip from the entrance to the food and the number of errors steadily decreased. The law of disuse is illustrated by the table for time and errors after 30 days. After a lapse of 30 days with no practice, or after 30 days disuse of the function learned, the time required for the rat to make the trip had almost doubled, and the number of errors in some instances had more than doubled.

c. The law of effect. The law of effect as stated by Thorndike is: *"When a modifiable connection between a situation and a response is made and is accompanied or followed by a satisfying state of affairs, that connection's strength is increased; when made and accompanied by an annoying state of affairs, its strength is decreased."* An annoying state of affairs is one which the individual attempts to avoid. A satisfying state of affairs is one which the individual attempts to prolong, and which he does nothing to avoid. If an action is followed by some external reward, or is in itself satisfying, the connection between that situation and response is strengthened, and the act is likely to be performed again if the situation arises. If, however, the act is followed by punishment, the connection between the situation and that response is weakened, and that response is not likely to follow the same situation again. The principle of the law of effect is being used when the reward of food or sex satisfaction is introduced in the maze-learning of rats. The law of effect, in its negative aspect, is clearly demonstrated in the experiment with the electric plates and the cheese, for every time the rat attempted to nibble the cheese, he got a shock, and the effects of these shocks were such that in the end the natural tendency of the rat to respond to the situation — the presence of cheese — by nibbling the cheese, was broken down.

d. The law of motives. In addition to the three laws stated by Thorndike, a fourth law could be included which may be stated as follows: The motive force of all learning is generated either directly or indirectly, by certain fundamental animal drives, and the stronger the drive the faster will be the learning. This is illustrated in the above experiments by the things which caused the animals to learn the maze. In one instance it was the hunger drive that produced the seeking behavior, another time the sex drive was utilized, and in a third instance the activity was produced by the animal's drive to escape punishment.

In human learning, particularly, a more immediate type of driving force consciously applied may stimulate learning or improvement. Certain factors entering into motivation have been measured. Ross [1] has traced the influence upon motivation during learning when the learner knew his progress and the influence when he knew very little or nothing about his progress. The individuals in one section were told nothing of their progress from day to day. Those in another section were given partial information, each day they were told that they were doing good, poor, or average, but they were not permitted to see their records. Those in the third section were given complete information, each person being shown his paper from the preceding practice period with corrections and scores indicated thereon, and a frequency table of results for that section was placed on the board. Each student of this section was urged to watch his relative and absolute progress from day to day and to make a learning curve.

Ross summarizes his investigations as follows: "All sections started off equal, . . . and for the second practice period they were still practically identical. After that the effect of the novelty wore off and the sections knowing their progress forged steadily ahead of the other two, but the section with no information made in general the poorest record of all."

The laws of learning described above operate in every learning process. They hold equally as well with the human as with the rat. The use of rewards and punishments as incentives and deterrents is made daily by teachers in the schools of to-day.

3. Rate of learning and forgetting. In learning any one thing it is found that the rate of improvement of various individuals tends to approximate certain typical learning curves for the specific problem to be learned. By studying the improvement of a number of individuals in typewriting, it is possible to establish certain typical curves of learning by reference to which we can predict

[1] Ross, Clay Campbell: "The Psychology of Motivation," *Industrial Psychology,* vol. III, 8 (August, 1928), 347.

with a fair degree of accuracy the improvement of any individual with a given number of hours of practice. The learning curve tends to assume the same general shape in all cases in learning any one particular thing, but the height which the curve reaches, and the speed of ascent will be influenced by such individual characteristics as differences in intelligence and in the strength of the motivating force.

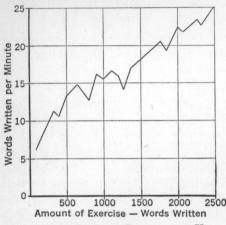

FIGURE 44. CURVE OF LEARNING TO USE A TYPEWRITER

From the curve shown in Figure 44 it is obvious that the amount of an individual's improvement fluctuates from time to time. In the first quarter of the curve there is a rapid rise. The rate of improvement slows up in the second quarter, and in the last half of the curve there is another rise in the rate of improvement. But even within a quarter the rate of improvement is not even, but shows various fluctuations.

Closely related to the rate of learning is the rate of forgetting. The rate of forgetting depends very largely upon the kind of material and consequently few generalizations can be made that apply to all kinds of material. Various investigators agree, however, that forgetting is very rapid at first, and that the rate of forgetting decreases as time goes on. This is shown in Figure 45.

In both cases from forty to fifty per cent was forgotten during the first day, followed by a marked slowing up in the rate of forgetting thereafter. If these curves represent the true state of affairs, ten hours of cramming just before an examination may be expected to yield better results than fifteen hours of study spread out over the course, but for permanency, cramming is a poor method. Knowledge shown on an examination for which a student has crammed is reproduced at too early a point on the forgetting curve. At the early point very little of the original learning has been forgotten, but a few hours or days later a large percentage will be forgotten.

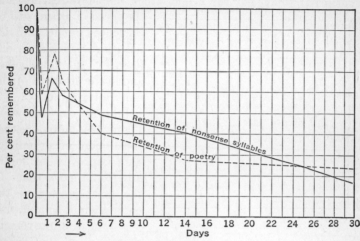

FIGURE 45. FORGETTING CURVES

A large number of very excellent investigations have been made into the factors influencing the rate and permanency of learning, but space will permit only a few brief statements summarizing the conclusions of these investigations.

1. The stronger the motive for learning the faster will be the learning process.
2. The less the number of habits formed simultaneously the faster will any given habit be learned.
3. Within certain limits, the less the frequency of practice, the more efficient is each practice period.
4. Motor habits are retained more easily than are verbal habits.
5. Meaningful material, like prose or poetry, is retained more easily than such meaningless material as nonsense syllables.
6. The rate of forgetting depends on the degree to which the material has been overlearned. Overlearning retards forgetting.
7. In general, those who learn fastest forget most slowly.
8. Pleasant experiences tend to be remembered longer than unpleasant ones.
9. In verbal habits the rate of forgetting is very fast at first, and becomes slower with time.

III. THE MEASUREMENT OF PUPILS

Nowhere are individual differences of greater importance than in the field of education, and nowhere has less provision been made for them than in this field. Until recent years, teachers totally disregarding the incontestable evidence to the contrary, have accepted the theory that all pupils are essentially equal in aptitudes and ability and have planned their work and taught their classes accordingly. It is true that in the olden days, Plato recognized the great variation in ability of different people, and even went so far as to organize his ideal republic around these individual differences. But down through the ages this part of Plato's teaching was overlooked, and education came to be based on metaphysics and impractical theories. So long as this medieval basis existed and education was controlled by impractical theorists, little or no provision was made for individual differences, but with the application of scientific methods in education, this condition is beginning to be remedied.

According to Cubberley, in the past, education was somewhat like "luck farming where the farmer looked at the moon, guessed at the weather, put in his crop and prayed to the Lord to pull him through another season." But in education as in farming, guessing is yielding place to measuring, for without measurement all opinions are mere guesses and all decisions unwarranted assumptions. It is the recognition of this fact and the desire to reduce education to a more scientific basis that has made the recent wave of objective tests so popular with educators.

Psychologists have contributed three types of objective measuring devices which are being generally adopted in the field of education. We shall consider them in the order of their development: 1. Intelligence tests; 2. Tests for special aptitudes; 3. Objective achievement tests.

1. **Intelligence tests.** Intelligence tests found one of their first uses in the field of education. Teachers have realized that in an ordinary school class the pupils differ as much in their intellectual ability as they do in their physical appearance. In the average schoolroom there are some whose intelligence is sufficiently high that they can learn four or five times as quickly as others in the

same room.   There are others who grasp a problem with one explanation; whereas the same problem must be explained four or five times to others.   This inequality of ability produced a condition ripe for the use of intelligence tests.   In Chapter XII several types of intelligence tests are described and we shall at this point consider only some of the more common uses that are being made of these tests in the field of education.

(a) *Admission.*   In recent years many of the privately endowed colleges and universities have begun using intelligence tests as a part of the regular entrance machinery.   And a number of state institutions, while barring none from admission as a result of low scores on intelligence, have established the precedent of giving all freshmen an intelligence test before they enter the institution, for they find the test data useful in so many administrative problems. The universities with the most extensive testing programs and with the longest programs in point of age are most enthusiastic about the value of the test.   Since 1919 both Columbia and Ohio State University have required tests of all new students.   During this time there have been over twenty-four thousand students tested in these two universities and for that reason their administration officers are in a position to know the real value of the tests.   When asked his opinion of the tests, Dean Hawkes of Columbia said, "Indispensable."   And when asked whether they would recommend the use of tests to other universities, without a single qualification, the officials at Ohio State replied, "Certainly."

Owing to the fact that in the public elementary and high schools attendance is not restricted but is usually compulsory, intelligence tests to determine whether or not a person should be admitted to one of these schools have not been very extensively used.   It is only a few of the more exclusive private secondary and elementary schools that have begun using tests for the purpose of admission.

(b) *Vocational guidance.*   In addition to the primary use of tests to determine the intellectual level of the students who apply for admission, vocational counselors and student advisors are beginning to make use of the test results in giving vocational guidance to the students, and assisting them in arranging courses to this end. In case a student is found low in abstract intelligence, he is advised against undertaking such courses as civil engineering or medicine. And in case he is low on social intelligence he is not advised to select courses leading to a career where the ability to get along with others is of major importance. Tests have many other uses in connection with vocational guidance, but the above cases will serve as an illustration.

(c) *Sectioning of classes.* In many of the larger institutions there are as many as four or five hundred students who take the same subject. For the purpose of teaching, the students are grouped into ten or twelve sections. A number of institutions have found it advisable to arrange these sections on the basis of the intelligence scores made by the students. Thus the group taught in the same class is homogeneous as to native ability and the instructor can develop his methods and make his assignments accordingly. Likewise in the large elementary schools where there are several classes of the same grade, the pupils of approximately equal intelligence are taught in the same class.

(d) *Amount of work.* Until recent years it was customary to require all students to spend the same amount of time, usually four years, at the university before being granted the A.B. degree. With the development of the present system whereby the degree is granted for the completion, with a standard degree of efficiency, of a specified amount of work, it is found that the more intelligent students can finish in three years, whereas the less intelligent ones may take five or six. Many of the college administrators are using the test results as a basis for granting or refusing requests of students to take more than the standard number of hours of work. Intelligence tests are also finding a limited use in some secondary schools in determining the amount of work students shall carry.

(e) *Problems of scholarship and discipline.* In the elementary and secondary schools intelligence tests are often used to determine whether a pupil shall be promoted or demoted. It sometimes happens that pupils who are doing unsatisfactory work and are a source of trouble and annoyance to the teacher, are to be accounted for by the fact that they are, in mental age, two or three years ahead of the pupils in their grade. By promoting these people to a grade where the work is in keeping with their ability and where increased interest in the work replaces trouble-making, it is found that both the problem of scholarship and that of discipline are solved.

In every large university, and in many of the secondary schools, students are occasionally found whose intelligence is high but who are failing in their work. But the vast majority of those who fail are found to be low in intelligence. If the school official whose duty it is to deal with these students has the data before him to show which are failing from lack of brains and which from lack of effort, he can deal much more effectively with the specific needs of the individual student. The dull student should be encouraged but not dealt with very severely; while the bright student should be told in no uncertain terms to "get to work."

2. Tests for special aptitudes. Recent experiments are indicating that instead of having a general faculty of intelligence, one has a number of special abilities, which are usually correlated. People are very unequal in these abilities and the fact that a man rates very high in one ability does not necessarily mean that he will rate high in other lines. Thorndike recognizes three types of intelligence. The first of these is general or abstract intelligence, which indicates one's ability to do school work and to think in terms of abstract symbols. This is what the average person means when he speaks of the ability measured by intelligence tests. Mechanical intelligence, or ability to see, and understand things in the proper mechanical relationships is a second type of intelligence. A third type is social intelligence, or ability to deal with people.

An individual may have high abstract intelligence and relatively low mechanical or social intelligence; or he may be high in any one of these and low in the other two. The failure of one's social intelligence to develop equally with his abstract intelligence accounts for the fact that so many men who lead their classes in college fail to make a success in later life. Success in life in most vocations depends more on social intelligence than on abstract intelligence.

Standardized tests are also being developed for measuring even more specialized abilities than those described above. An all-round estimate of an individual should include not only measures of the three types of intelligence, and more general aptitudes, but also of the various specific aptitudes or talents. Some have unusually high musical ability, some have high artistic and dramatic ability, while others are very deficient in these qualities. The school needs tests to measure all these abilities, so that it may know not only how far each child is retarded but just what each child can do best. A more complete discussion of the special ability tests is given in Chapter XII.

3. **Objective achievement tests.** For many years grades or teachers' marks have been considered the measure of student efficiency. All such problems in the management of a school as credit, failure, promotion, retardation, elimination, graduation, honors, recommendations for positions and indeed, the entire scholastic machinery of a school have been determined in no small part by the assignment of marks by the teachers. Since such importance is attached to the grades received, it is only right that the highest amount of accuracy and validity should be secured in assigning these grades.

That the grades commonly given by teachers are in general very unreliable is brought out in a number of studies. Starch and Elliott [1] had 114 teachers of mathematics, in as many high schools, rate a final examination paper in geometry. The variations in the grades assigned are shown in Figure 46.

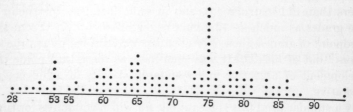

FIGURE 46. DISTRIBUTION OF MARKS ASSIGNED BY 114 MATHEMATICS TEACHERS TO A FINAL EXAMINATION PAPER IN GEOMETRY
(After Starch and Elliott.)

The differences in rating are astounding, and run all the way from 28 to 92 on the geometry paper. From such investigations as this, we are forced to the conclusion that teachers differ widely in

[1] Starch, D., and Elliott, E. C.: "The Reliability of Grading Work in Mathematics," *School Review*, 21 (1913), 254.

evaluating the same pieces of work in terms of the ordinary percentage scale. In a subsequent investigation Starch [1] had ten final examination papers in freshman English at the University of Wisconsin graded by ten instructors of English. The grades assigned these papers are shown in the following table:

MARKS ASSIGNED BY TEN INSTRUCTORS TO TEN FINAL EXAMINATION
PAPERS IN ENGLISH

PA-PERS	INSTRUCTORS										Average	Mean of Var.	Coefficient Variability
	1	2	3	4	5	6	7	8	9	10			
1	85	86	88	85	75	80	88	87	85	87	84.6	2.8	.004
2	77	80	87	80	62	82	82	87	85	87	80.0	4.6	.057
3	74	78	78	75	69	84	91	83	79	80	79.1	4.4	.056
4	65	65	62	20	26	60	55	68	55	50	52.6	2.3	.233
5	68	83	78	82	64	88	85	86	78	80	79.1	5.7	.070
6	94	87	93	87	83	77	89	88	88	89	87.5	3.2	.036
7	88	90	95	87	79	85	96	91	87	89	88.7	2.6	.029
8	80	84	73	79	72	83	85	91	77	76	80.0	4.6	.058
9	70	70	68	50	44	65	75	81	79	79	68.1	9.1	.118
10	93	92	85	92	81	83	92	89	84	85	87.6	4.0	.045
AVERAGE	79.4	81.4	79.8	73.7	65.5	78.7	83.8	85.1	79.7	80.2	78.7	5.3	.074

This table shows that in the same department of a university the gradings of instructors show wide discrepancies. Instructor 5, for example, gave grades on an average 20 points lower on the same papers than did instructor 8, and in some instances instructor 5 gave grades as much as 42 points below instructor 8. From the standpoint of grades, those whose papers were graded by instructor 5 were "out of luck." It was such facts as these that made the development of objective and standardized tests of achievement imperative.

By a standardized test is meant one for which standards for time of giving and standards for attainment for the various groups have been established by giving the test to a sufficient number of cases. In order to be capable of standardization a test must be purely objective, yielding the same result, regardless of who gives it, where it is given, or who corrects it. With the essay type of examination this is impossible. To answer this need there has been a development of short-answer examinations where definite an-

[1] Starch, D.: "Reliability and Distribution of Grades," *Science*, 38 (1913), 630.

swers which are either right or wrong have replaced long indefinite discussions. The relative merits of the two types of examinations are indicated by results obtained in the department of pathology at the George Washington University Medical School.

In order to compare the relative efficiency of the short-answer and the essay type of examination both types were subjected to the following test by the professors of pathology in the George Washington University Medical School. As a part of the final examination in pathology the students were given a three-hour examination consisting of ten questions in the traditional " discuss " form. They were also given a practical examination consisting of one hour and a half in the diagnosis of pathological tissues with the aid of a microscope. A short-answer examination which required one hour and a half to administer was also given.

It is generally recognized that the best criterion of an individual's knowledge of pathology is his ability to diagnose correctly pathological conditions in tissues. It follows, therefore, that the type of written examination that correlates most closely with the practical test in diagnosing tissues should be considered the most reliable kind of examination. Correlations were made between the grades on the three-hour free answer "discuss" examination and the scores in the practical test. The correlation secured was .24. A correlation was next run between the scores on the short-answer test and those on the practical test and in this case a correlation of .74 was secured. Taken at their face value, these correlations indicate beyond question that as an instrument for determining an individual's knowledge, the short-answer test yields much more reliable results than those obtained by the use of the traditional examination which required twice as long to give.

The reason for this may not be immediately apparent, but analysis indicates that the following are important in explaining the difference: 1. The short-answer test contained over two hundred items, and thus permitted a much wider sampling of the students' information than did the discussion type of examination which contained only ten questions. 2. The short-answer examination eliminated all extraneous factors such as handwriting, spelling, and grammatical errors which either consciously or unconsciously influenced those who rated the "discuss" papers. 3. The short-answer questions were more definite in their requirements than were the "essay" questions. In any question beginning with "discuss," difficulty is encountered in telling how much discussion is wanted, and this difficulty is avoided in the short-answer tests. 4. In the short-answer examinations several different types of tests were included, thus calling for a larger variety of mental operations than was the case in the "discuss" type of examination.

SCORE	4TH GRADE	5TH GRADE	6TH GRADE	7TH GRADE	
125–129			II	‖‖‖	
120–124		I	II	‖‖‖ III	
115–119			II	‖‖‖ ‖‖‖ I	
110–114	I	I	‖‖‖	‖‖‖ ‖‖‖ ‖‖‖	8TH GRADE STANDARD
105–109	‖‖‖	‖‖‖	‖‖‖ ‖‖‖ ‖‖‖ ‖‖‖ IIII	‖‖‖ ‖‖‖ ‖‖‖ ‖‖‖ ‖‖‖	7TH GRADE STANDARD
100–104		‖‖‖ ‖‖‖ III	‖‖‖ ‖‖‖ ‖‖‖ ‖‖‖ ‖‖‖ ‖‖‖	‖‖‖ ‖‖‖ ‖‖‖ ‖‖‖ ‖‖‖ II	
95– 99	IIII	‖‖‖ ‖‖‖ IIII	‖‖‖ ‖‖‖ ‖‖‖ ‖‖‖ ‖‖‖ II	‖‖‖ ‖‖‖ I	6TH GRADE STANDARD
90– 94	IIII	‖‖‖ ‖‖‖ ‖‖‖ ‖‖‖	‖‖‖ ‖‖‖ ‖‖‖ ‖‖‖ ‖‖‖ I	‖‖‖ ‖‖‖	
85– 89	‖‖‖ ‖‖‖ I	‖‖‖ ‖‖‖ ‖‖‖ ‖‖‖ II	‖‖‖ ‖‖‖ ‖‖‖ II	‖‖‖ III	
80– 84	‖‖‖ ‖‖‖ ‖‖‖ IIII	‖‖‖ ‖‖‖ ‖‖‖ ‖‖‖ ‖‖‖ III	‖‖‖ ‖‖‖ ‖‖‖ II	IIII	5TH GRADE STANDARD
75– 79	‖‖‖ ‖‖‖ ‖‖‖ ‖‖‖ IIII	‖‖‖ ‖‖‖ ‖‖‖	‖‖‖	II	
70– 74	‖‖‖ ‖‖‖ ‖‖‖ II	‖‖‖ ‖‖‖ IIII	III		
65– 69	‖‖‖ ‖‖‖ ‖‖‖ I	‖‖‖ ‖‖‖ I	III		4TH GRADE STANDARD
60– 64	‖‖‖ ‖‖‖ ‖‖‖ ‖‖‖ IIII	IIII			
55– 59	‖‖‖ ‖‖‖ ‖‖‖ I	I			3RD GRADE STANDARD
50– 54	‖‖‖ III	II			
45– 49	III	I	I		
40– 44	III				2ND GRADE STANDARD
35– 39	III				

Figure 47. Distribution of the Composites of the Scores on Three Standardized Educational Tests in the Fourth through Seventh Grade

Short-answer examinations are being developed in the various school subjects from the primary grades through college, and are gradually replacing the traditional type of examination. In addition to the use mentioned above, these tests when standardized are being used in all places where it is desired to compare the work of one grade with another, or the work of one school system with another, or the teaching efficiency of one person with another. They are also being used along with intelligence tests to secure a more homogeneous grouping of students in a grade. Figure 47 shows the scores made by the students in four grades in the same building in the public-school system of Alexandria, Virginia. The scores shown on the chart are composites of scores on a standardized reading test, arithmetic test, and spelling test. The reader should note the very wide spread of achievement in the same grade, and the overlapping of grades. For example, in the sixth grade the range of achievement varies from that represented by the upper quarter of the typical second grade to considerably above the average of the typical eighth grade. In other words, the sixth-grade teacher found it necessary to try to teach at the same time the same subject matter to children of second-grade ability and to children of eighth-grade ability. The inefficiency of such grouping is too obvious to need discussion.

The use of objective achievement tests is showing that a number of factors previously considered to be important are relatively unimportant in influencing the school achievement of pupils. For example, it is generally believed that there is a very close correlation between the amount and regularity of school attendance and the scholastic achievement of pupils. That such is not the case has been demonstrated by Denworth.[1] She studied the effect of length of school attendance upon the achievement of seven hundred pupils in New York City. Their achievement was measured by standard school tests. As a result of her study she concluded that differences in school attendance have a negligible influence on school achievement. Heilman's [2] study of the school records of 828 ten-year-old school children in Denver shows substantially the same thing. Both investigators agree that intelligence is the most important single factor making for achievement.

IV. MEASUREMENT OF TEACHERS

The use of objective measurement is not limited to the students. Teachers show wide differences both in innate teaching aptitude and in the success they have in making their pupils learn. We

[1] Denworth, Katherine M.: "The Effect of Length of School Attendance upon Mental and Educational Ages," *Twenty-Seventh Yearbook of the National Society for the Study of Education*, Public School Publishing Company, Bloomington, Ill., 1928.

[2] Heilman, J. D.: "The Relative Influence upon Educational Achievement of Some Hereditary and Environmental Factors." *Ibid.*

shall consider: 1. Measurement of teaching aptitude; 2. Measurement of teaching efficiency.

1. **Measurement of teaching aptitude.** It not infrequently happens that a student may be able to master in a very successful way, the textbook part of a teacher-training course, and yet may make a dismal failure when placed in complete charge of a class. It is universally recognized that some of the most important qualities making for teaching efficiency are innate, and that no amount of training can wholly overcome the lack of native ability.

Several attempts have recently been made to devise some method of predicting in advance whether a prospective teacher has the necessary aptitude for making a successful teacher. The George Washington University Teaching Aptitude Test [1] will serve as an example of these attempts. This test consists of five parts. Part 1 consists of thirty problems designed to measure one's judgment in dealing with typical teaching situations. Four solutions are suggested for each problem, and the person taking the test is instructed to indicate the best one. The following are samples:

1. Your supervisor unexpectedly comes into your classroom. If you were the teacher you should:
    —— Present some of your difficulties for him to solve.
    —— Explain that some of the children always make a poor showing before strangers.
    —— Do your best without comment.
    —— Ask the supervisor to take charge of the class.
7. You have difficulties with your principal. It would be best for you to:
    —— Give the facts to parents and teachers for your own protection.
    —— Have a talk with the principal.
    —— Get the advice of fellow teachers.
    —— Register the complaint with the school board.
15. You catch a fourth-grade pupil cheating for the first time. You should:
    —— Deny him promotion.
    —— Reprimand him before the class.
    —— Send him to the principal.
    —— Talk to him after school.
24. During the class period while you are explaining a lesson to a fifth grade, a circus parade passes your windows. You should:
    —— Allow the children to go to the windows.

[1] *Teaching Aptitude Test*, Center for Psychological Service, Washington, D.C., 1927.

—— Continue the class work, ignoring the parade.
—— Reprimand the children for their restlessness.
—— Have the children stand and go through setting-up exercises.

Part 2 consists of 80 questions in the true-false form designed to measure one's reasoning and information about school problems. The following are samples.

T F 7   A person may have had a considerable amount of schooling and yet have a low mentality.
T F 26 Good deportment is a reliable indication of high intelligence.
T F 66 The child who makes the best marks is usually the most popular with his fellow students.

A third part consists of a test in comprehension and retention, in which the person taking the test must study a fairly difficult reading passage and later answer, from memory, certain questions on it. A fourth part is a measure of ability to observe and recall what one has observed; and the last part is a test of one's ability to recognize emotional expressions of children.

Such a test is of considerable value in measuring the teaching aptitude and interests of students in teacher-training institutions and of prospective teachers who are applying for positions. An objective test measure of their ability will give a much more accurate indication than a superficial oral interview or questioning.

2. Measurement of teaching efficiency. In an address at the annual meeting of the American Association of Land-Grant Colleges, the writer [1] had the following to say concerning the measurement of teaching efficiency.

Nowhere are opinions so plentiful and measurements so inadequate as in evaluating teaching efficiency. Each school administrator has his pet scheme for rating teachers, and these various rating schemes have only two points in common: they are all subjective and they are all unreliable.

The cause of the unreliability of efficiency estimates lies primarily in two factors. In the first place, there is no general agreement as to the function of the teacher, and consequently there are no well-defined standards as to what constitutes teaching efficiency. In the second place, not knowing what they are trying to measure, school authorities naturally disagree as

[1] Moss, F. A.: "Eliminating Guesswork in Rating Teachers," *Industrial Psychology Monthly* (June, 1927), vol. II, no. 6.

to how it should be measured, the result being that present methods of measuring teaching efficiency are largely personal and incapable of standardization. In the olden days a teacher's efficiency was estimated by the number of pupils he flogged during the school year, and even to-day it is not infrequent that a teacher is rated by the number of pupils he fails in his classes.

One purpose of all teaching is to make desirable changes in students. These changes are indicated in the amount the students learn. It would be just as absurd to speak of teaching chemistry when no one is learning chemistry as to speak of a salesman selling an automobile when no one is buying it.

The purpose of teaching being thus defined, the teaching efficiency of any instructor is found to vary directly with the desirable changes produced in the students by his teaching.

To measure their improvement, it is necessary to know the mental status of the students at the beginning of the teaching. This calls for: first, the use of tests of mental alertness to ascertain the ability of the student to learn; and second, standardized achievement tests to indicate how much the student knows about the subject at the beginning of instruction. Having thus discovered the mental condition of the student at the beginning, the investigator must measure him again at the end of the period to see what has been the effect of the instruction.

Scores shown on the final achievement test should be compared with standards or norms for that subject and the efficiency rating of the teacher thus determined. The ratio between the amount of improvement as compared with the standards is the most reliable index of the efficiency of a teacher. Those whose students show little or no improvement should be rated low, while higher ratings should be reserved for those instructors whose students show more than average improvement.

For example, we have three teachers in the same school teaching American history to groups of thirty each. On the basis of standardized intelligence tests these groups are so divided that the intelligence of the students in the three groups is approximately the same. At the beginning of the school year a standardized achievement test in American history is given to each of these three groups, and the average score on this test for each of the three groups is found to be approximately fifty points. In this way we are assured that each of the three instructors has an equal chance to produce improvement in the students assigned to him.

At the end of the year all we need to do to measure the relative efficiency of these three instructors, other things having been kept equal, is to give another standardized test in American history. If it is found that the students of Instructor A make an average score of 75, while those of Instructor B make an average score of 85, and those of C only 60, it is quite obvious that the teaching efficiency of Instructor B is higher than that of either A or C.

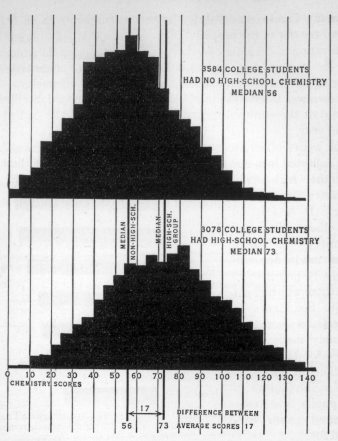

FIGURE 48. COMPARISON OF COLLEGE STUDENTS WHO HAVE HAD
HIGH-SCHOOL CHEMISTRY WITH THOSE WHO HAVE NOT

If it is desired to compare the teaching efficiency of these three instructors with that of instructors in other schools, all that is necessary is
to compare the score of their students with the scores made by other
students of equal intelligence who have had the same amount of instruction.

One advantage of the proposed plan is its eminent fairness. Just as the
wealth of a man can be estimated better from an inventory of his property
than from the opinion of his neighbors, so the teaching efficiency of an instructor can be determined more reliably by measuring the results of teaching than by the opinions of his administrative officers.

Twenty Land-Grant Colleges agreed to coöperate in an experimental try-out of the proposed plan.   It was decided to try it first in the rating of chemistry teachers.   The first step in the procedure was the construction and standardization of an objective test covering the material taught in first-year college chemistry.   The next step was to give the test together with a standard intelligence test to all the students in first year chemistry at the end of the school year.

The scores of all students who had had high-school chemistry were collected into one group and the scores of those who had not had the high-school chemistry into another. It was found that those who had chemistry in high school made approximately 17 points more than those who had not had it. See Figure 48. Corrections were accordingly made in all classes for this factor. The effect of the differences in intelligence of the pupils was next measured and corrected for.

These corrections having been made, the corrected scores of the pupils in any class give a fairly satisfactory index of the teaching efficiency of an instructor.   The study will not be completed for about two years, but the findings now available indicate the colossal differences in teaching efficiency of instructors.   The comparative efficiency of teachers of chemistry in the same large northern university is shown in Figure 49.

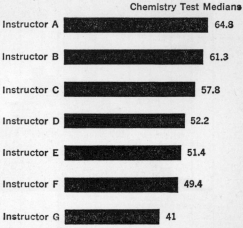

Chemistry Test Medians

Instructor A	64.8
Instructor B	61.3
Instructor C	57.8
Instructor D	52.2
Instructor E	51.4
Instructor F	49.4
Instructor G	41

FIGURE 49. COMPARATIVE EFFICIENCY OF TEACHERS OF CHEMISTRY IN THE SAME UNIVERSITY AS SHOWN BY MEDIANS ON CHEMISTRY TEST
Proper allowances have been made for differences in native intelligence and previous training of students.

INDEX

Ability: effect of past experiences on, 145–48

Abstract intelligence, sex differences in, 179, 180; measurement of, 209–12. *See also* Intelligence

Accidents, automobile, causes of, 388–93; chart showing distribution of blame for, 388; chart showing twelve most frequent causes, 389; circumstances attending occurrence of (Fig. 38), 390; and time of day (Fig. 39), 391; deaths from (Fig. 40), 392; four means of reducing, 393

Accomplishment, age of, 167

Accuracy, and speed, relation between, 256; of slow and rapid workers (Fig. 32), 357

Achievement, agreeableness of work and, 27; climate and, 65; race differences in, 112, 113; of college graduates, 148; training to equalize, 153, 154; heredity multiplied by environment, 156; sex differences in, 190–92; in school, and intelligence, 450

Achievement tests, in education, 446–50

Addiction, to drugs, stage of, 44, 45

Admission, to colleges and universities, intelligence tests for, 443

Adrenin, effect of, 57

Advertising, individual differences in, 85; amounts spent on, 298, 299; appeals to ignorance of consumer, 299–308; psycnology of, 309–30; emotional appeals in, 308, 309; specimen of ancient, 309; a community, 310; an organization, 310, 311; an individual, 311, 312; steps in, 313–24; goods, 313–30; getting attention, 313–17; holding attention, 315–17; arousing desire, 317–22; creating confidence, 319–22; repetition to create confidence, 319–20; stressing age of firm, 320; recommendations of users, 320; getting response, 322–24; argument, 323, 324; suggestion, 323; choosing medium, 324–27; newspapers as medium, 325; magazines as medium, 325, 326; outdoor advertising as medium, 326; street-car cards as medium,

326; window displays as medium, 327; preferred positions in, 327, 328; trade marks, 328–30; and salesmanship contrasted, 330

Age, strength of drive influenced by, 18; a factor in fatigue, 22; differences due to, 91, 157–71; individual's life regulated by, 157; chronological and mental, 158–60; labor turnover and, 159; and mental disorders, 159, 160, 252; optimum, for given occupation, 159; and mental disorders (Fig. 18), 160; physical, 160, 161; mental, 161, 162; of puberty, 161; rate of growth and, 161; educational, 162, 163; emotional, 163–71; and youth, battle between, 164; seven ages of man, 164–71; first — the helpless stranger, 164, 165; second — heir of the ages, 165, 166; third — youth, love, romance, 166, 167; fourth — the struggle, 167; fifth — victory or defeat, 168; sixth — regression, 168–70; seventh — helpless senescent, 170, 171; and age-group in auto accidents (Fig. 40), 392; in determining political party, 407; of politicians on entering politics, 415; of politicians on reaching height of political power, 415. *See also* Chronological age *and* Physical age

Air, constituents of, 74; circulation of and ventilation, 75; effect of changes in content of oxygen and carbon dioxide, 76, 77

Alcohol, weakening of resistance, to, 16; weather and desire for, 17; effect on behavior, 46–49; dotting-machine experiment, 47; effect on brain, 48; memory test, 48; delirium tremens, 49; delusions and hallucinations caused by, 49; feeble-mindedness and, 49; unreliability of information about, 55; cause of mental disorders, 250; as cause of auto accidents, 392

Alcoholic psychoses, among negroes and Irish, 96

Alexander the Great, Galton's study of, 123